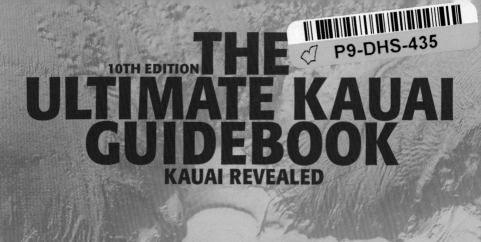

10TH EDITION THE
ULTIMATE KAUAI
GUIDEBOOK
KAUAI REVEALED

ANDREW DOUGHTY
DIRECTOR OF PHOTOGRAPHY LEONA BOYD

WIZARD
PUBLICATIONS
INC

Wai'ale'ale Crater, with its 3,000-foot, waterfall-etched walls, was the spiritual center of the ancient Hawaiian universe. Normally shrouded by clouds, this photo was taken from 10,000 feet after an explosive rainstorm passed on one of only two days a year when the sun is directly overhead, leaving no shadows on the walls.

The Ultimate Kauai Guidebook
Kauai Revealed 10th Edition

Published by Wizard Publications, Inc.
Post Office Box 991
Lihu'e, Hawai'i 96766–0991

ISBN: 978-0-9961318-4-1   4098
Library of Congress Control Number 2016946385
Printed in China

Cataloging-in-Publication Data

Doughty, Andrew
    The Ultimate Kauai guidebook : Kauai revealed / Andrew Doughty - 10th ed.
Lihue, HI : Wizard Publications, Inc., 2018
    p. 280: col. illus., col. photos, col. maps ; 21 cm.
    Includes index.
    Summary: A complete traveler's reference to the Hawaiian island of Kauai, with
full-color illustrations, maps, directions and candid advice by an author who resides in Hawaii.
    ISBN-13: 978-0-9961318-4-1
    LCCN: 2016946385
    1. Kaua'i (Hawaii) - Guidebooks. 2. Kaua'i (Hawaii) – Description and travel.
    I. Title.

DU628.K3   919.69'41_dc22

Cover space imagery courtesy of Earthstar Geographics (www.earth-imagery.com).
Cartography by Andrew Doughty.
All artwork and illustrations by Andrew Doughty.

We welcome any comments, questions, criticisms or contributions you may have, and we have incorporated some of your suggestions into this edition. Please send to the address above or e-mail us at **aloha@hawaiirevealed.com**.

Check out our website at **www.hawaiirevealed.com** for up-to-the-minute changes. Find us on **Facebook**, **YouTube** and **Twitter** (@hawaiirevealed).

Although the author and publisher have made every effort to ensure that the information was correct at press time, the author and publisher do not assume and hereby disclaim any liability to any party for any loss or damage caused by errors or omissions, whether such errors or omissions result from negligence, accident or any other cause. Information has been obtained from sources believed to be reliable, but its accuracy and completeness, and the opinions based thereon, are not guaranteed.

Dedicated to Sammie Dollar, who soars on the wind with the white-tailed tropic birds.

CONTENTS

CONTENTS

ACTIVITIES
122

ADVENTURES
192

ISLAND DINING
212

WHERE TO STAY
252

In a sense, this is not a guidebook; it's more of a love story. Having first seen the island as a tourist, I was immediately smitten. I had no idea that a place like this could exist anywhere in the world. Now as a resident, I marvel at its beauty every day.

Kaua'i is a unique place. People who visit here recognize this immediately. There are plenty of places in the world featuring sun and sea, but no other place offers the incomparable beauty, lushness and serenity of Kaua'i. Living here, we get to see first-time visitors driving around with their jaws open, shaking their heads in disbelief at what they see. Without a doubt, you will never see more smiles than during your visit to Kaua'i.

Our job is unusual, to say the least. We hike the trails, ride the boats, eat in the restaurants, explore the reefs and do the things we write about. It takes us two *years*, full time, to do a first edition book, and we visit places *anonymously*. We marvel at writers who can do it all in a couple of weeks staying in a hotel. Wow, they must be *really* fast. Our method, though it takes much longer, gives us the ability to tell it like it is in a way no one else can. We put in many long hours, and doing all these activities is a burdensome grind. But we do it all for you—only for you. (Feel free to gag at this point.)

We produce brand new editions of our books every year or two, but in the intervening time we constantly incorporate changes into the text nearly every time we do a new printing. We also post these changes on our website. This allows us to make some modifications throughout the life of each edition.

In this day of easy-to-access online reviews from countless sources, you can get "ratings" for nearly every company out there. What you get from our reviews is a single source, *beholden to* none, with a comprehensive exposure to all of the companies. There are two critical shortcomings to online reviews. One is that you don't know the source or agenda of the reviewer. Nearly every company that offers a service to the public *thinks* they are doing a good job. (But as you know, not everyone does.) So who can blame a company for trying to rig the system by seeding good reviews of their company at every opportunity or having friends write good reviews? Many also encourage *satisfied* customers to write favorable online reviews (obviously *not* encouraging *unhappy* customers to do so). But maybe their enemies or competitors retaliate with bad reviews. The point is, you never *really know* where those reviews come from, and it's almost impossible to reconcile terrible reviews right next to glowing ones for the same company. Which do you believe?

The other problem is a lack of a frame of reference. A visitor to Hawai'i goes on a snorkel boat and has a great time. (Hey, he snorkeled in Hawai'i, swam with a turtle—*cool!)* When he goes back home, he posts good reviews all around. That's great. But the problem is, he only went on *one* snorkel boat. We do 'em all. If only he realized that another company *he didn't even know about* did a much better job, had way better food, and a much nicer boat for the same price.

We are also blessed with hundreds of thousands of readers—from our books as well as our smartphone apps—who alert us to issues with companies and places. *Every single message* from our readers is received, placed in a special database that we constantly have available while we're out and about, and we personally follow up on every observation made by our readers. So when we walk into a business or restaurant, we check to see what our readers say and tips they send us, and we use them to our advantage.

(Thanks for the head's up about that incredible coconut cake at so-and-so restaurant—I know what *I'll* be ordering for dessert today.) With such a resource, and after two decades reviewing companies in Hawai'i full time, there ain't much that's gonna get past us.

A quick look at this book will reveal features never before used in other guidebooks. Let's start with the maps. They are more detailed than any other maps you'll find, and yet they omit extraneous information that can sometimes make map reading a chore. We know that people in unfamiliar territory sometimes have a hard time determining where they are on a map, so we include landmarks. Most notable among these are mile markers. At every mile on main roads, the government has erected numbered markers to tell you where you are. Where needed, we've drawn legal public beach access in yellow, so you'll *know* when you're legally entitled to cross someone's land. Most guidebooks have the infuriating habit of mentioning a particular place or sight but then fail to mention how to get there! You won't find that in our book. We tell you exactly how to find the hidden gems and use our own special maps to guide you.

As you read this book, you will also notice that we are very candid in assessing businesses. Unlike some other guidebooks that send out questionnaires asking a business if they are any good (gee, they *all* say they're good), we've had personal contact with the businesses listed in this book. One of the dirty little secrets about guidebook writers is that they sometimes make cozy little deals for good reviews. Well, you won't find that here. We accept no payment for our reviews, we make no deals with businesses for saying nice things, and there are no advertisements in our book. What we've seen and experienced is what you get. If we gush over a certain company, it comes from personal experience. If we rail against a business, it is for the same reason. All businesses mentioned in this book are here by *our* choosing. None has had any input into what we say, and we have not received *a single cent* from any of them for their inclusion. (In fact, there are some who would probably pay to be left out, given our comments.) We always review businesses as anonymous visitors and only later as guidebook writers if we need more information. This ensures that we are treated the same as you. (Amazingly, most travel writers *announce* themselves.) What you get is our opinion on how a business operates. Nothing more, nothing less.

Sometimes our candor gets us into trouble. More than once we've had our books pulled from shelves because our comments hit a little too close to home. That's OK, because we don't work for the people who *sell* the book; we work for the people who *read* the book. It's also true that a handful of local residents have become upset because we've told readers about places that they'd rather keep for themselves. Ironically, it's usually not people born and raised here who have this selfish attitude, but rather the newcomers who have read about these places *in our book* (of all things), then adopted the *I'm here now— close the door* mentality.

This book is intended to bring you independence in exploring Kaua'i. We don't want to waste any of your precious time by giving you bad advice or bad directions. We want you to experience the best that the island has to offer. Our objective in writing this book is to give you the tools and information necessary to have the greatest Hawaiian experience possible.

We hope we succeed.

Andrew Doughty
Kapa'a, Hawai'i

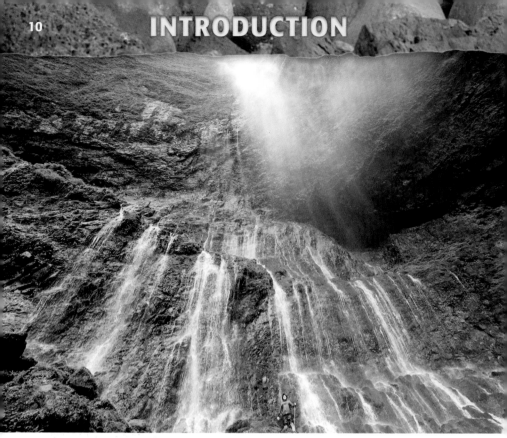

The walls of Wai'ale'ale Crater, from which the island of Kaua'i burst forth in a fiery cataclysm, are now home to innumerable waterfalls. This part of the crater is called the Weeping Wall.

As with people, volcanic islands have a life cycle. They emerge from their sea floor womb to be greeted by the warmth of the sun. They grow and mature and eventually die before sinking forever beneath the sea.

HOW IT BEGAN

The Hawaiian Islands were born of fire thousands of feet below the surface in the icy cold waters on the Pacific Ocean floor. A rupture in the earth's crust caused a vent to spew hot magma that built upon itself as it reached upward. When it began, no one knows exactly, but the first of the still-existing islands to boil to the surface was Kure. Nothing remains of that island today but its fringing coral reef, called an atoll.

As the Pacific plate shifted over the opening of the vent like steel over a cutting torch, more islands were created. Midway, French Frigate Shoal, Necker, Nihoa—all of these once-great islands were born and then mostly consumed by the angry ocean. What we call Hawai'i is just the last in a series of islands created by this vent. Someday these, too, will be nothing more than atolls, footnotes in the geologic history of the earth. But this vent isn't finished yet. The Big Island of Hawai'i is still expanding as lava from its active volcano continues even now to create additional real estate on that island. As we sit here, the future island of Lo'ihi is being created 20 miles southeast of the Big Island. Although still 3,100 feet below the surface of the ocean, in but a geologic moment, the Hawaiian volcano goddess Pele will add yet another piece of paradise to her impressive domain.

These virgin islands were barren at birth. The first life forms to appreciate these new islands of volcanic rock were marine creatures. Fish, mammals and microscopic animals discovered this new underwater haven and made homes for themselves. Coral polyps attached themselves to the lava rock, and succeeding generations built upon these, creating what would become a coral reef.

Meanwhile, on land, seeds carried by the winds were struggling to colonize the rocky land, eking out a living and breaking down the lava rock. Storms brought the occasional bird, hopelessly blown off course. The lucky ones found the islands. The even luckier ones arrived with mates or had fertilized eggs when they got here. Other animals, stranded on a piece of floating debris, washed ashore against all odds and went on to colonize the islands. These introductions of new species were rare events. It took an extraordinary set of circumstances for a new species to actually make it to the islands. Single specimens were destined to live out their lives in lonely solitude. On average, a new species was successfully deposited here only once every 20,000 years.

As the plants and animals lived out their lives, they broke up the rock, forming soil and organic debris. The ocean, meanwhile, was busily working to reclaim the horizon from these interruptions of land. Waves battered unmercifully against the fragile lava rock. In this battle between titans, there can be but one winner. While the creation of land eventually ceases on an individual island, the ocean never gives up. Wave after wave eventually takes its toll.

In addition to the ocean, rain carves up the islands. As the islands thrust themselves upward into the moisture-laden trade winds, their challenge to the rain clouds is accepted. As the air encounters the slopes of these tall islands, it rises and cools, causing the air to release its humidity in the form of rain. This rain forms channels that easily carve valleys in the soft lava rock.

Each successive wave is like a sculptor's hand, slowly shaping the island. Large storms can generate powerful waves, such as this one, which, over the eons, patiently return the island to the sea.

Ancient Hawaiian petroglyphs, such as this one near the banks of the Wailua River, can still be found tucked away in the jungle.

So what is the result of all this destruction? Paradise. Absolute paradise. There are few things more beautiful than Mother Nature reclaiming that which she gave birth to. The older the island, the more beautiful the landscape. A Hawaiian island is never more lovely than in its middle age, when the scars of constant environmental battles are carved into its face. Lush landscaped valleys, razorback ridges, long, sandy beaches—those things we cherish so much are the result of this destructive battle.

Kaua'i consists of 553 square miles of beach, rainforest, desert, mountains and plains. The island's landscape is as varied as its people. At Wai'ale'ale in the island's center, it rains nearly every day, making it one of the wettest places on earth. Just a few miles to the west, rain is rare, creating dry, almost arid conditions. The north shore is as lush as any place on the planet. The south shore is a sunny playground. The island's first inhabitants surely must have felt blessed at the discovery of this diversity.

THE FIRST SETTLERS

Sometime around the fourth or fifth century AD, a large, double-hulled voyaging canoe, held together with flexible sennit lashings and propelled by sails made of woven pandanus, slid onto the sand on the Big Island of Hawai'i. These first intrepid adventurers encountered an island chain of unimaginable beauty.

They had left their home in the Marquesas Islands, 2,500 miles away, for reasons we will never know. Though some say it was because of war, overpopulation or drought, it was more likely part of a purposeful exploration from a culture that had mastered the art of making their way through the featureless seas using celestial navigation and reading subtle signs in the ocean. Their navigational abilities far exceeded all of the other "advanced" societies of the time. Whatever their reasons, these initial settlers took a big chance and surely must have been highly motivated. They could not have known that there were islands in these waters since Hawai'i is the most isolated island chain in the world. Those who did arrive brought with them food staples from home: taro, breadfruit, pigs, dogs and several types of fowl. This was a pivotal decision. These first settlers found a land that contained almost no edible plants. With no land mammals other than the Hawaiian bat, the first settlers subsisted on fish until their crops could mature. From then on, they lived largely on fish and taro. Although we associate throw-net fishing with Hawai'i, this practice was introduced by Japanese immigrants much later. The ancient Hawaiians used fishhooks and spears for the most part or drove fish into a net already placed into the water. They also had domesticated animals that were used as ritual foods or reserved for chiefs.

As the culture evolved and flourished, it developed into a hierarchical system of order. The society was governed by chiefs, called *ali'i*, who established a long list of taboos called *kapu*. These kapu were designed to keep order, and the penalty for breaking one was usually death by strangulation, club or fire. If the violation was serious enough, the guilty party's family might also be killed. It was kapu, for instance, for your shadow to fall across the shadow of the ali'i. It was kapu to interrupt the chief if he was speaking. It was kapu to prepare men's food in the same container used for women's food. It was kapu for women to eat pork or bananas. It was kapu for men and women to eat together. It was kapu not to observe the days designated to the gods. Certain areas were kapu for fishing if they became depleted. This allowed the area to replenish itself.

While harsh by our standards today, this system kept order. Most ali'i were sensitive to the disturbance their presence caused and often ventured outside only at night, or a scout was sent ahead to warn people that an ali'i was on his way. All commoners were required to pay taxes to the ali'i in the form of food, labor and in other ways.

In January 1778 an event occurred that would forever change Hawai'i. Captain James Cook, who usually had a ge-

Who Were the Menehune?

Although the legend of Menehune exists throughout the Hawaiian Islands, the folklore is strongest on Kaua'i. Hawaiian legend speaks of a mythical race of people living in the islands before the Polynesians. Called the Menehune, these people were always thought of as being small in stature. The legend initially referred to their social stature, but it evolved to mean that they were physically short and lived in the jungle away from the Hawaiians. (The ancient Hawaiians avoided living in the jungle, fearing that it held evil spirits, and instead settled on the coastal plains.) The Menehune were purported to build fabulous structures, always in one night. Their numbers were said to be vast, as many as 500,000. Today, archeologists speculate that a second wave of colonists, probably from Tahiti, may have subdued these initial inhabitants, forcing them to live in the woods. It is interesting to note that in a census taken of Kaua'i around 1800, 65 people from the upper region of the Wainiha Valley identified themselves as Menehune.

Today, Menehune are jokingly blamed for anything that goes wrong. If you lost your wallet, Menehune took it. If your car won't start, Menehune have been tinkering with it. Kaua'i residents greatly cherish their legends of the Menehune.

nius for predicting where to find islands, stumbled upon Hawai'i. He had not expected islands to be there. He was on his way to Alaska to search for the Northwest Passage linking the Atlantic and Pacific oceans. As Cook approached the shores of Waimea, Kaua'i, on January 19, 1778, the island's inhabitants thought they were being visited by gods. Rushing aboard to greet their visitors, the Kauaians were fascinated by what they saw: pointy-headed beings (the British wore tri-cornered hats) breathing fire (smoking pipes) and possessing a death-dealing instrument identified as a water squirter (guns). The amount of iron on the ship was incredible. (Hawaiians had only seen iron in the form of nails on driftwood but never knew the source.) Cook left Kaua'i and briefly explored Ni'ihau before heading north for his mission on February 2, 1778. When Cook returned to the Big Island of Hawai'i after failing to find the Northwest Passage, he was killed in a petty skirmish over a stolen rowboat. The Hawaiians were horrified that they had killed a man they had earlier presumed to be a god.

Just after this, Kamehameha the Great of the Big Island began consolidating his power by conquering the other islands in the chain. Kaua'i, however, presented a unique problem. Cut off from the rest of the chain by the treacherous Kaua'i Channel, Kaua'i's King Kaumuali'i had no intention of submitting himself to Kamehameha. In the spring of 1796 Kamehameha tried to invade Kaua'i. He and his fleet of 1,200 canoes carrying 10,000 soldiers left O'ahu at midnight hoping to reach Wailua, Kaua'i, by daybreak. They were in the middle of the Kaua'i Channel when the wind and seas picked up. Many of the canoes were swamped. Reluctantly, Kamehameha ordered a retreat, but too late to stop some of his advance troops who were slaughtered after they arrived at the south shore beach of Maha'ulepu.

In 1804 Kamehameha tried again. He gathered 7,000 men, all heavily armed, and prepared to set sail for Kaua'i. Just before they were to leave, typhoid struck, decimating his troops and advisers. Kamehameha himself contracted the disease but managed to pull

Ancient Hawaiians lived off the sea. With reefs teeming with life, island waters have always been generous to the people of Hawai'i.

through. Kaua'i's king must have seen the writing on the wall and agreed to give his kingdom of Kaua'i over to Kamehameha. When Kamehameha died, his son, in order to solidify his power on Kaua'i, arranged to kidnap Kaua'i's King Kaumuali'i and forced him to marry his stepmother, the powerful widow of Kamehameha. Kaua'i's last king would never return and was eventually buried on Maui.

During the 19th century, Hawai'i's character changed dramatically. Businessmen from all over the world came here to exploit. Hawai'i's sandalwood, whales, land and people. Hawai'i's leaders, for their part, actively participated in these ventures and took a piece of the action for themselves. Workers were brought in from many parts of the world, changing the racial makeup of the islands. Government corruption became the order of the day, and everyone seemed to be profiting except the Hawaiian commoner. By the time Queen Lili'uokalani lost her throne to a group of American businessmen in 1893,

The earliest Hawaiians built elaborate terraces to grow taro, used to make poi. This terrace, in Limahuli Garden, is estimated to be 700 years old.

Hawai'i had become directionless. It barely resembled the Hawai'i Captain Cook had encountered in the previous century. The kapu system had been abolished by the Hawaiians shortly after the death of Kamehameha the Great. The *Great Mahele*, begun in 1848, had changed the relationship Hawaiians had with the land. Large tracts of land were sold by the Hawaiian government to royalty, government officials, commoners and foreigners, effectively stripping many Hawaiians of land they had lived on for generations.

The United States recognized the Republic of Hawai'i in 1894 with Sanford Dole as its president. It was later annexed and then became a territory in 1900. During the 19th and 20th centuries, sugar established itself as king. Pineapple was also heavily grown in the islands, and the entire island of Lana'i was pur-

What's it Like in the Wettest Spot on Earth?

The center of the island is called Mount Wai'ale'ale, meaning "rippling waters." It is here that you will find one of the rainiest spots on the planet with an average of 432 inches. Rain around the rest of the island is a fraction of this (see chart on page 27). The ancient Hawaiians recognized the importance of this spot and built a temple on the summit, its remains visible to this day. Unless you're up for an extremely adventurous hike (page 202), the only way you will get to see Wai'ale'ale up close and personal is by air.

The top of Mount Wai'ale'ale is somewhat barren. While this might sound strange given its moniker as the wettest spot on Earth, remember that few plants in this world are genetically programmed to deal with that much rain at that altitude. Plus the ever-present rain clouds prevent sunshine from enriching the plants. The bogs on top of the mountain make for a less-than-well-defined soil base, and fungi and lichen flourish in the constant moisture. The result is few trees. Those trees that do survive are stunted by nature's over-generous gift of water.

Just below the summit—3,000 feet straight down, to be precise—exists the unimaginable lushness one would expect from abundant rain. As the clouds are forced up the walls of Wai'ale'ale Crater, they shed a portion of their moisture. With the majority of the rain

falling on the summit, the crater floor is left with just the perfect amount. With volcanically rich soil left over from the fiery eruptions, the crater floor has become a haven for

The summit of Wai'ale'ale feeds the Wailua River 3,000 feet below the sheer cliffs.

anything green. Ferns rule the crater. The ground shakes beneath your feet as your footsteps echo through generations of water-saturated fallen ferns, which have created a soft underbelly on what was once a savage, lava-spewing giant.

There is a surprising lack of insect presence. And most that do live there are endemic, appearing nowhere else on earth. Aside from mosquitoes in the stream beds, we've encountered almost no insects in the dense fern growth of the crater. The only exception was a single flightless grasshopper. We have found some 'o'opu fish inhabiting streams between towering waterfalls. They live in these isolated pools and use their pelvic fins to actually climb the falls.

Everywhere one looks, plants have taken root. Every rock has moss, every fallen tree has other plants growing on it, every crevice has growth. Surely no other place on earth is as lush as Wai'ale'ale Crater.

chased for the purpose of growing pineapple. As the 20th century rolled on, Hawaiian sugar and pineapple workers found themselves in a lofty position—they became the highest paid workers for these crops in the world. As land prices rose and competition from other parts of the world increased, sugar and pineapple became less and less profitable. Today, these crops no longer hold the position they once had. In the 1990s the "Pineapple Island" of Lana'i completely shifted away from pineapple and started luring tourists. And where dozens of sugar companies once dotted the islands, the last one, on Maui, shut down for good in 2016. Former sugar workers have moved into other vocations, usually tourist-related or farming.

The story of Hawai'i is not a story of good versus evil. Nearly everyone shares in the blame for what happened to the Hawaiian people and their culture. Never-theless, today Hawai'i is struggling to redefine its identity. The Islands are looking back to the past for guidance. During your stay you will be exposed to a place that is attempting to recapture its cultural roots. There is more interest in Hawaiian culture and language than ever before. Sometimes the process is clumsy, sometimes awkward. There is no common agreement regarding how to do it, but in the end, a reinvigoration of the Hawaiian spirit will no doubt be enjoyed by all.

NI'IHAU

No man is an island, or so they say. But in Hawai'i, one family can own one. The island of Ni'ihau is a dry, somewhat barren island of 46,000 acres located 17 miles to the west of Kaua'i. When Scottish-born Eliza Sinclair was sailing in the islands with her family in 1863, they were looking for land on which to settle. Having turned down offers of several

On Kaua'i, the first settlers found an Eden more beautiful than any place they'd ever known.

The private island of Niʻihau has mile after mile of beautiful, untouched beaches. Unfortunately the only way you'll see this scene is to take a pricey tour with Niʻihau Helicopters.

tracts on Oʻahu (including Waikiki, which they dismissed as showing no promise), they were about to leave for California when King Kamehameha V offered to sell them Niʻihau. When Eliza's sons went to look at it, they found a green, wet island with abundant grass—perfect for raising cattle. What they were unaware of at the time was that Niʻihau had experienced a *rare* rainy period and was flourishing as a result. They offered $6,000, the king countered with $10,000, and they took it.

This was 1864 and, unfortunately for the Sinclairs, the residents of Niʻihau did not respect their ownership and resisted them. They had a further setback when an old Hawaiian showed them a deed indicating ownership to a crucial 50-acre sliver of Niʻihau deeded to the old man by King Kamehameha III. The Sinclairs were in a bind and solicited the aid of Valdemar Knudsen to negotiate the purchase of the remaining 50 acres. He spoke fluent Hawaiian and was well known and respected by the islanders. Knudsen went to Niʻihau and

offered $1,000 to the old man by slowly stacking the silver coins on a table while he explained how much better off the old man would be if he sold his land and lived in comfort on Kauaʻi. After repeated refusals from the man, Knudsen went to take the money away when the old Hawaiian's wife grabbed the money, and the deal was consummated on the spot.

When the Sinclairs discovered that the land was actually dry and barren, unsuitable for a cattle ranch at that time, they arranged to buy 21,000 acres of West Kauaʻi. (They would continue to buy land on Kauaʻi, eventually acquiring 51,000 acres of the island, which they own to this day.) If you take a helicopter ride, you may see their fabulous estate nestled high in the mountains near Olokele.

Today, about 130 Hawaiians live on Niʻihau. Most use bicycles for short trips on the unpaved roads, horses for trips more than a few miles and trucks for longer journeys. No telephones, except for a wireless two-way to Kauaʻi, no broadcast TV and no Internet, by order of the Robinsons—the descendants of Eliza Sinclair. Intermittent power is supplied by generator and solar.

Ni'ihau's one school hosts around 20 students K–12. The sense of family on the island is strong, and only Hawaiian is spoken in most homes. (Classes, however, are taught in English.) Ni'ihau residents are a deeply religious people, and crime against one another is almost unknown. They are intensely proud of their community and feel strongly that their people, their heritage and their way of life are special and are protected by God. They are quick to smile and laugh.

They live in one village called Pu'uwai (located in the only part of Ni'ihau where you can't see Kaua'i) and receive their mail once a week—the Post Office only delivers as far as Makaweli on Kaua'i. They shop for clothes and other durable items on Kaua'i, where most have family.

Time is fluid there. If someone says they'll see you on Wednesday, it could be any time of the day. There's no such thing as being late on Ni'ihau.

With a warehouse for staples and gardens for their fruits and vegetables, Ni'ihau islanders are reasonably self-sufficient. Travel to and from the island is via old military transport boats (like the kind that stormed the beaches of Normandy in WWII), and the rough, bumpy ride takes around three hours each way (during which many get seasick).

Life on Ni'ihau is certainly not without problems. No drugs or alcohol are allowed on the island, and families have been banished forever from the island for growing pakalolo (marijuana). Their mortality rate is high. Virtually everyone receives welfare and/or food stamps. With no permanent streams on the island, water is scarce, so they live off catchment. Although the largest lake in the state is on Ni'ihau, it is usually only a few feet deep, muddy and generally unpleasant.

The Robinson's land is valued at well over a *billion* dollars, but crushing tax burdens and losses (from Kaua'i operations) leave them relatively cash poor. Though the land has been in the family for over a century and a half, every time a land-owning relative dies, the government takes a huge bite out of the family in massive inheritance taxes. They claim that they can only afford to go out to dinner a few times a year. (You can dry your eyes now after that one.) They warmed to the idea of using some of their Kaua'i land for tourism for a few years, then backed away. They almost allowed the federal government to install (for a fee) rocket launchers on Ni'ihau as part of an expansion of the Pacific Missile Range Facility on Kaua'i's west side. The deal fell through when the government insisted on an ethnographic survey, which the secretive Robinsons feared would be used to create precedents that would allow native Hawaiians *from Kaua'i* to visit the island (for constitutionally allowed ritual or gathering purposes). Instead, they now lease much of their Kaua'i land to large, mainland seed growers cultivating genetically modified plants. They are also increasing their cattle operations, built a slaughterhouse here, raising eland (a large, African antelope), distributing venison from Maui and Moloka'i, and bring about 50 sheep a week over from Ni'ihau and market them to restaurants, calling it "forbidden lamb chops."

The Robinsons claim that their unique deed to the island gives them ownership of Ni'ihau's beaches—directly in conflict with state law that proclaims that *all* beaches in Hawai'i are public beaches. To date nobody has challenged them in court. If you land on a beach on Ni'ihau, you will be asked to leave. If you refuse, a truly *gargantuan* Hawaiian gentleman will be summoned, and he will ask you a bit more firmly. This request is usually sufficient to persuade all but the most determined individuals to leave.

Whether it's exotic and imported, such as this night blooming orchid, or native to Hawai'i, flowers abound on the Garden Island.

GETTING HERE

In order to get to the islands, you've got to fly here. While this may sound painfully obvious, many people contemplate cruises to the islands. Here's a tip—there isn't a single speck of land between the west coast and Hawai'i. And 2,500 miles of open water is a pretty monotonous stretch to cover.

When planning your trip, a travel agent can be helpful, though that method is becoming less and less common. The Internet has sites such as Orbitz, Expedia, Cheap-tickets, Cheapair, Pandaonline, Priceline, Travelocity, Kayak, etc. If you don't want to or can't go through these sources, there are large wholesalers that can get you airfare, hotel and a rental car, often cheaper than you can get airfare on your own. **Pleasant Holidays** (800-742-9244) provides complete package tours.

The prices listed in the WHERE TO STAY section reflect the RACK rates, meaning the published rates before any discounts. Rates can be significantly lower if you go through a travel company or book online.

When you pick your travel source, shop around—the differences can be dramatic. A diligent effort can make the difference between affording a *one-week* vacation and a *two-week* vacation.

Though most visitors fly into Honolulu before arriving, there are some direct flights to Kaua'i. Not having to cool your heels while changing planes on O'ahu is a *big* plus since interisland flights aren't quite as convenient—or cheap—as they used to be. If you fly to Kaua'i from Honolulu, the best views are usually on the left side (seats with an "A"). When flying to Honolulu from the mainland, sit on the left side coming in, the right going home. Interisland flights are done by Hawaiian (800-367-5320). Flight attendants zip up and down the aisle hurling juice at you for the short, interisland flights.

WHAT TO BRING

This list will be helpful in planning what to bring. Obviously, you won't bring everything on the list, but it might help you think of things you may otherwise overlook:

- Water-resistant, reef-safe sunscreen (SPF 30 or higher)
- Two bathing suits
- Shoes—flip-flops, trashable sneakers, water shoes, hiking or trail shoes
- Mask, snorkel and fins
- Digital camera
- Waterproof case for phone
- Hiking sticks (carbide-tipped ones are good for boulder-hopping hikes)
- Shorts and other cool cotton clothing
- Hat or cap for sun protection
- Light windbreaker jacket (for trip to Kalalau Lookout or helicopter trip)
- Cheap, simple backpack—you don't need to go backpacking to use one; a 10-minute trek to a secluded beach is much easier if you bring a simple pack.
- Long, lightweight pants for hiking if you are going through jungle country.
- Wool socks for walking on hot Polihale sand. (If you've been there before, you *know* what it's like.)

GETTING AROUND
Rental Cars

The rental car prices in Hawai'i *can be* (but aren't always) cheaper than almost anywhere else in the country, and the competition is ferocious. Nearly every visitor to Kaua'i gets around in a rental car, and for good reason. The island's towns are separated by distances sufficient to discourage walking. Many of Kaua'i's best sights can only be reached if you have independent transportation.

At Lihu'e Airport, rental cars can easily be obtained from the booths across the street from the main terminal. It's usually a good idea to reserve your car in advance since companies can run out of cars during peak times.

Below are the companies currently operating on Kaua'i:

The Big Guys

Alamo	**(877) 222-9075**
	(808) 246-0645
Avis	**(800) 321-3712**
	(808) 245-3512
Budget	**(800) 527-0700**
	(808) 245-9031
Discount Hawaii Car Rental	
	(800) 292-1930
	(808) 292-1930
Dollar	**(800) 800-4000**
Hertz	**(800) 654-3131**
	(808) 245-3356
National	**(877) 222-9058**
	(808) 245-5638
Thrifty	**(800) 367-5238**

The Little Guys

Island Cars	**(800) 246-6009**
	(808) 246-6000
Kaua'i Rent A Car	
	(808) 246-1881
Rent-A-Wreck Kauai	
	(808) 245-7177

The prices at Island Cars need to be much cheaper to justify some of the clunkers we've seen there. If you're 21–24 years old, most of the companies will rent to you, but you'll pay about $25 extra *per day* for the crime of being young and reckless. If you're under 21—rent a bike or moped or take the bus. Below are a few tips to keep in mind when you rent your car on Kaua'i.

Many **Collision Damage Waivers** will not cover vehicles on unpaved roads or beaches. Consider this when driving on dirt roads or at Polihale. Also note that some deals aren't as great as they might seem online. Discount car rental companies only allow a collision damage waiver if your personal auto insurance will cover you in Hawai'i and will *call your insurance company* before they let you drive off their lot. Many policies do not offer the kind of coverage they require, and so you are forced to buy their insurance (starting at $16/day).

Car break-ins can be a problem anywhere. They seem to be more frequent in the summer due to school vacations. The places usually hit are those that require you to leave your car in a secluded place for an extended period of time. Contrary to popular belief, locals are targeted nearly as often as tourists. To protect yourself, don't leave anything valuable in the car. (Well...maybe the seats can stay.) At secluded spots that have recently been robbed, savvy locals will often leave their doors unlocked and the windows partially open to prevent having their windows smashed, but doing so *might* negate your rental car insurance. If you park in a secluded spot and notice several piles of glass on the ground, it's evidence that some juvenile has a new hobby. Don't kid yourself into believing that trunks are safe—they are often easier to open than doors. One place thieves rarely look is under the hood. But don't put something there after you arrive at your destination since someone might be watching. We once drove up to the parking area at Se-

cret Beach, and there was a suspicious looking guy there. Mr. Slick acted busy by spending considerable time checking the oil in his car—*but the rusted hulk had no wheels all the way around.* Be alert and you should be OK.

All of this is not meant to convey the impression that car break-ins are rampant. In fact, the opposite is true. You could probably spend your entire life here and never experience one. (We haven't.) But if you lose your brand new $1,000 auto-everything digital SLR camera to some juvenile dipstick because you were one of the few...well, won't *you* feel sick?

4-Wheel Drive

With its many rugged roads, one of the best ways to see Kaua'i is by four-wheel drive. These can be difficult to come by at times. Ask the rental car company if they have disabled the 4WD mechanism. If you use a gold credit card for the automatic insurance, check with the card carrier to see if you are covered when you're on unpaved roads. Another tip is to avoid deep, soft sand. Even 4WD vehicles can get stuck in sand if they have the wrong tires. If you must drive on sand, let much of the air out of the tires to get more sand traction. (We'll leave it up to you how to get the air back in.) If you already *are* stuck in sand, try pulling the carpet from the trunk and driving on it to get out. (Oh, the car companies will love us for *that* one.) Rental car companies are always changing the vehicles to keep them new. At press time, all the *big* companies we list had SUVs or other 4WD vehicles. Expect to pay up to $60–$90 per day for the privilege of cheating the road builders.

Buses

Kaua'i has a bus system called the **Kaua'i Bus** (clever, eh?). It goes from

Hey, I Recognize That Place…

When Hollywood wants to convey the impression of beauty, lushness and the exotic, it's no contest what location they choose. Kaua'i has long been the location of choice for movie directors looking for something special. As you drive around the island, keep an eye out for the locations of scenes from some of these movies: Pirates of the Caribbean 4, The Descendants, Just Go With It, Soul Surfer, *all four* Jurassic Park *movies*, Tropic Thunder, Dragonfly, To End All Wars, Six Days/Seven Nights, Mighty Joe Young, George of the Jungle, Outbreak,

North, Honeymoon in Vegas, Hook, Lord of the Flies, Flight of the Intruder, Throw Momma From the Train, The Thorn Birds, Uncommon Valor, Body Heat, Raiders of the Lost Ark, Fantasy Island, King Kong, Acapulco Gold, Islands in the Stream, The Hawaiians, Lost Flight, Hawai'i, Paradise Hawaiian Style, Girls! Girls! Girls!, Donovan's Reef, Blue Hawai'i, South Pacific, Miss Sadie Thompson *and many more. Hollywood discovered Kaua'i years ago.*

Harrison Ford rehearsing at Maha'ulepu for the movie, Six days/Seven Nights.

It's cool when you literally stumble across movie props, as we did with this shipwreck from Tropic Thunder, *local resident Ben Stiller's film.*

Kekaha to Hanalei, and fares are $2. A monthly pass is $40, and most have bike racks. There are stops all along the main highway, but they aren't always marked as well as they should be. For a bus schedule or more information, call 246-8110.

Less Than 4 Wheels

If you really want to ham it up, try renting a HOG. (*Note:* The Supreme Court recently ruled that publishers cannot be held liable for bad puns.) **Kauaʻi Harley-Davidson** on the highway in Puhi (241-7020) rents HOGs. Good selection. Rates are $179 for 24-hours for HOGs. Expensive? You bet! But nothing else feels like a genuine Harley.

Scooters/mopeds are also available. We've seen some pretty close calls and consider them too unstable to recommend. Be *real* careful on hills, and stay off the highway between Lihuʻe and Kapaʻa. **Rent-A-Wreck Kauai** (245-7177) rents them for a confiscatory *$65* for 24 hours.

Taxis

If you want to tour the island by taxi… you have entirely too much money to burn. For those who need an occasional taxi service, you will find these available: **Sue's North Side Taxi** (635-0882), **Akiko's** (822-7588) or **Pono Express** (800-258-6880) on the east shore, or **City Cab** (245-3227) on the south shore.

Camper Vans

Want to take your accommodations with you? **Kauaʻi Camper Rental** (346-0957) rents out 1984–1991 Volkswagen Vanagon Westfalia Campers. That's right—see the tropics from a VW bus just like the hippies of yore. In all seriousness, Kauaʻi lends itself to being explored by camper van, especially the north and west shores. Having the versatility to just replant yourself at each camping location means getting to see a

Relics of a bygone era, the sugar industry is dead on Kauaʻi. Whether you love 'em or hate 'em, GMO crop research is the industry that is trying to replace it.

lot more of the island. Though not exactly cheap ($165/day or $1,050/week), the vans come loaded with everything you'll need (except refrigeration).

Wheelchair Accessible Vans

These are available from Wheelers Van Rentals (877-735-6365). Rates are $115 per day if you rent for a week, plus $200 for pickup at airport. Don't forget to bring your placard. Also, if you're looking to rent a wheelchair, Gammie HomeCare (632-2333) in Lihu'e has beach wheelchairs, but reserve them well in advance.

GETTING MARRIED ON KAUA'I

The beauty of Kaua'i has provided the backdrop for many engagements, weddings and vow renewals. And why not? It's in the air here. People are genuinely happy on Kaua'i, and the aroma of joy can make your life together even sweeter. Whether you choose a natural or manmade waterfall, a sunset on a beach, an elegant chapel, beautiful garden or an ancient Hawaiian temple, Kaua'i can create nuptial memories that will last a lifetime.

Thanks to e-mail and the Internet, you can arrange your own wedding, no matter how far away you are. All of the legal requirements, as well as possible wedding locations, are just a click away. Everything—from helicopter flights landing at private waterfalls to just the two of you on a beach at sunset with a minister—is available.

Some of the more popular wedding locations are at the St. Regis Princeville, Hanalei Colony Resort, Marriott, Hyatt, Sheraton and the Waimea Plantation Cottages. Many resorts have wedding coordinators and private wedding sites on property. You might also want to consider renting a private home for you and your guests. Don't let the RACK rates and wedding package prices scare you off. Nothing's carved in stone.

The number of details in planning a wedding is dizzying, and many couples prefer the assistance of an independent wedding coordinator. They can be tremendously helpful in navigating the complicated waters of your marriage. (Well, the ceremony, at least. After that, you're on your own.) Don't let yourself get herded into activities (for which they get a commission), and be on the lookout for add-ons that can ratchet up the price. Be especially selective of your photographer and videographer. This is a one-time event that can't be duplicated.

Some of the more reputable companies are listed below. Unlike most activities, we can't review each in depth. It's not possible to get married a dozen times and critique the way each coordinator did their job. We have, however, anonymously contacted virtually all of the coordinators on the island (in the guise of planning a wedding) and these stood out:

Ali'i Kaua'i Weddings
(808) 854-1003
Aloha Ever After
(877) 711-3003
Coconut Coast Weddings
(808) 212-7332
Island Weddings & Blessings
(808) 828-1548

WEATHER

Kaua'i doesn't have the best weather in the state, but the best weather in the state is on Kaua'i. What do we mean by that? Well, when it's good here, it's as good as weather can get—brilliant sunshine, crystal clear air, and gentle but constant breezes. That's when it's good.

Yeah, but I've heard it always rains on Kaua'i. We heard this many times before we came here for the first time.

The reality of Kaua'i is that it gets more rain than the other Hawaiian islands. In fact, one of the rainiest spots on earth is smack dab in the middle of the island. Mount Wai'ale'ale is an undisputed *year-round* rain magnet, receiving an average of 432 inches per year, which is a staggering 35 *feet* annually. (Though they've measured rainfall there for over a century, stating an average is more of an art than a science since there were times in the past they went up to read that gauge, perhaps after a year, only to find it overflowing—so they guessed.)

The mountain is shaped like a funnel pointing directly into the moisture-laden trade winds, which are forced to drop their precious cargo during their march up the slopes. The summit of Wai'ale'ale is other-worldly, with plants stunted and dwarfed by the constant inundation of rain. Moss, fungi and lichen flourish in the swamp just west of the actual peak. Alaka'i Swamp contains flora and fauna found nowhere else in the world. On the opposite side of the mountain, the spent clouds can do no more than drift by, making the west side of the island rather arid. What rain it does get comes from the sporadic Kona winds. (Throughout the islands, Kona winds refer to winds that come from the southwest and are often associated with inclement weather.)

All that said, the odds are overwhelming that rain will *not* ruin your Kaua'i vacation. The coast gets *far* less rain than the waterlogged central interior, and throughout Kaua'i the lion's share of rain falls at night. When it does rain during the day, it is usually quite short-lived, often lasting a matter of a few minutes. One of the things that takes a little getting used to is the fleeting nature of the weather here. In many parts of the country, rain or sunshine are words used *by themselves* to describe the day's weather. On Kaua'i, a warm, passing shower is to be expected and rarely signifies that a long period of rain is to follow. If you call the local telephone number for the National Weather Service (see page 27), you will probably hear something like this. "Today—mostly sunny, with a few passing windward and *mauka* (mountain) showers. Tonight—mostly fair with a few passing windward and *mauka* showers. Tomorrow—mostly sunny, with a few passing windward and *mauka* showers." So don't get bummed if it suddenly looks ominous in the sky. It'll probably pass within a few minutes, leaving happy plants in its wake.

If you want to know whether to take the top down on the convertible, look into the wind, and you'll be able to see the weather coming. Dark clouds drop rain—the darker the cloud, the harder the rain. It's as simple as that, and you will often see locals looking windward if they feel a drop on their heads. If you're inland, you will often be able to *hear* the rain approaching. When you hear the sound of a rushing river but there isn't one around, take cover until it passes. (Mango trees are ideal for this purpose and have ancillary benefits, as well.)

In planning your daily activities, a good rule of thumb is that if it is going to be a rainy day, the south shore will probably be sunny, and the west shore will almost certainly be sunny. The exception is during Kona winds when weather is the opposite of normal.

Storm systems do discover the state from time to time. Sometimes they're here for days. If one happens to hang around during your trip, don't despair. I first met Kaua'i during one of the wettest times in decades. There was even lightning, which is rare. And it was during that stay that I fell in love with the island and vowed to make it my home. Kaua'i in the rain is still Kaua'i.

As far as hurricanes are concerned, don't waste your time worrying about them. It's true, we had a real 'okole kicker back in 1992. Hurricane 'Iniki was a category 4 storm that stripped the island bare, ironically striking on September 11th of that year. But after this pruning, the island recovered and became greener than ever. Hurricanes are few and far between here. The only previous hurricanes to hit the island this century were 'Iwa in 1982 and Dot in 1959. When Isabella Bird traveled here in 1873, where she penned her excellent book, *Six Months in the Sandwich Isles,* she reported that "hurricanes are unknown in the islands," which means that there hadn't been one in living memory. (Of course, if one *does* strike during your stay, kindly disregard this last statement.)

As far as **temperatures** are concerned, Kaua'i is incredibly temperate. The average *high* during January is 78 °F, whereas our hottest time, late August/early September, has an average *high* of 85 °F. With humidity percent- ages usually in the 60s and low 70s, Kaua'i is almost always pleasant. The exception is the extreme west side, which is about 3 degrees hotter. (That might not sound like much, but you sure do notice it.)

Kaua'i's surface **water temperatures** range from a low of 73.4 °F in February to a high of 80 °F in October. Most people find this to be an ideal water temperature range. (Ocean water near a river mouth, such as Lydgate Beach Park, can get colder—we've seen the ocean get as low as 70 °F there during unusually cold Februarys.)

To get current weather or ocean information, call the **National Weather Service Weather Forecast** (245-6001).

Where Should I Stay?

If your decision about when to visit and where to stay takes rainfall amounts into account, the graph below should be of interest. Winter is our rainiest season. (But that's also when you will see the waterfalls at their best.) The north shore is a more popular place to stay in the summer, and

Median Monthly Rainfall Distribution

Inches

| Waimea | Po'ipu | Mt. Wai'ale'ale | Princeville | Kapa'a |
| 19" per year | 36" per year | 432" per year | 85" per year | 48" per year |

the south shore is more popular in the winter due to rainfall distribution and surf.

GEOGRAPHY

Kaua'i is located in the tropics at 22° latitude, meaning that it receives direct overhead sunlight twice each year three weeks before and after the summer solstice. (No part of the mainland United States ever receives direct overhead sunshine due to its more northern location.) The island is 553 square miles, with 50 of its 113 miles of shoreline composed of sand beaches. Compared to the other Hawaiian Islands, Kaua'i and O'ahu have by far the highest proportion of sand beach shorelines. You might read in brochures about "white sand beaches." Actually, they are *golden* sand beaches, unlike the truly white sand beaches found in other parts of the world. Kaua'i is too old to have any volcanic black sand beaches since the creation of *volcanic* black sand ends when the lava flow stops. (Waimea's black sand beach is from lava flecks chipped from riverbeds and from dirt.)

Kaua'i's interior is mountainous, with deeply eroded valleys and large plains around most of the coastal areas. Its rainfall is more varied than any place in the world. The northern and eastern parts of the island (called the windward side) receive the majority of the rain, with the southern and western sections (leeward side) considerably drier. (See rain graph on previous page.)

Looking at the map on the fold-out back cover, you will notice that a highway stretches *almost* all the way around the island. This means that Ke'e is as far as you can go by car on the north shore, and Polihale or the top of Waimea Canyon Drive is as far as you can go on the west side. An attempt to link the two a few years back ended with almost comic results. (See page 94 for more on that.)

The maps in this book are unique in that they show the roadside mile markers. These correspond to the little green signs you will see along the main roads of Kaua'i. This will give you a perspective regarding distances beyond the map scales. Another feature of our maps is

Thunderstorms are relatively uncommon on Kaua'i. But when we get 'em, they can be dramatic.

that north *usually* points up. We have found that many people get confused when they try to use a map where south is pointing to where east should be, etc. The only exceptions we made were a couple trail maps that benefited from using a specific elevated perspective.

In getting around, distances are usually measured in time, rather than miles. See the back fold-out map for a chart of driving times between towns.

HAZARDS
The Sun
Excluding our food prices, the hazard that affects by far the most people is the sun. Kaua'i's latitude means we receive sunlight that's more directly overhead than anywhere on the mainland. (The more overhead the sunlight is, the less atmosphere it is filtered through, and it's also more concentrated than it is farther north.) If you want to enjoy your *entire* vacation, make sure that you wear a strong sunscreen. We recommend a water-resistant sunscreen with *at least* an SPF of 30. Gels work best in the ocean, lotions are best if you're staying dry, and lotions meant for infants and kids work best on your face and head. (Less painful if it gets in your eyes.) Try to avoid the sun between 11 a.m. and 2 p.m. since the sun's rays are particularly strong during this time. If you are fair-skinned or unaccustomed to the sun and want to lay out, 15–20 minutes per side is all you should consider the first day. You can increase it a bit each day. *Beware of the fact that Kaua'i's ever-constant trade winds will hide the symptoms of a burn until it's too late.* You may find that trying to get your tan as golden as possible isn't worth it; tropical suntans are notoriously short-lived, whereas you are sure to remember a bad burn far longer.

Water Hazards
The most serious water hazard is the surf. During the winter, many beaches are not swimmable. Eastern and northern beaches are especially dangerous, and the sad fact is that more people drown in Hawai'i each year than anywhere else in the country. This isn't said to keep you from enjoying the ocean, but rather to instill in you a healthy respect for Hawaiian waters. See BEACHES chapter for more information on this.

Ocean Critters
Hawaiian marine life, for the most part, is quite friendly. There are, however, a few notable exceptions. Below is a list of those that you should be aware of. This is not mentioned to frighten you out of the water. The odds are overwhelming that you won't have any trouble with any of the beasties listed below. But should you encounter one, this information should be of some help.

Sharks—Kaua'i does have sharks. They are mostly white-tipped reef sharks with an occasional hammerhead or tiger shark. Contrary to what most people think, sharks are in every ocean and don't pose the level of danger people attribute to them. In the past 25 years, there have been so few documented shark attacks off Kaua'i—less than one per year—that they haven't been able to create a statistical average. (But the state as a whole had an unusually large number in 2013–14 in all.) When one *does* occur, it's usually tigers attacking surfers. Considering the number of people who swam in our waters during that time, you are more likely to choke to death on a bone at a lu'au than be attacked by a shark. If you do happen to come upon a shark, however, swim away slowly. This kind of movement doesn't interest them. *Don't* splash about rapidly. By doing this you are imitating a fish in distress, and you don't want to do that. The one kind of ocean water you want to avoid is murky water, typically found near river mouths. These are not interesting to swim in anyway. Most shark attacks occur in murky water at dawn or dusk since sharks are basically cowards who like to sneak up on their prey. In general, don't go around worrying about sharks. *Any* animal can be threatening, not just Jaws.

Sea Urchins—These are like living pin cushions. If you step on one or accidentally grab one, remove as much of the spine as possible with tweezers. See a physician if necessary.

Cone Shells—People tend to forget that shells are created by organisms to serve as housing. Most of these creatures are capable of protecting themselves by the use of a long stinger called a proboscis, which injects venom. You might hear that it's safer to pick up a shell by the large end. You should be aware that many shells have stingers that can reach any part of the shell and can penetrate gloves. Therefore, it is recommended that you do not pick up live shells. If you do find yourself stung, immediately apply hot water, as it breaks down the protein venom.

Portuguese Man-of-War—These are related to jellyfish but are unable to swim. They are instead propelled by a small sail and are at the mercy of the wind. Though small, they are capable of inflicting a painful sting. This occurs when the long, trailing tentacles are touched, triggering hundreds of thousands of spring-loaded

stingers, called nematocysts, which inject venom. The resulting burning sensation is usually very unpleasant but not fatal. Fortunately, the Portuguese Man-of-War is not a common visitor to Kaua'i. When they *do* come ashore, usually during the summer and fall on the east shore, they might do so in great numbers, jostled by a strong storm offshore. If you see them on the beach, don't go in the water. If you do get stung, immediately remove the tentacles with a gloved hand, stick or whatever is handy. Rinse thoroughly with salt or fresh water to remove any adhering nematocysts. Then apply ice for pain control. If the condition worsens, see a doctor. The folk cure is urine, and for some of us it comes in a handy applicator, but you might look pretty silly applying it.

Coral—Coral skeletons are very sharp and, since the skeleton is overlaid by millions of living coral polyps, a scrape can leave proteinaceous matter in the wound, causing infection. This is why coral cuts are frustratingly slow to heal. Immediate cleansing and disinfecting of coral cuts should speed up healing time. We don't have fire coral around Kaua'i.

Sea Anemones—Related to the jellyfish, these also have stingers and are usually found attached to rocks or coral. It's best not to touch them with your bare hands. Treatment for a sting is similar to that of a Portuguese Man-of-War.

Bugs

Though devoid of the myriad of hideous buggies found in other parts of the world, there are a few evil critters brought here from elsewhere that you should know about. The worst are **centipedes**. They can get to be six or more inches long and are aggressive predators. If you do happen to get stung, you won't die (but you might wish you had). You'll probably never see one, but if you get stung, even by a baby, the pain can range from a bad bee sting to a mild gunshot blast. Some local doctors say the only cure is to stay drunk for three days. (*Gotta* love a doctor who will prescribe rum.) Others say to use meat tenderizer or green papaya. Pain relievers like ibuprofen and ice are going to be your best bet.

Cane spiders are big, dark and look horrifying, but they're not poisonous. (But they seem to *think* they are. I've had *them* chase *me* across the room when *I* had the broom in

Hey...what are you looking at?

my hand.) We *don't* have no-see-ums, those irritating sand fleas common in the South Pacific and Caribbean.

Mosquitoes were unknown in the islands until the first stowaways arrived on Maui on the *Wellington* in 1826. Since then they have thrived. A good mosquito repellent containing DEET will come in handy, especially if you plan to go hiking. *Lotions* (not thin liquids) with DEET seem to work and stick best. Forget the guidebooks that tell you to take vitamin B_{12} to keep mosquitoes away; it just gives the little critters a healthier diet. If you find one dive bombing you at night in your room, turn on your overhead fan to help keep them away.

Bees are more common on the drier west side of the island. Usually, the only way you'll get stung is if you run into one. If you rent a scooter, beware: I received my first bee sting while singing *Come Sail Away* on a motorcycle. A bee sting in the mouth can definitely ruin one of your precious vacation days. Watch for them rolling around and disoriented at the beach.

Regarding **cockroaches**, there's good news and bad news. The bad news is that here, some are bigger than your thumb and can fly. The good news is that you probably won't see one. One of

their predators is the **gecko**. This small, lizard-like creature makes a surprisingly loud chirp at night. They are cute and considered good luck in the islands (probably because they eat mosquitoes and roaches).

One thing nearly all visitors have heard is there are no **snakes** in Hawai'i (aside from a rare, tiny, worm-like, blind burrowing snake said to be found here on occasion). There is concern that the brown tree snake *might* make its way onto the islands from Guam. Although mostly harmless to humans, these snakes can spell extinction to native birds. Guam has lost nearly all of its birds due to this egg-eating curse. Once they are fertilized, the snakes can reproduce for life from a single specimen. If there are any on Kaua'i (none are known to be on the island at this time), it would be a major disaster. Government officials aren't allowed to tell you this, but we will: If you ever see one anywhere in Hawai'i, please *kill it* and contact the **Pest Hotline** (643-7378). At the very least, call them immediately. The entire bird population of Hawai'i will be grateful.

Pigs

We're not referring to your dining choice. We mean the wild ones you may

Watch where you choose to take a nap.

encounter on a hiking trail. Generally, pigs will avoid you before you ever see them. If you happen to come upon any piglets and accidentally get between them and their mother, immediately bark like a big dog. Wild pigs are conditioned to run from local dogs (and their hunter masters), and Momma will leave her kids faster than you can say, "Pass the bacon."

Road Hazards

There are a couple things you should know about driving around Kaua'i. The speed limits here are probably slower than what you are used to, and Kaua'i police do have a few places where they regularly catch people. (That's code for speed traps.) We mention some in the tours. Also be aware that we have something on Kaua'i called **contra flow**. During commute hours, orange cones are placed on the lane divisions, forcing you to drive on the wrong side of the road. The area between Lihu'e and Wailua is an example of contra flow, and it can be a bit unnerving for the uninitiated.

Seat belt and **child restraint** use are required by law, and the police will pull you over for this alone. It's also illegal for drivers to use a **cell phone** without a headset. You should know that the Kaua'i Police Department regularly receives funds to enhance their seat belt violation enforcement, speeding enforcement and their sobriety checkpoints. So don't even think about violating these laws, or you'll likely get stung.

Lastly, even in paradise we have our **traffic**. Don't overlook the Kapa'a Bypass on the east shore, the Koloa-Po'ipu Bypass on the south shore and the Puhi Bypass near Lihu'e. In fact, driving *south* through Kapa'a can be a pain almost *any time* of day. If you don't take the bypass, consider taking the scenic route up 581 (at the ABC Store) to 580. Might not save any time, but it's prettier than someone else's bumper.

Dirt

Dirt? Yes dirt. Kaua'i's infamous red dirt has ruined many new pairs of Nikes. If you are driving on a cane road on the west side and have your window rolled down, you will eat a lot of it. It's always best to bring some trashable sneakers if you plan to do any hiking. And leave your silk argyle socks at home. If you want to know how staining it can be, just ask the makers of *Red Dirt Shirts*. They use one bucket of Kaua'i mud to dye *five hundred* shirts.

Dehydration

Bring and drink lots of water when you are out and about, especially when you are hiking. Dehydration sneaks up on people. By the time you are thirsty, you're already dehydrated. It's a good idea to take an insulated water jug with you in the car or one of those 1.5 liter bottles of water. Our weather is almost certainly different than what you left behind, and you will probably find yourself thirstier than usual. Just fill it before you leave in the morning and *suck 'em up* (as we say here) all day.

Swimming in Streams

Kaua'i offers lots of opportunities to swim in streams and sometimes under waterfalls. It's a fulfillment of a fantasy for many people. But there are several hazards you need to know about.

Leptospirosis is bacteria found in some of Hawai'i's fresh water. It is transmitted from animal (usually pig and cattle) urine and can enter the body through open cuts, eyes and by drinking. Around 100 people a year in Hawai'i are diagnosed with the bacteria, which is treated with antibiotics if caught relatively early. You should avoid swimming in streams if you have open cuts, and treat all water found in nature before drinking. (Some filters are ineffective for lepto—we've had good luck with Sawyer filters.)

Also, while swimming in freshwater streams, try to use your arms as much as possible. Kicking an unseen rock is easier than you think. Consider wearing water shoes or, better yet, tabis, while in

streams. (Tabis are sort of a fuzzy mitten for your feet that grab slippery rocks quite effectively.) You can get them at Kmart or Walmart in Lihu'e, or the Longs Drugs in Kapa'a.

Another bacteria to be aware of is **Enterococcus**, which can be found in rivers or the ocean in high concentrations after heavy rains. If the ocean water is looking brown, don't go swimming. The **Surf Rider Foundation's** Kaua'i chapter regularly tests water from 25 spots around the island and posts the latest findings on their website. Under normal conditions, if you don't have open cuts or swallow much water, your body will not be adversely affected by the bad stuff.

Though rare, **flash floods** can occur in any freshwater stream anywhere in the world, even paradise. Be alert for them.

Lastly, remember while lingering under waterfalls that not everything that comes over the top of the falls will be as soft as water. Rocks coming down from above could definitely ruin the moment.

Grocery Stores

Definitely a hazard. Restaurants may be expensive, but don't think you'll get off cheap in grocery stores. Though you'll certainly save money cooking your own food, a trip to the store here can be startling. Phrases like *they charge how much for milk?* echo throughout the stores. One tip: **Foodland** and **Safeway** both offer discount cards (called Maika'i Cards and Safeway Club Cards, respectively) that can bring pretty big savings off their otherwise confiscatory rates. Kapa'a's stores are easily seen along the highway; north shore has Foodland at Princeville Shopping Center and **Big Save** in Hanalei. The south shore has Big Save in Koloa on Koloa Road. If you're a **Costco** member, we have one near Kukui Grove in Lihu'e. If you're not a member and will be here awhile, consider joining as they have the best prices. If you just don't want to shop, **Kaua'i Island Shopping Service** (822-5477) will shop and deliver for a fee plus cost of food—certain areas only.

Roosters

OK, so you don't normally think of roosters as hazards. And normally they're not. These guys are wild in many parts of the island and can be charming. But our roosters have proliferated since Hurricane 'Iniki freed so many back in 1992, and they are particularly stupid here. They don't seem to know when they're supposed to crow, so they do it *all day long* just to cover themselves. (Probably for liability purposes.) If any of these two-legged alarm clocks are near where you're staying, you may find yourself waking up *real* early.

TRAVELING WITH CHILDREN (KEIKI)

Perhaps we should have put this section under HAZARDS.

Kaua'i (and Hawai'i in general) is very kid friendly if you know the best places to go, have the right gear, and enjoy the great outdoors. Your kid's age and your comfort level are the biggest factors to consider when planning your trip. Sun protection is a must (keiki-sized UV blocking rashguards and hats) as is having plenty of water. Personal hydration packs (such as CamelBak) are great for hiking and going to the beach. They even come in kids' sizes (which is nice since you'll be carrying most everything else). If your crumb crunchers are 5 or younger and you want to do some hiking, a baby-frame backpack (like those made by Kelty) is essential. Not only do they keep your keiki out of harm's way, but most of these packs also have a surprising amount of room for hauling other gear. Sure, you might look and feel like a pack mule, but

sharing the outdoor experience with your little ones is sure to make for lifelong memories. (Plus your kid is already well-positioned for taking selfies with you.) These packs can be checked *for free* with most airlines since they count as child transport (as do car seats and strollers). Otherwise, they can be rented on island for around $35 a week from the companies listed below.

Hiking trails here are plentiful, but many are too strenuous for kids. If you have a baby frame pack, then your options increase, but you don't want to be clambering up and down cliffs either. Listed here are trails that can easily be done with kids aged 5–10. We assume that kids older than this can handle some of the more varied terrain of other, more difficult hikes. In general, we think anything more than 3 miles would be pushing it for kids (gotta include rest stops), but only you can make the judgment call on what is appropriate. Trails don't have guardrails or fencing to keep you from dropoffs, and often the surrounding vegetation hides some steep hillsides. Keep your kids close and don't let them wander.

Koke'e Trails—Kaluapuhi Trail, Water Tank Trail and Berry Flat (see map page 142).

North Shore—Kilauea Historic Stone Dam Trail.

East Shore—Sleeping Giant, Kuilau Ridge Trail, Ho'opi'i Falls.

South Shore—Po'ipu Shoreline Sandstone Hike. (You'll definitely need sun protection and water; be sure to take breaks whenever you find shade.)

If you need a crib, stroller, car seat, baby-frame pack and things you never even thought you needed (especially if you're staying at a condo), **Ready Rentals** (823-8008), **Babylicious** (652-4273) or **Rainbow Rentals** (212-5031) have it all.

As far as swimming in the ocean with your little one, **Lydgate Beach Park** in

Wailua has a boulder-enclosed keiki (kid) pond that is wildly popular. (See the aerial photo on the inside back cover.) It also has two playgrounds (Kamalani), the best free one on the island. Overall, it's a nice place for keiki. Also check out **Salt Pond Beach Park** in Hanapepe and **Baby Beach**, both in BEACHES. **Po'ipu Beach Park** in Po'ipu is popular with local parents, as well as visitors. These are considered the best places for children, except during periods of high surf. Obviously, surf and keiki don't go well together.

During calm summer surf, **Kalihiwai Beach** can be a pleasant place to bring kids. While not as protected as Lydgate or Salt Pond, it's picturesque, and your kids will make many new local friends.

Train lovers might want to check out **Kaua'i Plantation Railway** (245-7245). They cruise through 2.5 miles of the Kilohana Plantation in Lihu'e. You'll stop and feed pigs along the way, which the kids go crazy over.

Kaua'i Mini Golf (828-2118) is a pretty good putt-putt. Grounds are lush and there are lots of water hazards here. (You're going in the water at some point, so deal with it.) A good selection of sandwiches, snacks and ice cream for sale, and the price is $18.50 for adults (who will enjoy it), $15 for youngun's 11–17, and $11 for keiki ages 5–10. Easy to recommend. Only complaint is the closeness to the highway there in Kilauea. They also have a small, well-marked botanical garden.

If going to the **movies** is your thing, Kaua'i is more lim-

ited than any other island. We don't get all the movies you find on the mainland. The largest theater, **Kukui Grove Cinema** (245-5055) in Lihu'e has a whopping *four* screens. They have a funny policy about not selling tickets early, so people start lining up about 30 minutes before the start time. Cash only. The other theater is on the west side. The historic, one-screen **Waimea Theater** (338-0282) was built in the 1930s. They've done a nice job restoring it, and it has a lot of charm. They can be a bit behind in new releases.

If you are looking for babysitters, nearly every lodging on the island has lists of professional services, as well as employees who baby-sit. **Babysitters of Kaua'i** (632-2252) and **Kaua'i Babysitting** (652-5373) charge around $25 per hour. Some hotels, such as the **Hyatt** and the

Baby Beach in Lawa'i lands another satisfied customer.

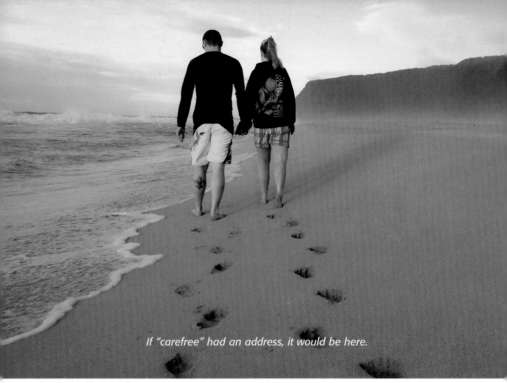

If "carefree" had an address, it would be here.

Marriott, offer rather elaborate services that can be a rug-rat's dream. If you are staying at a place that has no front desk, contact your rental agent for an up-to-date list of sitters.

Traveling With Children Best Bets

Best Kid Friendly Beaches—'Anini on right side or Kalihiwai (Rock Quarry) in summer on North Shore. Boulder Ponds at Lydgate on East Shore. Po'ipu Beach Park, left side on South Shore. Salt Pond Beach Park, far left side on West Shore.

Best Playground—Kamalani Playground at Lydgate Beach Park

Best Library—Princeville Library

Best Big Resort Pool—Grand Hyatt Kaua'i in Po'ipu

Best Resort Pool That Won't Drown Your Wallet—Waipouli Beach Resort in Kapa'a.

Best Lu'au to Keep Your Kid's Attention—Lu'au Kalamaku at Kilohana

Best Fancy Restaurant to *Not* Take Your Kids—Kaua'i Grill in Princeville

Best Shops to Find a Unique Toy—Beachrail Lines in Nawiliwili, Magic Dragon Toy & Art Supply in Princeville, or Sand Kids in Po'ipu.

Best Place to Have a Locally Made Root Beer—Kaua'i Beer Company

Best Weekly Event for Kids & Adults—Hanapepe Art Night

Best Place for Family Camping—Koke'e State Park

THE PEOPLE

The people of Kaua'i are the friendliest people in the entire country. "Oh, come on!" you might say. But this is not the admittedly biased opinion of someone who lives here. This conclusion was reached by the participants in the *Condé Nast Readers' Choice Awards*. This is a sophisticated and savvy lot. *Condé Nast* is the magazine of choice for world travelers. When asked in their yearly poll, readers rate Kaua'i at or near the top of the list in friendliness nearly every year.

What does this mean? Well, you will notice that people smile here more than other places. Drivers wave at complete strangers (without any particular fingers leading the way). If you try to analyze the reason, it probably comes down to a matter of happiness. People are happy here, and happy people are friendly people. It's just that simple. Some people compare a trip to Kaua'i with a trip back in time, when smiles weren't rare, and politeness and courtesy were the order of the day.

Ethnic Breakdown

Kaua'i has an ethnic mix that is as diversified as any you will find. Here, *everyone* is a minority; there is no majority. The last census count revealed the ethnic makeup below.

White	34%
Asian	31%
Hawaiian or other Pacific Islander	9%
Hispanic	11%
Black	0.7%
Native American or Alaska Native	0.6%
Mixed or didn't respond	25%
Total population	**67,091**

SOME TERMS

If you are confused regarding terms in Hawai'i, this should help. A person of Hawaiian blood is Hawaiian. That is a racial term, not a geographic one, so only people of the Hawaiian race are called Hawaiian. They are also called Kanaka Maoli, but only another Hawaiian can use this term. Anybody who was born here, regardless of race (except whites), is called a local. If you were born elsewhere but have lived here a while, you are called a kama'aina. If you are white, you are a haole. It doesn't matter if you have been here a day or your family has been here for over a century, you will always be a haole. The term comes from the time when westerners first encountered these islands. Its precise meaning has been lost, but it is thought to refer to people with no back-

ground (since westerners could not chant the kanaenae of their ancestors).

The continental United States is called the mainland. If you are returning home, you are not "going back to the states" (we *are* a state). When somebody leaves the island, they are off-island.

HAWAIIAN TIME

One aspect of Hawaiian culture you may have heard of is Hawaiian Time. The stereotype is that everyone in Hawai'i moves just a little bit more slowly than on the mainland. We are supposed to be more laid back and don't let things get to us as easily as people on the mainland. This is the stereotype...OK, it's *not* a stereotype. It's real. During your visit, if you get in the rhythm, you'll notice that this feeling infects *you* as well. You might find yourself letting another driver cut in front of you in circumstances that would incur your wrath back home. You might find yourself willing to wait for a red light without feeling like you're going to explode. The whole reason for coming to Hawai'i is to experience beauty and a sense of peace, so let it happen. If someone else is moving a bit slower than you would like, just go with it.

THE HAWAIIAN LANGUAGE

The Hawaiian language is a beautiful, gentle and melodious language that flows smoothly off the tongue. Just the sounds of the words conjure up trees gently swaying in the breeze and the sound of the surf. Most Polynesian languages share the same roots, and many have common words. Today, Hawaiian is spoken *as an everyday language* only on the privately owned island of Ni'ihau, 17 miles off the coast of Kaua'i (see INTRODUCTION chapter). Visitors are often intimidated by Hawaiian. With a few ground rules you'll come to realize that pronunciation is not as tough as you might think.

When missionaries discovered that the Hawaiians had no written language, they sat down and created an alphabet. This Hawaiian alphabet has only 12 letters. Five vowels: A, E, I, O and U, as well as seven consonants: H, K, L, M, N, P and W.

The consonants are pronounced just as they are in English, with the exception of W. It is often pronounced as a V. Vowels are pronounced as follows:

A—pronounced as in *Ah* if stressed or *above* if not stressed.

E—pronounced as in *say* if stressed or *dent* if not stressed.

I—pronounced as in *bee*.

O—pronounced as in *no*.

U—pronounced as in *boo*.

One thing you will notice in this book are glottal stops. These are represented by an upside-down apostrophe ' and are meant to convey a hard stop in the pronunciation (and are quite awkward to type). So if we are talking about the type of lava called 'a'a, it is pronounced as two separate As (AH-AH).

Another feature you will encounter are diphthongs (no, that's not a type of bathing suit), where two letters glide together. They are ae, ai, ao, au, ei, eu, oi and ou. Unlike many English diphthongs, the second vowel is always pronounced. One word you will read in this book, referring to Hawaiian temples, is heiau (HEY-YOW). The e and i flow together as a single sound, then the a and u flow together as a single sound. The Y sound binds the two sounds, making the whole word flow together.

If you examine long Hawaiian words, you will see that most have repeating syllables, making them easier to remember and pronounce.

Let's take a word that might seem impossible to pronounce. When you see how easy this word is, the rest will seem like a snap. The Hawai'i state fish is the humuhumunukunukuapua'a. At first glance it seems like a nightmare. But if you read the word slowly, it is pronounced just like it looks and isn't nearly as horrifying as it appears. Try it. Humu (hoo-moo) is pronounced twice. Nuku (noo-koo) is pronounced twice. A (ah) is pronounced once. Pu (poo) is pronounced once. A'a (ah-ah) is the ah sound pronounced twice, the glottal stop indicating a hard stop between sounds. Now you should try it again.

Humuhumunukunukuapua'a.

Now, wasn't that easy? OK, so it's not easy, but it's not impossible either.

Below are some words that you might hear during your visit:

'Aina (EYE-na)—Land.

Akamai (AH-ka-MY)—Wise or shrewd.

Ali'i (ah-LEE-ee)—A Hawaiian chief; a member of the chiefly class.

Aloha (ah-LO-ha)—Hello, goodbye, or a feeling or the spirit of love, affection or kindness.

Hala (HA-la)—Pandanus tree.

Hale (HA-leh)—House or building.

Hana (HA-na)—Work.

Hana hou (HA-na-HO)—To do again.

Haole (HOW-leh)—Originally foreigner, now means Caucasian.

Heiau (HEY-YOW)—Hawaiian temple.

Hula (HOO-la)—The storytelling dance of Hawai'i.

Imu (EE-moo)—An underground oven.

'Iniki (ee-NEE-key)—Sharp and piercing wind (as in Hurricane 'Iniki).

Kahuna (ka-HOO-na)—A priest or minister; someone who is an expert in a profession.

Kai (kigh)—The sea.

Kalua (KA-LOO-ah)—Cooking food underground.

Kama'aina (KA-ma-EYE-na)—Longtime Hawai'i resident.

Kane (KA-neh)—Boy or man.

Kapu (KA-poo)—Forbidden, taboo; keep out.

Keiki (KAY-key)—Child or children.

Kokua (KO-KOO-ah)—Help.

Kona (KO-na)—Leeward side of the island; wind blowing from the south, southwest direction.

Kuleana (KOO-leh-AH-na)—Concern, responsibility or jurisdiction.

Lanai (LA-NIGH)—Porch, veranda, patio.

Lani (LA-nee)—Sky or heaven.

Lei (lay)—Necklace of flowers, shells or feathers. The mokihana is the official flower of Kaua'i.

Liliko'i (LEE-lee-KO-ee)—Passion fruit.

Limu (LEE-moo)—Edible seaweed.

Lomi (LOW-me)—To rub or massage; lomi salmon is raw salmon rubbed with salt and spices.

Lu'au (LOO-OW)—Hawaiian feast; literally means taro leaves.

Mahalo (ma-HA-low)—Thank you.

Makai (ma-KIGH)—Toward the sea.

Malihini (MA-lee-HEE-nee)—A newcomer, visitor or guest.

Mauka (MOW-ka)—Toward the mountain.

Moana (mo-AH-na)—Ocean.

Mo'o (MO-oh)—Lizard.

Nani (NA-nee)—Beautiful, pretty.

Nui (NEW-ee)—Big, important, great.

'Ohana (oh-HA-na)—Family.

'Okole (OH-KO-leh)—Derrière.

'Ono (OH-no)—Delicious, the best.

Pakalolo (pa-ka-LO-LO)—Marijuana.

Pali (PA-lee)—A cliff.

Paniolo (PA-nee-OH-lo)—Hawaiian cowboy.

Pau (pow)—Finish, end; *pau hana* means quitting time from work.

Poi (poy)—Pounded kalo (taro) root that forms a paste.

Pono (PO-no)—Goodness, excellence, correct, proper.

Pua (POO-ah)—Flower.

Puka (POO-ka)—Hole.

Pupu (POO-POO)—Appetizer, snacks or finger food.

Wahine (vah-HEE-neh)—Woman.

Wai (why)—Fresh water.

Wikiwiki (WEE-kee-WEE-kee)—To hurry up, very quick.

A beautiful sunset can mean only one thing—time for a mai tai.

Quick Pidgin Lesson

Hawaiian pidgin is fun to listen to. It's like ear candy. It is colorful, rhythmic and sways in the wind. Below is a list of some of the words and phrases you might hear on your visit. It's tempting to read some of these and try to use them. If you do, the odds are you will simply look foolish. These words and phrases are used in certain ways and with certain inflections. People who have spent years living in the islands still feel uncomfortable using them. Thick pidgin can be incomprehensible to the untrained ear (that's the idea). If you are someplace and hear two people engaged in a discussion in pidgin, stop and eavesdrop for a bit. You won't forget it.

Pidgin Words & Phrases

Ainokea—I don't care. (Say it out loud.)
An' den—And then? So?
Any kine—Anything; any kind.
Ass right—That's right.
Ass why—That's why.
Beef—Fight.
Brah—Bruddah; friend; brother.
Brok' da mouf—Delicious.
Buggah—That's the one; it is difficult.
Bus laugh—To laugh out loud.
Bus nose—How one reacts to a bad smell.
Chicken skin kine—Something that gives you goosebumps.
Choke—Plenty; a lot.
Cockaroach—Steal; rip off.
Da kine—A noun or verb used in place of whatever the speaker wishes. Heard constantly.
Fo days—plenty; "He got hair fo days."
Geevum—Go for it! Give 'em hell!
Grind—To eat.
Grinds—Food.
Hold ass—A close call when driving your new car.
How you figga?—How do you figure that? It makes no sense.
Howzit?—How is it going? How are you? Also, Howzit o wot?

I owe you money or wot?—What to say when someone is staring at you.
Lolo—Crazy or stupid.
Mek ass—Make a fool of yourself.
Mek house—Make yourself at home.
Mek plate—Grab some food.
Mo' bettah—This is better.
Moke—A large, tough local male. (Don't say it unless you *like beef*.)
No can—Cannot; I cannot do it.
No mek lidat—Stop doing that.
No, yeah?—No, or is "no" correct?
'Okole squeezer—Something that suddenly frightens you ('okole meaning derrière).
O wot?—Or what?
Pau hana—Quit work. (A time of daily, intense celebration in the islands.)
Poi dog—A mutt.
Shahkbait—Shark bait, meaning pale, untanned people.
Shaka—Great! All right!
Shoots, den—Affirmative/roger that.
Shredding—Riding a gnarly wave.
Slippahs—Flip-flops, thongs, zoris.
Stink eye—Dirty looks; facial expression denoting displeasure.
Suck rocks—Buzz off, or pound sand.
Talk stink—Speak bad about somebody.
Talk story—Shooting the breeze; to rap.
Tanks eh?—Thank you.
Tita—A female moke. Same *beef* results.
Yeah?—Used at the end of sentences.

MUSIC

Hawaiian music is far more diverse than most people think. Many often picture Hawaiian music as someone twanging away on an 'ukulele (pronounced OO-KOO-LAY-LAY, not YOU-KA-LAY-LEE) with his voice slipping and sliding all over the place, as though he has an ice cube down his back. In reality, the music here can be outstanding. There is the melodic sound of the more traditional music. There are young local bands putting out modern music with a Hawaiian beat. There is even

Hawaiian reggae and hip hop. If you get a chance, check out iTunes or stop by **Wal-mart** (246-1599) in Lihu'e. They have a good selection of Hawaiian music.

THE HULA

The hula evolved as a means of worship, later becoming a forum for telling a story with chants (called mele), hands and body movement. It can be fascinating to watch. When most people think of the hula, they picture a woman in a grass skirt swinging her hips to the strumming of an 'ukulele. But in reality there are two types of hula. The modern hula, or hula 'auana, uses musical instruments and vocals to augment the dancer. It came about after westerners first encountered the islands. Missionaries found the hula distasteful, and the old style was driven underground. The modern type came about as a form of entertainment and was practiced in places where missionaries had no influence. Ancient Hawaiians didn't even use grass skirts. They were brought in later by Gilbert Islanders.

The old style of hula is called hula kahiko (also called 'olapa). It consists of chants and is accompanied only by percussion and takes years of training. It can be exciting to watch as performers work together in synchronous harmony. Both men and women participate, with women's hula somewhat softer (though no less disciplined) and men's hula more active. This type of hula is physically demanding and requires strong concentration. Keiki (children's) hula can be charming to watch as well.

Kaua'i was the home of the most prestigious hula school in all the islands. People came from every part of the island chain to learn the hula at the Ka-ulu-Paoa. Great discipline was required, and the teachers could be very strict. The remains of this school are still evident on a plateau above Ke'e Beach.

The lu'au around the island usually have entertaining hula shows, though not as "authentic" as some of the festival demonstrations seen on occasion. Some resorts and shopping centers also have hula shows on occasion.

FARMERS' MARKETS

Called Sunshine Markets locally, you'll find them every day of the week, great places to pick up locally grown fruits and produce. Get there before they open, because things go fast. Below is a list; each is also shown on the various maps.

Monday—In Lihu'e at Kukui Grove Shopping Center off Nawiliwili Road at 3 p.m., and Koloa Ballpark on Maluhia Road at noon. In Kapa'a at Kealia Farm across from Kealia Beach at 3 p.m.

Tuesday—In Kalaheo at the Kalaheo Neighborhood Center on Papalina Road off the Hwy at 3 p.m. West of Hanalei at Waipa Farm (near Lumaha'i Beach) at 2 p.m.

Wednesday—In Kapa'a at the Kapa'a New Town Park on Kahau Street at 3 p.m.

Thursday—In Hanapepe at Hanapepe Park at 3 p.m., and in Kilauea at the Kilauea Neighborhood Center on Keneke off Lighthouse Road at 4:30 p.m.

Friday—In Lihu'e at Vidinha Stadium on Hoolako Road at 3 p.m. In Kapa'a at Kealia Farm across from Kealia Beach at 3 p.m.

Saturday—In Kekaha at Kekaha Neighborhood Center on Elepaio Road at 9 a.m. Also a large private farmer's market in Hanalei at 9:30 a.m. at the Hanalei Neighborhood Center and Ballpark just past the post office, mauka side of the highway. In Puhi at the Kaua'i Community College parking lot at 9:30 a.m.

Sunday—In Anahola on Hokulele Rd. (first left past/north of Duane's Ono Char Burger) from 10ish a.m. to 3ish p.m.

BOOKS

There is an astonishing variety of books available about Hawai'i and Kaua'i. Everything from history, legends, geology, children's stories and just plain ol' novels. In Hanapepe, **Talk Story Bookstore** (335-6469) has a very nice selection, as well as hard-to-find used books. And don't forget the **Kaua'i Museum** (246-2470) in Lihu'e. They, too, have interesting and hard-to-find books.

A NOTE ON PERSONAL RESPONSIBILITY

In past editions we've had the sad task of removing places that you can no longer visit. The reason, universally cited, is *liability*. Although Hawai'i has a statute indemnifying landowners, the mere threat is often enough to get something closed. Because we, more than any other publication, have exposed heretofore unknown attractions, we feel the need to pass this along.

You need to assess what kind of traveler you are. We've been accused of leaning a bit toward the adventurous side, so you should take that into account when deciding if something's right for you. To paraphrase from the movie *Top Gun*, "Don't let your ego write checks your body can't cash."

You will probably be more physical during your trip, so *train* for it. Doctors and officials strongly believe that the biggest cause of injury and death of visitors stems from people who aren't active at home, coming here and blowing a gasket from all the recreating they've dreamed of doing here. If you plan on doing any hiking, snorkeling or other activities, spend the month before coming here exercising as much as you can. Your body will reward you, we promise.

Please remember that this isn't Disneyland—it's nature. Mother Nature is hard, slippery, sharp and unpredictable. If you go exploring and get into trouble, whether it's your ego that's bruised or something more tangible, please remember that neither the state, the private landowner nor this publication *told* you to go. You *chose* to explore, which is what life, and this book, are all about. And if you complain to or threaten someone controlling land, they'll rarely fix the problem you identified. They'll simply close it... and it will be gone for good.

Sometimes even good intentions can lead to disaster. At one adventure, a trailhead led hikers to the base of a wonderful waterfall. There was only *one* trail, to the left at the parking lot, that a person could take. Neither we, other guides nor websites ever said, "Stay on the trail to the left," because at the time there was only one trail to take. The state (in their zeal to protect themselves from liability at an unmaintained trail) came along and put up a DANGER KEEP OUT sign at the trailhead. Travelers encountering the sign assumed they were on the wrong trail and started to beat a path to the right instead. But that direction started sloping downward and ended abruptly at a 150-foot-high cliff. Hikers retreated and in a short time a previously non-existent trail to the right became as prominent as the correct (and heretofore *only*) path to the left. Not long after the state's well-intentioned sign went up, an unwitting pair of hikers took the new, incorrect trail to the right and fell to their deaths. They died because they had been dissuaded from taking the correct trail by a state sign theoretically erected to keep people safe. The result? You'll now see more warning signs than ever in Hawai'i.

Our point is that nothing is static and nothing can take the place of your own observations and good judgment. If you're doing one of the activities you read about in our book or someplace else and your instinct tells you something is wrong, *trust your judgment* and go do another activity. There are lots of wonderful things to do on the island, and we want you safe and happy.

And also remember to always leave the island the same way you found it.

A NOTE ABOUT ACCESS

If a lawful landowner posts a NO TRESPASSING sign on their land, you need to respect their wishes. That seems simple enough. But here's where it gets tricky.

It's common in Hawai'i for someone who doesn't own or control land to erect NO TRESPASSING, KEEP OUT and ROAD CLOSED signs. Picture a shoreline fisherman who doesn't want anyone else near his cherished spot, putting up a store-bought sign to protect his solitude. Or a neighbor on a dirt road who hates the dust from cars driving by, so he puts up a sign that he knows locals will ignore, but it might dissuade unwary visitors.

In the past we did our best to try to ferret out when NO TRESPASSING signs were valid and when they were not, and we took *a lot* of heat from residents who mistakenly thought we were encouraging trespassing when we weren't. But the current environment doesn't permit us to do that anymore. So if you're heading to one of the places we describe and you encounter a NO TRESPASSING sign, even if you think it's not authorized by the landowner (and even if it's on *public* land), we have to advise you to turn around and heed the sign. All descriptions in our book come with the explicit assumption that you have obtained the permission of the legal landowner, and unfortunately, it'll usually be up to you to determine who that is and how to get it. But please, under no circumstances are we suggesting that you trespass. Plain and clear. Don't trespass...ever...for any reason...period.

MISCELLANEOUS INFORMATION

Kaua'i has no distinct **visitor season**. People come here year round to enjoy the island's blessings. However, certain times of the year are more popular than others. Christmas is always a particularly busy time, and you may have trouble getting a room if you are determined to stay at a particular resort. The graph on page 44 illustrates typical visitor distribution here.

Waterfalls and wild chickens—It doesn't get more Kaua'i than this.

The island never feels crowded the way other destinations can feel. This might sound surprising, given poll results. When pollsters ask people where they would like to go, Kaua'i is always in the top 10.

If you're looking to dump your **digital images** onto a CD, **Walmart** (246-1599) on Hwy 56 in Lihu'e has good prices or, if you're member, try **Costco** (241-4000) near Kukui Grove Shopping Center in Lihu'e.

Travelers' checks are usually accepted, but you should be aware that some merchants might look at you like you just tried to offer them Mongolian money. You should also know that the American Express Card seems to be less welcome here than at some destinations. A number of places will not accept it.

The **area code** for the entire state is 808.

Plastic bags are banned on the island, and rather than springing for paper bags, many stores will simply hand you your purchases, no matter how numerous. Consider bringing your own reusable bag.

If you are planning to see either the **National Tropical Botanical Garden** or the **Grove Farm Sugar Plantation Museum**, make your reservations before you get here to assure admittance. Campers should also obtain their permits before they arrive, especially for the Na Pali Coast. See CAMPING in the AC-TIVITIES chapter.

If you have an **early checkout** (or a **late flight**) and need a place to freshen up

before your flight, consider the bathrooms at Lydgate State Park, several miles north of the airport, which have showers. Upon entering the road to Lydgate, the showers to the right on Nehe Street are a bit more private.

If you wear **sunglasses**, *polarized* lenses are highly recommended. Not only are colors more brilliant here, but the lower latitudes of Hawai'i make polarized lenses particularly effective.

It is customary on Kaua'i for *everyone* to remove their shoes upon entering someone's house (sometimes their office). Kaua'i's **red dirt** can be particularly pernicious, and nobody wants to spend their day cleaning floors.

Daylight saving time isn't observed in Hawai'i.

If you are going to spend any time at the beach (and you really should), woven bamboo **beach mats** can be found all over the island for about $3. Some roll up, some can be folded. The sand comes off these more easily than it comes off towels.

If you want to arrange a **flower lei** for you or your honey as you arrive at the airport on a direct flight (no interisland flights), call **Greeters of Hawai'i** (800-366-8559) or **Honolulu Lei Greetings** (800-665-7959) before you arrive. You can get a nice lei on Kaua'i for around $27. (I know where you're going with that—stop it!) While on island, **JC's Flowers** (822-5961) in Kapa'a across from Kinipopo Shopping Center has nice leis for reasonable prices. A plumeria lei is $8 and up, and they're gorgeous. (Not bad!)

Finally, if you're staying on the south shore and you have a medical issue, **Po'ipu Mobile MD** (652-7021) makes house (hotel/condo) calls 24 hours a day for non-emergency care. Fees range from $400 to $700. It may sound pricey, but I'd rather be in my hotel room sipping a mai tai than sitting in the ER with a sprained ankle.

Thousands J F M A M J J A S O N D

Visitors Per Month

If you came to Hawai'i to get leid, this is the place that lovers lay them.

VOLUNTEERING ON VACATION

There are many opportunities to give back while you are visiting from building homes to beach cleanups. One of our favorites is the **Kaua'i Humane Society** (632-0610) Shelter Dog Field Trip program. Basically, you spend the day with an unloved dog by picking one up in the morning (as early as 10 or 11 a.m.) and returning one hour before closing in the afternoon. They provide all the supplies you need, and you supply a $200 credit card deposit. This has led to many adoptions, and they'll help with that, too.

FIND US ONLINE

You will find recent changes, links to cool sites, the latest satellite weather shots and more on our website **www.hawaiirevealed.com**. We also show our own aerial photos of nearly every place to stay, so you'll know if oceanfront *really* means oceanfront.

In earlier editions we had a **Calendar of Events** mentioning festivals, island celebrations and special events. Waste of time! Organizers make changes so often (including days before scheduled events) that it wasn't reliable enough to continue printing it in advance. But the Internet is perfect for that. So our website has updated listings of island events.

HAWAII REVEALED APP

OK, we have to toot our own horn here. If you have a smartphone or tablet and want a version of this book that is geo-aware (a book that literally knows where it's at) visit the iTunes store or Google Play and check out **Hawai'i Revealed**. We have re-GPSed the island (not relying on existing public domain maps) and created an interactive version of this book. (You haven't really lived until you've spent a whole day *GPSing all the mile markers on the island* so they will be precise on the moving map. Or spending seven days in Waimea Canyon getting all the trails precise and correct.) Just tap the map, and everything we describe in the book appears along with the distance to your current location.

A beautiful sunny day on the North Shore delivers on the dream.

Kaua'i's north shore...where lushness takes on a whole new meaning. Every shade of green imaginable is represented in its myriad plant life. Its beaches are exquisite and its mountains unmatched in their sheer majesty. After a heavy rain, you will literally be unable to count the number of waterfalls etched into the sides of the north shore mountains.

For the sake of clarity, we will identify the north shore as everything north of Kapa'a. (Look at the fold-out back cover map to orient yourself.) While this description includes Anahola (which some may consider east shore), it is easier to remember it this way, and anyone driving north of Kapa'a is usually going to the north shore anyway. The main highway, which stretches around the island, occasionally changing its name, has mile markers every mile. These little green signs can be a big help in knowing where you are at any given time. Therefore, we have placed them on the maps represented as a number inside a small box 16. We will often describe a certain feature or unmarked road as being "0.4 miles past mile marker 16." We hope this helps.

Everything is either on the *mauka* side of the highway (toward the mountains) or *makai* (toward the ocean). Since people get these confused, we'll refer to them as *mauka side* and *ocean side*.

All beaches we mention are described in detail in the chapter on BEACHES.

Driving north of Kapa'a, you'll see **Kealia Beach** on your right, just past mile marker 10. This is a popular boogie boarding beach. At this beach you can often see water spitting into the air from the collision of an incoming and outgoing wave, called *clapotis* for the trivia-minded. (Doesn't that sound more like something a sailor might pick up while on shore leave?)

ANAHOLA

Next, comes the town of Anahola. This area is designated Hawaiian Homelands, meaning it is available to persons of Hawaiian descent. The spike-shaped mountain you see on the *mauka* side is **Kalalea Mountain**, also called **King Kong's Profile**. As you drive north of Anahola, look back, and you will see the striking resemblance to King Kong. To the right of the profile is a small hole in the mountain called (this is clever) **Hole-in-the-Mountain**. It used to be bigger, but a landslide in the early 1980s closed off most of it. You can see it best between mile markers 15 and 16. One legend says that a supernatural bird named Hulu pecked the hole in order to see Anahola on the other side. Geologists say that there was once a long lava tube stretching from Wai'ale'ale to the sea. The mountain mass on either side of the ridge has been removed by ceaseless erosion, leaving only the ridge and its ghost of a lava tube.

Duane's Ono-Char Burger is in Anahola. This is a good place for burgers and shakes if you're hungry but not in a hurry.

There are several secluded beaches north of Anahola that require walks of

Perched on a bluff overlooking the vast Pacific Ocean, the Kilauea Lighthouse stands as a silent sentry.

Wyllie Beach
'Anini Channel
Moku'ae'ae Island
Kilauea Lighthouse
Kilauea Pt. National Wildlife Refuge
Kahili Beach (Rock Quarry)
Makapili Rock
Pools of Mokolea
Secret Beach

'Anini Beach
'Anini Rd
Kalihiwai Beach
1st Kalihiwai Rd
Lighthouse
Kilauea Rd
Crater Hill
Kilauea Bay

2nd Kalihiwai Rd
Kalihiwai Falls
24
Kong Lung Center
Kilauea
Farmer's Mkt Thurs. 4:30 p.m.
Na 'Aina Kai Botanical Garden

The Prince Golf Course
26
Oka St.
Keneke Rd
Wailapa Rd

Map continued on page 51

56
27
25
Unnamed Twin Falls
Kahiliholo Rd
23
Kolo Rd
22
56

Princeville Airport

Stop kayaking here

Stop kayaking here

Kalihiwai Falls (Visible from bridge)

Ho'okui Rd

Kilauea Falls is also privately owned and only accessible by kayak (and even this is contested!).

Kapa ka Rd

Kalihiwai River

Kilauea Stream

Kilauea Slippery Slide is privately owned, closed and not accessible to the public.

Hanalei River

Powerline Trail

2,814'   Mt. Namahana

Power poles are marked to serve as a navigational aid.

∿ Indicates Foot Trails
⋰ Kapa'a Bike Path
18 Roadside Mile Marker
⋰ Unpaved Roads
‒ Public Access
⛺ Campsite

‒Trail overgrown from here going north

0 ————————— 1 Mile
0 ————————— 1 Kilometer

© 2017 Wizard Publications, Inc.

Anahola to 'Anini

Waiakalua
Beaches

Arch

Pakala Channel
(which you won't swim in...right?)

*The reef edges are denoted by ••••••••••
and come directly from government topographic
maps. The task of verifying the precise location
of all underwater reefs would be herculean and
has not been attempted by us.*

Pila'a Beach

White
Tank

Larsen's Beach

N. Waiakalua Rd

Zuckerland

21

56

20

N
W — E
S

Ko'olau Rd

Moloa'a Bay

19

Moloa'a Rd

18

17

Ko'olau Rd

16

Papa'a Bay

Papa'a Rd.

'Aliomanu Beach

15

Aliomanu
Road
(Broken Loop)

King Kong's Profile &
Hole-in-the-Mountain

Anahola
Beach
Park

Kahala
Point

14

Anahola
Anahola

Kukuihale

Anahola Stream

Gate

Secluded
Cove

12

Kealia Rd

Spalding Monument
A monument built by a long-dead
sugar baron to himself, now in
disrepair. Kind of embarrassing
when you think about it.

Hauaala Rd
4WD

Kealia Rd

Donkey
Beach

56

11

Map continued on page 61

various lengths, including Waiakalua Beach and Larsen's Beach. See map on the previous page and the BEACHES chapter. In 2014 the founder of a fairly successful website reportedly paid *$200 million* for the land fronting Larsen's so he could build a vacation home. We have it labeled on the map as Zuckerland.

Near mile marker 17 is the Moloa'a Sunrise Juice Bar (822-1441) A good place for smoothies and juices (but the selection of fresh fruit is hit or miss and overpriced, and the food is expensive and underwhelming).

At the end of Wailapa Road (on the ocean side of the highway between mile markers 21 and 22) are the Na 'Aina Kai Botanical Gardens (828-0525). This is what happens when you have someone with obvious big bucks (in this case the first wife of the late *Peanuts* creator Charles Schulz) with a dream and vision to create 240 acres of tropical gardens, sculptures, a teak wood plantation, a desert garden, secluded beach and stream,

all scrupulously maintained. Guided tours are expensive—$35 for the recommended 1.5-hour tour—but it's such an exceptionally beautiful area that it's worth it. Arrange in advance. Other guided tours of different lengths also available.

KILAUEA

The former plantation town of Kilauea is just past mile marker 23 and is accessible off Kolo Road. It is known for the Kilauea Lighthouse (828-1413). This is a postcard-perfect landmark perched on a bluff and represents the northernmost point of the main Hawaiian Islands. When it was built in 1913, it had the largest clamshell lens in existence and was used until the mid '70s when it was replaced by a beacon. Directly offshore is Moku'ae'ae Island, a bird sanctuary. Self-guided tours of the lighthouse area are available, though you can't go upstairs and visit the light itself. The view from the bluff is smashing and worth your time. Open 10 a.m. to 4 p.m., it's $5 per person to

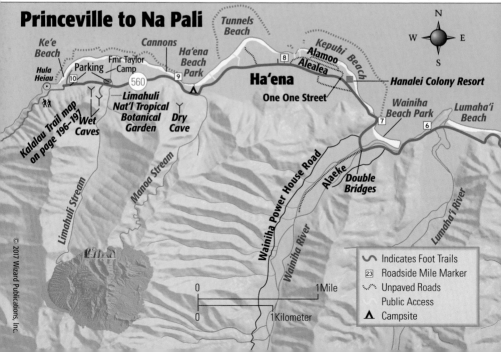

Princeville to Na Pali

Tunnels Beach

Ke'e Beach
Cannons
Ha'ena Beach Park
Kepuhi Beach
Alamoo
Alealea

Hula Heiau
Parking
Fmr Taylor Camp
10
560
9
Ha'ena
One One Street

Limahuli Nat'l Tropical Botanical Garden
Dry Cave

Wet Caves

Kalalau Trail map on page 196–197

8
Hanalei Colony Resort

Wainiha Beach Park
7
6
Lumaha'i Beach

Limahuli Stream

Manoa Stream

Wainiha Power House Road

Alaeke
Double Bridges

Wainiha River

Lumaha'i River

N
W E
S

0 ——— 1 Mile
0 ——— 1 Kilometer

⌢ Indicates Foot Trails
23 Roadside Mile Marker
⋯ Unpaved Roads
Public Access
▲ Campsite

1 Mauna Kai
2 Puamana
3 Westin
4 Kamahana
5 SeaLodge
6 Plantation at PV
7 Nihilani at PV
8 The Cliffs
9 Ali'i Kai I
10 Emmalani Court
11 Pali Ke Kua
12 Hanalei Bay Villas
13 Pu'u Poa
14 Hanalei Bay Resort
15 St. Regis Princeville
16 Villas of Kamali'i

Princeville

Queen's Bath

SeaLodge Beach

Falls

Building A

Punahele

Kapiolani

Kaweonui

Keoniana

Kamehameha

Kaui

Pepelani

Albert

Hideaways Beach
(Pali Ke Kua)

Liholiho

Honoiki

Princeville
Makai Course
Clubhouse

Lei O Papa

Ka Haku Road

Wyllie

Pu'u Poa Beach

Hanalei Plantation Rd

Hanalei River

Princeville
Center

Queen
Emma's

Hanalei Pier
(Black Pot)

0   1/2 MILE

28

Kuhio Highway

© 2017 Wizard Publications, Inc.

The reef edges are denoted by ············
and come directly from government topographic
maps. The task of verifying the precise location
of all underwater reefs would be herculean and
has not been attempted by us.

See Princeville detail map above.

Hideaways
(Pali Ke Kua
Beach)

Wyllie
Beach

St. Regis Princeville

Pu'u Poa
Beach

Princeville

Princeville Makai Course

Hanalei Plantation Rd

Kahalahala
portion of
Lumaha'i

Grocery
Store

Last Gas on
North Shore

Hanalei
Bay

Hanalei Pier
(Black Pot)

560

28

5

1

56

Waikoko
Beach

Wai'oli
Beach Park

Pine
Trees

Waipa
Beach

Wete

Aku

Hanalei River

Hanalei
Bridge

2

Parking
Lot

4

3

Hanalei
Inn

Ching Young
Village

Okolehao Trail

Stop
kayaking
here

Kumu

Farmer's
Market
Sat. 9:30 a.m.

Hanalei
Center

Hanalei

Map continued on page 48

get in (kids are free). Closed Sundays and Mondays. Take Kilauea Road.

Kilauea has also become a high-priced refuge for the super rich. Many exotic compounds are sprinkled about the area, just beyond sight.

Just north of Kilauea, on the *mauka* side, is **Banana Joe's** fruit stand with a decent selection of produce. They also carry numerous locally made products such as Popsicles. The frosties are excellent. (Frozen bananas ground through a Champion Juicer, which creates a consistency similar to ice cream.) Nearby is **Kaua'i Mini Golf & Botanical Gardens** (828-2118). See TRAVELING WITH CHILDREN on page 35 if you're in a putting mood. It's a pretty nice putt putt.

KALIHIWAI

After Kilauea you will notice two Kalihiwai Roads on the map. It used to be a loop connected at the bottom via a bridge. The bridge was erased by a tsunami in 1957, and the state hasn't replaced it yet. (Give 'em time; they're still debating whether smart phones are just another passing fad.) The first Kalihiwai Road leads to a beautiful little bay, **Kalihiwai Bay**. (Keep an eye out for a small, pretty hidden falls on your right after a bridge.) Kalihiwai is a good place to stretch your legs and enjoy the scenery.

Back on the highway, there's a road 0.5 miles past mile marker 24 called Kahiliholo Road. It's the only place you can park to walk to an **unnamed falls** 0.5 miles farther up the road on the left. (The falls are sometimes used by people to rinse off saltwater after they've been to **Secret Beach**.) The stream flows under the road and falls again into the valley. The long bridge past the falls has a narrow walkway. Visible on the *mauka* side is **Kalihiwai Falls**, a gorgeous, two-tiered falls. The cars on this bridge *seem* to go by at 110 mph, so be careful. Sometimes

they let the brush over-grow along the side of the road and it becomes hazardous to walk there. (You might have a tough time seeing the falls unless you walk out onto the bridge.) You might see the remains of a vehicle turnout right at the bridge. The state closed it because of our old buddy, *liability*.

As you continue, take the second Kalihiwai Road to 'Anini Road, which leads to **'Anini Beach**, where many of the rich and famous choose to build their homes. This is one of the safest places on the north shore to swim and is protected by a long, fringing reef.

PRINCEVILLE

Continuing on Highway 56, the resort area of **Princeville** beckons. It was named after Prince Albert, the visiting 2-year-old son of King Kamehameha IV. Although the young lad died two years later, the name stuck. The resort is renowned for its ocean bluff condominiums.

Princeville's cliffs lead many to think that it has no beaches to offer. *Au contraire.* Beaches don't get much better than **Hideaways**, a very pleasant little pocket of coarse sand. The catch is that you need to hike down about 5–10 minutes to it. Another gem (in the summer) is **Queen's Bath**. This is a natural pool located on a lava bench. See BEACHES on page 104. The **St. Regis Princeville** is a good place to dine, shop or just gawk. If you are staying in Princeville, you may choke over the prices at Foodland or Big Save in Hanalei. Consider stocking up on food in Kapa'a where it's *somewhat* cheaper.

A REAL GEM

As you leave Princeville, note that the highway changes names again and the mile markers start at 0. The gas station here is the last place to get gas on the north shore (and they have the prices to prove it!). Across the street is the **Hanalei**

Lookout. Many postcards have been sold featuring this view. This valley is where most of the taro in Hawai'i is grown. Taro corm (the root portion) is pounded to make poi. This is the stuff everyone told you not to eat when you came to Hawai'i. If you go to a lu'au, try it anyway. Then you can badmouth it with authority.

HANALEI

Going down the road, you come to the old-style **Hanalei Bridge**. Its wood planks are slippery when wet. This is a good time to tell you about Kaua'i's one-lane bridge etiquette. All vehicles (up to seven or eight) on one side proceed, so if the car directly in front of you goes, you go. Otherwise, stop and wait for cars on the other side to go first. Most bridges from here on have one lane. Hanalei Bridge has a 15-ton weight limit, so you won't see big tour buses past this point. One bridge, called

the Waipa Bridge, was built in 1912 for $4,000. It's so sturdy that it has *never* needed a major repair. The state found this intolerable and planned to replace it with a $5 million bridge that would hopefully require *lots* of maintenance. Local residents banded together in the late '90s and successfully fought 'em off.

The area around **Hanalei** (meaning wreath-shaped or crescent-shaped) **Bay** is a pretty little community. The surfing here is famous throughout the islands for its challenging nature during the winter. The entire bay is ringed by beach. A wide assortment of people live in Hanalei, including longtime locals, itinerant surfers, new age types, celebrities and every other type of individual you can imagine. You're as likely to see locals driving a Mercedes or Hummer as you are a car held together with bungee cords and duct tape.

The Hanalei Lookout is a postcard waiting to happen...

Sunset from Hanalei Pier is a great place to end your day.

After Hanalei, you ascend the road to a turnout overlooking **Lumaha'i Beach** (if the vegetation next to the turnout is not overgrown). This is a fantastic-looking beach made famous when Mitzi Gaynor washed that man right out of her hair in the classic Kaua'i-made movie *South Pacific* in 1957. (If you haven't seen the movie, that last statement must sound awfully stupid.) The eastern portion is the best but requires a hike down. Otherwise, you can walk right onto it just before the Lumaha'i Stream.

Notice how lush everything looks from here on? This part of the island gets the perfect amount of rain and sunshine, making anything green very happy.

HA'ENA

Wainiha Beach Park, past mile marker 6, is often a great place to beachcomb, but the swimming is not good.

One of the best **snorkel** and shore SCUBA spots on the island, **Tunnels Beach**, is past mile marker 8. See BEACHES chapter. This is the same spot that the world renowned surfer, Bethany Hamilton, lost her arm to a tiger shark in 2003. Her story got the Hollywood treatment in the film *Soul Surfer*. Don't let this deter you from seeing this amazing beach. See the HAZARDS section for reassurance.

Before you get to mile marker 9, the road dips at **Manoa Stream**. The stream flows over the road and is always creating potholes. It often creates a hole big and deep enough to pop your tire, so look for it as you cross. You are now at **Ha'ena Beach Park**. Camping is allowed with a county permit, and the beach is lovely year round (but the *swimming* isn't always lovely; see BEACHES chapter). Across the street is the **Manini-holo Dry Cave**. Manini-holo was said to be the chief fisherman for the Menehune. He and other Menehune dug the cave looking for supernatural beasts called akua who had been stealing their fish, but they didn't find *da buggah*.

Below mile marker 9 is a pile of rocks, all that remains of a heiau that was destroyed when they built the road. Called **Hale Pohaku**, it was where they raised small white dogs that served two purposes. One was food for the chiefs. The other was for chiefesses who gave birth. Often times children born to important chiefesses were removed and raised by others. So the small dogs would have their teeth pulled so they could nurse from the chiefesses to relieve the pressure in their breasts from the milk. If you look around, you'll find that one of the rocks has a petroglyph of a dog still on it.

Past mile marker 9 you will come to **Limahuli Stream**. Many people (including us) use this stream to rinse off the saltwater after their day at **Keʻe Beach**, which is still ahead, or use it to rinse SCUBA gear after a dive at Tunnels.

Above Limahuli Stream is the **Limahuli Garden** (826-1053). It is part of the National Tropical Botanical Garden. They have guided tours (by reservation only) of the gardens for $40, self-guided tours for $20 Tuesdays through Saturdays. The variety of endangered plants is refreshing. A real treat is the ancient terrace system, crafted by some of the earliest Hawaiians, estimated to be 700 years old and in fantastic condition.

Just past the Limahuli Stream are the **Wet Caves**, called **Waikapalaʻe Cave** (reachable by a short trail) and **Waikanaloa Cave** (right there on the road). The upper **Waikapalaʻe Cave** contains a clean, freshwater pool. Until some years ago the back portion of the cave (reachable only by swimming in the cold water) hid a phenomenon called the **Blue Room** (a chamber where the light turned everything blue). But the water level is now too low, and too much light has erased the blue from the blue room. The wet and dry caves are former sea caves, gouged by waves when the sea level was higher than it is today. We were silly enough to SCUBA dive the upper cave and can report that there is not much to see, but it was kind of fun anyway (and spooky when we swam past where you could see the light entering the cave). Hawaiian legend has it that these caves were dug by the fire goddess

Shave Ice: An Island Delicacy

One local treat everyone should try is shave ice. Lest you be confused, shave ice is not a snow cone. Snow cones are made from crushed ice with a little fruit syrup sprinkled on. True shave ice (that's shave, not shaved) uses a sharp blade to literally "shave" a large block of ice, creating an infinitely fine powder. (Keeping the blade sharp is vital.) Add to this copious amounts of exotic fruit flavors, put it all on top of a big scoop of ice cream, and you have an island delight that is truly broke da mouf. In our constant quest to provide as thorough a review as possible, we have unselfishly tried nearly every combination of shave ice. The result: We recommend the rainbow shave ice with macadamia nut ice cream. But by all means, engage in research of your own to see if you can come up with a better combination. The best shave ice on the island is at Hee Fat General Store or Tege Tege in Kapaʻa, Jo-Jo's Anuenue in Waimea and Wishing Well Shave Ice in Hanalei. These can be found in the ISLAND DINING chapter.

Pele. She dug them for her lover but left them when they became filled with water.

At mile marker 10, you have gone as far as you can go by car. This is **Ke'e Beach,** marked by a fabulous lagoon that offers great swimming and snorkeling when it's calm. The well-known **Kala-** **A REAL GEM** **lau Trail** begins here. Eleven miles of hills and switchbacks culminate in a glorious beach setting, complete with a waterfall. The first leg of the hike leads to **Hanakapi'ai Beach** with a side trip to **Hanakapi'ai Falls.** You sure ain't gonna do this trail on a whim, so for more on the **Kalalau Trail,** see ADVENTURES on page 196.

Ke'e is where **Na Pali Coast** begins. You can see its edges from here. Numerous movie scenes have been filmed at this location. If you walk past Ke'e Beach on the shoreline trail beside the

Walk the shoreline trail past Ke'e Beach for a great view of Na Pali.

rocks (when seas aren't raging), you'll get an enticing look at the rugged **Na Pali coastline.** Look up toward the mountains, and you'll see **Bali Hai** (Hawaiian name **Makana Peak**). Clever photography turned the peak into the mystical island of Bali Hai in the movie *South Pacific.* As you stare at this peak with its incredibly steep sides, picture the following scene that took place in ancient times.

Men would climb the 1,600-foot peak carrying special spears made of hau and papala. The trail was so difficult in spots that they had to cling to the side of the mountain for dear life. When it got dark, they would light the spears and hurl them as hard as they could toward the ocean below. The spears were designed to leave a fire trail behind and were light enough to get caught in the updrafts. The light show was immensely popular.

From the end of Ke'e Beach, a trail cuts through the jungle up to the **Ka-ulu-Paoa Heiau,** still visible by the pavement of stones outlining its foundations next to a lava cliff. All the land here is state or county, even the run-down house in the jungle. (Despite an oddly out-of-place PRIVATE PROPERTY sign on land deeded to the county *decades* ago.) But nearby residents—and sometimes bullhorn-equipped lifeguards—not legally authorized by the state to control access, often dissuade people from walking on this public land to the heiau due to its sacred nature. Whether they have the authority or not, if you are dissuaded, you should respect their wishes. For over 1,000 years this heiau served as the most important and prestigious school for hula in the islands. Would-be students came from around the island chain to learn from the *kumu hula,* or hula master. Please don't disturb any rocks lying about. Just past the heiau a short trail leads to a small waterfall (which is merely a trickle during dry times). *Fifty* generations of hot, thirsty students came to this tiny waterfall, sat on these very rocks and talked about their lives, hopes, fears and dreams. It's humbling to share these rocks with their spirits. It's as if you can still hear the echo of their lives in the sound of the gurgling water.

Just east of **Ke'e** is where the infamous **Taylor Camp** used to be. This is where Howard Taylor, brother of the late Elizabeth Taylor, owned a piece of land in the 1960s and encouraged other "hippies" to come and live off the land. The camp swelled to more than 100 people who mostly ended up living off residents or the government. Before the state condemned the property in 1977, camp residents began what would become the national *puka shell* craze when one of the residents fashioned a necklace of shells and gave it to Howard, who in turn gave it to his famous sister Liz.

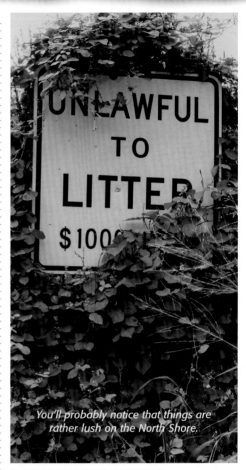

You'll probably notice that things are rather lush on the North Shore.

NORTH SHORE SHOPPING

Across from mile marker 20 on your way north to Kilauea is **Hawaiian Hardwoods** for mostly large furniture pieces, following the natural forms found in the original wood. In Kilauea at Kong Lung Center try **Kong Lung Trading** for outstanding Japanese ceramics, housewares, toys and other items. In the same building don't miss **Banana Patch Studio** for Hawaiian style ceramics and other island items for the home. In the back is **Cake**, a women's boutique with some unique clothing and accessories. Outside at the back of the center is **Coconut Style** for unique island batik designs. **Island Soap & Candle** has just what the name implies, all made locally. And for jewelry, stop in at **Lotus Gallery**. Across the street in the Kiluaea Plantation Center, tucked in the back, is **Hunter Gatherer**. They have a treasure trove of home goods, jewelry and other locally made gift items.

In the Princeville Shopping Center, **Magic Dragon Toy & Art Supply** has many options to keep the young and old entertained, including books, games, puzzles and, of course, dragons. **Walking in Paradise** has all kinds of sandals from fancy to functional. The **Princeville Wine Market** has a small but discerning selection of wines and spirits, as well as a chill barrel outside for your convenience. **Live A Little** has a great selection of sunglasses and island-designed hats.

As you approach Hanalei, the north shore's shopping mecca, stop at Hanalei Dolphin Center and have a look at **Ola's** for fine arts and some pretty unusual gifts and **I Love Hanalei** for island-style clothes. On the same side of the road is the green Halele'a Building where **Titus Kinimaka Kai Kane** has some good buys on surf wear. On the main highway before Ching Young Village, behind the main road in Kauhale Center, visit **Crystals & Gems Gallery** for some unusual handcrafted jewelry. Back on the main highway, **Kokonut Kids** has adorable children's island wear and some toys. Browse **The General Store of Hanalei** for art and *sometimes* music created by local artists. Next door is one of our favorite shops **On The Road To Hanalei** for Asian-inspired housewares, pottery and jewelry.

In Ching Young Village there are many shops and places to eat. **Pedal 'n Paddle** has great outdoor gear for sale and rent, and if your shoes have taken a beating on your trip, this is a great place to pick up island-friendly, surf-and-turf footwear.

The **Backdoor Surf** is good for surf wear. **Hanalei Strings** has a small selection of Hawaiian music and 'ukulele. **Robin Savage Gifts and Gourmet Hanalei** is a great stop for housewares and Hawaiian foodstuffs.

Across the street in Hanalei Center be sure to walk behind the building and see **Havaiki Oceanic and Tribal Art**, which has extensive and unique artworks from all over the pacific islands and is not to be missed. **Yellowfish Trading Co.** carries vintage Hawaiiana, antiques and collectables. **Tropical Tantrum** has batik print clothing; **Sand People** also has women's clothes and island-style items for your home. **Hanalei Surf Co.** has the best wetsuits. **Jewel of Paradise** has some unusual glass paperweights of celestial bodies that are worth a look. If you are heading up to Ha'ena, stop in at the Hanalei Colony Resort and check out **Na Pali Art Gallery & Coffee House**.

NORTH SHORE BEST BETS

Best Beach—Ke'e or Hideaways
Best Snorkeling—Tunnels, Hideaways or Ke'e
Best Treat—Apple Cobbler at Village Snack & Bakery or any flavor at Kaua'i Nut Roasters
Best Lava Swimming Pool in the Summer—Queen's Bath
Best Secluded Beach—Waiakalua
Best Swimming When Calm—Ke'e
Best Shore SCUBA Dive—Tunnels Beach
Best Beachcombing—Wainiha Beach
Best View—Sunset from Ke'e Overlooking Na Pali, or from Hanalei Pier
Best Parking Spot—One of the Few Available at Tunnels
Best Place to Gas Up *Only When Desperate*—76 Station in Princeville
Best Place to be Glad You're Wearing Comfortable Shoes—The End of the 11-Mile Long Kalalau Trail

Wailua is known as the coconut coast.

Kaua'i's east shore is where the majority of the population resides. The kings of yesteryear chose the Wailua River area to live, making it forever royal ground. All members of Kaua'i royalty were born in this area. Kuamo'o Road, designated as 580 on the maps, is also called the King's Highway. In ancient times only the king could walk along the spine of this ridge. (Kuamo'o means the lizard's spine.)

Today, the east shore is often referred to as the Coconut Coast. One drive through Wailua and it's obvious why: thousands of coconut trees planted over a century ago by an idealistic young German immigrant who dreamed of overseeing a giant copra (dried coconut) empire. Unfor-tunately, nobody told him how long coconut trees took to mature, and the plantation was not economically successful, but his legacy lives on in the form of a gigantic coconut grove. These trees have already lived longer than their expected lifespan, so the grove is starting to thin out a bit. The resort across from Wailua Beach ensconced in all those coconut trees was called **Coco Palms**. It got whacked by a hurricane on September 11, 1992, and has been closed ever since. Even with its rich Hawaiian history (and even though Elvis Presley filmed *Blue Hawai'i* there), none of its subsequent owners has been able to figure out a way to reopen it, though the current owner has ambitious plans.

Detailed map on page 200

Kahuna Rd

Kawaihau Rd

Kainahola Rd

Moalepe Trail

Bridge

Intersection of Moalepe & Kuilau Trails

Ignore

Waipouli Rd

Kuilau Ridge Trail

1,000'

'Olohena

Powerline Trail

Puuopae

Keahua Arboretum

600'

520'

Wailua Reservoir

Kaua'i Research Station

4 (Again)

5

Kamalu

Farmer's Market Tues. 3 p.m.

581

'Opaeka'a

Kuamo'o Rd

Kaua'i's Hindu Monastery

580

Kuamo'o-Nounou Trail

Electrical Substation

4

3

5

Wailua Forestry Management Rd

North Fork Wailua River

Kuamo'o Rd

280'

2

Map continued on page 208

Secret Falls
22°02.951
159°22.369

Private

Indicates Foot Trails
Kapa'a Bike Path
18 Roadside Mile Marker
Unpaved Roads
Public Access
⊙ Heiau (Temple)

South Fork Wailua River

Kayak Landing
22°02.486
159°21.837

Wailua Falls

Cliff Jump

Trails to bottom

22°02.209
159°21.753

583

Ma'alo Rd

Detailed map on page 157

Ho'opi'i Falls

Kahuna Rd

Kapahi Rd

2 Miles ↑
To Anahola

Kealia Rd

56

11

Kapa'a Stream

Kawaihau Rd

Hauaala Rd

Kaehulua Rd

Kealia Beach

10

Ka'apuni Rd

Mailihuna

Kawaihau Rd

Lookout

Hauiki Rd

Moikeha Stream

'Olohena Rd

Farmer's Market Wed. 3 p.m.

581

9

Walking / Biking Path

Kahau

Lehua

Road

Lokelani

Nounou (Sleeping Giant)

Kukui St

Roxy Square

Kapa'a Beach Park

Lihi Boat Ramp

400'

Nounou Mt Trail

Kapa'a Shopping Center

8

Waipouli Beach Park

Cook Island Pine Trees

1,241'

200'

Kaua'i Village Shopping Center (Whale Mural)

Waipouli Complex

Moanakai Rd

Waiouli Plaza

3
4

Haleilio Rd

Waipouli Town Center

Kapa'a

56

"Temporary" Kapa'a Bypass

Kinipopo Shopping Center

7

Aleka Loop

7

Wailua

Kuamo'o Rd

5

Papaloa

6

580

Waipouli Beach

'Opaeka'a Falls

1

14

Smith's Tropical Paradise

13 12 1 10 8

Coconut Marketplace

Kamokila Hawaiian Village

Wailua

6

Wailua Bay

683'

15

Lydgate Beach Park

Fern Grotto

Leho Dr

16

Playgrounds

Kalepa Ridge

Kuhio Highway

5

707'

Wailua Golf Course

Nukoli'i Beach (Kitchens)

4

Map continued on page 67

56

1 Honu'ea International Hostel
2 Hotel Coral Reef Resort
3 Kaua'i Kailani
4 Waipouli Beach Resort & Spa
5 Courtyard Kaua'i Coconut Beach
6 Plantation Hale Suites
7 Kaua'i Coast Resort
8 Islander on the Beach
9 Kaua'i Shores
10 Lae Nani
11 Lanikai
12 Kapa'a Sands Resort
13 Wailua Bayview
14 Coco Palms Resort (still closed)
15 Hilton Garden Inn Kaua'i
16 Kaha Lani

N
W ⊕ E
S

0   1 Mile
0   1 Kilometer

Wailua & Kapa'a

For our description, the east shore means the Wailua/Kapa'a area to Lihu'e. (Take a look at the fold-out back cover map to orient yourself.) Both areas are heavily populated. (This is a relative term; together they have about 25,000 residents.)

The same descriptive ground rules that we discussed at the beginning of NORTH SHORE SIGHTS apply here.

Unlike other areas of the island where a single road dominates your tour, this area has many significant sights located off the main road. Therefore, we will describe them in a more scattershot manner and generally work our way from north to south.

WAILUA/KAPA'A

In the extreme northern part of Kapa'a is a delightful waterfall called Ho'opi'i Falls, which you can hike to. See HIKING on page 157.

While we are up the road off the main highway, there are several hikes in this area that provide excellent views. The Nounou Mountain Trail (also called the Sleeping Giant), the Kuilau Ridge Trail, the Jungle Hike and the Secret Tunnel to the North Shore Hike are all located inland and all are worthy of consideration. (See HIKING in the ACTIVITIES chapter for more information.)

One aspect of ancient Hawaiian culture that can be seen to this day is the heiau, a structure carefully built from lava rocks and used for religious purposes. There are seven heiau stretching from the mouth of the Wailua River to the top of Mount Wai'ale'ale. All except the Wai'ale'ale heiau are marked on the map on the previous page. The mouth of the Wailua River was well known, not only throughout the Hawaiian Islands, but also in parts of central Polynesia as well. Ancient Polynesians are thought to have come all the way from Tahiti to visit it.

Wailua is also known for ghosts and spirits. It was thought that during a certain phase of the moon, spirits of those who had recently died would paddle down the river in large numbers and work their way around the island to a cliff at Polihale (described on page 91) where they would leap to the next life. Known as night marchers, these ghosts are still believed by many Hawaiians to exist, and sightings are most prevalent along the highway between Wailua and Lihu'e. Interestingly, this stretch of road has also been responsible for many bad car accidents. Of course, police blame the wrecks on another type of spirit—the kind that comes in a bottle.

The first heiau, near the mouth of the Wailua River on the southern side, is called Hauola, City of Refuge. It is part of what was a larger structure called Hikina-akala, meaning the rising of the sun. If a person committed an offense worthy of execution (such as allowing his shadow to touch the shadow of a chief or interrupting an important person), he would attempt to elude his executioners by coming here. By staying at the site and performing certain rites prescribed by the priest, he would earn the right to leave without harm.

The second temple is on the *mauka* side of the highway between the north end of Leho Road and the road to Smith's Tropical Paradise. This is called Malae and at 273 by 324 feet, it is the largest heiau on Kaua'i. Legend states that it was built by Menehune. There is not a lot to see. If you decide to visit it, be wary of your footing.

The third heiau is just up Kuamo'o Road (580) on the left side. This area had several names and several functions. The first portion that you see is called Holoholoku. Some archeologists say that this area was used for human sacrifice. Most of the time those sacrificed were prisoners of

Kealia Beach is so easy to access, local residents even drive onto the sand at the south end.

war. If none could be found, however, the kahuna would select a commoner and have the executioner strangle him secretly at night. Some archaeologists find this interpretation of Hawaiian history in spiritual bad taste, given its very close proximity to the **Birthstones**, described below, and assume that the area was used for animal sacrifices. The heiau was later purposely desecrated and used as a pigpen by the wife of the last king of Kaua'i, who did so as a signal that the ancient religious ways should be abandoned in favor of Christianity.

Just a few dozen feet up the road from **Holoholoku** is the **Birthstone**. It was essential that all kings of Kaua'i be born here, even if they were not of chiefly origin. One of the two stones supported the back of the mother-to-be while the other was where she placed her legs while giving birth. The outline of stones near here indicates where a grass shack once stood, where the pregnant mother stayed until it was time to give birth. The flat slab of sandstone that you see on the ground covered the remains of a sacrificed dog, indicating that the place was kapu, or forbidden to commoners. The giant crack in the rock wall was where the umbilical cord of the newborn was placed. If a rat came and took the cord, it was a sign that the child would grow up to be a thief (or worse, a tax collector); otherwise, all was well.

Continuing up 580, a short way past mile marker 1, there's a dirt road angling back toward the ocean. (You're allowed to walk around the yellow gate.) Located at the end of the road are two large boulders probably surrounded by weeds. Though few residents are aware of it, the rocks' position is no accident and dates back over 1,000 years.

The ancient Hawaiians didn't live in a world of well-defined seasons. They didn't even measure their own lives in years, but rather stages of life. But they did need to keep track of the passage of the sun for planting and religious reasons. These two multi-ton rounded and shaped **solstice rocks** are perfectly offset so that if you align yourself with them so they appear to touch with the right one closer to you, the sun will rise from the intersection on the summer solstice. (Winter solstice involves aligning the right side of the left boulder with the thumb-like hill on Sleeping Giant behind you.) Imagine the importance they must

Lacy 'Opaeka'a Falls is a Wailua landmark. At press time you could only see half due to invasive species trees blocking it. If the state cuts them down, it will look like the photo inset.

have attributed to this task by considering the difficulty of hauling these boulders up from the Wailua River, perhaps one boulder from each fork for symmetry. (Hawaiians *loved* symmetry.)

Past those boulders, if you walk down the path about 100 feet past the guardrail, there are several large stones. One of them was known as the **Bellstone** and, if thwacked properly, can produce a metallic clank (not the gong we have come to expect from metal bells). This sound supposedly carried throughout the entire Wailua Valley. The stone was struck in ancient times to signal the birth of what would be a new chief. Unfortunately, the state has allowed vegetation to swallow up the giant solstice rocks, and the Bellstone is so overgrown you'd need to buy our GPS-aware smartphone app and a machete to find it.

Still on 580 just before you get to the 'Opaeka'a Falls turnout is the last heiau

you will see. Called **Poli'ahu**, this is a rather mysterious heiau and the one that is most worth your time. Legend states that it was built by Menehune, the legendary people of small stature, and was devoted to the interests and activities of the gods, demigods and high ali'i. There is also a nice **Wailua River Lookout** here.

The actual final heiau in this chain rests atop the rain-soaked plateau of **Wai-'ale'ale**. The remnants of this most sacred heiau are still visible today. Called **Ka-'awako**, the altar itself stood 2 feet high, 5 feet wide and 7 feet long. Toward the rear, standing on one end was a phallic stone. It is located on one of the wettest spots in the entire world. According to the USGS, this spot receives 432 inches of rain per year. (You read a lot of numbers about the annual rainfall on **Wai'ale'ale**—this number comes straight from the people who read the rain gauges. The original gauge is in the Kaua'i Museum.)

The ancient Hawaiians were bothered that the small, sacred pool on top of Wai'ale'ale didn't feed their most sacred river, the Wailua. Not to worry. In a project that would make the Army Corps of

Engineers proud, they cut a trench at the top of the mountain from the small pool to the edge of the cliff so the water would add to the waterfalls that feed the Wailua River. Then they could say the most sacred pool fed the most sacred river.

While on Kuamo'o Road *(a well-known speed trap)*, stop by the **'Opae-ka'a Falls Lookout.** These lacy 151-foot falls flow year round. Late morning light is best, around 10:30 a.m. There is another **Wailua River Lookout** across from the 'Opae-ka'a Lookout.

NOT TO BE MISSED!

Kamokila Hawaiian Village (823-0559) is across the street from 'Opae-ka'a Falls. It's 4.5 acres of private land with numerous huts scattered about. Some might find it interesting; others might get antsy, but it's only $5 per person to get in and wander around. It'll probably take 40 minutes or less to see it, and it's certainly *not* indispensable. If you are guided, it will be *very* slow paced, but delivered from the heart. You can also rent a canoe, stand-up paddleboard or kayak (all for $35) for a trip to Secret Falls from here. (See the Kayaking section in ACTIVITIES on page 160.)

Further up Kuamo'o Road, past some hairpin turns, is a road on the left called Kaholalele. At the end is **Kaua'i's Hindu Monastery** (888-735-1619). This is an *incredible* place, but they only give free 90-minute tours by reservation once a week. (It varies depending on the Hindu calendar—call for dates, and you may want to call again the day before to confirm you will actually get to see the temple up close. They sometimes close it without warning depending on the type of work they are doing.) It's set in an absolutely idyllic environment next to the Wailua River. This temple is built entirely of hand-carved stones from India. Some stones take as long as seven years to carve, and there are 4,000 of them. And their special Roman-inspired fly ash concrete foundation is designed to be crack-free for a thousand years. (When we had our driveway paved, they guaranteed it *would* crack within a month—and it did.) They say it's the only pure stone temple being built anywhere in the world and should be complete in 2017, but their narrative, details and completion date seem to change with every visit. They have a strict dress code, so wear long pants and shirts with short or long sleeves or use one of their free sarongs. Hindu worshipers can visit at 9 a.m., other visitors between 10:30 a.m and noon. If you get a chance, a tour is highly recommended, though we've noticed that when groups get too large, the quality suffers. They also have self-guided tours that'll only take 10 minutes or so. You won't see the temple, though you'll get to check out their incredible sprawling banyan tree. An interesting gift shop featuring all things Hindu. Bring mosquito repellent.

Continuing several miles up Kuamo'o Road, the road eventually crosses over a stream and becomes unpaved. The second crossing is literally in the stream and it occasionally flows too heavily over the road to cross in your car. See the detailed map of this area on page 208. A 4WD is often a necessity beyond the stream crossing while regular cars are at the mercy of the maintenance cycle of the road and the weather. (Sometimes the wimpiest Neon can make it; other times pre-maintenance ruts become too much for some 4WDs.) Large puddles are usually lined with small rocks, not mud. Several trailheads are in this region. A pretty one, before the road becomes unpaved, is the **Kuilau Ridge Trail.** The **Keahua Arboretum** is located near here, but it's been rather unkempt for years, so don't knock yourself out to see it.

The unpaved section of this road is Wailua Forest Management Road. The

Lihu'e & Puhi

1 mile to
Wailua Falls

*Kilohana
Crater*

∿ Indicates Foot Trails
23 Roadside Mile Marker
Unpaved Roads
Public Access

0   1 Mile
0   1 Kilometer

Map continued on page 77

Farmer's Market
Sat. 9:30 a.m.

Kilohana

Kukui Grove
Center
(Farmer's Mkt
Mon. 3 p.m.)

58

*Kaua'i
Community
College*

1

50

Hokulei
Village

Kalepa

Puhi

Nuhou

Costco

Pika

Kaumuali'i Hwy

2

Kaumuali'i Hwy

50

Puhi Rd

Hanalima

Puakea
Golf Course

← **9 Miles
to Po'ipu**

50   3

(Puhi Bypass)

Kipu Rd

Haleukama

Hulemalu Rd

Kipu Rd

Halehaka Rd

Bridge

*Papakolea
Stream*

Hulemalu Rd

Falls

Kipu Falls

(Puhi Bypass)

*Cook
Island
Pines*

Hule'ia Stream

As far as you can go by kayak.
21°56.588
159°23.719

Falls

Map continued on page 61

area feels like a giant oxygen factory. Take a big whiff, and you'll almost get a buzz from the purity of the air. The **Jungle Hike** on page 156 and the **Secret Tunnel to the North Shore** in ADVENTURES are back here, as well as stunning forests. This area is excellent for mountain biking.

Back on the main highway, you'll find that traffic in downtown Kapaʻa (on the highway) can get congested at times, *especially* going south. The county opened up a "temporary" bypass road across from Coconut Marketplace on the south end, and up mauka from the ABC store at the north end. (See map on page 61.) The "permanent" bypass road is scheduled to be completed sometime during the next ice age. All the land around the bypass area was for sale some years back. Kauaʻi residents were worried that someone would buy the 1,400 acres and develop it, connecting Kapaʻa to Wailua and creating a big-city feel. Entertainer Bette Midler (a part-time resident) bought it instead and promised never to put anything other than trees on it.

One of Kapaʻa's notable views is the **Sleeping Giant**. The best angle is from

These petroglyphs are usually submerged in the mouth of the Wailua River, but they can appear after heavy rains.

the small turnout kitty-corner from the Chevron station (on the main highway). Look *mauka* and you will see the outline of a giant. (This is your *ink blot* test for the day.) According to legend, the giant you see (you *do* see it, don't you?) was a friendly sort who flattened areas where he sat. Local villagers liked this and also planted bananas in his footsteps. One day the chief ordered a heiau to be built. Villagers were too busy, so the giant volunteered. It took two weeks and he did a great job. Villagers threw a party to celebrate, and the giant ate a bit too much. (If you've been to a luʻau, you can relate.) He fell asleep and has not been roused since, but is expected to wake up any time (maybe during your visit).

Local folklore says that if Kauaʻi's people learned of an attempt to invade their island, they would light fires behind the **Sleeping Giant** in order to illuminate his profile at night. This would frighten invading warriors into thinking that Kauaʻi had some really big dudes and that intruders should rethink their invasion plans.

While you are in Wailua, riverboat trips up the **Wailua River** can take you to the **Fern Grotto** for $25 per person. This is a natural amphitheater filled with ferns and is a popular place for weddings. See RIVER TRIPS in the ACTIVITIES chapter. The **Wailua River** is usually called the only navigable river in all Hawaiʻi, but that depends on your definition of navigable. The mouth of the river has several stones with ancient **petroglyphs** carved in them. After heavy rains, the river sometimes washes away large amounts of sand, revealing these stones for a short period of time. The mouth itself is always changing, and watching it wash over its banks after a heavy rain can be wild. The river mouth can go from not flowing at all to carving up the mouth in a matter of hours.

There is a paved beachside walking path behind the Courtyard Kauaʻi at Coconut Beach, and a longer path from Kapaʻa Beach Park north to Donkey Beach. They are great for a stroll or to ride a bike. A good place to take a *sandy* beach walk is from **Lydgate Beach Park** south as far as the Kauaʻi Beach Resort. The sand is continuous almost the whole way.

Lydgate Beach Park is one of the safest places to swim on the island. It has a boulder-enclosed pond that allows water and fish in but keeps out the ocean's force, though the water clarity is not very good due to some well-intentioned but harmful work done in 2011. See BEACHES on page 112. There is even a keiki (kid) pond, which is shallower. Add to this showers, restrooms and two playgrounds, and you have a nice little park for a day at the beach for those who don't want to expose themselves to the open ocean.

On the southern side of the Wailua River is **Smith's Tropical Paradise**. Here you will find a nice garden (not in the same league as other nicer island gardens) in which to stroll, filled with tropical plants and wailing peacocks (which sound like cats being tortured). Entrance is $6 per person. They also hold a pretty good luʻau here. See ISLAND DINING chapter for more information.

As you pass the **Wailua Municipal Golf Course** going south toward Lihuʻe, realize that the entire coast fronting the course is a sandy beach. Called **Nukoliʻi Beach**, there are rarely more than a few people on it.

LIHUʻE

Coming from Kapaʻa and just before you enter Lihuʻe from Highway 56, you see Maʻalo Road (583) on the *mauka*

side. This leads to **Wailua Falls**. In ancient times (and as recently as 2016,

 which you can see on YouTube), men would jump off the top of the falls to prove their manhood (which was often left on the rocks below). This test can be fatal. Government maps list the falls' height at 80 feet. That always bothered us because it sure *looks* taller. So, a while back we dropped a fishing line and sinker to the bottom from the lip of the falls (boy, did *we* look stupid) and measured it. To our amazement, it was 173 feet of solid drop. (We measured it *twice* to be sure.) That's actually taller than Niagara Falls, though the latter has a tad more water flowing.

You might see people splashing about in the pool below the falls. It's a wonderful scene and lots of fun. Those people got down there by hopping the stone wall (at the far end of the lookout, away from the falls) and then walking behind the chain link fence about 100 feet to a steep trail with exposed tree roots for handholds. That, or they took the less steep trail 0.3 mile back down the road from the end of the turnaround. (See map on page 60.) The latter is easier but requires a much longer walk and includes awkward river walking. Neither are professionally maintained, and both can be slippery when wet. The state, in their paranoia about liability, has erected signs telling you not to take the trails to the bottom. They even cut the ropes (but users keep replacing them) that get strung to make it safer and easier. (Making it *less* safe apparently makes some bureaucrats *feel* safer.) Those people below ignored the signs—and might be local residents who have played at the bottom of the falls for generations—but state bureaucrats don't want you down there, so you should stay on top.

The falls plunge into a pool that's 33 feet deep. Why so exact? Because in one of those *just because* moods (before the state put up the signs), we hiked down with some friends, hauling SCUBA gear (gee, those ropes sure did help), and SCUBA-dived the pool. (We also brought a kayak—what were we *thinking?*) There we found 14-inch long small-mouthed bass and some Tahitian prawns with bodies over 8 inches long, plus arms. Lingering beneath the falls, the scene is like an upside-down battlefield with explosions of white that will cause percussive waves to sweep through your entire body, your air-filled chest shuddering from the blasts. We also found rental car keys (perhaps tossed by an irate but shortsighted spouse), bolt cutters, a cane knife, and other odds and ends.

Back on the highway, if we're just trying to get *through* Lihu'e during traffic, we usually take 51 to 570 (Ahukini Road) to Hwy 56. (See map on page 67 for this to make sense.) It bypasses Hanama'ulu and much of Lihu'e.

In Lihu'e, one place worth stopping for if you have a strong love of culture and history is the **Kaua'i Museum** (245-6931) on Rice Street. This isn't exactly the Smithsonian, but they have a mildly interesting display of Hawaiian artifacts and a permanent display called *The Story of Kaua'i* as well as other rotating displays. Their gift shop is well stocked with books, maps and assorted items. If you are looking for topographic maps of the various areas (serious hikers prefer these as traveling companions) or just an obscure book on Kaua'i or Hawai'i, this is a good place to stop. Admission is $15 per person unless you are going to the gift shop, which is free.

If museums ain't your cup of tea, maybe a pint of beer is. One of Hawai'i's best breweries is a little farther down Rice Street just past Kress St. The **Kaua'i Beer Company** brews several tasty adult beverages as well as their own root beer. See DINING for more info.

Taking Rice Street east leads you to Nawiliwili Harbor. There are two shopping centers here called **Harbor Mall** and **Anchor Cove Shopping Center.** **Kalapaki Beach**, behind Anchor Cove, is a good place to watch sailboats, outrigger canoes and cruise ships, in addition to the beach's other attributes.

On Rice Street, you will pass the main entrance to the **Kaua'i Marriott.** Its other entrance is off Kapule Highway (51) and leads through **Hokuala Kaua'i** to either **Ninini/Running Waters Beach** or the **Ninini Lighthouse.** The lighthouse uses a 4.7 million candlepower light. We remember how that sounded like *a lot* the first time we heard it, until we realized you can go to the store and buy *15 million* candlepower flashlights for $30. To get to the lighthouse, you pass a golf course.

Rice Street loops around and becomes Nawiliwili Road. It is here that you will find **Grove Farm Sugar Plantation Museum** (245-3202). This was the private home of George N. Wilcox and his nieces. It was turned into a museum by Mabel Wilcox shortly before her death in 1978. With 80 acres and several buildings to browse through, it is quite popular. (And they make an awesome sugar cookie here.) Groups of about six are escorted around the grounds and house for 2 hours for $20 per person. Even if this isn't normally your cup of tea, you will probably find it interesting. It's the story of an incredible family's rise to prominence in the old, sugar-dominated Kaua'i. Reservations are required. Tours on Mondays, Wednesdays and Thursdays.

Off Nawiliwili Road is Wa'apa Road. Take this road to Hulemalu Road, and you will come to a scenic overlook for the **Menehune (Alekoko) Fishpond.** This is a large, impressive fishpond adjacent to

Wailua Falls is one of the easiest falls on the island to access—just drive up and gawk.

the **Hule'ia Stream**. According to legend, it was built in one night by the Menehune as a gift for a princess and her brother. Estimates of its age range as high as 1,000 years. Today, it is privately owned and has fallen into disrepair as a fishpond. Nonetheless, it is a remarkable landmark that is worth a look.

Back on the main highway (which has changed its name to Hwy 50, the Kaumuali'i Hwy), you'll find yourself heading south. Before mile marker 1 is **Kukui Grove Shopping Center**, the biggest shopping center on the island. It's more geared toward locals but might have something to offer you. Past it is our island **Costco**.

Past mile marker 1 you will see **Kilohana** (245-5608) on your right. This was the home of Gaylord and Ethel Wilcox and has been lovingly restored to its former glory. Gaylord Wilcox was manager of the Grove Farm Plantation. Walk through the door of this 16,000-square-foot mansion, and you get a sense of Kaua'i in days past. The furniture, fittings and motif all harken back to a simpler day when sugar was king. Inside is a good restaurant called **Gaylord's**, as well as several shops, galleries, a lu'au and the tasting room for **Koloa Rum**, distilled here on the island. Their spiced rum is the best we've ever tried. They also have a train ride for $20 that kids ($14) might enjoy. See BASICS on page 35 for more.

Across from mile marker 3 on the main highway is Kipu Road, which also acts as a bypass road. Located off this road is a glorious little waterfall called Kipu Falls. Though people have been swinging off a rope swing and jumping into the pool here for over a century, and though you may read about it elsewhere, the current landowner does *not* allow access. There is now a fence to keep you out and trust me—they *don't* want you here due to safety and liability concerns. In 2011 these falls became notorious in the islands when a bill passed through the state house that would have effectively *ended all travel writing of any kind*

Baby Beach in Kapa'a has a natural sandstone breakwater that is a hit with little kids.

about Hawai'i because of controversy (in part) over access to these falls. So do everyone a favor: Keep the peace, and stay away from Kipu Falls.

If you were to continue on Kipu Road, you would quickly come to a magnificent strand of Cook Island pines. These trees were highly valued as ship's masts in the Age of Discovery. This entire area is called **Kipu** and is currently leased to the Rice family and the Waterhouse Trust. William Hyde Rice was a cattle rancher, and a monument to him was erected here by his Japanese workers. Behind Ha'upu mountain is the fabulous beach called **Kipu Kai**. This long crescent of sand is a beachgoer's dream. Unfortunately, the only way to reach it is by boat or over the private road owned by Kipu Ranch and the Waterhouse Trust. This road is closed to the public, though you can get a glimpse of Kipu Kai from the ATV tour on page 123. John Waterhouse ordered that the 1,096 acres of leased state land revert to the state at the time of death of the last of his nieces (all in their 70s). We've tried walking to Kipu Kai from Ha'ula Beach. The horse path up and over the tall mountain is riddled with evil plants with thorns that turned our exposed legs to hamburger.

EAST SHORE SHOPPING

Though not as unique as the north shore, east shore shopping still has its gems. Starting in northern Kapa'a, there's the **Kaua'i Products Fair.** Most of the products, ironically, are *not* made on Kaua'i—so ask—but a few are and may be worth a look.

In downtown Kapa'a, try **The Root, Island Hemp & Cotton, Deja Vu** and **Denim Patch** and **Tropical Tantrum** for clothing. A great find, but easy to miss, is **a.ell atelier** for unique men's Hawaiian shirts and *outstanding* one-of-a-kind formal gowns, as well as casual clothes made

on the premises, along with gifts and art. Look for vintage-style Hawaiian clothing and gifts at **Hula Girl. Bamboo Works** proves practically anything can be made out of bamboo—even a bicycle frame. **Serendipity: A Vintage Boutique** is a charming shop for stuff you wish you'd find at a garage sale, but never do (only open Fridays and Saturdays). **Larry's Music Boutique** has a vast selection of Kamoa 'ukulele. There are also some small galleries worth a stop sprinkled around town. A couple of our favorites are **Earth & Sea Gallery** in the Dragon Building and **Kela's A Glass Gallery,** which has fantastic glass artworks across from the soccer field. Look on the mauka side of the highway for **Calabash Wearable Wood** with unique koa wood hats, belts, wallets, jewelry and more. Next door, **Garden Isle Bath & Body** has great products made on site. **Orchid Alley** will ship their plants to the mainland.

Continuing south just before the (faded) whale mural, **Sweet Bikinis** behind Lemongrass Restaurant offers great bikinis and cover-ups. **Marta's Boat** is a women's boutique (across the street from Foodland). Plan to shop here in the afternoons to be sure they're open.

In Kaua'i Village Shopping Center, if you enjoy making your own jewelry, visit **Divine Planet** for a huge selection of beads, as well as textiles for the home. **Crush Boutique** features clothing for women and keiki plus some locally made hats and jewelry.

Coconut Marketplace is a mall that is getting more life with a remodel, but it's still a little depressing—most things are pretty kitschy. A couple stand outs are worth a look, though. One bright light is **Style World** for unique women's clothes and accessories. Visit **By the Sea** for nice footwear.

At Kinipopo Shopping Village across from Haleilio Road in Kapa'a, stop by

Goldsmiths Kauai, which has been around for more than 30 years and designs their own jewelry. Across the highway is **Pagoda** with Asian accessories and antiques for your home.

Before or after your visit to Wailua Falls, stop by **Kapaia Stitchery**. In addition to the *unrivaled* Hawaiian print and batik fabric selection, they also have beautiful Japanese kimonos and everything any quilter could need. Koa wood items can be seen at **William & Zimmer Woodworkers** next door.

In Lihu'e, many visitors stop at **Walmart** or **Hilo Hattie** (on Hwy 56 near Ahukini) before that last rush to the airport. Always something here for everyone. Walmart is also a good first stop on the island for tabis, water shoes and all kinds of outdoor gear, Hawaiian music CDs, flower leis, Hawaiian coffee and macadamia nuts.

Kukui Grove Shopping Center at the corner of Hwy 50 and Nawiliwili Road is a sprawling mall in two large sections. One section contains **Pier 1**, and the other portion has some good places to grab a treat or a sandwich while shopping at **Macy's** or any of the other specialty stores. There are also **Longs Drugs**, **Starbucks** and **Jamba Juice**.

Across from Kalapaki Beach is **Harbor Mall**, and one of our favorite stops for the kid in all of us is **Beachrail Hobby & Collectibles**.

Back on Hwy 50, heading west, is **Kilohana Plantation**, a former plantation manager's private home. The pottery at **Clayworks of Kilohana** (behind the main house) is worth a stop, and you or your young one can make a keepsake to take home or have shipped. **Koloa Rum** is where you'll find the best rum made in the islands, and their tasting room is beautiful. *Love* their spiced rum. **Grande's Gems**, above the restaurant, has some of the most beautiful fine gem-

stone jewelry on the island. There are other galleries in the main house worth a browse.

Puhi Village Plaza at the stoplight in Puhi has specialty wines (including Hawaiian), liquors and champagne at **The Wine Garden**. They also carry Kaua'i Cigars—at least the tobacco comes from Kaua'i. They're not bad but smoke a bit young and simple, and they are pretty pricey, too.

If you'd like to arrange a shipment of tropical flowers or a plant grown on lava rock, try **Kaua'i Nursery & Landscape** (245-7747) on the left side as you head toward Po'ipu.

EAST SHORE BEST BETS

Best Beach Walk—Lydgate Beach Park to Kaua'i Beach Resort

Best View—From the Top of Sleeping Giant for Hikers; Sunrise over Lydgate for Non-Hikers

Best Place to Let Little Ones Swim in the Ocean—Baby Beach

Best Treat to Share With 10 Friends—One Slice of Hula Pie at Duke's

Best Hidden Gem—Ho'opi'i Falls

Best Uncrowded Beach—In Front of Wailua Golf Course

Best Playground—Kamalani Playground at Lydgate Park

Best Boogie Boarding—Kealia Beach

Best Evening Stroll—Paved Beach Path between Kapa'a Beach Park and Kealia)

Best Lu'au—Smith's Tropical Paradise or Kalamaku at Kilohana

Best Way to Spend 7 Years—Carving One Stone for the Kaua'i Hindu Monastery

Best Place to Grab a Drink and Head to the Beach—Poolside Bar at Islander on the Beach

Best Place to Make Your Pupils Big—Mile-Long Secret Tunnel to the North Shore

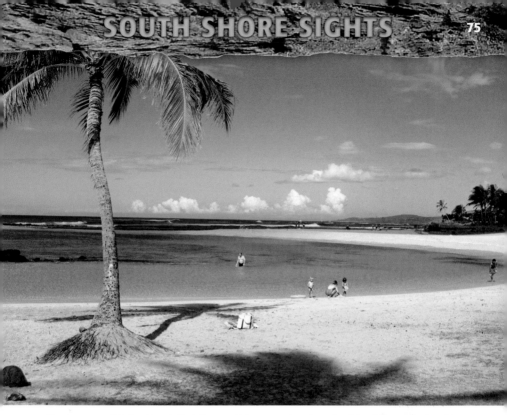

Semi-protected Po'ipu Beach Park is one of the many beaches that bless the south shore.

The sunny south shore... where rainfall is less frequent, and sunshine is abundant. Many people prefer the sunnier quality of the south shore to the lushness of the north shore. Fortunately, you can have it all.

For the sake of this discussion, we will consider the south shore as everything past Puhi to Kalaheo. (Look at the fold-out back cover map to orient yourself.) Past Kalaheo, the character of the island changes again, and we will cover that in the WEST SHORE SIGHTS chapter.

The same descriptive ground rules that we discussed at the beginning of NORTH SHORE SIGHTS chapter apply in this chapter.

All beaches we mention are described in detail in the chapter on BEACHES.

Driving to Po'ipu from Lihu'e along the main highway, you will pass through the Knudsen Gap between mile markers 6 and 8. A century ago this was the scariest part of the island. The small gap between the mountains was the only route you could take to the south shore and was a perfect place for an ambush. Even the local sheriff always dreaded going through the Knudsen Gap.

Past mile marker 6 you will come to Hwy 520, or Maluhia Road. This road to Koloa and Po'ipu is called the Tree Tunnel. When Walter Duncan McBryde was landscaping his home in the early 1900s,

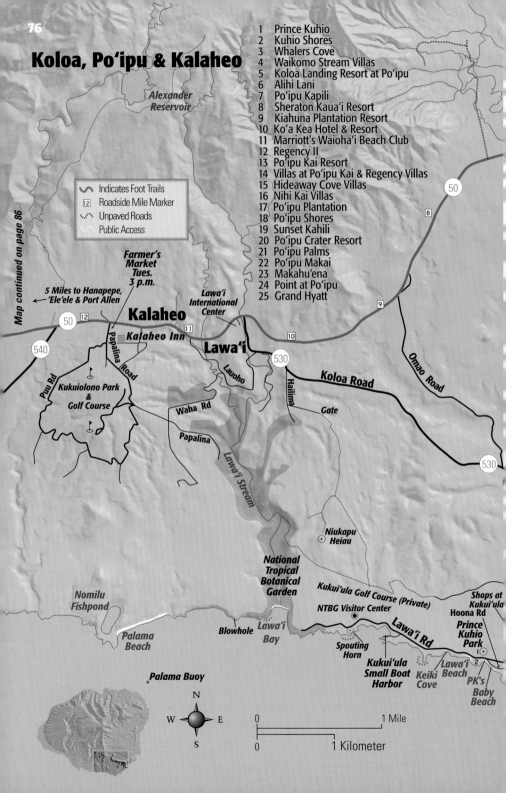

Koloa, Po'ipu & Kalaheo

1 Prince Kuhio
2 Kuhio Shores
3 Whalers Cove
4 Waikomo Stream Villas
5 Koloa Landing Resort at Po'ipu
6 Alihi Lani
7 Po'ipu Kapili
8 Sheraton Kaua'i Resort
9 Kiahuna Plantation Resort
10 Ko'a Kea Hotel & Resort
11 Marriott's Waioha'i Beach Club
12 Regency II
13 Po'ipu Kai Resort
14 Villas at Po'ipu Kai & Regency Villas
15 Hideaway Cove Villas
16 Nihi Kai Villas
17 Po'ipu Plantation
18 Po'ipu Shores
19 Sunset Kahili
20 Po'ipu Crater Resort
21 Po'ipu Palms
22 Po'ipu Makai
23 Makahu'ena
24 Point at Po'ipu
25 Grand Hyatt

Alexander Reservoir

ᔕ Indicates Foot Trails
12 Roadside Mile Marker
Unpaved Roads
Public Access

Map continued on page 86

Farmer's Market Tues. 3 p.m.

5 Miles to Hanapepe, 'Ele'ele & Port Allen

Lawa'i International Center

Kalaheo

Kalaheo Inn

Papalina Road

Puu Rd

Kukuiolono Park & Golf Course

Lawa'i

Lauoho

Waha Rd

Papalina

Koloa Road

Omao Road

Hailima

Gate

Lawa'i Stream

Niukapu Heiau

National Tropical Botanical Garden

Kukui'ula Golf Course (Private)

NTBG Visitor Center

Shops at Kukui'ula
Hoona Rd

Prince Kuhio Park

Nomilu Fishpond

Palama Beach

Blowhole

Lawa'i Bay

Spouting Horn

Kukui'ula Small Boat Harbor

Lawa'i Rd

Keiki Cove

Lawa'i Beach

PK's Baby Beach

Palama Buoy

N
W   E
S

0   1 Mile
0   1 Kilometer

Halfway Bridge

Kaumuali'i Highway

To Puhi →

50

4

5

Knudsen Gap

6

Kipu Road

Puhi Bypass

Hulemalu

50

7

Bridge

Hule'ia

Cook Island Pines

Kipu Falls (Closed)

Ha'upu Tunnel

520

(Tree Tunnel)

Maluhia Road

Private Road–Gated

Waita Reservoir

Private Road–Gated

Ha'upu 2,297'

Map continued on page 66

520

Anne Knudsen Park (Farmer's Mkt. Mon. Noon)

Ala Kinoiki

Koloa

Note: Since none of the cane roads in this area have street signs, relevant telephone poles are indicated on the map to assist in navigating the roads if gates are unlocked.

Grocery Store

530

Koloa Road

Weliweli

Waikomo

Old Koloa Sugar Mill

Gate

Telephone Poles

Maha'ulepu Beaches

Ha'ula Beach

Lithified Cliffs

Koloa–Po'ipu Bypass

Guard Shack

Cliff Cracks

Po'ipu Rd

Kiahuna Plantation Dr.

Cave

Gillin's Beach

Kawailoa Bay

Dry Blowhole

Kiahuna Golf Course

Po'ipu

Gate (closes at 6 p.m.)

CJM Stables

Po'ipu Rd

Po'ipu Bay Resort Golf Course

Lithified Cliffs

Poipu Shopping Village

Ala Kinoiki

Po'ipu Rd

Mokewehi Lithified Cliffs

4

Po'ipu Rd

Hoonani

5

Kapili

6 7

25

The reef edges are denoted by ⋯⋯⋯⋯ and come directly from government topographic maps. The task of verifying the precise location of all underwater reefs would be herculean and has not been attempted by us.

8

9

Koloa Landing

Kiahuna Beach

Hoowili

10 11

Pee

12

14 15

3

Sheraton Caverns

Po'ipu Beach Park

Hoone

16 17

13

20

24

Brennecke Beach

18 19

21 22 23

Shipwreck Beach

Makahu'ena Arch
21°52.124
159°26.697

© 2017 Wizard Publications, Inc.

The south shore is all about beaches and resorts and snorkeling and... well, that about covers it.

he found that he had over 500 eucalyptus trees *left over*. He donated these trees, called swamp mahogany, to the county. Many residents showed up to help plant the trees. The result is the Tree Tunnel. (Part of it was torn down in the '50s when they rerouted the highway.) The beginning part is the most beautiful; farther south the branches don't intertwine at the top the way they did before either Hurricane 'Iwa in 1982 or 'Iniki on September 11, 1992.

KOLOA

Driving down Hwy 520 you come to the town of Koloa, sometimes called Old Koloa Town. This was the first sugar plantation town in all the islands when Kamehameha III leased the land to Ladd and Company in 1835. The town has much charm and is worth a stop. Perusing the historic plaques and taking in the sights can be done in an hour. Next to the Crazy Shirts store there is a marvelous monkeypod tree whose branches seem to meander forever.

Across the street (kitty-corner) from the shops are the remnants of an old sugar mill built over 170 years ago. There you will also find a plaque dedicated to the sugar plantation workers and a good (if somewhat dated) synopsis of sugar history on the island.

Looking at the map, you will see a dirt road leading to Waita Reservoir and Ha'upu Range Tunnel. They are gated and not available to visit unless you book an ATV or 4WD van tour. We used to think these gates were a relatively modern annoyance until we stumbled across an old local newspaper from 1934. In a letter to the editor the writer warned people not to accept an invitation from a well-known plantation manager when he said he "wanted to show you something interesting." Apparently the crafty manager did this whenever he had a long way to drive and wanted to have somebody along to open and close all the gates.

PO'IPU

Continuing to Po'ipu on Hwy 520 and doglegging onto Po'ipu Road, watch your speed. This is a notorious speed trap and sobriety checkpoint area, and the limit is 25 mph, slowing to 15 mph near the school. (The Koloa-Po'ipu Bypass shown on the map on page 77 is an even more effective speed trap because you are easily lulled into going over 40 mph.)

Past mile marker 4 as you approach Po'ipu, the offshoot on the far side of the traffic circle instead takes you onto Lawai Road where you'll come to Prince Kuhio Park. (Enter the park from the left side of the wall.) There you will find a monument to Prince Kuhio, the last royally designated heir to the Hawaiian throne. He went on to become a delegate to Congress until the early 1920s. In this park you will also find the Ho'ai Heiau, impressive in its perfection and almost chiseled appearance. The entrance is toward the rear on the left side.

The palm trees between here and Baby Beach often fill dramatically at sunset with vast numbers of non-native parakeets, who leave just as suddenly at sunrise. They will spend the night clinging to the bottom of the fronds in even the strongest of winds.

Continuing along Lawa'i Road, you will come to Spouting Horn Beach Park. This wonderful delight is a small lava shelf where water from waves is thrust through an opening, causing water and air to squirt out a blowhole. This particular site distinguishes itself from other blowholes around Hawai'i in that it has an additional hole that blows only air, causing a loud moaning and gasping sound. Legend has it that the entire coastline in this area was once guarded by a giant female lizard called a mo'o. She would eat anyone who tried to swim or fish in the area. One day a man named Liko went fishing. The mo'o went to attack Liko, who threw a spear into the mo'o's mouth. The angry mo'o chased Liko into the lava

NOT TO BE MISSED!

tube. Liko escaped, but the mo'o became trapped in what we now call Spouting Horn, where its cries of hunger and pain can be heard to this day.

The Spouting Horn was formerly dwarfed by an adjacent blowhole called the Kukui'ula Seaplume. That seaplume would shoot much higher—as high as 200 feet into the air. But on an early Sunday morning back in the 1920s a sugar company manager ordered one of his workers to drop blasting powder into the hole to widen it so the plume wouldn't

Spouting Horn is often more dramatic at high tide.

Watch your step around these ficus roots at the Allerton Garden in Lawa'i. This beast of a tree was planted from a sapling in 1952. Now you know why they call this the Garden Island.

shoot into the air. The reason? The salt spray from the geyser was stunting the growth of 10 acres of cane (among the company's many thousands of acres), and the manager would not stand for that. Looking down on the lava shelf you can see its remains in the form of a large rectangular aperture to the left of the current blowhole opening.

The view from the lookout can be quite dramatic during large, summer swells. (Watching the spout from Kukui'ula Small Boat Harbor across the bay can be more picturesque, especially at sunset.) At one time you could walk down onto the lava bench, but there have been incidents where people have been swept to their deaths into the Horn. Now you can be fined for going past the guardrail.

If you ever happen upon another blowhole in Hawai'i where there are no signs forbidding you to get close, *never* stand between the hole and the ocean. A very large wave would have no difficulty dragging you in. Some years ago two visitors from San Francisco were knocked in while they stood between the Spouting Horn and the ocean. One was *on crutches* at the time. They were lucky—rather than being crushed inside the hole, they were immediately sucked out of the blowhole and into the open ocean where they were rescued by some phone workers on their break.

Just before Spouting Horn is the entrance to the National Tropical Botanical Garden. This incredibly beautiful garden consists of 252 acres called the McBryde Garden and 80 acres called the Allerton Garden (742-2623). Even if you normally wouldn't visit a garden, you'll probably like this one. See LAND TOURS on page 166.

Going back the way you came, just before the fork is a road leading to Koloa Landing. This is a popular SCUBA shore dive. Until the 1900s this was Kaua'i's main port. Whaling ships used to winter here, and all goods brought to Kaua'i came through either Koloa Landing or Waimea.

Going back to the traffic circle, take the branch toward Po'ipu, which is turtle country. Look out at the water for any reasonable length of time, and you'll see green sea turtles swimming nearby. This area was developed in the '70s and '80s and has become a much sought-after visitor destination. Swanky hotels and condominium resorts line the road. (See WHERE TO STAY chapter for more information.) The beaches in this area are fantastic, with the best of the best located past the resorts at a place called Maha'ulepu. This beach (see BEACHES chapter) sports lots of places

A REAL GEM

to walk and some incredible sandstone cliffs. The dirt roads around here can be good places to ride mountain bikes. Horseback riding, snorkeling, fishing and more are all available in this area. The lithified cliffs from Maha'ulepu to Shipwreck Beach offer delicious shoreline hikes. See HIKING in the ACTIVITIES chapter.

One thing that totally escaped our attention until an alert reader pointed it out to us was the presence of a cool-looking lava arch at the shoreline between the Point at Po'ipu Resort and Makahu'ena

at the southern tip of the island. Park at Pe'e and Oluolu Streets and walk toward the shoreline. If that fenceline boundary of Makahu'ena condos were to continue, it would lead to the arch. Don't let the ocean smack you around here.

There's lots of cactus along this part of the island. It was imported in the 1800s because it made a perfect natural cattle fence—and you don't even need to repair it.

KALAHEO

After Lawa'i comes Kalaheo. There are a handful of good restaurants and shopping opportunities here (including

These lithified sand dunes of Maha'ulepu are a stunning testament to the power of the ocean.

some pretty good pizza—see ISLAND DINING). One of Kalaheo's lesser known gems is the Kukuiolono Park and Golf Course (see GOLFING in the ACTIVITIES chapter). This is the private course and garden donated by Walter McBryde to the people of Kaua'i. If you want to try your hand at golf, this is the place to learn. The price is $10 *per day* (cash only). The small Japanese garden located on the course was Mr. McBryde's pride and joy. This is where he chose to be buried, near the 8th tee.

Although it was sugar that drove the economy along here for over a century, it was phased out in the 1990s to grow coffee, on the assumption it would be more profitable. It struggled for years, and the company was sold in 2011 to the same Italian coffee conglomerate that owns Hills Bros. The Kaua'i Coffee Company has 3,100 acres under cultivation. To be honest, it's not very good coffee. Most of the trees are an unimpressive breed called *yellow catuai.* Don't confuse it with the *far* superior coffee grown on the Kona coast of the Big Island where the coffee-growing environment is ideal. Also, most Kaua'i coffee is machine-picked, so beans slightly under and over their peak get picked in the process. Kaua'i Coffee has smaller fields of *blue mountain,* and *red catuai,* which is better, but it's expensive, and we've only found this coffee at their visitor center located on Hwy 540 just past mile marker 12 on Hwy 50. That 4-mile-long road, sometimes called the Coffee Highway, cuts through much of the coffee plantation. The visitor center is popular with tour buses but is only marginally interesting, and their museum is particularly scant. Only for hard-core coffee groupies.

Incidentally, any fixed-wing pilot on the island will tell you they *love* coffee trees.

Their leaves are dark and dense, which capture the sun and heat the air around them. This makes them exceptional generators of thermal currents, providing free lift when the heated air rises.

Just after mile marker 14 you will come to the Hanapepe Valley Lookout. As you gaze over the peaceful vista, it's hard to believe that this was the scene of the bloodiest and most savage battle known to have taken place on Kaua'i. The embittered son of Kaua'i's last king started a revolt against government rule. Remember that Kaua'i had never been conquered by Kamehameha the Great. Both of his invasion attempts had been costly in terms of men, and neither had even reached Kaua'i in large numbers. Even though Kaua'i's last king voluntarily accepted Kamehameha's rule, it forever stuck in the royal craw that Kaua'i had not been *forced* into submission. So when this revolt occurred, it was a perfect excuse to send Hawai'i troops over to show those Kauaians who was boss. Government troops sent to put down the revolt were unimaginably brutal, and their methods were reviled even among their supporters. Men, women and children were needlessly slaughtered, and the wanton killing continued for 10 days.

Everything past here is covered in the WEST SHORE SIGHTS chapter.

SOUTH SHORE SHOPPING

Following Koloa Road will take you right into Koloa Town, where there are many shops and galleries to browse. Among the more interesting, starting from the east end of Koloa Road, is The Wine Shop, which has a great selection of wines, spirits and gourmet foodstuffs. At Island Soap & Candle Works, you can watch the items for sale being made. Behind their store is Discount Variety for reasonably priced beach mats, etc., and Under The Sea Gallery for cute keiki items. Jungle Girl carries some funky island accessories and fabrics. Christian Riso Fine Art is our favorite art gallery in town. The 'Ukulele Store has a wonderful selection and knowledgeable staff. On down Poipu Road Pohaku T's carries only locally made items and has a huge selection of T-shirts, all designed and printed on Kaua'i.

Continuing on Poipu Road toward Po'ipu, is Poipu Shopping Village. You will find many boutique fashions from $3 flip-flops to $30,000 pearl necklaces. If you forget your swimsuit or just want to look more island-style, try Making Waves or Bamboo Lace for women or Overboard for men. For kids' fashions, you can't beat Sand Kids, where they also have lots of toys to entertain your keiki. James Coleman Art Gallery is one of the better art galleries. Black

The Tree Tunnel is your entrance to the South Shore. You can thank a wealthy resident who had all these trees left over from his gardening project.

Pearl Kaua'i has stunning (not just black) pearls.

Farther along are The Shops at Kukui'ula with a nice mix of restaurants, shops and galleries. We like Palms Gallery for Hawai'i artists and Galerie 103 for rotating exhibits. Visit Latitudes for home accessories. Martin & MacArthur has great koa jewelry. Ocean Jewelry & Gifts has some outstanding and unusual pieces. For clothes try Tommy Bahama, Quicksilver or Blue Ginger for kids' clothes. Malie Organics has their main store here—they only use indigenous organic flora to create their beauty products. There is also Living Foods Market & Café, which sells local produce, foodstuffs and a large selection of wines and beers.

Just off Highway 50 in Lawaʻi on Koloa Road is Hawaiian Trading Post, which has the largest selection of Niʻihau shell leis and Tahitian Black Pearls on the island, as well as other jewelry and gift items.

If you are out by Spouting Horn, check out the jewelry vendor stalls there, especially for pearls.

In Kalaheo, if you have decided to take up the ʻukulele, hit Kalaheo Music & Strings on the main highway. -

SOUTH SHORE BEST BETS

Best Strolling Beach—Mahaʻulepu
Best Short Cliff Stroll—To the Left of
    Shipwreck Beach near Hyatt
Best Snorkeling—Around the sandy
    point at Poʻipu Beach Park
Best Sunset View—At Spouting Horn

Best Hot Dog—Puka Dog
Best Treat—Chocolate Gelato at
    Lappert's
Best Place To Watch Fools Jump Off A
    Cliff—Shipwreck Beach in Front of
    the Hyatt Poʻipu
Best Secluded Beach—Haʻula Beach
Best Swimming—Poʻipu Beach Park
Best Pizza—Brick Oven Pizza
Best Beachcombing—Kawailoa Bay
Best Golf—Poʻipu Bay Resort
Best Hotel Grounds—Grand Hyatt
Best Chance of Seeing a Beached
    Monk Seal—Poʻipu Beach Park
Best Massive Burrito to Go—Da Crack
Best Romantic Restaurant—Tidepools
    at Grand Hyatt or Beach House
    at Sunset
Best Place for a Sunset Cocktail—The
    Sheraton Kauaʻi Resort

Niʻihau Shell Lei

The women of Niʻihau carry on a tradition dating back centuries. With indescribable patience, they collect tiny Niʻihau shells, then clean, drill, string and pack them with fiber, creating fabulous lei. This is no easy task. An entire day's labor often reaps only four or five useable shells. And it requires thousands of shells to make a lei. Some women only search for shells at night, believing that the sunlight dulls the shell's luster. Though they cost from several hundred to several thousand dollars each, this is a relative bargain given the amount of labor that goes into one. It can take several years to complete the more ornate lei. The result is a perfect, handcrafted and tightly packed lei representing one of the last truly Hawaiian art forms. There are fewer and fewer people on Niʻihau who are willing to participate in this process, and many consider it a matter of time before this art form will be lost.

If you purchase one, the best selection on the island is at the Hawaiian Trading Post on the corner of Highways 50 and 530 (Koloa Road) in Lawaʻi. Make sure it was actually made on Niʻihau, and not a copycat made on Kauaʻi.

One last caveat: If you buy one, do it for yourself. It would be crushing to spend all that money only to show your lei to someone and have 'em say, "Oh, yeah, I got one for free at Hilo Hattie's." While Niʻihau shell lei are infinitely more beautiful, some might not appreciate the difference.

Polihale is where the Na Pali coastline gives way to 12-plus miles of uninterrupted sand beach.

If the south shore is called the sunny south shore, western Kaua'i should be called the *very* sunny west shore. That's because rain is very scant indeed, and the temperature is 3 to 4 degrees hotter than most of the rest of the island. The first two things visitors notice on this side of the island are the relative aridity of the land and the red color of the soil. Trade winds coming from the northeast lose the bulk of their rain on Mount Wai'ale'ale, creating a rain shadow on the west side. Unless there are Kona winds (meaning from the south or west), you can pretty much be assured that it will be dry and sunny on the west side. The red dirt is especially vibrant because of the high iron content of our volcanic soil. This combined with lots of moisture and time has made the iron oxidize. The soil is literally rusty.

This part of the island is dominated by two attractions: the 12.5-mile-long sand beach stretching from Waimea to Polihale and the incredible Waimea Canyon in the interior.

HANAPEPE

As you drive along the main highway leaving Kalaheo, you will come to the Hanapepe Valley Lookout, described in SOUTH SHORE SIGHTS chapter. After you go through 'Ele'ele (where many of the boat tours leave from), you come to Hanapepe. Called Kaua'i's "Biggest Little Town," Hanapepe is but a shadow of its former self. It was founded by Chinese rice farmers in the mid to late 1800s. They were opium-smoking bachelors, and underground opium shops could be found there as recently as the 1930s. Hanapepe was the only non-plantation

West Shore & Waimea Canyon

N W E S (compass)

Kalalau Beach

Honopu Beach & Arch

Nu'alolo Kai

Miloli'i

Kalalau Valley

Detailed map of Koke'e on page 142–143

Kalalau Lookout

Awa'awapuhi Trail

18

Pu'u o Kila Lookout (better)

Nu'alolo Trail

Koke'e Museum

17

Makaha Ridge Tracking Station

Miloli'i Ridge Rd

Don't go past here in the rain.

16

2000 ft. Descent–Watch Your Brakes

22°07.589
159°41.343

15

Koke'e Rd

Koke'e Ditch

Pine Forest Drive & Picnic Area

Makaha Ridge Rd

Ka-uhao Ridge Rd

14

Pu'u Hinahina Viewpoint

Po'omau Canyon

Ka'aweiki Ridge Rd

Contour Rd

Waipo'o Falls

13

Polihale Ridge Rd

Soft, sandy spot in road

Ha'ele'ele Ridge Rd

Polihale State Park

Pu'u Ka Pele Lookout

12

Waimea Canyon

Koai'e Canyon

Lonomea Camp

550

Queen's Pond

Ancient Hawaiian jumping off point for spirits

Pu'u Lua Reservoir

Hipalau Camp

Kaluahaulu-Wai'ale Trail

Nohili Point

Monkeypod Tree

Kolo Ridge Rd

Picnic Area

11

Waimea Canyon Lookout

Kaluahaulu Camp

Barking Sands

Mana Ridge Rd

10

Wiliwili Camp

Poachers Camp

Kahelu Ridge Rd

These ridge roads are hunter roads and only open to vehicles on most weekends and holidays. The state's website implies you can hike at any time. The views from the ends of these ridge roads (especially Polihale and Ka-uhao) are extraordinary.

9

Kukui Trail

8

Hunter Check-in Station

7

Waimea Canyon Trail

Military Boundary

32 (Again)

33

Mana (gone)

Ka-boom Mountain

32

31

6

Waimea River

Pu'u Ki Wai'alae

Major's Bay

30

5

Pacific Missile Range Facility

29

Waimea Canyon Plaza

552

4

Waimea Canyon Dr

3

Kokole Point

28

27

Koke'e Rd

Kekaha

2

550

Menehune Ditch & Waimea Swinging Bridge

Mana Drag Strip

Farmer's Market Sat. 9 a.m.

26

Kekaha Rd

25

Waimea

24

1

In Waimea, check your gas gauge before going up to the canyon.

Kekaha Beach Park

Kikiaola Small Boat Harbor

Waimea Plantation Cottages

23

22

Beach access is usually obvious along this part of the island. Only Pakala Beach needs to be pointed out.

Lucy Wright Beach Park

Russian Fort Elizabeth

21

Pakala Beach (Infinities)

20

Hanapepe/ 'Ele'ele

Gay & Robinson Sugar Mill (now closed)

19

18

50

South Shore map on page 76

Legend

- ∿ Indicates Foot Trails
- 23 Roadside Mile Marker
- ⋰⋱ Unpaved Roads
- ⛺ Camp Sites

The reef edges are denoted by ⋯⋯⋯ and come directly from government topographic maps. The task of verifying the precise location of all underwater reefs would be herculean and has not been attempted by us.

0 ————— 5 Miles

0 ————— 5 Kilometers

Salt Pond Beach Park

Port Allen Airport (Burns Field)

Glass Beach

17

© 2017 Wizard Publications, Inc.

town on the island, and it gained a reputation as Kaua'i's wildest spot. In 1924 they had a riot that killed 16 Filipino workers and four police officers. This was a violent and flamboyant town that had as many bars as churches. It began to decline in the late '70s. The 1982 opening of Kukui Grove Shopping Center in Lihu'e marked the end of an era for Hanapepe's business community.

A good analogy for Hanapepe today is that of an old chair. While some people look at an old stick of furniture and see a priceless antique, others see it as an old, used item to be replaced by a newer one. Depending on your outlook, you will either find downtown Hanapepe charming or a quasi-ghost town. Although Hanapepe is rising out of the ashes with some nice rehabilitation work, during most of the week we probably agree with the ghost town description. If you have a couple minutes to spare, you might want to blow through downtown just to decide for yourself. There are several shops and galleries that might be worth exploring. Friday night is *art night,* and it's when the town really wakes up with live music, good food options, craft vendors and a changing roster of other activities. Check out some of the galleries we mention on page 95. There's a swinging footbridge over the Hanapepe River. It replaced the old bridge that swung off during the 1992 hurricane.

This area is where most of our power is generated. People assume that, living on a tropical island, we must have some exotic way of making our electricity. Sorry to burst your bubble, but we burn oil—it's just that simple—and we have the elec-

tricity bills to prove it! In a few years we hope to burn wood chips from local tree farms to help supplement that.

If you take Lele Road (Hwy 543), you come to **Salt Pond Beach Park**. This is where they continue to make salt out of seawater (see BEACHES chapter). This park usually offers very safe swimming as well as restrooms. (Hard to find in this area.)

Before you get to Waimea, you will see a road to **Fort Elizabeth** just past mile marker 22. (The sign has been misspelled for years.) Here are the vague remains of a Russian fort built in 1816 by George Scheffer.

Scheffer was a German-born doctor working for a Russian company. A difficult, quarrelsome and conceited man, he had a habit of eventually alienating most people he met. (Know the type?) He did make a good *first* impression, however, and managed to sufficiently impress a Russian official, who sent Scheffer to Hawai'i to ingratiate himself with King Kamehameha and recover a lost ship's cargo. When Kamehameha eventually

Hanapepe

Indicates Foot Trails
11 Roadside Mile Marker
Unpaved Road

N W E S

Map continued on page 86

Map continued on page 76

Moi Rd
Awawa
Swinging Bridge
Kona
Ko
50
15
18
Hanapepe Rd
Hanapepe Rd
17
Lele
543
'Ele'ele Shopping Center
16
540
Kaua'i Coffee Visitor Center
Salt Pond Beach Park
Port Allen Marina Center
Small Boats
Port Allen
Big Boats
Hanapepe Bay
Awaialo
Aka Ula
Glass Beach
Port Allen Air Strip
Wahiawa Beach

0   1/2 MILE

© 2017 Wizard Publications, Inc.

became suspicious of Scheffer, the German moved on to Kaua'i. There he found a receptive King Kaumuali'i who, although he had officially given his kingdom to Kamehameha, still resisted offshore rule. Kaua'i's king-in-name-only saw a chance to get the Russians involved and perhaps restore his power. The two men realized how much they could help each other and soon hatched plans to conquer the other islands using Russian ships. By this time Scheffer had become intoxicated by his status on Kaua'i and lost sight of the fact that he could not deliver on any of the promises he was making to Kaua'i's king. He built a second fort where Princeville is today and even renamed Hanalei Valley, calling it Schefferthal, with the king's blessing.

As Scheffer began building the Russian Fort in honor of Elizabeth, a Russian consort, his sponsors back in Russia were beginning to get a hint of Scheffer's tactics. They sent a ship to Hawai'i to tell Scheffer that he was to pack and leave the island. Scheffer ignored the message and continued building the fort. By this time Kaua'i's king was becoming suspicious, and a group of American businessmen saw an opportunity to rid the island of Scheffer and Russia. They started the rumor that Russia and America were at war. Kaua'i's king abandoned Scheffer, who fled the island in a leaky old ship and set sail for O'ahu. Once there, Scheffer was told he would be taken prisoner. He fled to Brazil where he changed his name to Count von Frankenthal and tried to lure colonists to his estate of the same name.

Why are we telling you all this? Because the story's more interesting than the actual site—little more than a perimeter of rocks from the foundation. (By the way, there are lots of bees here.)

If you drive through Fort Elizabeth and take the dirt road, you'll come to the **mouth of the Waimea River**. This can be a beautiful area to linger and watch the interaction of the ocean with the river, especially when the river flow is low. The dark, rich sand separating the ocean from the river is saturated with water from the river. White waves sometimes gently lap up and down the sand without sinking in, creating a delicate show of contrasts. You'll notice an olive green tint to the sand here. This is from a semi-precious gem called olivine, which the Waimea River tirelessly mines from its lava bed along with black flecks of lava, making the floor of the Waimea Canyon lower and lower in the process.

The dark sand at the mouth of the Waimea River beautifully contrasts with the ocean foam slithering into the river.

WAIMEA

Back on the main highway you come to the town of Waimea. This part of the island usually looks best (and greenest) in the winter. Off to your right you will see the Captain Cook Monument. It was in Waimea that the great explorer first set foot in Hawai'i in January 1778. (He was later killed on the Big Island in a petty dispute over a stolen rowboat.)

Travel 1.3 miles up Menehune Road on the *mauka* side of the highway to see the Menehune Ditch, a smooth, lined irrigation ditch designed to bring water from the Waimea River to the taro fields. Only the top of a tiny section is now visible because previous roadbuilders literally *paved* right up to this ancient structure. It's mostly buried and not visually striking. But it's impressive to think that the rocks used for its construction are said to have come from a quarry more than 6 miles away. This is one of the few Hawaiian relics that almost certainly wasn't created by the current race of Hawaiians who came from Tahiti around 1,000 AD. *That* group didn't cut and dress stones—as is the case at Menehune Ditch—they simply stacked them. This irrigation ditch is much older and was probably built by the initial inhabitants—the original "native Hawaiians"—who came from the Marquesas Islands around 500 AD. These first settlers lived a peaceful though less structured life until the Tahitian invaders displaced them and their culture 500 years later, establishing the Hawaiian culture we know today.

Across from the ditch is the Waimea Swinging Bridge. Like the one in Hanapepe, it, too, is a replacement for the old one blown away in 1992. *Sometimes* seedy characters hang out here making visitors feel unwelcome.

The Waimea (meaning red water) River is full of sediment that dyes the water red. All the beaches in the vicinity of the river are murky due to river runoff,

and the swimming is correspondingly poor. According to legend, there was a beautiful chief's daughter named Komali'u who was sought after by many men in the village. One day a man named Mano asked her to marry him. When she refused, he killed her at a waterfall where her blood ran into the river. The chief named the village, canyon and river Waimea in memory of his daughter.

To help cool down while in Waimea you have a few frosty options. JoJo's Shave Ice (across from mile marker 23) and Jo-Jo's Anuenue (on the mauka side of the Hwy behind the statue of Capt. Cook) are the go-to shave ice shops in town. Both have similar offerings and choosing our favorite changes almost yearly—let us know which you think is best. If you're wanting a heartier and healthy option, G's Juicebar next to the Waimea Theater has some killer juices and smoothies.

KEKAHA

From Waimea, most people go up the road to the Waimea Canyon, but we will get to that later. Assuming you are continuing along the coast, you arrive in Kekaha. This is the last town on this side of the island. Past mile marker 25 the highway hugs the beach for 2 miles. It's a nice place to stop and enjoy views of Ni'ihau past mile marker 26, and beach access here is accomplished by simply falling out of your car onto the sand.

Waimea Canyon Plaza is the last area with food along here. The Menehune Food Mart has sandwiches and hot dogs. Things aren't as hideously expensive there as you'd expect, given the remoteness of the location.

While driving along the west side past Waimea, take note of the cliffs to your right. Those are former sea cliffs cut off from the sea. The land you are driving on is different than most other land in the island chain. It's not technically volcanic.

When the massive Waimea Canyon (described later) was formed, the river carried the rock and soil out of the canyon where the ocean's current drove it along the shore to the northwest (as it still does today). Some of it washed up on shore. There it joined a gigantic amount of sand that was actually made by sea creatures *on the north shore* and transported down the Na Pali coast by the ocean. The result is one kickin' place to grow sugar—just ask the Robinsons, who grew thousands of acres of it here until 2009. In that year they shut down the island's last sugar mill, though some of the remaining sugar cane under cultivation is used by the Koloa Rum Company to make Kaua'i rum. The Robinsons, along with the state of Hawai'i, now lease 12,000 acres to several mainland seed companies that take advantage of the perfect year-round growing conditions to grow mostly GMO (genetically modified) seed corn and soybeans in the former sugar cane fields. They also raise shrimp on the makai side of mile marker 29, using a 500-foot deep well that taps into clean ocean water. Kaua'i Shrimp is available at some restaurants and from an outlet in downtown Hanapepe and is probably the tastiest shrimp we've found.

Many maps list a town farther north called Mana. It was once a thriving little community until the mid-1900s. This area was formerly marshy and famous for its mirages. Now the town of Mana is a mirage, nothing more than two mango trees and a mule. Some of its homes were moved and are now part of Waimea Plantation Cottages Resort. You can tell a former Mana cottage because it always had a door facing north and one facing south so passing spirits wouldn't get stuck inside.

From here on, the coastline is pure sand from the same north shore source described above. There's a great opportunity to have a huge stretch of sand to yourself along here. See Kokole Point on page 120.

You will pass the Pacific Missile Range Facility. About every two months they do a Star Wars missile test. (When they fire missiles, rather than move the rockets, they literally move the building out of the way.) Offshore, submarine hunting exercises take place almost continuously. This is a repository for some of the most sophisticated sensing equipment in the world, and they are capable of detecting a bottle bobbing up and down in the choppy water. (But for some reason, when a fishing boat is missing in the area, they seem incapable of finding it.) Fronting part of the base is Barking Sands Beach. The sand grains at this beach have a thin coating of silica and are supposed to make a barking sound if you walk on them when conditions are right (see BEACHES). Access is a problem, though. See BEACHES chapter for more.

A well-known surf site here is Major's Bay, so called because it's off the old commanding officer's quarters. *Hey, wait a minute. This is a Navy base. Isn't major an Army rank?* True, but it *used* to be an Army base, and the name stuck.

POLIHALE

Looking at the map, you'll notice that the highway ends after the first mile marker 32. Follow the map, and the first dirt road will take you to Polihale. (It's a public access, misleading signs notwithstanding.) On the very rare occasions that it rains heavily here, the road to Polihale can get pretty sloppy. (It also gets potholed at times, and officials at State Parks like to close it once in a while as they wait to rescrape it.) From the extreme northern end of the beach, the magnificent cliffs of Na Pali beckon you with their sheer majesty. The dunes of Polihale are up to 100 feet high. The BEACHES chapter provides more information on Polihale.

Beware of large, low-flying birds at the south end of Salt Pond Beach.

As soon as you leave Hwy 50 on your way to Polihale, look at the mountain in front of you. It's a military restricted area. They've bored caves into the mountain where they store ammunition, such as bombs and bullets. With so much explosives, you're about as welcome there as a pack of matches.

If it's summer, you might see kayaks coming (or rolling) in for a surf landing. From here you could walk to the left for 12.5 miles in the sand. (Maybe another day, huh?) Winds are usually calm here. There are facilities, including showers, restrooms and drinking water.

The Hawaiians believed that the cliffs at the end of Polihale Beach, called Ha'ele'ele, were the jumping off point for spirits or 'uhane leaving this world. There they would leave this life and join their ancestors forever. If there was no 'aumakua, or family of spirits, to receive them, they would wander around the area, attaching themselves to rocks and generally causing mischief. That's why it's considered unwise to take anything, such as stones, from this area. You may bring back a wayward spirit itching to get back home.

WAIMEA CANYON

Waimea Canyon is a spectacular gorge that defies description. Island legend states that when Mark Twain was here, he dubbed it "the Grand Canyon of the Pacific." (Unfortunately, when you read his biography, you find that when he visited Hawai'i, he never set foot on Kaua'i. Oops, there goes another urban legend.) Regardless, the layers evident on the sides of the canyon are reminiscent of the grander canyon in Arizona. Each layer represents a different eruption and subsequent lava flow. The canyon is 10 miles long, 1 mile wide and more than 3,600 feet deep.

To get to the canyon, take Waimea Canyon Drive from Waimea. They want you to go up from Koke'e Road in Kekaha because they hope you'll buy something there, but the views are better going up from Waimea. On your return from the canyon, you can take Koke'e Road (between mile markers 6 and 7) down for a different view of the coast.

Before you go up the road, check your gas gauge. There are no stations up there (but restrooms are available at the major lookouts), and you've got a 40-

mile round trip ahead of you with a 4,000-foot elevation rise. The temperature is 10–15 degrees cooler up there, and a sweater or light jacket might be wise, depending on conditions. There are more good hiking trails in this area than anywhere in Hawai'i. For more hiking information and a detailed map of the trails in the Waimea/Koke'e area, see HIKING on page 142.

To reach the canyon, turn *mauka* onto Waimea Canyon Drive just past mile marker 23 near a church. The road twists and turns its way up the canyon's side. On the way, keep an eye out to the west for Ni'ihau. There are some great views of that private island from up here. (Even on cloudless days there's almost always a cloud over Ni'ihau. Its land mass causes them.) Past mile marker 10 is the Waimea Canyon Lookout. This is one of several vantage points and definitely worth a stop. From here on, you will probably see lots of wild chickens about. They thrive in this environment.

NOT TO BE MISSED!

The canyon lookout is an awesome vista. At one time three rivers, fed from the island's center by the Alaka'i Swamp on Mt. Wai'ale'ale, all ran down the gently sloping shield volcano, emptying into the ocean at separate points like the spokes of a wheel. That's what created the now-dry valleys you see on your way out to Polihale. When a fault caused the collapse of part of the volcano's flank, the three rivers were forced to combine as they ran down into the fault. This new, opportunistic river carved a place for itself in the splintered and fractured lava flows. The results are extraordinary.

As you drive upward, there are numerous areas along the road from which to view the canyon. From the Pu'u Ka Pele Lookout, the Waipo'o Falls are visible after a heavy rain, especially in the winter. The hike there (see HIKING in the ACTIVITIES chapter) is fabulous. The Pu'u Hinahina Lookout, located past mile marker 13, has a Ni'ihau Viewpoint in addition to its canyon lookout. If it's clear, the view of Ni'ihau is great.

Shortly after this lookout, there is a paved road on your left leading to the Makaha Ridge Tracking Station run by the military in conjunction with the Pacific Missile Range Facility. The road drops 2,000 feet over a relatively short distance and can be a real brake burner. Not far before the gate at the station you will see several dirt roads leading into a pleasant forested area with picnic tables.

Looking at the map, you'll see that there are dirt hunter-roads all along this part of the coast. The views from the edge of the ridges are mind-boggling, but they are only open certain weekends and are *supposed* to be used by hunters. The only one that's always open and available is Miloli'i Ridge Road. See AD-VENTURES on page 202.

Past mile marker 15 is the Koke'e Museum (335-9975). This is a good place to stretch your legs, and the parking lot is usually loaded with wild chickens. The small, free museum won't take up much time but has several interesting displays, and its three-dimensional map of the canyon really gives you a sense of what you are seeing. The Koke'e Lodge (335-6061) next door is the *best place in Koke'e* to get lunch. (It wins first place in a contest of one.)

As you ascend the road, note how different the vegetation is up here. Remember how dry it was down at the bot-

tom near Waimea? Here it is always cool, and there is more rainfall than on the plain below.

Just past the lodge (on the opposite side of the road), driving Waineke Road to Mohihi Road makes a wonderful diversion if you happen to have a 4WD vehicle. You can drive 6 miles into the interior of Koke'e, visiting beautiful sights along the way. The map of the area is on page 142.

At mile marker 18 is the Kalalau Lookout where most people stop. We suggest that you drive right past it and go to the *far* superior, but less used, Pu'u o Kila Lookout. You are not about to see another canyon lookout. You are about to be treated to one of the greatest views in the Pacific. The Kalalau Valley is the largest valley on Na Pali. It was inhabited until 1919, and its beach is only reachable by an 11-mile hike or by kayak (see ADVENTURES chapter). For now, just revel in the view. Clouds are always moving in and out of the valley, so if it's cloudy, wait a while before you give up. It's well worth it. The earlier you go, the fewer clouds there tend to be. You can

A REAL GEM

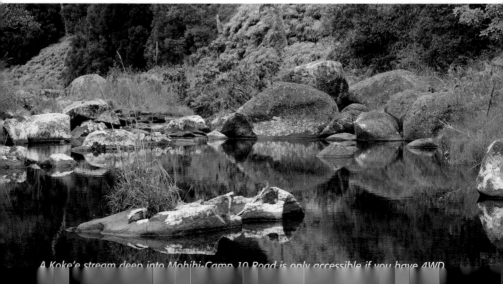

A Koke'e stream deep into Mohihi-Camp 10 Road is only accessible if you have 4WD

usually see clouds coming from the interior of the island. When they encounter the valley, they sink. Sinking air warms, and warmer air can hold more moisture. So if conditions are right, during normal trade winds, the clouds disappear into humidity in less than a minute right before your eyes. If the winds are coming from the ocean (not the norm), clouds back up in the valley, and it won't clear up.

According to historians, there used to be a *steep* trail into the valley from here leading down across a ridge called *ka-pea*, a Hawaiian word for scrotum. It was so-named because the trail was so steep that it made your…well, *you* figure it out.

Hawaiian geese, called **nene**, tend to hang out at the lookouts. These are endemic to Hawai'i (found nowhere else) and are what you get when you take wayward Canada geese and isolate them in the tropics for a million years. They've adapted to higher altitudes, lost most of the webbing on their feet and have no fear of cars or people, so be careful driving around at the lookout. They also try to make their living begging food from visitors. Please try to resist.

This is the end of the road. As the crow flies, Ha'ena on the north shore is less than 7 miles away, but you ain't no crow. They tried to build a road from here to Ha'ena in the '50s. Anybody who has ever hiked the **Alaka'i Swamp Trail** before they installed a boardwalk could tell you that a road in these parts is next to impossible. The results of this boondoggle are monuments in the form of heavy earthmoving equipment still stuck in the swamp where the prison work crews left them. A stroll from here down part of the **Pihea Trail** can be a pleasant diversion. This is where the road to Ha'ena was supposed to start.

In 1870, Queen Emma made a famous trek through the **Alaka'i Swamp** to the Kilohana Lookout. (As an aside, Alaka'i means "to lead," because it's impossible to get around in there without a guide.) She had a hundred people accom-

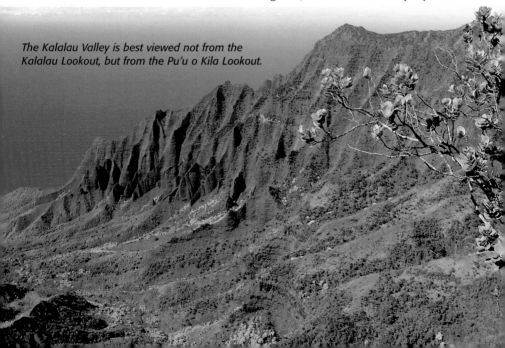

The Kalalau Valley is best viewed not from the Kalalau Lookout, but from the Pu'u o Kila Lookout.

pany her and stopped at awkward times to insist on hula demonstrations. Her guide vowed never to go into Alaka'i again, and the trip became legendary throughout the islands.

By not having a road completely encircling the island, Kaua'i has been able to escape the fate that has befallen O'ahu. As long as the dots aren't connected, there will always be parts of Kaua'i that are remote.

WEST SHORE SHOPPING

Hanapepe has many galleries and shops. Some of our favorites are starting from the east are: **Kaua'i Fine Art** has historical maps and prints. **Banana Patch Studio** is where artists can be seen making a multitude of pottery items for sale. **Blu Umi** has unique Japanese-inspired home accessories and baby items. **Becky Wold: Art of Marbling** showcases fine silk scarves in one-of-a-kind marbleized print designs. **Aloha Spice Company** is great for foodstuffs like flavored macadamia oils. Get a custom Hawaiian shirt made at **Jacqueline on Kaua'i**. **Island Art Gallery** has spectacular modern artwork and jewelry from around the world. **Amy Lauren's** features contemporary Kaua'i artists. Behind them is **Puahina** for original silk-screened Hawaiian warrior T-shirts and clothing items screened with native plant motifs. Across the street is **Talk Story Bookstore** specializing in used and rare books, as well as new works by local authors. Slightly farther west of the main part of town, don't miss **Keiki Kovers** for adorable island-made clothes for babies and young kids. On the main highway is **Salty Wahine** that makes gourmet salt blends using tasty local ingredients.

In Waimea, check out **Sea Shell Diamond Gallery** for beautiful and unusual jewelry. **Aloha N' Paradise** has a nice selection of local artwork for sale. Pick up your fresh deli foods and local beef from

The nene of Koke'e are accomplished beggars. This one flew off in a huff when we said no.

Ishihara Market or for staples **Big Save** across the street. Don't miss **Aunty Lilikoi** (near Big Save) for outstanding passion-fruit products made on premises. They'll even share recipes. On the west end of town is **Kaua'i Granola/Sugar Cane Snax**. If you like your coffee and granola in the morning, they have Espresso Bytes, which combines both. Chocolate Macaroons are also very yummy.

WEST SHORE BEST BETS

Best Sunset View—A Couple Miles Up Waimea Canyon Drive

Best Treat—Shave Ice at Jo-Jo's Anuenue or JoJo's Shave Ice in Waimea

Best Hearty Food—Chili and Cornbread at the Koke'e Lodge

Best Place for Quiet Contemplation— To the Right of the Viewing Platform at Pu'u o Kila Lookout

Best Swimming—Salt Pond Beach Park or Queen's Pond at Polihale (if calm)

Best Place to Get Away From it All and Write the Great American Novel— Waimea Plantation Cottages

Best Place to Have Good Brakes— Makaha Ridge Road

Best Thing to Wear While Walking on Hot Sand—Wool Socks, No Shoes

Ke'e Beach and its reef lagoon offer some of the best swimming on the north shore. This is how it looks from the Kalalau Trail.

Because Kaua'i is older than the other major Hawaiian islands, it is blessed with having more sand beaches per mile of shoreline than any other. No part of the island is without sandy beaches. Many are accessible by merely driving up and falling into the sand. Others are deliciously secluded, requiring walks of various lengths. Some are local secrets; others are unknown even to most locals. In this section we will describe virtually all of Kaua'i's beaches starting from the north shore and working our way around the island clockwise. All of these beaches are located on the maps of the various areas. A few beaches are in the ADVENTURES section because that's the only way you'll see 'em.

BEACH SAFETY

The beaches of Kaua'i, and Hawai'i in general, are beautiful, warm and, unfortunately, can be dangerous. The waves, currents and popularity of beachgoing have caused Hawai'i to become the drowning capital of the United States. If you're going to swim in the ocean, you need to bear several things in mind. We are not trying to be killjoys here, but there are several reasons why Hawai'i's beaches can be particularly dangerous. The waves are stronger here in the open ocean than in most other places. Rip currents can form, cease and form again with no warning. Large "rogue waves" can come ashore with no warning. These usually occur when two or more waves fuse at sea, becoming a larger wave. Even calm seas are no guarantee of safety. Many people have been caught unaware by large waves during ostensibly "calm seas." We swam and snorkeled most of the beaches we describe in this book on at least two occasions (usually more than two). But beaches change. The underwater topography changes throughout the year. Storms can take a very safe beach and rearrange the sand, turning it into a dangerous beach. Just because we describe a beach as being in a certain condition does not mean it will be in that same condition when *you* visit it.

Consequently, you should consider the beach descriptions as a snapshot in calm times. If seas aren't calm, you probably shouldn't go in the water. If you observe a rip current, you probably shouldn't go in the water. If you get caught in a strong rip current that pulls you away from the shoreline, *don't* panic and *don't* try to fight your way back in. Swim parallel to shore and try to signal for help. If you're at a remote beach, consider asking a local person about conditions. Most will be helpful. If you aren't a comfortable swimmer, you should probably never go in the water, except at those beaches that have lifeguards and protected pools, such as Lydgate State Park. But during abnormally high seas, even these are potentially hazardous. Kaua'i averages nine drownings per year—most of these are visitors. We don't want you to become part of that statistic. There is no way we can tell you that a certain beach will be swimmable on a certain day, and we claim no such prescience. There is no substitution for your own observations and judgment. And though it might sound obvious, one of the biggest contributors to drownings is alcohol. Hey, we're not lecturing. Go ahead, *suck 'em up* if you like. But stay on dry land and off the roads when you do.

Sprinkled among remote island beaches are yellow rescue tubes. If you see someone in distress and you're a good swimmer with fins, you can grab one and take it out and possibly save a life.

In general, the north shore beaches are calmest during the summer months (meaning April–September). The south shore is calmest during the winter months (meaning October–May). North shore high surf is stronger than south shore high surf since our location in the northern hemisphere makes us closer to northern winter storms than southern hemisphere storms. But drownings have occurred all too frequently even on the south shore.

A few of the standard safety tips apply. Never turn your back on the ocean. Never swim alone. Never swim in the mouth of a river. Never swim in murky water. Never swim when the seas are not calm. Don't walk too close to the shore break; a large wave can come and knock you over and pull you in. Observe ocean conditions carefully. Don't let small children play in the water unsupervised. (In fact, it's best to keep them at the protected ponds such as Lydgate.) Fins give you *far* more power and speed and are a much underappreciated safety device (besides being more fun). If you are comfortable in a mask and snorkel, they provide considerable peace of mind, in addition to opening up the underwater world. Lastly, don't let Kaua'i's idyllic environment cloud your judgment. Recognize the ocean for what it is: a powerful force that needs to be respected.

To get **ocean safety information**, visit: www.hawaiibeachsafety.com.

When frolicking at a beach, especially a rocky one, **water shoes** are invaluable for protecting your feet from cuts. They can turn a marginal beach into a fun beach.

People tend to get fatigued while walking in sand. The trick to making it easier is to walk with a very gentle, relaxed stride while lightly striking the sand almost flat-footed.

Beach conditions are usually best in the first half of the day. And remember that weekends—like weekends everywhere—are more popular with local beachgoers, so it's best to plan your beach activities for weekdays, if possible.

The Hawai'i Supreme Court ruled in 2006 that *all* beaches are public to "the upper reaches of the wash of the waves… at high tide during the season of the year in which the highest wash of the waves occurs." This means that you can park yourself on any stretch of shoreline sand you like. The trick, sometimes, can be access. You might have to cross private land to get to a public beach. We've pointed out a legal way to every beach on the island, and some of the maps have access routes in yellow to show you the way. This, along with descriptions and directions, will assist you in finding the beach of your choice. But public access is an involved and often murky subject. We did our best to get it right, but there *may* be some that are marked where *somebody* may object. (E.g., "This *used* to be public access, but the county easement wasn't filed properly when the moon was full, and my attorney talked to their attorney, and together they drafted this 85-page document describing the protocols necessary when accessing every fourth Tuesday…") You get the idea. Use your best judgment.

The beaches that are *supposed* to have **lifeguards** are highlighted with this ⊕ symbol. They are Ke'e, Ha'ena Beach Park, Hanalei, Kealia, Lydgate, Pine Trees, Po'ipu, Salt Pond, Lucy Wright, and Kekaha.

When we mention that a beach has **facilities**, it usually includes restrooms, showers, picnic tables and drinking water. Facilities are sometimes less than pristine.

A WORD ABOUT SHELLS

A walk along Hawaiian beaches reveals that seashells are relatively rare here compared to other parts of the world. This is due, in part, to rough seas and the obstacles between where the shell making creatures live and the shore. As a result, it's especially rare to find a whole shell without some kind of damage. So please do your part by resisting the desire to bring one back as a souvenir. Once we were snorkeling at Larsen's when a visitor asked us, "How come I don't see any such and such type of shells anymore? We were here five years ago and saw *lots* of them. I have a whole bag of 'em back home in my garage." We told him, "Maybe we don't have 'em anymore because they're all in that bag of yours in the garage."

NORTH SHORE BEACHES

⊕ Ke'e Beach

A REAL GEM

This is as far as you can go *by car* on the north shore. The beach here is called Ke'e (also called Ha'ena *State* Park), and it's a swimming, snorkeling and sunbathing favorite that can get crowded. The sand volume here varies tremendously. Some summers the sand fills the lagoon, creating a knee-deep sand swimming pool. During these times *on flat calm days* the snorkeling just *outside* the reef is unreal. Tons of fish, clear water and so many turtles you'll lose count as you cruise out the reef opening on the left side and head right. But calm seas are the *only* time you should consider *leaving* the lagoon. During winter months and at other times, large waves may wash over the reef, creating an excess of lagoon water. During these times the beach usually closed to swimming. Since Ke'e has the only reef opening, this water has only one place to go to equalize the volume—

out the reef opening on the left side. That's why it's important to observe ocean conditions carefully. Big waves mean big currents in the reef openings and big problems for you unless you stay away from the reef opening.

The park is equipped with facilities and is often crowded—too crowded— and parking is an issue after 8 or 9 a.m. If the showers are full, the stream you crossed 0.3 miles back makes an ideal place to rinse off the saltwater, but be careful—the rocks can be slippery.

The highway's end is also where the Kalalau Trail begins. It leads to **Hana-kapi'ai Beach** and **Kalalau Beach**, which are described in the ADVENTURES chapter.

➕ Ha'ena Beach Park

This very pretty beach has complete facilities and lifeguard. It is located across from the **Dry Cave**. Plenty of parking in the pothole-filled lot near the beach. Sand is very coarse (and therefore, comes off very easily). Although you might see people swimming here, the shore is totally exposed, lacking any reef protection. The smallest of waves has a surprising amount of force.

Lifeguards often close the beach to swimming in the winter months. A popular surf spot off to the left of the beach is called **Cannons**. Since the beach is very steep, a small wave could knock you over and the backwash could pull you in; therefore, swimming is hazardous except during very calm seas. Camping with county permit.

❖ Tunnels Beach / Makua Beach

A REAL GEM One of Kaua'i's snorkeling nirvanas. This superb beach has a wide-fringing reef that is so large it can be seen from space. There is often a lateral rip current, but it's *normally* quite weak, making Tunnels a good snorkeling spot most of the time. The beach is quite popular, and you will often see SCUBA divers here, as well as surfers and windsurfers. All this makes it sound crowded, but a lack of street parking keeps the numbers relatively low. The kaleidoscope of underwater life is usually profuse and definitely worth your time to explore. See section on SNORKELING on page 183 for some useful tips. See also the SCUBA section; both are in the chapter called ACTIVITIES. Public access is by either of two short dirt roads

Walking on the rocks next to the ocean may seem safe, but both photos are of Queen's Bath. Don't put yourself into a position where you're relying on Mother Nature smiling. She can be moody.

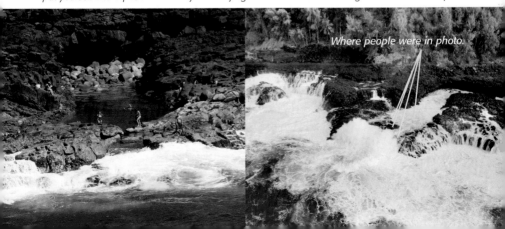

Where people were in photo.

past mile marker 8 on Hwy 560. The first (and best if you're snorkeling) one is 0.4 miles past mile marker 8. It is actually privately owned (by the seven surrounding land-owners), and they don't want you parking on it. Fortunately, one of the nearby landowners wrote to us pointing out that the deed to the road says, "There is an easement in favor of the county of Kauai." Perhaps this is why the county has listed it as a public access. The second one is almost 0.6 miles past mile marker 8 and has shorter access to the sand. Get there early to assure a parking spot. If they're full, park at Haʻena Beach Park and walk to the right. You could also take Alealea Street before mile marker 8, park near the sand, and walk to the left along the beach. (It's a half-mile walk in sand that way, but it's pretty.) You should know that if you park on the highway itself, they *do* give tickets.

❖ Kepuhi Beach

The snorkeling is good here but not nearly as good as Tunnels. You'll rarely find

many people on this beach, so if you're in the area and want easy access but no crowds, this is the beach for you. This long strip of sand is fronted by an even longer coral reef. The makeup of this reef causes a slightly stronger current. Check out conditions before you snorkel. Because most of it is not located directly off the main highway, it tends to be forgotten, even by locals. It is, however, still used on occasion by throw-net fishermen. Access is at the eastern end of Alamoo Road. See map on page 50. Limited parking.

❖ Wainiha Beach Park

Hazardous surf and its location at the mouth of the Wainiha River make it murky and unsuitable for anything other than shoreline fishing and beachcombing.

❖ Lumahaʻi Beach

This is the long, wide, golden, glorious beach you see just after you've passed Hanalei Bay. Pictured on countless postcards and posters, this beach was first made famous as a location for the movie *South Pacific*, where Mitzi Gaynor spent considerable time washing that man right out of her hair. If you're looking for a huge, picture-perfect stretch of sand on

Lumahaʻi is the widest beach on the north shore. But the better swimming is at the far, narrower end.

The Hawaiian Monk Seal

The endangered Hawaiian monk seal occasionally comes ashore after a heavy meal or to avoid a predator. Many people assume the seals are sick or injured and attempt to coax them back into the water. If you are lucky enough to encounter one, please leave it alone. Beaching is perfectly normal. The fines for disturbing one can range as high as $25,000. The seals dive as deep as 1,500 feet to feed and are considered the most primitive seals in the world with ancient social behavior. Unlike other seals, they don't come ashore in large numbers.

Leave me alone. Too many mai tais last night.

the north shore, Lumaha'i shouldn't be missed. If you're looking for safe swimming, Lumaha'i shouldn't be touched. This beach and Hanakapi'ai on the Na Pali Coast are the two most dangerous beaches on Kaua'i. Exposed to open ocean, the waves here, even small ones, are frighteningly powerful. We've come to this beach after seeing it absolutely flat at Ha'ena Beach Park, a few miles away, only to be utterly assaulted by Lumaha'i's waves. Put simply, most of Lumaha'i is almost never safe to swim. The waves, currents and backwash are not to be underestimated. Lumaha'i Stream on the left side is sometimes crossable during calm seas and low stream flow. It serves as an estuary for 'o'opu during the summer when the shifting sands tend to cut off the river from the ocean. During this time, the closed river mouth is sometimes safe to swim. But absent these conditions, swimming in Lumaha'i Stream has caused numerous individuals to be swept out to sea. Surfers and boogie boarders often use the left side of the beach near the rocks, but unless you're an expert on Hawaiian surf, this should not be attempted.

Separated by lava rock to the right (east) of Lumaha'i is **Kahalahala Beach** (technically part of Lumaha'i, but who's quibbling?). Swimming here is a different story. You access it from a marvelous 3–4 minute walk down through lush jungle to the beach 100 feet below. During calm summer days the water here can be like a crystal-clear swimming pool. There's a tidepool for keiki to splash about, a fair amount of shade, and a tall rock that some people love jumping off. (Our general rule

If you can negotiate the steps and path on the right side coming down to the sand, Hideaways delivers the right ingredients that make a great beach. And in the summer it's twice as long as this.

is to never jump off anything you haven't checked out first.) When seas are calm here, this area is utter paradise. Big surf, however, which is not uncommon in the winter, makes this part of the beach nearly as dangerous as the rest of Lumaha'i.

Access to these beaches can be obtained either via a trail from the top of the lookout at the eastern edge of the beach *before* mile marker 5 on Hwy 560 (this gets you to the eastern part, which is the best part), or from the parking area just before you get to the Lumaha'i River. See map on page 50.

❖ Hanalei Bay

The four beaches described below are all part of Hanalei Bay. With its single long crescent of sand, the bay is beautiful to look at but not great to swim in. Pounding shore break, backwash and rip currents, especially during the winter months, make Hanalei Bay less than ideal as a swimming beach. But that doesn't make it any less

pretty. Large surfing waves make Hanalei Bay very popular with surfers, who come from other islands to experience the extremely long-lasting waves.

❖ Waikoko Beach

Easy access and good reef protection at this one portion of Hanalei Bay make this a popular beach during moderate surf periods, but the water is shallow, which makes for marginal swimming conditions. The snorkeling is better than the swimming if stream flow isn't high. Located between mile markers 4 and 5 as the road begins to ascend. Access is near the 25 MPH sign. See map on page 51.

➕ Wai'oli Beach Park

Located at the end of either He'e or 'Ama'ama Roads in Hanalei and often referred to as **Pine Trees** (though there are no pine trees there—only ironwood trees). The underwater topography focuses more of the ocean's force here, making the swimming hazardous except during very calm seas. Swimming is much better at nearby Hanalei Pavilion Beach Park. Access is from Weke Road in Hanalei. A reader pointed out (and we verified) that this beach has particularly good sand for building sand castles. The stuff sticks together like cement.

➕ Hanalei Pavilion Beach Park

Also located on Weke Road in Hanalei, it includes facilities and a lifeguard. Popular with boogie boarders and surfers, the shore break and backwash make for less-than-ideal swimming conditions most of the time, but it's better than Wai'oli Beach Park.

❖ Black Pot

Located near the mouth of the Hanalei River, swimming conditions are marginal. (We've had several readers tell us that this is a favorite for swimming but, they probably aren't taking into account the high bacteria levels from the river.) During calm summer surf, boogie boarding is possible near the pier area. Black Pot refers to a large black cooking pot residents used to keep at the beach. This is the area where kayakers put in to paddle up the Hanalei River. The picturesque pier here makes a good sunset photo. Facilities available at beach. Camping with county permit. Super busy on weekends.

❖ Pu'u Poa Beach

Located next to the St. Regis in Princeville, the beach has a fringing reef and offers good snorkeling possibilities during calm seas. During the winter, the waters off the outer edge of the reef offer some of the best and most challenging surfing in the state (for experts only). Access is through a cement path starting just to the left of the gate house at the St. Regis. Free valet parking for going to the public beach, except for the tip, though. Getting to the beach necessitates negotiating 632 steps. (Yes, we counted...it was a slow day.) From here you can walk all the way to the mouth of the Hanalei River. Another access is

from Black Pot Beach and requires wading to come across the usually shallow water at the mouth of the Hanalei River. The final access is from the end of Hanalei Plantation Road (see map page 51). It's an easy walk but a half mile (described in HIKING), so pack light.

❖ Pali Ke Kua Beach / Hideaways

A REAL GEM Fifty feet before the St. Regis in Princeville gate house is a corridor off to the right (next to the Pu'u Poa tennis courts). This path leads *down* (120 feet below) to Pali Ke Kua Beach, also called Hideaways. Parking is pretty limited. The first half of the descent consists of stairs and a railing. The remainder is trail. All told, it takes 5–10 minutes to get there. There are actually two beaches here, with the second one off to the right separated by a rocky point. Both offer excellent snorkeling during calm seas. The salient underwater features are good relief and a diverse fish community punctuated by the occasional turtle. With marvelous coarse sand, large false kamani trees for shade and good snorkeling when calm, this beach is a wonderful place to spend the day. You won't usually find too many people here since parking near the trailhead corridor is limited.

While the beach can be a nice place to bring the kids, some may have trouble negotiating their way down the path. (In fact, *you* might have trouble, too, if it has been raining and the path below the steps is muddy. Ropes might be there to help, if that's the case.) When seas aren't calm, rip currents can form. Check ocean conditions carefully. Unusually high surf has been known to generate waves that can sweep across the entire beach. The *other* part of Pali Ke Kua beach can be reached by swimming to the right from Hideaways or by walking a paved trail leading down

The 2-mile long fringing reef at 'Anini usually gives this beach the calmest water on the north shore.

from the Pali Ke Kua condominiums. That _other_ path is a private trail available only to guests at Pali Ke Kua.

❖ Queen's Bath

A REAL GEM

Queen's Bath is actually a large pool the size of several swimming pools carved by nature into a lava shelf with an inlet from the ocean for fresh seawater to flow. If the surf is too high, you would never recognize this place as anything special. But _during calm seas_, Queen's Bath is a marvelous pool to swim in. Fish get in through the inlet, making it all the more charming. (Bring your mask and water shoes; no fins needed.) It's a great place to take your underwater camera. During mid-summer, if the ocean is _too_ calm, the water is not refreshed as much as it should be. During high surf, it's dangerous as the water flows in and out of the pond. Queen's Bath has claimed numerous lives because people got nailed by large waves during times that they should not have gone. During winter months (generally October–April), high surf assaults the area, and you should always stay away. Even when the ocean appears calm, it's always possible for a rogue wave to snap at this part of the shoreline, knocking people around, may-

be even dragging them back into the open ocean. Some people think we shouldn't even mention this attraction. But this is the information age—you're _gonna_ hear about it—and we'd rather you know about the safety issues than leave you with no information at all. And it _is_ a GEM—just one to experience only during calm seas. To get there, follow the trail off Kapiolani Road near Punahele Road in Princeville. See map on page 51. The trail (slippery when wet) passes a marvelous seasonal waterfall on your right after a few minutes. (Good for rinsing off the salt when you're done.) After dropping 120 feet, the trail encounters the ocean at the lava shoreline where a small waterfall drops directly into the ocean. Go to the _left_ along the lava for 260 yards following the dire warning signs. (It'll seem like more.) Queen's Bath is recessed in the rock and is part of a horseshoe-shaped lava cut. Use the photo on page 99 or the inside cover to identify it. If you can't find it, the ocean probably isn't cooperating.

❖ SeaLodge Beach

A REAL GEM

This wonderful pocket of sand is set in an indentation in the cliff. With plenty of shade courtesy of false kamani trees and heavenly coarse sand (the kind that won't stick to you with the tenacity of a barnacle), SeaLodge Beach is a real find. This beach is sometimes empty of people because most don't know it's there. During the summer in particular, it's an ideal secluded beach. Access is found in SeaLodge Resort at the end of Kamehameha Road in Princeville. Parking is an issue here. The resort dedicated seven stalls "Trail". Don't park in any of the other stalls because they belong to residents or on the road because you will get a ticket or towed. The trail is next to the stalls. See map on page 51. Where the trail encounters the ocean, it veers to the left. Look for turtles in the water here. The snorkeling can be outstanding during very calm seas, but entry and currents need to be respected. Depending on the weather, the trail can be slippery and a bit tricky in areas. During periods of unusually high surf, waves have been known to travel all the way to the base of the cliff. Don't come here if this is the case. Once at the trailhead, the entire picturesque hike should take

between 10 and 15 minutes and is well worth it. (If you had taken a right at the ocean instead, a short hike along the coastline would bring you to small, pretty waterfall.)

❖ 'Anini Beach Park

A REAL GEM Protected by a *long* fringing reef, 'Anini Beach has become a popular place for the rich and famous to build homes. The water can be very shallow, and the snorkeling *can* be good in many areas when visibility cooperates, though it seems to have been overfished. The swimming is among the safest you'll find on the north shore if you stay near the shoreline. Better snorkeling is near the outer reef edge, but it's not as safe there. The channel at the western end of the beach is where the water flows out, so stay away from this part. (See the left side of the map on page 48.) There are numerous areas along this stretch of sand to swim, snorkel or just frolic. There is a polo field across from the beach; check it out if you're there during summer. 'Anini

Local children often play in the shallow stream at Kalihiwai Bay.

Beach is a good place to learn windsurfing. Camping is allowed with county permit, facilities at the pavilion. The name used to be *Wanini Beach,* but the "W" was blasted away with a shotgun by an irate resident who felt it had been misspelled. Other residents assumed the gun-toting spell-checker must have corrected a mistake and the "new" name stuck. (*That's* typical Hawai'i.) Take the northern Kalihiwai Road (between mile markers 25 and 26) and stay to the left on 'Anini Road.

The far (west) end of the beach, on the other side of the channel, is known as **Wyllie Beach**. Residents of Princeville access it by taking a 0.25 mile-long trail from the end of Wyllie Road, which drops 20 stories. The easier way is to park near the channel on 'Anini Road (if you see a PRIVATE ROAD sign, you've gone too far) and wade across the stream. Wyllie Beach is a thin ribbon of sand with lots of shade from false kamani trees (whose fallen leaves turn yellow, red, orange and brown). It makes a very nice stroll as the ocean gently laps at your feet (though the sand can disappear during high tide and surf). There is a touch more sand in nearshore waters (though still plenty of rocks) than at other parts of 'Anini. Be aware that when the surf is breaking over the reef offshore, a rip current can form leading to the channel.

❖ Kalihiwai Beach

Located at the mouth of Kalihiwai Stream, you drive down from either Kalihiwai Road. (It used to be a loop, but the bridge was knocked out by a tsunami in 1957, and they haven't rebuilt it.) At the bottom of the road, you encounter a picturesque bay with a wide sand beach lined with ironwood trees to park under. There are houses on the other side of the road. The beach is popular with boogie boarders in the summer and is a good place to see local keiki learning to ride waves. It's also a good place to just enjoy the water during the summer. During the winter, surfers ride the large waves under the cliff area. The eastern (first) Kalihiwai Road is the best road to take to the beach. The only ding is that local dogs occasionally roam free, leaving—well, *you* know what they leave behind.

❖ Secret Beach

A REAL GEM Also known as Kauapea Beach and known to most locals by the more enticing name of Secret Beach, this is a stunningly beautiful beach only accessible via a more-tiring-than-you'd-think 10–15 minute hike. This fact, along with its former anonymity, caused it to become Kaua'i's premier nude beach. For the record, public nudity is illegal in Hawai'i, and police issue tickets there, so it's not as prevalent as it once was. This long, golden sand beach is narrower and not swimmable during the winter, but on calm summer days it can be a delight for swimming and offers good snorkeling. It's worth the trip year-round just to see its exceptional scenic beauty. There is usually a small waterfall to rinse off your gear and a few places where water squirts from the side of the cliff. The island off to your right is Moku'ae'ae Island, a bird sanctuary. To get to Secret Beach, turn right off the first (eastern) Kalihiwai Road, then right on the first dirt road you encounter. (See map on page 48.) Take the trail to the bottom. (It's real slippery when it's raining.) Make a mental note of where it encounters the beach for your return. If you go to the *left* at the bottom of the trail, the shoreline leads to the **Secret Lava Pools**, pretty tidepools that are visitable on calm summer days. But a rash of deaths from people being swept out to

Mark Zuckerberg paid a reported $200 million for the land behind Larsen's Beach. All you gotta do is hike down the trail to it.

sea during high winter seas (conditions which we *specifically* advised people to avoid) has left us thinking that these tidepools should probably be avoided.

❖ Kahili Quarry Beach

Where Kilauea Stream encounters the ocean is a beach sometimes called **Rock Quarry Beach**. There is good swimming on the left (western) side and good snorkeling on the right side during calm seas. Since this is a river mouth, the water can get murky at times. (Sharks, which like murky water, have been sighted here during periods of heavy stream flow.) This is a popular boogie boarding and surfing site. The river mouth can cause rip currents. Easiest access is from a dirt road off N. Wailapa Road. Avoid Rock Quarry Road from the north side as it was impassable, even with 4WD, at press time. See map on page 48. A good hike near here is described under HIKING on page 151.

❖ Waiakalua Beach

A marvelous and undiscovered north shore beach. Although from your car it requires a steep, 5–10 minute walk to the beach 160 feet below, Waiakalua is an undisturbed, serene place to spend the afternoon. Medium coarse sand, a long, fringing reef, numerous pockets of shade and a freshwater spring at the far end add to the charm. Observe the reef from up on the bluff. Calm summer snorkeling can be interesting but shallow; watch out for rip currents. During other times, swimming can be hazardous. To the north is a rocky point separating the two halves of the beach. The snorkeling around this point is exciting, featuring clear water teeming with big life. However, the rips, surges and surf make this area tricky—only advanced snorkelers need apply. Otherwise, just enjoy the beach. The cool spring at the far end offers sweet, fresh water. Bring an empty container and some way to filter the water—all fresh water obtained anywhere in nature should be treated to prevent bacterial disease. (It barely trickles during dry months.) To get to Waiakalua, turn onto North Waiakalua Road and take the dirt road on the left side just before the end of the road. Park when you can't drive any more, and take

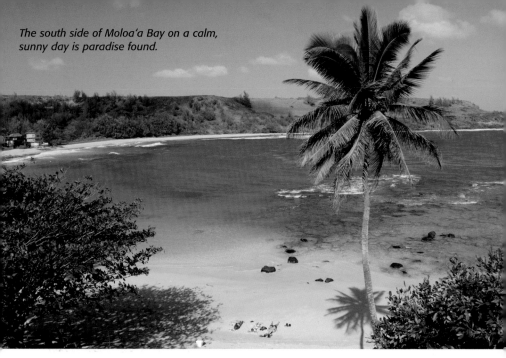

The south side of Moloa'a Bay on a calm, sunny day is paradise found.

the trail off to the left. The beach on your left at the bottom is Waiakalua Beach. The path off to your right leads to **Pila'a Beach**, which has lots of coral and good snorkeling. It can take 10–30 minutes to reach **Pila'a Beach**, depending on your boulder-hopping prowess. Otherwise, just stay at Waiakalua Beach. You'll probably have either one all to yourself. See map on page 49.

❖ Larsen's Beach / Lepe'uli Beach

 This has crystal-clear water, lots of beachcombing and seclusion. The beach is named **A REAL GEM** after a former manager at Kilauea Plantation named L. David Larsen (the rascal who introduced the hated blackberries to Koke'e). This beach is splendidly isolated but can be accessed by walking down a county access trail. Off to the right are a bunch of lava rocks that make for good snorkeling if conditions are right. To the left is a long crescent of sand broken by occasional outcroppings of rock and reef. Underwater topography creates good conditions for beachcomb-

ing. Pakala Point is on the left side where the first beach ends and lava rock protrudes out into the ocean. Just before these rocks is **Pakala Channel**. (Shown near the top of the photo and on the inside back cover.) Most of the water you see breaking over the reef drains through this channel; therefore, *don't swim in or near the channel*. The water leading just up to the channel moves so swiftly at times that it seems more like rapids than a rip current. If the ocean is calm and you stay away from the channel, if the tide is right and you have some experience snorkeling, this place can be a snorkeler's paradise. Lots of coral and fish in shallow, crystal-clear water greet the eye. Relatively few beachgoers use this beach during the week. This beach is *not* a swimming beach, just for snorkeling, due to the sharp reefs and shallow water.

One thing that can be *very cool*—if you're careful—is to get in the water at the southeast end (where the trailhead is) and let the current take you toward (but not into!) the Pakala Channel. Then get out and walk back.

The end of summer is when water at reef-fringed beaches like Larsen's has the poorest visibility because it has usually been many months since it has had a good flushing by the high surf.

During periods of high surf, waves *tower* above the reef, breaking on the edge, which can be quite a spectacle.

On the opposite side of Pakala Point are two pockets of sand that are even more secluded and offer good snorkeling and a chance of spotting a monk seal. Avoid the path on the rocks if the surf is up. Larsen's is about 20 minutes north of Kapa'a; take the *north* end of Ko'olau Road (the second Ko'olau if you're coming from Kapa'a) just before mile marker 20. 1.2 miles from the north end of Ko'olau Road, take the left Beach Access road all the way until it ends—it looks like a driveway at the beginning. (See map on page 49.) Follow the steeper trail to the bottom, which is 140 feet below you. (The easier path to the left is private property.) The beach is a 5–10 minute walk down the hill. Note where the trail hits the beach for your return. We've noticed that the far end of the beach often attracts nudists.

Lastly, consider posting a selfie of yourself here on your Facebook page. The landowner behind the beach, Mr. Zuckerberg to you and me, reportedly paid *$200 million* for land and will probably get a kick out of it. Or maybe not…

❖ Moloa'a Beach

A REAL GEM A wonderful beach on calm days. The right (southeast) side is much nicer than the northwest side. Very pretty, but not great for swimming when seas aren't calm. It's off the main highway and not as well known as other beaches. Take the first (southeastern) Ko'olau Road (before mile marker 17). Hang a right on easy-to-miss Moloa'a Road, next to a large fruit stand. The public access is near the end of Moloa'a Road. Parking is *very* limited. There are a few stalls toward the end of the road; otherwise, park where there are *no* NO PARKING signs to dissuade you. You might have to walk a ways to the beach, but it's worth it. To get to the southeast side, you'll have to walk 100 yards along the beach. There you'll find the wading, swimming and boogie boarding the best, and shade is plentiful. See map on page 49.

❖ Papa'a Bay

Very picturesque. The beach access involves a 5-minute trail through the brush down to some rocks below. After that you'll have to boulder-hop about a hundred yards. You need to use the access to North 'Aliomanu Beach (see map on page 49) and look for a beach access when the road turns to the right. In addition, it is one of the few beaches on Kaua'i where you may detect a fishy smell. When the producer of the movie *Six Days/Seven Nights* was here to film the plane crash scene, he apparently liked the location so much, he purchased all *174 acres* around the bay and built quite a compound, which sold in 2009 for $28 million. Although the land and house around the bay are private, the *beach* is public.

❖ 'Aliomanu Beach

This is really two beaches with different access points. The long, fringing reef offshore of the south beach is used heavily by locals for throw-net fishing, octopus hunting, pole fishing, torch fishing and limu harvesting. This beach, along with Pila'a and Larsen's, attracts families who have been limu (an edible seaweed) harvesting on the outer parts of the reef for generations. They pick the top part of the plant, leaving the roots to regenerate.

The northern (and better) beach is accessed from a parking lot 80 feet above the beach, requiring a 5-minute walk. (See map on page 49.) Although the nearshore waters are rocky, the beach is sandy and very pretty.

⊕ Anahola Beach Park

The area around Anahola is designated Hawaiian Homelands, and most of the beach users are Hawaiian. Visitors aren't common but are welcome. Swimming is safest where it is protected on the right (eastern) side of the bay to just before Kahala Point. Watch for rip currents near the remains of a pier. Also nice is the northern end, which is lightly used and can be accessed from the first Aliomanu Road.

EAST SHORE BEACHES

❖ Donkey Beach / Paliku Beach

So named by drifters in the '60s who observed burros and mules being used by

A REAL GEM the sugar company to haul seed cane to the fields nearby. Donkey Beach was once a popular nudist beach on Kaua'i due to its location, but the land's current owners have done much to end this practice. (After purchasing the land from a defunct sugar company and selling house lots for $2 million plus, they're not too thrilled with the idea of naked beachgoers.) This long stretch of sand is also popular with surfers. Interestingly, surfing in ancient times was usually done nude. (I wonder if that's where the term *hang loose* came from...)

Access is 0.5 miles north of mile marker 11 north of Kapa'a. Look for a hiking sign guiding you to the parking lot with facilities. The uncrowded beach is very attractive, with a convenient tree in the middle for shade. The foreshore at the beach is steep, creating a pounding shore break and strong backwash. Swimming is often hazardous. It's about a 10-minute (550 yard) walk on the paved path to the

You won't find any donkeys at Donkey Beach. In fact, you might not even find any people either.

beach. As you near the shoreline, veer to the right for the beach. To the left (north) past the stream and over the small hill is a secluded cove (cleverly labeled "secluded cove" on our map) where the snorkeling can be very good at times. You will probably have that cove all to yourself. During rainy times, there might be a small waterfall and swimming hole behind the cove. There is yet another cool cove if you keep hiking north, but we're embarrassed to point it out because all too often it seems to be used as a dumping ground for abandoned vehicles and other litter by people who don't believe in taking care of the land the way past generations did.

⊕ Kealia Beach

Drive north of Kapaʻa and you will often see lots of boogie boarders and surfers in the water here. (See map on page 61.) The powerful waves are fantastic but can be treacherous. The currents and backwash are sometimes ferocious. The northern end of the beach is more protected by a breakwater and can be good for wading and occasionally snorkeling on a calm day. If you have never ridden waves, be very careful here or you might get drilled into the ground. If the surf is high, definitely leave it for the big boys. If you choose to try boogie boarding here, water shoes or short fins are a must. Lifeguard and facilities.

❖ Kapaʻa Beach Park

Located in the heart of Kapaʻa, this is heavily used by locals. Like any beach located close to a population center, Kapaʻa Beach Park is not as pristine as other beaches you will find. That said, the northern section (the part just before the lookout as you leave Kapaʻa going north) offers interesting but shallow snorkeling. Check for currents. The rest of the park is not as memorable. It is, however, a good place for a beach stroll or to watch the sunrise. There are a few large sand pockets along the beach that are swimmable when the surf isn't high. Regular facilities here plus a swimming pool. The best thing about Kapaʻa Beach Park is watching the kite surfers on a windy day.

❖ Waipouli Beach

Pretty, but not a good swimming beach. There are a few small pockets along the southern portion of the beach that are relatively safe for swimming during calm periods, but be cautious. The area seaward of the beachrock fronting the beach is subject to strong currents year-round. This is normally considered a dangerous beach. There is a paved shoreline trail along much of this beach, which is perfect for jogging or a leisurely stroll.

Just north of Waipouli Beach is **Waipouli Beach Park**, also called **Fuji Beach** and sometimes **Baby Beach**. Conditions there are different. This can be a nice place to let keiki splash around in the ocean. Part of it (on Moanakai Street between Pahihi and Makana) is often protected by a long, natural sandstone breakwater. Only when the tide or surf are high does water flow over the sandstone and form a current to the left. If the tide is especially high or there's a large eastern swell, keep small children away as the current can get surprisingly strong. The most protected spot is the right (south) end of the beach near the sea wall. Most of the time, however, it's flat calm. The sand is coarse, so you'll sink a bit more into it. Check to make sure the ocean isn't making a liar out of us and that it's clean enough. Since it's located in the middle of town, it sometimes gets a little dirty.

❖ Wailua Beach

Across from the closed Coco Palms Resort, from the mouth of the Wailua

River to a rocky point to the north, this is an easily accessible beach. Just drive right up. It is popular with surfers and boogie boarders who appreciate the unprotected waves. Winter swells sometimes keep even these users out of the water. Swimmers should be aware of rip currents in several areas along the beach and pounding shore break during high seas. (Frank Sinatra learned this the hard way. During some down time while filming *None but the Brave* in 1964, Old Blue Eyes was swept 200 yards out and had to be saved by local surfers.) The river itself, which is crossable only during periods of *low flow*, can cause tricky water conditions, so caution is advised. The ocean and the river are constantly battling for supremacy, and the struggle can be dramatic. The ocean builds up a sandbar, and the river attempts to erode it. Sometimes the river is completely stopped up. When it finally breaks through the sandbar, it can be fascinating. The sandbar can erode in a matter of an hour or two, taking large amounts of sand with it. For a short time thereafter, ancient Hawaiian petroglyphs are exposed on rocks in the river mouth.

➕ Lydgate Beach Park

Located just south of the Wailua River, Lydgate is composed of a picnic area, **A REAL GEM** a large patch of grass, restrooms, two nice playgrounds, showers, lifeguard and two marvelous, boulder-enclosed ponds. These ponds are nearly always safe to swim, with the smaller one meant for keiki (kids), but after a heavy rain should be avoided due to debris and water quality. These ponds were created to allow fresh seawater and fish into the pond, while protecting you from the ocean's force. And they worked well until the county dredged the ponds in 2011 to

deepen them. When they dug, they tapped into goo below the sand, and the wound to the sea floor has never really healed, meaning the visibility and fish count are much lower than before the county "fixed" the pond. Nevertheless, the park facilities along with usually safe swimming make it a good place to get into the ocean. Access is just off Leho Drive in Wailua. (See map on page 61.) Camping is allowed. Note that if Portuguese man-o-wars happen to be present, they're usually near the rocks at the far right end.

❖ Nukoli'i Beach Park

From Lydgate to the far end of the Kaua'i Beach Resort is a long sand beach called Nukoli'i Beach, known locally as *Kitchens*. This beach includes the area fronting the Wailua Golf Course. This entire stretch of sand, more than 2 miles long, is never crowded, often deserted. This is surprising given its proximity to Kapa'a, but good for you. There is a road fronting much of the golf course, until it erodes at the very end. If you just want to easily claim a large spot of beach for yourself, this is as good a place as any. The swimming conditions vary along the beach but are usually marginal. Currents and surf are the usual villains. The area in front of the golf course is the only part worth considering for swimming purposes. The snorkeling can be good when it's calm, and it's fun to hunt for golf balls in the water. You might even find a club hurled by someone having an off day. Access? Just drive right up from the dirt road between the golf course and the resort entrance (not far from mile marker 4). Or take the Kaua'i Beach Resort entrance to access the southern portion of the beach. Facilities near the resort. One caveat: Natural currents often bring to this beach flotsam, such as netting and ropes from passing ships.

❖ Hanama'ulu Beach Park

Water is usually murky (and sometimes so are its beachgoers) due to the Hanama'ulu Stream. Sharks are often seen in the area. The waters around Ahukini Pier can offer interesting snorkeling when it's very calm. In general, a mediocre beach with fairly good park facilities that tends to attract a marginal crowd. You probably won't want to hang here.

❖ Ninini Beach / Running Waters

Located below the golf course near the Marriott, there's good snorkeling off to the left in front of the rocks on a calm day. However, even then it can be surgy and a bit tricky. Access via a walk along a golf cart path, then a right turn before the beach turning into a steeper dirt trail to the water; see map on page 67.

❖ Kalapaki Beach

With a gently sloping sand bottom and partial protection from the open ocean, Kalapaki is popular with visitors and locals alike. Swimming, bodysurfing, stand-up paddleboarding (no kite surfing because of the nearby airport), beginner surfing and boogie boarding conditions are usually good except during periods of high surf. Adjacent Nawiliwili Park behind the Anchor Cove Shopping Center is a popular picnic spot. Canoes and twin-hulled sailing catamarans often come ashore here. Facilities near Anchor Cove Shopping Center. Access is by a road behind the shopping center or through the Marriott. See map on page 67. This is a good place to be when a cruise ship goes by. Because it's at Nawiliwili Bay (where the Hule'ia and Nawiliwili streams empty), the water won't be as clear as other water around the island. When calm (which is most of the time), it's a good place to teach your little one how to ride a boogie board.

❖ Niumalu Beach Park

Good place to launch kayaks for trips up the Hule'ia Stream (where the opening

Kawailoa Bay at Maha'ulepu is a great place to spend a beach day.

The water is nice, but entry can be a bit awkward from this spot. Shipwreck Beach can be a good place to sit and watch frustrated fishermen cast off (literally).

scenes from *Raiders of the Lost Ark* were filmed). Camping by county permit, but you wouldn't want to. Other water activities are lousy due to its location so far up the river and general ickiness to the water.

SOUTH SHORE BEACHES

❖ Maha'ulepu Beaches

A REAL GEM This marvelous coastline is wild and undeveloped, actually consisting of three separate areas known as **Gillin's Beach,** **Kawailoa Bay** and **Ha'ula Beach.**

The whole of Maha'ulepu makes for fantastic exploring and beach walking, hence the gem. The swimming can be hazardous, and seas here are often choppy. Winter is best. Ocean entry is difficult in many places. The land is privately owned and the company is good about allowing access, so locals bend over backward not to give 'em a reason to shut it off. There is an abandoned guard shack on the road to the beaches, and they close off access between sunset and sunrise. (They will fine your *da kines* off if you have to call them to open the gate after closing.) Please take everything out that you bring in.

Maha'ulepu is located past the Hyatt on Po'ipu Road after the road becomes dirt. Turn right when the road ends and drive past an old guard shack. See map on page 77. There can be long stretches between road maintenance past the horse stable, and it might be difficult to navigate in a regular car. Those with 4WD (and those drive a rental car like it's stolen) will have no problem.

To get to **Gillin's Beach,** park at the lot where the road otherwise continues to the left. A short trail from the right side of the lot takes you to the beach. (See map.) This beach is named after the late Elbert Gillin whose rebuilt house (now a pricey vacation rental) is on the beach just off to your right. If you walk past it, you'll see a stream that may or may not reach the ocean. Take the trail *before* the stream and look for an offshoot to the left that has a bridge. (Generously provided by the makers of *Pirates of the Caribbean 4*.) Upstream you'll see a small, triangle-shaped opening off to your left. This is an ancient, open-roofed sandstone sinkhole called Makauwahi Cave with some cool features. Seven thousand years of protected sediment in one corner of the cave acts as a time machine and hides the bones of extinct birds, now-vanished palm tree species and evidence of a large pre-contact tsunami.

Local paleoecologists have been doing some studies here and sometimes have it gated off. This area is identified as a cave on the map rather than as an amphitheater because we didn't want the casual map reader to think that rock concerts were held there. If the cave is locked, there's a trail to the left that overlooks the amphitheater from above. Look for reintroduced endangered plant species up on top, salvaged from this former shallow lake.

To get to **Kawailoa Bay**, continue on the dirt road until it is directly next to the beach. Kitesurfing is popular from here to **Gillin's Beach**. They ride the waves faster than the wind, and it is a real treat to watch.

The trail to **Ha'ula Beach** (see map on page 77) requires a walk along an elevated field of lithified sand. (The trail starts where a fence ends at the cliff's edge, which doesn't leave a lot of margin for error if your balance is off.) The constant assault from sea spray has caused the sandstone to erode into short but fantastically sharp and strangely shaped pinnacles. This is a great place to observe the power of the ocean as it smashes into the cliff. Local fishermen drop their lines into the water from here since they can see their prey before they cast. When you reach **Ha'ula Beach** (about a 10–15 minute walk), you will almost certainly

have it all to yourself. The beach is backed by high sand dunes. Behind one you will find an old picnic table. The beach is rarely visited except by occasional horseback tours from CJM Stables. The swimming isn't very good; in fact, it can be quite hazardous, depending on conditions. But the beach is a beautiful place to enjoy your solitude. Over the ridge to the northeast is **Kipu Kai Beach**. Totally isolated, the only way to get to it is by sea or over that ridge. And the horse trails over the ridge are generously sprinkled with evil, spiked stickers. Bring your Kevlar pants.

The area between **Ha'ula Beach** and **Kawailoa Bay** contains other lithified sand dunes as well. Fishing from the top (labeled Cliff Cracks on the map) is incredible, but be careful—the dunes can be brittle, so don't fall in. The beach area just north of these lithified dunes often provides lots of goodies for the beachcomber. Check out the dry, sometimes gasping blowhole near the shoreline at the eastern edge of Kawailoa Bay.

Maha'ulepu was the scene of a terrific slaughter in the spring of 1796. When King Kamehameha launched the first of two invasion attempts, he and his fleet of 1,200 canoes carrying 10,000 soldiers left O'ahu at midnight, hoping to reach Wailua on Kaua'i by daybreak. They were in the middle of the treacherous Kaua'i Channel when the wind and seas picked up. Many of his canoes were swamped. Reluctantly, Kamehameha ordered a retreat, but too late to stop some of his advance canoes. When they landed at Maha'ulepu, they were exhausted. They awoke to the sound of enemy troops who proceeded to kill all but a few escapees. The last thing these escapees wanted to do was go back to O'ahu and tell their boss what happened. So they bolted all the way to the Big Island and kept their mouths shut.

❖ Shipwreck Beach

This beach was named for an old, unidentified wooden shipwreck now long gone. Also called **Keoniloa Beach**, it fronts the Hyatt. The public access road is between the Hyatt and the Po'ipu Bay Resort Golf Course. The beach is used mostly by surfers, boogie boarders, body surfers and people staying at the Hyatt. High surf can create very unfavorable conditions. Even during calm seas, swimming is sometimes difficult. The Hyatt erects colored flags to signal ocean conditions—green meaning safe. (Though we've *never* seen a green flag. Their lawyer probably confiscated it.) The cliff off to your left is called Makawehi Point and is a popular place for pole fishermen. You will often see foolhardy young men jumping off the cliff into the waters below. In 2013 Justin Bieber took a flying leap, then one of his bodyguards reportedly roughed up a photographer who caught the scene. The cliffs are a fascinating place to hike and are described in HIKING on page 159. The Hyatt has some outdoor showers near the beach area to rinse off, but they are technically only for the guests.

❖ Brennecke Beach

Great boogie boarding and lots of turtles. Since it is so small, surfboards are not allowed near the shore. The waves are usually great and tend to break both far away and close to shore—perfect for both beginners and advanced. You can rent boogie boards across the street at Nukumoi Surf Co. Observe conditions carefully before you go in. Since this beach is more susceptible to change than most island beaches, you'll have to evaluate its boogie viability. Be careful bodysurfing here. The local ER nickname is Break Neck Beach since body surfers sometimes get drilled into the sand.

➕ Po'ipu Beach Park

A REAL GEM This is the major center of beach activity on the south shore. The swimming is nearly always safe just to the left of the tombolo/sandbar, which disappears for stretches after major storms and during those times can bring a rip current. To the left is an area semi-protected by a breakwater along with some shade. It's very popular with children. Park facilities and lifeguard are present. This park is a nice place to enjoy the ocean, though it can get very crowded. The far right side isn't as protected but features excellent snorkeling with lots of fish and good swimming if the surf isn't high.

❖ Kiahuna Beach / Sheraton Beach / Po'ipu Beach

A REAL GEM Take your pick with regard to the name. This beach fronts the Sheraton Hotel and Kiahuna Resort. It is postcard pretty and often safe to swim, thanks to an offshore reef. Surfers ride waves outside the reef, but you should stay inside unless you really know your stuff. Boogie boarding and snorkeling help make this one of the most user-friendly beaches around. Access from the end of Hoonani Road. See map on page 77.

❖ Koloa Landing

An old boat launch used as a SCUBA spot. See SCUBA in the ACTIVITIES chapter.

❖ Baby Beach / Kaheka Beach

This stretch of sand is partially protected from surf by a natural breakwater of lava boulders forming a quasi-protected pool. The sand only extends a little way into the water, giving way to a lining of lava stones, so you'll be grateful for those cheap water shoes you brought with you. These same shallow stones also capture some of the sun's heat, making the water a little warmer here. A REAL GEM for people terrified of the ocean, as well as little crumb-crunchers, hence the name. Check conditions first. On Hoona (loop) Road off Lawa'i Road. Parking is pretty limited. See map on page 76.

❖ PK's

Named after the Prince Kuhio monument across the street on Lawa'i Road in Ho'ai Bay. Almost no sand and entry can be awkward, but snorkeling is good at times. Also used for SNUBA and SCUBA.

❖ Lawa'i Beach / Beach House

This tiny pocket of sand next to the Beach House Restaurant nearly disappears at high tide. The snorkeling in front of the restaurant is great, but the water is subject to currents during periods of high surf and needs to be respected. At other times it can be calm and a good place for the less-experienced snorkeler. SNUBA (not SCUBA) is also done here. Just stay near the shore around the restaurant.

❖ Keiki Cove

A minuscule pocket of sand just past Lawa'i Beach where the road almost clips the ocean. (A break in the low stone wall between two houses hides stairs.) It's usually protected and an excellent place to let rug-rats experience the ocean, but check it yourself first.

❖ Kukui'ula Harbor

Probably the most forgotten beach on the South Shore. When tiny little Lawa'i Beach is jammed with people, this protected harbor with a very pretty mountain backdrop, a great view of Spouting Horn, is lightly used during the week and there's plenty of parking. (Weekends are more crowded with locals launching their boats.) There's plenty of sand, a huge lawn and facilities. Snorkeling isn't great, but swimming is often protected by the boat jetty.

Pulverized bits of glass, rounded by the ocean, color the sand at Glass Beach.

❖ Lawa'i Bay

Access is the problem here. There's no way to get here by land without crossing private property. But you can kayak here from Kukui'ula Harbor, which is only a mile to the east. The beach is in a particularly lovely setting, backed by the National Tropical Botanical Garden. If you visit the beach, you're not allowed to venture into the private garden. Garden personnel say that this is one of the rare places on the island where green sea turtles nest. (Most of Hawai'i's green sea turtles are born in French Frigate Shoals, 500 miles away.)

❖ Palama Beach

The only way to get to this beach is to take Kaua'i Coffee's dirt road past their visitor center in Kalaheo off Hwy 540. You'll have to fill out a waiver, take it to the nearby main office and pay $25, then wait several weeks for it to be processed. And permits are not available during coffee harvesting. If you're still with me, the beach is quiet and nearly always deserted, often visited by a monk seal or two.

WEST SHORE BEACHES

There aren't a lot of listings under West Shore Beaches. That's because it's almost *all beach*.

❖ Glass Beach

If someone told you that you gotta check out the beach near an old dump, would you believe 'em? Then if they said the reason to check it out was because stuff from the dump washes ashore, would you go? Well...you should. Glass Beach makes a rotten first impression. It's in the industrial part of 'Ele'ele backed by huge, ugly tanks full of gasoline. Add to that millions of pieces of broken glass, washed in from broken bottles and auto glass. The result?

A colorful tapestry of sand and multicolored glass. (Come to think of it, doesn't glass *come* from sand?) This isn't a beach to frolic at or swim in. It's a good strolling beach, especially if you want to tie in a visit here with a hike along the Swiss cheese-type of lava farther east. until a sign dissuades you further. The amount of glass varies with tides and surf—sometimes there's almost none here or ultrafine; sometimes it's everywhere. Please don't take any of the glass litter. (Now *there's* a bizarre statement if taken out of context.) To get to Glass Beach, drive toward Hanapepe, turn left on Waialo Road going toward Port Allen. Before the ocean, go left on Aka Ula until it's dirt. (You may want to park there.) Then take a right on the dirt to the beach. A 20-minute or so walk further east leads to **Wahiawa Beach**, a dark sand beach where tour boats sometimes moor for lunch and kayaks visit in the winter. See map on page 87.

➊ Salt Pond Beach Park

This area is distinguished in that it has the only natural salt ponds in Hawai'i still used to make salt. Seawater is pumped into containers and allowed to evaporate. More water is added, and then it is transferred to shallower pans. The process is repeated until the water is loaded with salt. This is allowed to evaporate completely, leaving crystallized salt behind. (Excellent in kalua pig.) During the summer you'll likely see people practicing this process. The nearby park and its facilities are a popular place for locals to bring their families. The beach is separated by two rocky points. A natural ridge of rock runs between the two points, creating an area of relative calm inside. Swimming is usually safe, and children play in the semi-protected ocean water. The exception is during periods of high surf, which can make it unsafe. In Hanapepe past mile marker 17 off Lele Road. Usually windy, especially in the afternoon. Camping with county permit, full facilities and lots of wild cats. The parking lot and restroom area may turn you off, but the beach is very nice.

❖ Pakala Beach

Those cars you might see parked on the side of the road shortly after mile marker 21 belong to surfers carrying their boards to a very famous surfing site also known as **Infinities**, so named because the ride seems to last forever. The water is murky and only used for expert surfing.

➕ Lucy Wright Beach Park

Lucy Wright was a prominent member of the Waimea community when she died in 1931. It is a testament to how the townsfolk felt about her that the beach was named in her honor, especially in light of the more historic event that happened here. For it was at this spot that Captain James Cook first set foot in the Hawaiian Islands in January 1778. The beach itself is not a particularly good beach. The Waimea River mouth is nearby, and the silty water is less enticing than clear waters elsewhere. Some guidebooks label this a black sand beach, like the black sand beaches on the Big Island or Maui. That's not quite accurate. Though there *is* lots of black sand here—flecks of lava along with a green stone called olivine chipped from the riverbed by the Waimea River—much of the "black sand" is simply fine sediment carried by the same river. The best part of the beach is watching the interplay of the ocean and river mouth, described on page 88. Full facilities. The river mouth is also a popular place for beginner stand-up paddleboarding.

❖ Polihale

A REAL GEM This area consists of more than 12.5 *miles* of uninterrupted sand beach. (It used to be 17 miles, but the beachwall near the highway east of Kekaha Beach Park is too sporadically sandy to consider it a beach.) There are three regions, called **Kekaha Beach Park**, **Pacific Missile Range Facility** and **Polihale State Park**. Except for a few small areas, the entire stretch is unprotected, which means it is exposed to the ocean's force. During periods of high surf, waves can travel up the beach and pull you in, so be wary. When the seas are calm, you might enjoy the water. The sand can get pretty hot out on this side—hot enough to fry your feet—so watch it. Take water with you. It's available only at Kekaha Beach Park and at the other end at Polihale State Park.

➕ **Kekaha Beach Park** is the first region you encounter. High surf generates a particularly powerful rip current, and waves can be unbelievably strong; stay out or ask the lifeguard unless the water is real calm.

Past Kekaha is one of the least appreciated (and used) stretches of beach on the island. **Kokole Point** marks the beginning of PMRF (below). The dirt road 0.7 miles past mile marker 27 leads to the shoreline. 4WD drivers should read the part about driving on sand under the Polihale description below if you want to drive on the beach. At the beach here you can often walk for a mile (especially to the west) and not find a soul. Ni'ihau seems so close from here. There's no shade, and the same swimming warnings apply as Kekaha Beach Park. But it's a great place to enjoy a wide, sandy beach and awesome for a late afternoon BBQ.

Pacific Missile Range Facility (PMRF) is operated by the U.S. Navy. Access *through the facilities* these days for visitors is pretty hard to get. It's a long and arduous process. But you are allowed to *walk along the beach* from Polihale, past the great sand dunes described below until a turnaround point. Just make sure you stay within 20 feet or so from the shoreline so you don't venture onto base property, and expect to be turned around if a rocket launch is imminent. The beach on the northern part (adjacent to Polihale State Park) is **Barking Sands Beach**. If conditions are right, the sand dune (which has numerous kiawe trees) is supposed to make a barking sound with your every step. The likely cause is a combination of uniform grain size coupled with a thin coating of silica that sticks when dry. Don't feel bad if it doesn't happen. We've jumped up and down like idiots on that sand until we were blue in the face, and we haven't even gotten it to whine. The sand needs to be *real* dry. Local legend has it that the barking sound comes from nine dogs buried in the sand. They belonged to their master, a fisherman, in the days when dogs didn't bark. (Sometimes I wish those were *still* the days.) One day, they started acting antsy after the master tied them up before he went fishing. While he was out, a storm broke and forced him off course. A god gave the dogs the power to bark so they could guide their master home. Unfortunately, the dogs were so fearful waiting for their master that they ran around the stakes they were tied to. Around and around and around they ran until they buried themselves in the sand. The fisherman was depressed when he returned and couldn't find his dogs. He would go down to the shore every day looking for them, but he never found them. The dogs remain there to this day, barking for their master, hoping he will find them. (My neighbor's dog seems to bark for the same reason.)

Polihale State Park is the end of the line. You can't go any farther north on this part of the island without a boat. This is where the Na Pali Coast starts. (Sunsets can be dramatic here—the cliffs light up red as the sun gets close to the horizon.) Rain is rare in these parts. On the few occasions that it does rain hard, the road can get pretty sloppy. Other times potholes might slow you down, but regular cars can almost always make it. The sand can get *real* hot in the summer. Hot sand can slip into your shoes and burn you. A smart beachgoer will wear only wool socks (no shoes, despite how goofy it looks) to keep the blisters away. The four facility areas here tend to be poorly maintained but include showers, restrooms, picnic tables and drinking water (which you'll need).

The dunes of Polihale are famous throughout the islands. The beach averages 300 feet wide, and the dunes can get up to 100 feet high. Walking down a dune like that can be fun; walking up is a monster. Better to walk around unless you are training for the *Ironman Triathlon*. Locals drive their 4WD vehicles right onto the beach. If you try it, be aware that you are a *long* way from Lihu'e. The first thing a tow truck driver will probably ask you is, "Do you own your own home?" It's probably cheaper to buy a new car. And AAA won't tow a *stuck* car, only one that won't start, so yank an important-looking wire before you call them. Remember the 4WD drive trick to driving on sand is to have low air pressure in your tires (15 psi is what we use), be gentle on the gas, and *don't stop* in soft sand; let your momentum carry you. A cheap air pump from Walmart that plugs into the cigarette lighter can refill the air. Even with all that,

it's still possible to get stuck. Consider taking the carpet out of the trunk and driving on it if you're stuck.

To get there, take Hwy 50 till it ends, veering right at the fork. (See map on page 86.) The first dirt road leads 3.2 miles to a large monkeypod tree. To the left is **Queen's Pond**. This is the one part of Polihale that often offers safe swimming. It is partially protected by a small fringing reef, and the swimming inside the reef is good except during periods of high surf.

If you go to the right at the monkeypod tree, there's a soft sandy spot in the road 4.5 miles from where you left the pavement. If you drive past it *(don't stop in the sand)*, look for the large parking lot on your left with three small pavilions and restrooms. You'll be able to fall out of your car onto the sand.

Beaches along **Na Pali** are not reachable unless you're up for an adventure. That's why they are described in the ADVENTURES chapter.

Two lovers live their sunset dream at a west side beach.

Wet, warm and happy. Life is good...

If you want more from your Kaua'i vacation than a sun-tan, Kaua'i offers a multitude of activities that will keep you happy and busy. Among the more popular activities are helicopter tours, ocean tours of Na Pali, golfing, hiking, SCUBA diving and kayaking. You will find lots more to do here as well.

We've listed the activities here in alphabetical order. Beware of false claims on brochures. We've seen many fake scenes in some brochure racks. Computers have allowed photo manipulation to imply realities that don't exist (which *we* don't do).

Activities can be booked directly with the companies themselves. Ask them if they have any coupons floating around in the free publications or if there is a discount for booking direct. You can also book through **activity brokers** and **booths**, which are numerous and usually have signs such as FREE MAPS or ISLAND INFORMATION. Allow me to translate: The word FREE usually means I WANT TO SELL YOU SOMETHING.

What we're about to tell you has gotten this book pulled from some shops and badmouthed in some circles, but the truth's the truth. Their objective, as is the case with many concierges, is to sell you activities for a commission. *Occasionally,* you can get better deals through activity booths or your concierge, but not often, because 25–30 percent of what you're paying is their commission (which they call a "deposit") for making the phone call. That's why calling direct can sometimes save money. Companies are so happy they don't have to give away one-quarter to one-third of their fee to activity booths, they'll sometimes give you a discount.

Many of the activity booths strewn about the island are actually forums for selling timeshares. We are not taking a shot at timeshares. It's just that you need to know the real purpose of some of these booths. They can be very aggressive, especially with so many timeshares on the market. (To use a wilderness analogy—they are the hunters; you are the hunted. Don't let them see the fear in your eyes.)

Selling activities is a *big* business on Kaua'i, and it's important to know *why* they're pitching a certain company. If an activity booth or desk steers you to XYZ helicopter company and assures you that it's the best, that's fine, but consider the source. That's usually the company that the booth gets the *biggest commission* from. We frequently check up on these booths. Some are reputable and honest, and some are outrageous liars. Few activity sellers have ever done any of the activities unless they got it *free* and the company *knew* who they were. On the other hand, we *pay* for everything we do and review activities *anonymously*. We have no stake in *any* activity company we recommend, and we receive *no* commission. We just want to steer you in the best direction we can. If you know who you want to go with (because you read our reviews and decided for yourself), call them direct first.

A warning: Many of the companies listed have a 24-hour cancellation policy. Even if the weather causes you (not them) to cancel the morning of your activity, *you will be charged.* Some credit card companies will back you in a dis-

pute if the 24-hour policy is posted, some won't. Fair? Maybe not. But that's the way it is.

Lastly, consider booking online before you come. Good companies can fill up in advance, and the Internet can pave the way for your activities. Our site at **www.hawaiirevealed.com** has links to *every* company listed here that has a site, even the ones we recommend *against*.

ATVs (also called quads) can be a fun way of seeing the back country. They are like Tonka Toys on steroids with knobby tires. The companies here offer *very* different experiences. Unfortunately, none currently offers single-person ATVs.

Kipu Ranch Adventures (246-9288) is our favorite. The scenery is the nicest, the vehicles (Kawasaki Teryx 4's and Mulepro 6's) are top quality and the most comfortable of the three companies, plus their guides are the most customer-oriented. Their tour is of the beautiful Kipu Ranch. In the 3-hour tour ($146 per person), you're treated to the lump-in-your-throat backdrop of Ha'upu Range along the pastures. They'll descend into woodsier areas, along the stream where *Raiders of the Lost Ark* was filmed (bring a swimsuit and water shoes in case you "fall" in) and usually end up at a viewpoint almost no one on Kaua'i ever gets to see—the hidden valley and beach of Kipu Kai from the road that drapes across the mountain. (Because it's private and closed, we *never* thought we'd get to see this sight.) You pay for two seats whether you have a second person or not. Both the 2-hour and 4-hour tours ($104 and $168 per person, respectively) omit Kipu Kai but visit a small waterfall. If you prefer not to drive, any tour can cost $96 by riding with a guide.

Their machines are ridiculously stable (you'll get a demonstration), and they run their tours well. Their training is excellent if you're new to these. You won't be allowed to totally cut loose on your bike, but your overall moving speed is similar to Kaua'i ATV. It's a tour, and you will get dusty or muddy. But it's a fun way to see exceptional scenery. Minimum age for riders (*drivers* must be 18) is 9 years old for all tours except the 2-hour waterfall tour, which is 7 years old.

Princeville Ranch Adventures (826-7669) is a lot of fun and has more variety than the other ATV companies. Besides the ATV ride, you get to try out two ziplines, followed by a dip in a secluded, waterfall-fed swimming hole. The vehicles hold two people, but be warned if you have an odd man out—single drivers will have to pay an additional *$159* for the empty seat. Cruising through the ranch lands, you'll encounter varied terrain with plenty of hills, dips and turns to test your skills (and opportunity to get your passenger filthy). Because this is the wetter side of Kaua'i, you'll have more chances for mud than dust, giving dramatic effect to your before and after selfies. You'll stop early on to take in the views of Kalihiwai Ridge before strapping back in for the muddiest stretch of the course. Next you park and walk jungle trails, crossing a few streams (you will get wet and muddy) while the guides narrate and share knowledge of Kaua'i's plant and animal life. Overall, they're accurate and do a good job, though some guides might be more interested in talking shop with coworkers. You get a taste of their zipline course with two zips and a suspension bridge crossing above the swimming hole (you start and end in the same place). This part is optional and can be a good opportunity for

those with kids too small to be part of regular zipline tours—the kids wait with a guide while you get your zip on. The deli lunch is good, but no drinks are provided—you're expected to bring your own. The 4 hour tour is $169 for drivers (18 and up), $159 for passengers ($129 for kids 5 to 11). $129 to ride along with a guide. Closed-toe shoes are required—we recommend renting theirs for $5. (Let them clean 'em up.) Our biggest complaint is that whoever starts driving has to finish—no switching. Minimum height to drive is 5 foot 4 inches, maximum weight per person is 280 pounds, and 5 years and 50 pounds minimum to zipline).

On the other hand, **Kaua'i ATV** (742-2734) in Koloa is the exact opposite in almost every way. They lack the good views of Kipu Ranch and lush surroundings of Princeville Ranch. Instead of mostly trail riding here you usually stick to dirt roads. The average moving speed is 15 MPH, and you may reach 25 MPH at times; it depends on the guide. If it's been raining, you're encouraged to crash through every puddle. During dry times, it's super dusty. Either way you'll get dirty. They almost never cancel due to weather. Like Kipu Ranch, they have up to 12 vehicles per group. Service is pretty blank at the check in. Their playground is mostly old sugar cane roads plus two stops at small waterfalls and a cool trip through a half mile-long tunnel. Two-, three- and four-person mud buggies make up the fleet (try to get one of the newer looking ones), and they allow qualified drivers to take turns. Narrations are minimal, which is good, because when they do talk, the information is often inaccurate. Our safety concerns stem from personal observations, including seeing another customer complain that his brakes were not working. (He was told to simply "keep his distance" in-

Beachside biking along the east shore.

stead of replacing the brakeless ATV.) The waterfall tour is $315. It's $253 for the shorter tour. A plus here is that they allow drivers as young as 16 and riders as young as 5. Maximum weight per person is 320 pounds.

BIKING

Bike lanes or shoulders of some kind line the main highway from Princeville all the way around to Mana on the west side (though some are narrow in spots, and some bridges force you into the traffic). Past Princeville, forget it. And for what it's worth, we find that Kaua'i drivers are more likely to crowd bikes off to the side than other islands. Don't know why, but it's true.

For mountain biking, the dirt roads in Po'ipu, especially near **Maha'ulepu,** can be fun, though a bit dusty. Another good place is the cane road between **Kealia Beach** and **Anahola.** (Start at Kealia Beach and pedal north; give way to ATV riders.) And the 2.5-mile paved road from **Kealia Beach** up to **Spalding**

Monument is really scenic and sparsely driven. You'll gain 400 feet of elevation in the process. The **Kuilau** and **Moalepe Trails** can be exciting. (Described under HIKING on page 156.) The roads past the end of **Kuamo'o Road** in Kapa'a leading toward Wai'ale'ale and the **Jungle Hike** described on page 156 are excellent for mountain bikes.

If you don't mind a long drive, the roads of Koke'e offer good choices. See the Koke'e map on page 142 and the west side map on page 86. Pay attention to **Mohihi-Camp 10 Road** on the Koke'e map. The **contour road** in Koke'e is always fun. You can even travel down the spine of some of the ridges, such as Kauhao and Ka'aweiki, if you have the stones to pedal back up.

If you're interested in renting a mountain bike, call any of these companies: **Kaua'i Cycle** (821-2115) in Kapa'a, the friendliest bike shop on the island (with some great prices), or **Outfitters Kaua'i** (742-9667) in Po'ipu. **Pedal 'n Paddle** (826-9069) in Hanalei has beach cruisers and hybrids only. You'll pay $30–$45 per day. Bikes with shocks are better but more expensive.

If you just want to go downhill, road trips down Waimea Canyon Drive are available. They're fun but pretty short. With **Bicycle Downhill/Outfitters Kaua'i** (742-9667) you meet at 6 a.m. or 2:30 p.m. in Po'ipu, then drive up to the canyon in their van. (Don't worry, they provide coffee for the 6 a.m. tour.) Near mile marker 12 you get out and coast downhill almost the entire way on 550 and 552, ending up in Kekaha before noon. $113.

Kaua'i is in the process of spending 50 million federal dollars to construct a shoreline walking/biking path from Nawiliwili to Anahola, scheduled to be completed about the time that Lady Gaga draws her first Social Security check. Currently the only completed section is the 6-mile section from Waipouli Beach Resort in Kapa'a to just north of Donkey Beach and a 2-mile chunk from Lydgate to Coconut Marketplace. The northern section is the prettiest, and the smooth concrete path is easy to ride on beach cruisers. Shops in Kapa'a rent them. **Coconut Coasters**

(822-7368) is near the north end of town and has a great selection of cruisers, hybrids, mountain bikes, a range of kids' bikes, and tandems. We really like **Hele On Kaua'i** (822-4628) near Pono Market. They make the rental process very simple, and it's the best bang for your buck. You can get a bike for 1 hour for $5—enough time to do the whole paved portion. They only carry cruisers and child trailers, but anything more for the bike path is overkill. They also have several satellite offices along the path, including across from Kealia Beach.

Boogie Boarding

Boogie boarding (riders are derisively referred to as *spongers* by surfers) is where you ride a wave on what is essentially a sawed-off surfboard. It can be a real blast. You need short, stubby fins to catch bigger waves (which break in deeper water), but you can snare small waves by simply standing in shallow water and lurching forward as the wave is breaking. If you've never done it before, stay away from big waves; they can drill you. Smooth-bottom (hard shell) boards work best. If you're not going to boogie board with boogie fins (which some consider difficult to learn), you should do it with water shoes or some other kind of water footwear. This allows you to scramble around in the water without fear of tearing your feet up on a rock or urchin. Shirts are *very* important,

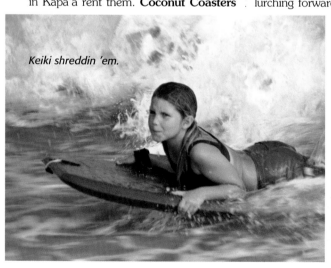

Keiki shreddin 'em.

especially for men. (Women already have this aspect covered.) Sand and the board itself can rub you so raw your *da kines* will glow in the dark.

Your hotel activity desk may have boards. It should cost you $5–$9 per day, $15–$30 per week. Other places include:

North Shore—Hanalei Surf Co. (826-9000) or **Pedal 'n Paddle** (826-9069).

East Shore—Seasport Divers (823-9222) and **Boss Frog** (822-4334).

South Shore—Seasport Divers (742-9303) in Po'ipu, **Po'ipu Surf** (742-8797) in The Shops at Kukui'ula or **Nukumoi Beach & Surf Shop** (742-8019) across from Po'ipu Beach.

Below are some beaches worth considering. Also check the BEACHES chapter for more.

- **Kealia Beach** in Kapa'a is excellent, but the waves are powerful.
- **Kalapaki Beach** in Lihu'e is a smart choice for beginners and the timid.
- **Brennecke Beach** has returned to its former glory. (For a decade it was poor after being chewed up by a hurricane.)

CAMPING

The ultimate in low-price lodging is offered by Mother Nature herself. Kaua'i is a great place to camp with 13 different areas—six state camping areas and seven county campsites. See map on next page. To camp at a state-controlled site, you need to contact the **Hawai'i DLNR, State Parks** in Lihu'e at (808) 274-3444. (Our website has a link to a page where permit applications can be filled out online.) You are *strongly* advised to get your permit before you arrive because the sites can fill up, especially during peak season (May–December). The state requires that you enter the driver's license or passport number of every adult who will be camping, as well as the names of any minors, along with your dates of travel. The permits are $18 per group per night (except Na Pali, which is $20 *per person*) and should be acquired as far in advance as you can. They recommend at least six months in advance during the busy months. *More* for Na Pali.

The state enforces permits with uncommon zeal, so when officers swoop in to check your permits, stand at attention and wipe that smile off your face.

For more on beach campsites see BEACHES chapter.

County campsites require a county permit. They will send you an application, or you can get it online. The cost is $3 per adult per night. Call:

County of Kaua'i Parks & Recreation
4444 Rice St., Suite 105
Lihu'e, HI 96766
(808) 241-4463

Car camping from 4WDs at Koke'e State Park is lovely—especially Sugi Grove—and is convenient if you plan to hike much there.

If you need to rent camping or hiking gear, your best sources will be **Pedal 'n Paddle** (826-9069) in Hanalei or **Kayak Kaua'i** (826-9844) in Kapa'a. **Kaua'i Camper Rental** (346-0957) has VW camper vans as well as camping equipment for rent.

Propane can be found at **Walmart** in Lihu'e. For butane, call **Gaspro** (245-6766) in Lihu'e.

Good places to buy gear include: **Da Life** (246-6333) in Kalapaki Bay, **Pedal 'n Paddle** (826-9069) in Hanalei, **Aloha Exchange** (332-5900) in Kalaheo and **Discount Variety** (742-9393) in Koloa or **Walmart** and **Costco** in Lihu'e for food.

Camping Sites–County Sites in Black, State Sites in Purple.

Na Pali Coast State Wilderness Park
Haena Beach Park
Hanalei (Black Pot Beach)
'Anini Beach Park
Hanakoa
Kalalau Beach
Miloli'i Beach
Koke'e State Park
Polihale State Park
Anahola Beach Park
Lydgate Beach Park
Lucy Wright Park
Salt Pond Beach Park

Lastly, TSA can be fussy with camp stoves, even when checked. Just so you know… Readers have been enraged when stoves they bought here have been confiscated, even when they're clean.

Kaua'i's waters contain abundant fish. Of course, it's one thing to have 'em and another thing to catch 'em. Whether you want to go deep sea fishing, sit by a lake or cast off a cliff, you will be pleased to know that all are available on Kaua'i. Anyone can fish in the ocean—no permit needed (check size and season regulations, though). Freshwater fishing does, however, require a permit.

Deep Sea Fishing

If deep sea fishing's your game, there are several charter companies around. They all provide the necessary gear. Tuna, wahoo (ono) and marlin, among others, are all caught in these waters. The seas around the islands can be rough if you're not used to them, and it's fairly common for someone on board (maybe you) to spend the trip feeding the fish. We advise that you take Dramamine or Bonine *before you leave*. Scopolamine patches work well but have side effects that can temporarily affect vision. (It can make close-up vision poor for a week.) Other alternatives may be available. See your doctor. (I've always wanted to say that.) Some people feel that greasy foods or citrus before or during your trip is a no-no; *many* swear by ginger tablets. Some seriously suggest putting a cherry seed in your bellybutton (and hope the fish don't laugh at you).

Most boats troll nonstop since the lure darting out of the water simulates a panicky bait fish—the favored meal for large game fish. On some boats, each person is assigned a certain reel. Experienced anglers usually vie for corner poles on the assumption that strikes coming from the sides are more likely to hit corners first.

You should know in advance that in Hawai'i, the fish belongs to the boat. What happens to the fish is entirely up to the captain, and he'll usually keep it. You may catch a 1,000-pound marlin and be told that you can't have as much as a steak from it. If this bothers you, you're out of luck. If the ono or another *relatively* small fish are striking a lot and there is a glut of them, you might be allowed to keep it—or half of it. You *may* be able to make arrangements in advance to the contrary.

Before deciding *who* to go with, decide if conditions warrant going at all. It might be calm on one side of the island and rough on another. Current ocean conditions can be obtained by calling the **National Weather Service** (245-6001) for weather.

Prices below do not include taxes, harbor fees, fuel surcharges or tip.

Reputable charter companies are:

West Shore Charters

In the past, we've had astonishingly bad experiences with **Deep Sea Fishing Kaua'i** (634–8589) based out of Port Allen. They have improved considerably. Four-hour charter (shared with five others) is $169.

East Shore Charters

Hawaiian Style Fishing (635-7335) has a 25-foot boat that goes out of Kapa'a. Unlike most boats there's no deckhand, so it'll be a bit more hands-on (literally). If the trolling's not working, they'll bottom feed. A good, flexible outfit. $140 for a half day.

Leaving from Nawiliwili Harbor, **Lahela Sportfishing** (635-4020) uses a 34-foot Radon. They allow you to take the catch up to 30 pounds. Shared charters are expensive at $225 per angler (three minimum/four maximum) or a better deal at $750 for up to six anglers as a private charter.

Kai Bear (652-4556) has a 38-foot and a 42-foot Bertram, making them some of the largest (and most comfortable) fishing boats on island. An ownership change has greatly improved the attitude and overall feel at Kai Bear. Half day is $175; 6-hours is $235. Half day private is $825 (less if you use cash). Prices include taxes and fees.

Freshwater Fishing

There are dozens of lakes (actually manmade reservoirs) strewn throughout the island. Largemouth bass are plentiful. You'll also find smallmouth bass and a tough-fighting South American import called tucunaré or peacock bass. Avoid fishing when the water is real muddy after a heavy rain; fish won't bite. **Tom Christy** is the local tucunare guru, and you can book time with him from **Sportfish Hawai'i** at (877) 388-1376. A pricey $265 for half-day trips, which includes gear, bait and beverages. Some readers haven't been impressed with this tour, but but we haven't observed that.

Though **fly fishing** isn't very big in Hawai'i, die-hards now have an option on Kaua'i. **Fly Fish Kaua'i** (652-9038) offers both fresh and salt water tours. The 4–5 hour tour is $350 for either type and only one person is preferred, so as not to spook the fish. Most gear and lunch is provided, but you'll need to get your own tabis.

The **Pu'u Lua Reservoir** in Koke'e (on the west side, see map on page 86), as well as several feeding streams, are stocked yearly with rainbow trout fingerlings. Lake waters are too warm for trout to spawn. Trout season in Koke'e is restricted to the first Saturday in July until the end of September. The rules are complicated. **Division of Aquatic Resources, Department of Land and Natural Resources** (274-3344) can fill in any additional blanks you may have.

Places to obtain licenses are: **Walmart** (246-1599) in Lihu'e and **Salt Pond**

Country Store (335-5966) in 'Ele'ele/ Hanapepe. Squid and shrimp can be obtained from most supermarkets.

GOLFING

With its bountiful nightly rainfall and warm, sunny days, Kaua'i is a perfect environment for golf. Its seven golf courses are diverse, ranging from a wealthy sugar magnate's private course donated to the island to a world-class resort course rated in the top five for the all the islands by Golf Digest in 2016. If golf is your game, Kaua'i is sure to please.

The prices described under Fees in the table reflect the highest category of fees. Check the specific course descriptions in our app for more information and possible discounts. Many have additional twilight specials. If you're planning on golfing multiple days at different courses, consider renting clubs from a third party. **Kauai Golf Club Rentals** (346-0626) has Callaway clubs available for five days at $109, and they'll deliver them to your hotel. The **Kaua'i Bound Store** (320-3779) in Nawiliwili has Wilson clubs for $70 per week.

Below we'll give you the skinny on the island's courses. We have detailed reviews of each course in our smartphone app, **Hawaii Revealed**, but didn't have space to fit it all in the book.

Kaua'i Golf Courses

Golf courses are located all around the island. You'll notice that greens tend to break *toward the ocean* more than your eye will tell you. We'll start from the north shore and work our way down. If you only have time for one course, and money is no issue, we'd recommend Po'ipu Bay.

On the north shore, **Princeville Makai Golf Club** offers an impressive 18 holes with commanding and outstanding views and is one of the best on the island. The greens and fairways are in great shape and the layout fairly open.

On the east shore, **Wailua Municipal Golf Course** is pretty darned good for a muni and is reasonably priced (for Hawai'i). As it parallels the beach on Kaua'i's Coconut Coast, Wailua constantly reminds you that you are near the ocean. In Lihu'e, **Ocean Course at Hokuala** embraces the ocean like no other and the views and layout are *outstanding*. Their renovations in 2016 improved the infrastructure and brought golf-

Course	Phone	Par	Yards	Rating	Fees
Kiahuna Golf Club	742-9595	70	5,878	69.1	$110*
Kukuiolono Golf Course (9 holes x 2)	332-9151	72	6,154	69.1	$20
Ocean Course at Hokuala	241-6000	71	6,252	71.6	$205*
Po'ipu Bay Golf Course	742-8711	72	6,959	68.9	$250*
Princeville Makai Golf Club	826-1912	72	6,134	69.6	$239*
Puakea Golf Course	245-8756	72	6,061	68.8	$105*
Wailua Municipal Golf Course	241-6666	72	6,585	71.3	$48–$60

* Indicates power cart included in fee.

boards (which are fun to ride). In Puhi, **Puakea Golf Course** is a fun and moderately difficult course. It's not in the same league as some of the resort courses, conditions—including the hazards—are poor, but the fees reflect this.

On the south shore, **Po'ipu Bay Golf Course** is a sprawling 210 acres of wide-open golfing. It has spectacular scenery, impeccable grooming and attention to detail. Greens are real consistent. They try to keep them as fast as they can, given the windiness. At nearby **Kiahuna Golf Club** the fairways seem to be getting more love these days than we've seen in the past. Homes are all around the course, detracting from the natural beauty, and ocean views are scarce.

Heading west a bit, in Kalaheo **Kukuiolono Golf Course** is the personal nine-hole golf course of a sugar magnate from the 20th century. It's simple, dirt cheap and has a certain charm. Cash only.

HELICOPTERS

If ever there was a place made for helicopter exploration, it's Kaua'i. Much of

For those who venture off the fairway here at Po'ipu, we have some advice: Take the stroke.

the island can be seen only by air, and helicopters, with their giant windows and their ability to hover, are by far the preferred method for most. Going to Kaua'i without taking a helicopter flight is like going to see the Sistine Chapel and not looking up. You will see the ruggedly beautiful Na Pali Coast and marvel at the sheerness of some of its cliffs. This is an area where razor-thin, almost two-dimensional mountains rise parallel to each other, leaving impossibly tall and narrow valleys between them. You will see vertical spires and shake your head in disbelief at the sight of a goat perched on top. The awe-inspiring Waimea Canyon unfolds beneath you. A good pilot will come up over a ridge, suddenly exposing the glorious canyon, often timed to coincide with a crescendo in the music you hear in your headphones. You will see the incredible Olokele Valley with its jagged twists and turns and stair-step waterfalls. It is impossible to keep track of all the waterfalls you will see on your flight. You

Welcome to dreamland…

will get a different view of Kaua'i's fabulous north shore beaches and reefs. You might see whales, depending on the time of year. And best of all, you will be treated to the almost spiritual splendor of Wai'ale'ale Crater. You have never seen anything like the crater—a three-sided wall of waterfalls 3,000 feet high, greens of every imaginable shade and a lushness that is beyond comprehension. Many people find themselves weeping when they enter the crater. Others find that they stop breathing—it happened to me the first time. If it has been dry lately, it's simply great; if it's been *pumping* rain in the interior, the waterfalls are spectacular.

When you are finished with the flight, you will either be speechless or babble like a fool—it happens to everyone.

Bear in mind that we're not rabidly pro-helicopter statewide. In our Maui book, *Maui Revealed*, we were lukewarm on flights there (fearing a bang-for-your-buck deficit). O'ahu, too, doesn't lend itself well to air tours. But on Kaua'i it's absolutely worth it.

One concern you may have is safety, and that's a valid point. As far as the industry safety record is concerned, there have been crashes and "incidents," when a craft has had to make an unscheduled landing. You can ask the companies directly about safety, but you should be aware that over the years when we've tried it, we were often misled or directly lied to. Not every time, but many times.

When we checked with the FAA, we discovered that, like many things, safety evaluations aren't that simple. A company might be cited for maintenance violations—*that* sounds ominous. Then you find out that the maintenance was carried out properly, but a log was dated incorrectly, or the company didn't fill out a particular form. Should we steer you away from them for this reason?

In the end it comes down to a matter of judgment. Below is a list of companies that we feel are qualified. Not all have spotless safety records. Things happen—a warning light comes on, and they have to land immediately. Even if it was a false alarm, it is still considered an "incident." These companies struck us as honest and forthright in their concerns about safety.

One issue that all the companies have to deal with is weather. As a pilot myself, I appreciate a company that will *cancel* due to marginal weather. Setting aside the safety factor, if cloud base is super low and it's dumping rain, how much will you get to see? When we don't like the weather, we call the companies to see which ones are canceling. The companies that seem most willing to fly when we wish they *wouldn't* are **Safari** and **Island**. Safari, especially, has really disappointed us by flying during what we consider very ugly conditions.

As far as seating is concerned, the front seat is the best. To console you, some companies might tell you otherwise when they direct you to a back seat. From the front, the island rushes at you with incredible drama. The problem is that seating arrangements are *supposed* to be made on the basis of weight. (They will discreetly weigh you at check-in.) Lighter people are generally seated up front. If you are seated in the back, the **right seat** is the best since much of the action will be on the right side. (By common agreement, companies fly clockwise around the island, making Na Pali and other areas best from the right side, though good pilots will rotate the chopper often to accommodate left seat passengers.) Although companies won't guarantee you the *front* seat, ask them if they'll at least keep you on the *right side* of the craft and let them know you'll consider them weasels if they don't comply. Most will accommodate. If they don't, consider going elsewhere.

There are four different types of helicopters. **A-Stars** seat two passengers up front and four in the back, leaving two people in the middle. Helicopter companies like these crafts since they can fly six passengers at a time. There are usually no windows to open, so glare may be a factor with your pictures. **Eco-Stars** are a roomier and more luxurious version of A-Stars. They have lots of window space, are quieter and cost more (over $3 million a pop), so tours are more expensive. **Blue Hawaiian** and **Sunshine** use Eco-Stars. At press time nobody was using **Bell Jet Rangers** on Kaua'i, but it's a popular tour helicopter nationwide and one we try to avoid due to poor seating. **Hughes 500** aircraft seat two passengers in the front and two in the back, a great arrangement. The Hughes has the pilot sit on the left side, out of the way. (*Some* A-Stars like Jack Harter's do, as well.) Hughes have large, removable windows. While the back is a bit cramped and doesn't allow the forward view that other back seats do, their side views are better. Currently, only one, **Jack Harter** has one because the Hughes cost more per person to oper-

ate per passenger than A-Stars. They'll fly with the doors off. Windy and cold in back but an awesome experience. Lastly, **Mauna Loa** flies **Robinson R-44s**. These are piston-driven (as opposed to much more reliable turbine-driven) helicopters with one-third the horsepower. Though these birds are much cheaper to buy and operate, it's not reflected in their tour prices.

All helicopters on Kaua'i are allowed to fly 500 feet over most scenic areas. (Companies that claim *only* they can fly that low…are full of beans.)

This is a hard section to write. You're going to spend a lot of money, and we *really* want to point you in the right direction. Most of the companies do a pretty good job, but they're very different. (Of course, like another activity that comes to mind—*wink, wink*—even when a helicopter ride over Kaua'i is bad…it's still good.) The difference between helicopter companies is the difference between a very pleasant flight and really experiencing the island. It's the difference between coming off the craft with a pleasant smile and leaving with a stupid grin on your face that won't leave you all day—between having a tale to tell and experiencing something so moving that it will stay with you for a lifetime. All this said and done, our favorites are **Blue Hawaiian** and **Jack Harter**.

Company	Phone	Helicopter Type	2-Way *	Departs
Blue Hawaiian Helicopters	245-5800	Eco-Star	Yes	Lihu'e, Princeville
Jack Harter Helicopters	245-3774	A-Star, Hughes	Yes	Lihu'e
Mauna Loa Helicopters	245-7500	Robinson R44	Yes	Lihu'e
Safari Helicopters	246-0136	A-Star	Yes	Lihu'e
Sunshine Helicopters	245-8881	A-Star, Eco-Star	No	Lihu'e
Island Helicopters	245-8588	A-Star	Yes	Lihu'e
Ni'ihau Helicopters	335-3500	Agusta	Yes	Hanapepe

* Indicates whether craft contains a microphone for you to talk to the pilot.

Scale on Na Pali is hard to convey. The arch on the right side of the photo is big enough to fly an airplane through.

Prices

The prices we list in this section are the "out-the-door" prices (including taxes, fees and fuel surcharges), but remember that companies adjust them all the time. Flight times are the guaranteed minimum amount of time in the air. You can almost always get a discount by calling the company and asking, or booking directly on their website. Charter rates for the whole bird are between $700 and $3,000 per hour.

Most Recommended

Blue Hawaiian Helicopters (245-5800)—This is the company to go to if you want the cushiest flight and a great location at the airport instead of a van ride from off-site. Their Eco-Stars are the most comfortable choppers on the island and the roomiest. Giant windows (with gobs of glare, too, if you're into photos) provide a great viewing area. $269 per person for a 50-minute tour from Lihu'e, but there is a $20 discount if you book online at least five days in advance. They also do a 45-minute tour from Princeville Airport for $289. For an extra $40 you can get a recording of your flight made from four on-board cameras.

Jack Harter Helicopters (245-3774)—Named after the guy who started it all on Kaua'i in the early '60s, his company's tours are still in demand, so book in advance. Harter has 60-minute flights for $289 (get $30 off if you book online) and an excellent comprehensive 90-minute flight for about $145 *more*. They're the only one with such a flight, and the experience is relaxed and unhurried. Pilots come and go at all helicopter companies, so the quality of the pilot's narration can come down to training. For what it's worth, the accuracy of Jack Harter's narrations seems pretty high. If you want a sportier trip (we think it's more fun), they also have a four-passenger Hughes that flies with the doors off for $309. *Very* cool and great for photographers. Unlike their A-Star flights,

Vantage points like this are things mere mortals will never achieve—unless they spring for a pricey but highly memorable helicopter ride.

the Hughes has no background music. For this there's a 250-pound weight limit, 400 pounds *per couple*.

Other Qualified Companies

Safari Helicopters (246-0136)— We're not a big fan of their tours. ($239 for 55 minutes.) They record your entire trip from multiple on-board cameras. (It's $40 extra.) The quality may be pretty bad (we get hypnotized by watching the dirt on the camera lens moving back and forth), and frankly, we think you'd be *much* happier with a professionally made video, rather than one taken on the fly (so to speak). But at least you'll get to hear your voice if you ask the pilot questions. Readers have told us that they are the most accommodating to larger passengers. They also have

a trip that lands at a remote canyon where you get out and listen to a lecture about the Robinson Family history and their plans. Overpriced at $314, but Safari often has exceptional discounts on their website.

Island Helicopters (245-8588) has 50-minute tours in their A-Stars for $297. For $385 (check for discounts— all their prices are outrageous, but they offer deep discounts for booking online) they'll land at the waterfall in Jurassic Park called Manawaiopuna Falls (they should offer half off if you can pronounce *that* one properly) and let you get out for photos and some area info. No swimming, and people over 250 pounds (couples over 420 pounds) may have to purchase an additional ticket.

Mauna Loa Helicopters (245-7500) out of Lihu'e Airport stresses private tours in their marketing for two or three passengers, and they do a pretty good job. It's $325 per person for the 60-minute island tour or $408 for the extended 75-minute flight that visits more waterfalls. (You have the option of flying either tour with the doors off for the same price.) Photographers may want to try their pricey photo tour, for $693 *per hour* for up to two people. You get to choose the locations. 275 pound per person maximum weight limit.-

Sunshine Helicopters (245-8881)— Our least favorite company. They won't let you talk to the pilot the way most companies do (no two-way intercom). Sunshine uses A-Stars and Eco-Stars (which they call Whisper-Stars) from Lihu'e (the 50-minute tour is $244 for the A-Star and $264 for the Whisper-Star). Although helicopter companies always claim that weight distribution decides who sits up front, if you pay an extra $50, they'll distribute your butt up front. They call them "first class seats." The $60 recording of your flight is pricier than elsewhere.

Be wary of some of the information imparted during some of these flights, especially from bigger companies that may have pilots from the mainland with little knowledge of Kaua'i. They mean well, but often their "facts" are way off.

Helicopter Tips

- Never take a flight of less than 50 minutes; you will only get your appetite whetted. It's too rushed.
- With a still camera, zoom lenses work best since the size of the field changes rapidly.
- Use a fast ISO speed of 400 or higher.
- Beware of the glare from the inside of the windows, and don't let your camera touch a vibrating window while shooting. Circular polarizers (which you'll have to adjust constantly) are *vital* for reducing glare. Wearing dark clothing helps, too. Polarized sunglasses help in the glare department.

- Don't get so caught up taking pictures that you lose the moment. It's hard to soak up the magic of your flight through a camera viewfinder.
- If you're in a craft that has two-way communication, don't be afraid to ask the pilot to turn so you can take a shot of something. Most will.
- If you're prone to motion sickness, take something *before* you fly.
- Remove any earrings before putting on the headphones.
- If you can't hear the pilot over the music, ask him to adjust the sound.
- If there are four or more of you, consider chartering an A-Star helicopter. It might actually be cheaper and will allow you to call many of the shots during the flight: "Pilot, please hover here for a few minutes, and turn a little more to the right." If only your group is on the flight, you are effectively chartering the flight whether you realize it or not, so take advantage of it.
- Morning is usually the best time for flights (though Na Pali looks best in the afternoon). Rainy weather brings more waterfalls.
- If you take a helicopter trip, do it early in your stay. It'll help orient you to the island.
- When you see people getting off a helicopter after their tour, try not to be downwind from them. They are often foaming at the mouth from their experience and might drool on you.

For an off-island helicopter experience, **Ni'ihau Helicopters** (335-3500), owned by the powerful Robinson family, flies groups to their privately owned island of Ni'ihau. For $440 you fly for 1-hour, circumnavigating Ni'ihau from a thrillingly low altitude, and land at one of its beaches for snorkeling, beachcombing and a pic-

No buffalo roam here, but the deer and the antelope play on the Forbidden Island. And the only way to see 'em is with Ni'ihau Helicopters.

nic. Bring your own snorkel gear and towel. This is an awesome trip, and if you've already seen Kaua'i by air, it's highly recommended. Ni'ihau's beaches are achingly beautiful, especially when they land on the northern tip of the island. Nowhere will you find cleaner water or better beachcombing, and you can keep whatever you find. The problem you encounter with them is that they require at least five people on a flight and don't usually have enough customers to ensure a flight for you. Even if they do, their twin-engine Agusta is often being chartered for commercial work (such as the military, which uses it for electronic warfare exercises). If you are determined to take the flight, contact them as much in advance as possible to maximize the chance that they can organize a flight, but don't be surprised if it doesn't work out. Less than a thousand people a year get to visit this place. Count yourself special if you're one of them. Tours depart from Port Allen Airport on Kaua'i's west side.

Airplane Tours

If you don't like helicopters and still want to see Kaua'i by air, **Wings Over Kaua'i** (635-0815) has a three-passenger Cessna 172 and a six-passenger Airvan with circle island tours for $135. Visibility is better with the Airvan, but it scoots along pretty fast. Airplanes can't go into the narrow valleys the way helicopters can. It's nowhere *near* as thrilling as a helicopter tour, and if your objective is to see the sights, go with helicopters. But if you just want a plane ride over Kaua'i, here's your chance, and they're friendly folks. Weight limits are higher (310 pounds). You can charter the whole plane for $600. Try to sit on the right side because they fly clockwise around the island.

Air Ventures Hawai'i (651-0679) also does tours in their six-seat Airvan for $145 for the hour. They also have a YMF-5 Super biplane that would make Snoopy drool. They call their pilot the

"Red Baron" (who, in real life, actually flew a *triplane*.) At $525 per couple for an hour-long flight, it's similarly priced to helicopters, but they only take two passengers at a time, so tours are more personalized. Biplanes have fairly rotten views. The wings dominate everything you see. But you'll *look* cooler in your photos. (They have a mount for your GoPro, but the wings vibrate too much for video—set it to time-lapse photo and use a high ISO setting.)

Of all the Hawaiian Islands, none offers more trails or better hiking than Kaua'i. You could spend an entire month on Kaua'i, hiking every day and not see half the trails that the island has to offer. And those are just the officially *maintained* trails.

We have *lots* of hikes in this book. We've also made some close-up maps to assist on specific hikes. Additionally, there are several *excellent* hikes listed in the ADVENTURES chapter since they're a bit…different.

If you plan to do a lot of hiking, contact the agencies below for information packets on their trails:

Hawai'i DLNR Division of State Parks
3060 Eiwa St., Suite 306
Lihu'e, Hawai'i, 96766
(808) 274-3444

County of Kaua'i Parks & Recreation
4444 Rice St., Suite 105
Lihu'e, HI 96766
(808) 241-4463

If you need to **rent** camping or hiking gear, your best sources will be **Kayak Kaua'i** (826-9844) in Kapa'a or **Pedal 'n Paddle** (826-9069) in Hanalei. For walking in streams or anything slippery, nothing beats **tabis**. Like felt-covered mittens for your feet, they provide impressive traction on mossy rocks. (No ankle support, though—duct tape helps remedy that.) **Walmart** in Lihu'e or **Discount Variety** in Koloa are your best bets.

Good places to buy other gear include: **Village Variety** (826-6077) in Hanalei and **Discount Variety** (742-9393) in Koloa. In Lihu'e, **Da Life** (246-6333), has lots of outdoor clothing, shoes and camping gear. *Some* specialty gear (stuff the REI fans might like) can also be found at the **Aloha Exchange** (332-5900) in Kalaheo. Don't forget **Walmart** in Lihu'e.

A **hiking stick** can be helpful on some trails. We sometimes even use two on long hikes and find that they greatly ease climbing and descending and give better balance, in addition to their usefulness in probing mud puddles. It's also handy during the months when tiny **crab spiders** are active. Their minor bites aren't dangerous, just annoying, especially if you get one in the face. Just wave a stick in front of you if you notice any on the trail. In a flash of brilliance, they were brought to the islands *on purpose* to attack a farming pest. Didn't work—smooth move, guys! (Next, they'll probably want to bring in *tarantulas* to get rid of the mosquitoes.)

Lastly, it's nice to be able to visually see *where* you are on a trail and know you're going in the right direction. But many of the trails on the island do not show up on a typical GPS or Google maps. *Well,* it just so happens that we GPSed every trail on the island, and they are in our smartphone apps available online.

KOKE'E/WAIMEA CANYON AREA

In Koke'e State Park you'll find exceptional hiking, with the additional benefit of higher altitude and its accompanying cooler temperatures. The map on page 142 shows the layout of the trails and dirt roads. The dirt roads, even when graded well, become *very* slick when wet. As a result, you may have to walk to some of the trailheads, lest you find yourself stranded. It's a good idea to check in at the **Koke'e Museum** (335-9975, open 9 a.m. to 4 p.m.) before you hike to get up-to-date information.

By the way, some of the trails in Koke'e require a 4WD vehicle (or a *long* walk) to get to them. As an alternative to a 4WD, consider renting a mountain bike and bringing it up to the canyon in your car. Then ride it out and hide it in the forest near the trailhead (since you can't use it on Koke'e trails themselves), and you will find that your hiking options greatly increase.

Pihea Trail   Kids?
(2 miles round trip)

If you only do one hike while visiting the canyon area, this is the one you want. This short trail is only about a mile, but it wraps around the upper rim of the Kalalau Valley, so give yourself plenty of time because you are going to be constantly stopping to take pictures. The view just keeps getting better and better.

The (often *muddy*) trail starts at the end of Waimea Canyon Drive at the Pu'u o Kila Lookout. (See map on page 143.) The beginning part skirts the edge of the valley, and then passes through native 'ohi'a and fern forests until reaching the backside, where the whole valley is laid out before you, with the ocean in the background 4,000 feet below. At the end, a very short but *steep* spur trail leads to Pihea Vista. Nice, but tricky to walk up to—it's optional. (Long legs help). Turn around whenever you are ready, or continue on to the Alaka'i Swamp Trail.

Alaka'i Swamp Trail
(8 miles round trip)

This trail starts in the canyon area on the island's west side and leads to a magnificent view of Hanalei Bay on the north shore, while taking you through the highest swamp in the world along the way. Thankfully, you're insulated from the mud most of the time by a boardwalk.

Start by taking the Pihea Trail (see page 143) until you hit the Pihea Vista junction. Just past here, the trail is covered in most spots by a boardwalk. (The part of the trail before the boardwalk is sometimes pretty muddy and slippery, so be forewarned.) After about a mile when the trail intersects the Alaka'i Swamp Trail, go left (east); it's 2 more miles to the end. (Many readers have said it's *way* more than that—hey, sorry, the GPS don't lie.) The Alaka'i Swamp Trail leads to the edge of a cliff where the Kilohana Lookout affords a majestic view of Ha'ena on the north shore, clouds permitting. Imagine hiking to this point before the boardwalk was installed. Then imagine that the hard part was *still to come*. That's because the ancient Hawaiians used this trail to get to the north shore when the surf precluded going by sea. Once at Kilohana, they went over and down the 3,400-foot cliff to the valley floor and along the sloping valley to the ocean. All this for westsiders to visit family on the north shore in the winter. (Remember this the next time you think you're too busy to drive across town to see Mom.) Along the trail you'll see old telephone poles. They were erected by the military after the attack on Pearl Harbor and stretched across the swamp, down the cliffs of Kilohana and into Hanalei. They served as a backup communications line in case the Japanese captured Lihu'e. Even without the view at the end, it's probably the most unusual hike on the island. Full grown trees on the flats rarely exceed 5 feet tall. Submerged grasses, vines and moss-covered trees sheltering endemic birds (found nowhere else) make this a memorable hike. Fog rolls in and out constantly, adding to the mystery of the scenery. You've *never* seen wilderness like this. While you're on this boardwalk, you'll have the same thought as everyone else—"My *God*, this must have been a wretched hike before they installed this." Darned straight! It's about 8 miles round trip from your car, but you can just go as far as your desire takes you. The boardwalk system was created in the late '90s and was quite a task. Even with it, expect to get a little muddy from patches where the boardwalk was left out, and watch for areas where the metal mesh will want to snag your innocent, unsuspecting foot. If you want to avoid the sometimes sloppy stretch of the Pikea Trail, you can an just do the Alaka'i Swamp Trail from its beginning off Mohihi-Camp 10 Road. (See map.) You'll probably need a 4WD or mountain bike to get to the Alaka'i Trailhead off Mohihi. Pihea's car access from the end of Waimea Canyon Drive makes it the better route.

Po'omau Canyon Ditch Loop

(Distance varies by route and vehicle capabilities)

This is an outstanding loop hike and one of our favorites in the park. It sports incredible views, lush and exotic surroundings, and a dizzying finger of land that sticks out into the canyon and overlooks two glorious waterfalls at one shot. This is a truly beautiful trail. Originally cut in 1926 to assist Koke'e Ditch workers, it's unofficially kept up by volunteers, such as the Sierra Club. Long pants can be useful if the blackberry bushes (and their evil thorns) are sticking

These two people on the Alaka'i Swamp Trail's boardwalk are in for a treat: a spectacular sheer cliff overlooking the island's north shore 4,000 feet below the lookout.

Koke'e Trails

The nature of the terrain at Koke'e makes it difficult to convey the type of hiking each trail provides. This accurate, computer-generated, shaded relief map is drawn from an angled perspective to give you a feel for the lay of the land. Since this is a perspective map, the mileage scale should be a little smaller at the top of the map (since it's "farther away" from your eyes) and a little bigger at the bottom of the map.

0   1 MILE

Honopu Valley
Airplane Trail
Kalalau Lookout
18
Honopu Trail
Awa'awapuhi Trail
See Nu'alolo Hike map on page 147
Kaluapuhi Trail (2.0)
Koke'e Rd
17
Water Tank Trail
4WD From Here
Nu'alolo Trail
Koke'e Museum
Chlorine Water Valves
Pu'u ka Ohelo Trail
Berry Flat
Pole #320
16
Pumping Station
1.3
1.6
Mohihi-Camp 10 R
Cabins at Koke'e Park on Dr
Koke'e Rd
0.0
Waineke
Mohihi
0.9
Kumuwela
Spur Rd (0.75)
Miloli'i Ridge Rd
15
Unnamed Trail
Halemanu-Koke'e Trail
0.5
Camp Sloggett (0.8)
Waininiua Trail
Makaha Ridge Rd (Paved)
Hale
Waineke 4WD
14
Kumuwela Trail
Kumuwela Rd (2.0)
End of Ditch Trail
Po'omau Canyon
Pu'u Hinahina Lookout
Black Pipe Trail
Koke'e Ditch
Grassy Bank
22°06.599
159°38.638
13
Waimea Canyon Dr
Canyon Trail (2.4)
Waimea Canyon
Waipo'o Falls

Publications, Inc.

Note: Distances given for trails are one way. Distances listed along Mohihi-Camp 10 Road are from the intersection of Waineke Road and Kokee Road near telephone pole 320. Don't be fooled by a sign at that intersection saying Kumuwela.

Kilohana Lookout
22°09.375
159°35.624

Pihea Vista

Kalalau Valley

Pu'u o Kila Lookout

Pihea Trail (1.8 to Intersection)

Alaka'i Swamp Trail (2.0 to the end)

End of Road

Alaka'i Swamp Trail (1.2 to Intersection)

Pihea Trail (1.75 to Intersection)

22°08.799
159°37.070

N
W   E
S

Bridges with Metal Slats

Tall Rock & Cliff Face

Kawaikoi Stream Trail (1.75)

2.25

22°07.919
159°37.902

3.0

3.7

Sugi Grove Campground

Ditch Trail (3.6)

Short Spur Road Above Small Dam

4.2

Excellent Views

Mohihi-Camp 10 Rd

Foot Bridge

4.5

5.2

6.0

Po'omau Canyon Vista (0.3)

Po'omau Canyon

Mohihi-Wai'alae Trail

Kohua Ridge Trail (2.5)

Koaie Canyon

Indicates Foot Trails
17 Roadside Mile Markers
Unpaved Roads
Waimea Canyon Drive
▲ Campsites
▪ Restrooms
Water Tunnel

The Po'omau Canyon Ditch Trail sports some awesome views of the valley 1,500 feet below you.

out into the trail. The footing is occasionally obnoxious, and there are opportunities for the genetically clumsy or the vertiginous to take a long roll.

To get there, take Waineke Road (across from the Koke'e Museum) to Mohihi-Camp 10 Road. Park at the intersection of Mohihi and Kumuwela Road, then walk about a mile on Mohihi Road to the trailhead. The unmarked trailhead is *on your right*, angling back toward the road. (If you come to a bridge with metal slats, you've gone 600 feet too far. The trailhead is *just before* a road turnout and might be marked with a near-invisible metal signpost (missing a sign). Look for it on your right when the road-cut wall of rock and dirt on your left is about to end. If you have to cross a concrete walkway at a small dam at the beginning of the trail, *you're on the wrong trail.* Using the map feature of our smartphone app is really helpful on this hike. The GPS works even when you don't have a cell signal, which is really useful in the remote canyon area where coverage is spotty.

Almost as soon as you start the trail, you will come to a small valley with a running stream. This is your canary in a coal mine. If the vegetation is too thick to walk through, it means you are unlucky enough to be here toward the end of this trail's volunteer-run maintenance cycle, and that the rest of the trail is overgrown as well. Might want to do a different hike.

The trail winds its way through primordial-looking jungle with ferns, birds and often the sound of running water to keep you company. Toward the end of the first half, there is a narrow finger of land jutting out into the canyon on your left; look for it. This is only for the intrepid The trail is plenty wide, but still choose your steps carefully, as the drop on either side is rather conclusive. At the end is a vista from a poet's dream. *This* is what you came for. On the far wall to your left a thunderous cascade of water pounds its way down. Next to it on the other side of a horseshoe-shaped canyon, a multi-step waterfall plunges into a deep pool. Expect it to take 1.5–2 hours of moderately strenuous hiking to get to this point.

After taking in the view, head back up the ridge to rejoin the main trail and then continue on it for a short distance until you encounter an easy-to-recognize spur road. Hikers used to have the option of continuing on the path to a second trail segment that eventually led to another scenic overlook, but that part of the trail is closed now, and for good reason: getting there requires traversing an unstable landslide area more than 200 feet wide and growing.

So instead of going that way, take the spur road to where it hits Kumuwela Road and then take a sharp right. Kumuwela will hit Mohihi, completing the loop and depositing you at your awaiting car. Now *there* is a hike to savor!

Canyon Trail to Waipo'o Falls
(4 miles round trip)

Another favorite, this one is also moderately strenuous and will probably take you 2–3 hours, depending on how long you linger. Along the way you will get unparalleled views of the canyon from the other side, visit two waterfalls and find a cold pool to swim in, if you like.

You park your car at the Pu'u Hinahina Lookout between mile markers 13 and 14, walk to the back of the parking lot, through a clearing and to the trail to your left. If there's no parking, you can park at the top of Hale Manu Valley Road between mile markers 14 and 15 on Waimea Canyon Drive and walk 0.8 miles down the road (with a 240-foot loss in elevation) to an-

other trailhead, unless you have a 4WD. (See map on page 142.)

About 0.5 miles into the trail from Pu'u Hinahina (which is steeper than the road option above) you have the option of going to the lookout off to your right. You might want to save that for the end, since other views will be better.

You'll end up at the top of these two falls when you do the Waipo'o Falls hike. These falls can shrivel to a trickle during dry times and when they divert water to feed farm fields in Kekaha.

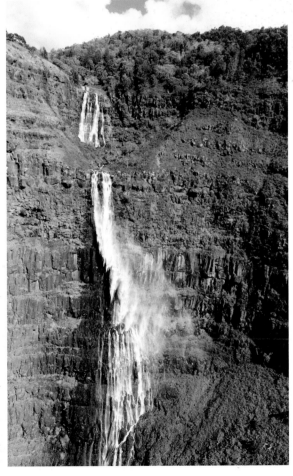

After you are exposed to the great canyon views, you will come to the top of a ridge. Keep an eye out for goats on the opposite walls. Look south for a provocative-looking rock arch, out where it's impossible for man to have created it. (You will see it closer from the larger waterfall ahead.) The light in this part of the canyon is usually best in the late afternoon.

Just past and below the ridge, you'll come to an intersection, with a small falls to your left and a bigger one to your right. The first one is tiny, but the pool is cool and refreshing. The bigger set of falls takes a two-step plunge down 800 feet. You come out at the top of the first step, so you won't get to look over the side at the largest drop. These falls sometimes have pretty low flow, especially in the summer or when they're diverting lots of the water for the fields below in Kekaha, so don't be disappointed. Just enjoy the delicious scenery, complete with wild ginger everywhere, before making your way back.

If you are feeling extra adventurous, it's possible to go beyond the stream and hike for about another mile to get even better canyon views.

Awa'awapuhi Trail
(6.5 miles round trip)

This is a fairly strenuous upside-down hike (down then back up) that will reward you *big time* at the end. It's fairly short getting there (1.5–2 hours), but coming back up can be a bit longer, making this a half-day hike.

The trailhead parking lot is just past mile marker 17 on Koke'e Road (550). The first mile or so usually has a few muddy spots, and hiking boots are recommended. It is consistently downhill with many sections having a staircase-like effect due to the many tree roots across the

trail. Mixed native and non-native forest greets you over the first 1.5 miles with ginger plants and guava trees. You don't start getting glimpses of the valleys the ridge sits between until about 2 miles in—even then clouds tend to obscure what surrounds you. (The lookout at the end is often cloud free even when the upper sections seem socked in.) Some stretches will have you walking through narrow corridors of ferns, while in other sections the trail is wide enough for three people to walk side by side. Keep an eye out for blackberry bushes, both for a possible snack and for their nasty thorns. Native plants such as koa trees and 'ohi'a lehua envelop the trail with shade the farther you go.

Just beyond mile marker 3 you'll notice a trail to the left called the **Nu'alolo Cliffs Trail**. A tiny section suffered a landslide in 2013, and the state closed this glorious trail for 4 long years until they could repair it. If you want to combine it with the Nu'alolo Trail as a loop, do go down Nu'alolo first and come back up Awa'awapuhi. It's way better that way.

Continuing past the closed trail, you're less than .25 miles away from your goal. Nothing can prepare you for what you are about to see. Just when you thought it couldn't get any better, the Awa'awapuhi Lookout steals your heart with cliffs so sheer and green they can't possibly be real. High altitude-flying, white-tailed tropic birds laugh and soar *beneath* you. Knife-edge ridges you didn't even know were there stand against the cliff. This is a side of God's handiwork that you never knew existed. Revel, savor, remember.

The view from past the guardrail is even better, but you're unprotected. If you fall, the first step is a fairly jarring 2,000 feet. To the right is the almost vertical Awa'awapuhi Valley. Check out the spires at the valley mouth. To the left is the glorious Nu'alolo Valley. And you are the lucky buggah who's there to soak it all in.

Rested? Good. It's time to pay the piper. You're at 2,600 feet, and the road is 3 plus miles away at 4,120 feet. Fortunately, it's fairly gentle most of the way and you brought a ton of water, right?

Nu'alolo Trail
(7.6 mile loop trip)

This trail takes you to the other side of Nu'alolo Valley (compared to the Awa-'awapuhi Trail). The downside is that the terrain is not as smooth as Awa'awapuhi, the upside is that it goes out closer to the shoreline, with a stupendous vista at the end. You're gonna surrender 1,600 feet of altitude over 3.8 miles going down and *somebody's* gotta pay for it on the return. *Coming from* the Koke'e Lodge and Museum 15 miles up from the shoreline Hwy, the trailhead is on your right. After a short climb you'll descend through a landscape that will change from bird-filled koa forest to patches of wild flowers to dryland forest to exposed ridge. All are a tribute to the rain's infatuation with increasingly higher altitudes. The trail will split in a few places but quickly rejoins. By the way, part of this trail is open to hunting during some parts of the year. It's highly unlikely that you'll encounter a hunter, but it's probably best to avoid practicing those new pig calls you just learned.

Less than 3 miles into the hike is the turnoff for a hunter trail. Bypass it and stay to the right. At 3.2 miles is the intersection of **Nu'alolo Cliffs Trail**. Continue another 0.3 miles to Lolo Vista Point. Swallow hard. You're on the upper edge of an Eden-like valley. The view will take your breath away—and then some. Nu'alolo Valley is unimaginably beautiful, and the Na Pali Coast looks endless beneath you. This is the bluff where Harrison Ford had his tree-choking tantrum in *Six Days/Seven Nights*. (Though *he* got here by helicopter.)

Some warnings: You should start this hike no later than 10 a.m. (earlier if possible). Hiking boots are a good idea. This is not a good trail if it's been raining a lot in Koke'e. Avoid when muddy, or bring your bobsled. Hiking *up* Nu'alolo when it's muddy is awful. As for water, bring at least twice as much as you think you'll need. After all, it's downhill at first, so lugging

Nu'alolo/Awa'awapuhi & Honopu Trails

Kokee Rd

550 — 3,660' — 15

16

4,120' 17

Kalalau Lookout — 4,000'

17

Kalalau Valley

Nu'alolo Trail (3.8)

Awa'awapuhi Trail (3.1)

Honopu Trail (2.1)

Seasonal Waterfall

Nu'alolo Cliffs Trail

2,980'

Honopu Valley — 3,000' 22°09.325 159°40.347

2,600' 22°09.207 159°40.824

Nu'alolo Valley

2,400'

Lolo Vista — 2,234' 22°09.020 159°41.803

Map continued on page 196

Kalalau Trail

"Fat Man's Misery" rock

Nu'alolo to the left of you, Awa'awapuhi to the right. This is a great time to be a hiker.

the water that far is relatively painless. Drink up before you start your ascent, and dump any water you don't want to carry.

Kuku'i Trail
(5 miles round trip)

While gazing into Waimea Canyon, you may wonder if there's a trail down into it. Yup. And lucky for you, it's down the road at a lower elevation near mile marker 9, so you *only* have to descend (and, of course, *ascend)* 2,300 steep, unrelenting feet. Ah, but what views you'll see on your way down as the canyon changes in appearance. It's 2.5 miles to the river below. (Not much distance to lose almost half a mile in elevation, so the grade is steep.) At the bottom is Wiliwili Camp (which has a restroom). Make *sure* you bring enough water for the trek back up. Too many people underestimate the climb, and they're fantasizing about water on the way up. The climb back up is pretty grueling, and you'll be sore for a few days.

If you don't want to go all the way down, there's a good viewpoint 0.3 miles into the trail and a *spectacular* viewpoint 1 mile into (and 750 feet below) the trailhead. Past this, the trail goes through forest, which is sometimes pretty mosquito-infested. The state is sometimes slow to keep up with the annoying buffalo grass that adorns parts of the trail.

Mohihi-Wai'alae Trail
(7 miles round trip)

First things first. If you don't have a 4WD vehicle, you probably won't be doing this trail unless it's *real* dry, you have *lots* of confidence it won't rain, and you're willing to beat your car like a rented mule. That's because it starts at the end of Mohihi-Camp 10 Road, 6 miles from Waimea Canyon Drive (Hwy 550). See map on page 143 and the description of the road in the Po'omau Canyon Ditch Trail hike.

If you are blessed with a 4WD vehicle, you'll be treated to one of our favorite trails on the island. Not for any sweeping views—you only get one or two of those.

This trail shines because it passes through one of the finest forests you'll ever see.

After parking at the end of Mohihi Road near picnic tables, you'll take the trail down a few minutes, across a footbridge, and walk toward and to the right of more picnic tables.

Down through a forest of sugi trees, you'll have to cross a stream that you can usually boulder-hop. A few dozen feet uphill after the stream there's an old metal sign with MOHIHI TRAIL and an arrow. The trail angles back uphill to the right.

From here it's not so confusing. The trail gains 250 feet, levels out, undulates and climbs a bit more until you come to a broken bench. From here there's a grand view of Koai'e Canyon, part of Waimea Canyon.

For another 1.5 miles the trail undulates then emerges onto a plateau with a rain gauge. Until now the trail has been fairly wide. From here it's narrower, with passages through ferns, and there are a few areas that require care since they're on the side of a hill. Zip-on pant legs are nice to keep the ferns from clawing at your legs.

If you're game, the next mile is well worth it. It will drop to a luxuriant fern forest, then keeps getting better and better. When you're about 2.5 miles from your car, the trail completely levels out. The forest has gotten more and more exotic looking. Gone are the introduced plants of Koke'e. This is an old growth, native forest that looks utterly primeval. It's as if someone had a bucket of life and splashed it all over the ground. Be careful not to walk on the mosses themselves.

The ground is soft and gentle, like walking on a thickly padded carpet, and the area feels ancient and undisturbed. The 87 inches of rain this area gets per year are absorbed by the forest floor. Walk slowly and observe how life bursts from every nook and cranny. Native birds, though not numerous, show little or no fear of humans. We've been lucky enough to be here on a sunny day, but

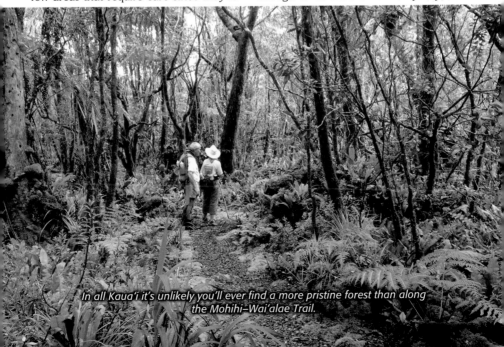

In all Kaua'i it's unlikely you'll ever find a more pristine forest than along the Mohihi–Wai'alae Trail.

even rain won't obscure the healthiest, happiest and most prosperous forest you may ever walk through.

Although the trail keeps going for many, many miles, 3–3.5 miles is a good turning-around point since it'll get swampy and harder farther on. (There are mile markers.) Though this last portion is *reasonably* marked, keep track of where you've been for your return. Try to start early—by 9 a.m., if possible, so you can take your time on this trail. Camping at Sugi Grove can be handy for this.

NORTH SHORE HIKES

Hanalei 'Okolehao Trail
(4 miles round trip)

So you've been especially gluttonous since you've been here, and the guilt is keeping you awake at night. Here's your chance to work off that lu'au you attended. This trail is a puffer. It gains 1,250 feet in less than 2 miles. That means the grade is steep, tiring and unrelenting. It will seem much longer than it is.

Most of the first 0.7 miles is on the dull remains of a steep old dirt road. By the time the road ends and the *real* trail starts (at a huge power pole whose lines swoop into the valley below), you'll probably hate the trail and hate us for mentioning it. Look to the left, and the trail continues through forest. It's prettier, as it quickly starts climbing the ridge, but just as strenuous. Climb, climb, climb, climb. Then climb some more. There are breaks in the vegetation affording grand views, but you couldn't care less because you're puffing so hard. After about 30 miles (really 1.8, but you'll swear we're lying) you are richly rewarded. A lovely plateau dotted with ti plants can offer impossibly sweeping views if it's not too overgrown. (Just before the trail ends at the plateau, a different spur trail to the right leads to a separate ridge. Nasty, scary, hard-core and death-defying make that a *must-miss* alternative.)

From the trail's end at the plateau you can see one-fifth of the entire island, weather cooperating, from Anahola all the

Ti plants grace the end of the 'Okolehao Trail. Turn around and you'll see more of the island from up here than perhaps any other trail on the island.

way around to the end of the road at Keʻe. Behind you, you'll see Waiʻaleʻale and the Hanalei River chiseling its way out of the mysterious center of the island, the Kilauea Lighthouse, Hanalei Bay...nowhere is there a more expansive view.

Was it worth it? Only you can say, but we think so. Is the hard part done? 'Fraid not. Coming down is also hard because the constant downhill is hard on the knees...and ʻokole if it's wet and you slip.

To get to the trailhead, drive past Princeville and turn left just after you cross the Hanalei Bridge at the bottom. (See map on page 51.) At 0.7 miles from Hwy 560 is a parking lot on your left. The trailhead's on the opposite side at a small footbridge. After 500 feet you'll encounter a chain gate with an old road rising steeply to your left. Climb till the end or until you run out of sweat.

Incidentally, the word ʻokolehao refers to liquor made from ti roots. In the old days, bootleggers planted ti up here to supply them with raw materials.

Hike Through Old Club Med
(1 mile round trip)
This is a short, sweet hike that affords beautiful views of Hanalei Bay and gives an alternative way to Puʻu Poa Beach. The land is privately owned, but the owner has been generous enough to allow walking access. The grounds are dotted with the foundations and skeletons of old cottages and bungalows, with the jungle slowly trying to reclaim the them, giving it an abandoned *Jurassic Park* feel. (Don't climb on these structures, or the owner might take away access.) The trail is a gently sloping old road and the grounds are maintained (mowed), making for a very leisurely hike. At the end of the trail, the road splits. If you go left, you can go around the old clubhouse to reach the point that gives the best views of the bay.

(The spot once was the site of the gazebo used in South Pacific as part of the Frenchmen's estate.) Go to the right and it leads downhill to the west end of Puʻu Poa Beach. To get here, drive to the end of Hanalei Plantation Road (the last right as you exit Princeville towards Hanalei). The road becomes unpaved for the last 300 yards. Once you reach the gate at the end, find a place to park along the side of the road. (Make sure to face the correct direction, or they'll ticket you.) Parking may be limited. The trail access is on the left side of the gate.

Pools of Mokolea
(1 mile round trip)
For those looking for a beautiful, wild shoreline hike but who don't want something too long and strenuous, this may be the ticket. It only travels 0.5 miles from you car but has some tasty rewards.

From Kahili (Rock Quarry) Beach, cross Kilauea Stream and head to the right. (The stream is usually shallow—don't cross if it's raging.) You'll see a road, but earlier portions are on private land—hence your need to start the hike the way we're describing it. You'll eventually either go up and down next to a wire fence, or around—either way ending on the lava bench. You'll soon see tide-pools. Fish and crabs scatter at your approach. Lots of ancient metal equipment and parts are scattered along the shore. For 100 years the sugar company dumped worn-out gear here. What was once junk has been transformed by a century of melting rust into an intriguing part of the landscape.

More tide-pools and more lava. It's slow going because you're mostly boulder-hopping on lava rocks, so take your time. Only 800 feet from the end of the road is a large, Jacuzzi-sized hole in the lava where the ocean surges in and out. It's great to watch, but beware of large

The Pools of Mokolea top off a short but sweet shoreline hike.

sets of waves that can surprise you. (This goes for much of the walk along here. Monster surf needs to be evaluated.)

Soon you reach Mokolea Point. What a spectacular place! Waves often pummel the area, creating rivulets of water flowing across the lava bench. During low surf a wonderful lava pool graces the area. Several small pools behind the large rock make nice soaking pools if the surf isn't too high. Moderate waves sometimes wash over the bench, replenishing the pools. Overhead, white-tailed tropic birds and shearwaters often soar on the thermals. Kilauea Lighthouse and Crater Hill are 1.3 miles across the water with Makapili Rock in front. During winter (October–April) the surf may overwhelm the area, and this hike should not even be considered. Low tide is best.

Just past the pools is the end of your hike. The ocean has cut a trench in the lava all the way to the cliff. When there's surf, the ocean comes roaring into the trench, which gets narrower and narrower, eventually undercutting the cliff in a small pocket. The result is a violent ricochet as the water and compressed air explode out of the trap that the lava has set for it. It's like a dragon breathing water instead of fire. Some waves even hiss as they are expelled. Sometimes rogue waves pound with such ferocity you think the ground will split beneath your feet. Some explosions of water may shower you, so be careful.

To get to the marginally defined trailhead, take Wailapa Road between mile markers 21 and 22 off Hwy 56 near Kilauea. Then take the smooth dirt road to Kilauea Bay. Park and find the best place to wade across the stream.

Historic Kilauea Stone Dam Hike
(5 miles round trip)

This is one of the better hikes for those with kids. Serious hikers might not be as impressed. Though this trail is often very muddy (it is the north shore, after all) it is one of the least strenuous hikes to be found—there's not much elevation gain, it is well maintained and has lots of shade. You can also do this with a mountain bike. The payoff is a lovely garden and historic stone dam with plenty of spots to sit and enjoy the scenery. The dam was built in the 1880s to supply water to Kilauea Sugar Plantation and still supplies water to the Wai Koa farming community. The swimming hole isn't that great, but local teens are often there enjoying the rope swing.

The trail is part of a larger loop trail called the **Wai Koa Loop Trail**. It passes through Wai Koa Plantation where a number of farmers utilize the idyllic conditions for a variety of crops including banana, avocado, breadfruit and mahogany. In fact, you'll spend awhile walking through some of the 200 acres of the largest mahogany plantation in the U.S. The entire loop trail is 5 miles in length, but the best half is the one to the stone dam, which is the latter half if you were to walk the whole loop. The section we recommend skipping is much more exposed (hot and sunny) and has you walking on a dirt road used as ac-

cess for the farms rather than an actual trail a lot of the time. You'll see more of the farms and have a chance to see some resident pigs, but all in all it is expendable.

You'll first need to sign a waiver either at Kaua'i Mini Golf or online at the Anaina Hou Community Park website. Drive to the back of the community park past the mini golf, and you'll find the signs for the trailhead. You start on a single path that undulates through a wooded area (the most elevation gain you see is around 40 feet). In less than half a mile you encounter the mahogany plantation. The long corridors of trees create unique perspective along the way. Just under a mile into the trail you'll come to where it intersects the loop. The signs will suggest you go right, but this is where you want to turn left to stay in the shade and reach the dam. Look for where the trail skirts the edges of the mahogany trees to avoid the often rutted and muddy road. Signs are posted along the way to keep you going in the right direction. Once you reach the trail down to

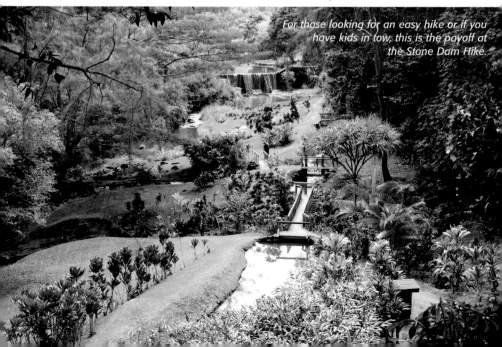

For those looking for an easy hike or if you have kids in tow, this is the payoff at the Stone Dam Hike.

the dam, before descending into the garden, take the time to view it from the covered picnic area visible up ahead. If you're here in the late afternoon, the light shines directly onto the dam, making for great photos. Small bridges over the irrigation ditches add to the ambiance here. Look for the path to the right that goes uphill to a bamboo thicket and Buddha statue—it is also a back way to the dam swimming hole. In all, the trail will probably take around two hours. You'll want to bring shoes that can get a little muddy, water and some snacks (the dam is a great spot for a picnic).

Kalalau Trail
(22 miles round trip)

The ultimate hike is also the most famous hike in all Hawai'i. Eleven miles of switchbacks, hills and beautiful scenery. This hike can be a real adventure. Because of this, we discuss it in detail in ADVENTURES on page 196.

EAST SHORE HIKES

Sleeping Giant (Nounou Mountain)
(2, 4 or 5 miles round trip)

This is a moderately difficult trail. Actually, it's three different trails. The vertical elevation you will gain from the East Trail is 1,000 feet. A thousand feet sounds like a big rise (OK, it *is* a big rise), but this is a hike worth experiencing. Nearly the entire hike is through forests with pretty views. This is a real trail, not an abandoned road like some hiking trails. Of the three trails, the East is the prettiest and the least steep, though it involves the most elevation gain. If you take the eastern route, at the third switchback after the 0.5 mile stake, the trail seems to split into two paths. *Do not take the left fork, which is on the side of the mountain!* This is probably a pig trail and not part of the main trail. You won't like it. In fact, other trails that deviate from the main

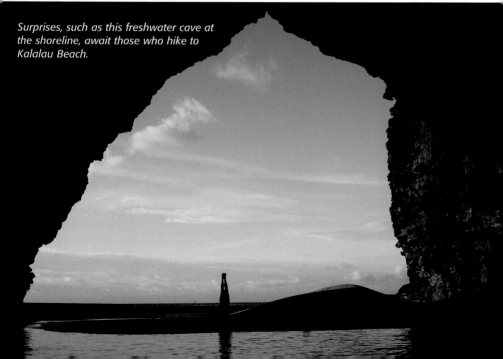

Surprises, such as this freshwater cave at the shoreline, await those who hike to Kalalau Beach.

trail are usually bad. Take the time to savor some of the luscious views of the entire east shore from spots. When you get to the main fork in the trail (diligently guarded by hala trees with their A-frame, cage-like roots), take the fork to the left for 3 or 4 minutes to the picnic table. From here you can see the entire Wailua Valley from Anahola to Lihu'e. The view is not to be missed and well worth the climbing effort expended. Anyone who becomes dizzy from heights should be aware that there are areas along the east side trail where the beautiful sweeping view off to one side is quite steep.

Up at the picnic table, there is a short trail dipping south across the giant's neck up to his forehead and nose. Or is it his chin? Hard to say. The view from up there is, literally, a once-in-a-lifetime experience. The vista is without rival. Think *real hard* before you take this part. It is steep, and the spine is almost vertical on both sides. A wrong step, or a slip anywhere near the nose, would almost certainly cost you your life. Just before the summit there is a short trail to your left

The Sleeping Giant's chin offers an incredible panoranic east shore view, for those with the nerve to go past the end of the official trail.

leading to the hole in the giant's chin, seen from the bottom of Kuamo'o Road. This part of the Nounou Trail is what they call a real 'okole squeezer. Stop at the picnic table unless you are very brave, very foolish and very well insured.

If you take the West Trail or the Kuamo'o-Nounou Trail, you'll find the climbing steeper. It's a good workout; we like to climb it every other day if we've enjoyed a few too many restaurant reviews lately. Kuamo'o-Nounou Trail and West Trail combine at a magnificent strand of Cook Island pines (a very tall and straight pine tree thought, during the Age of Discovery, to make good ships' masts).

Of the three trails to the top, we recommend either the East Trail or the Kuamo'o-Nounou Trail. (The latter has a stretch where mosquitoes might mug you. Use a repellent.) The map on page 60 makes it easy to find the three trailheads.

This jungle hike is fairly easy and rewards you with a nice place for a picnic.

Kuilau Ridge Trail
(3.5 miles round trip or 4.3 miles one way)

This trail begins 1.75 miles past the Kaua'i Research and Extension Center. The trailhead marker is on the right side as you are driving west on Kuamo'o Road, and there are a few parking stalls. Otherwise, park at the nearby Keahua Arboretum.

This is a very nice hike. The first part is a gentle but constant incline that takes you past a myriad of birds. Watch and listen for them. At the end of the incline (about 30 minutes), you will come to a small picnic area overlooking a lovely valley. If it's clear, you will get a stunning view of Mount Wai'ale'ale. This is a nice place to have lunch or just enjoy a long sip of water. *Make sure you go past the picnic tables.* The payoff is 5 minutes later. You will be rewarded with a wonderful razorback, winding, rolling, trek into paradise. *Gorgeous!* There are lush hillsides filled with ferns of every size and shape. Off in the distance you can see the ocean at Kapa'a and all the way to Lihu'e at another point. Very nice. Turn around where

the Kuilau Trail ends and the Moalepe Trail begins (see map on page 60) at a quaint wooden bridge. (Or continue onto Moalepe Trail, if you like, though Moalepe isn't in as good condition due to horses stomping the snot out of the trail base.) The entire hike should take you 2.5 to 3 hours if you hike at a semi-steady pace. Bring water. Hiking boots recommended, but tennis shoes OK. You can wash the mud off at the stream at the arboretum.

Jungle Hike
(1 mile round trip *plus* however much road you need to walk)

If you want a *taste* of the steamy jungle and forest (but without the need for a machete and a gallon of insect repellent), this might be what you're looking for. It leads to a government stream gauging station and passes through some magnificent scenery. Your reward at the end is a small, picturesque stair-step little falls where two streams come together adjacent to a water diversion ditch. (The word ditch has ugly connotations, but often these small dams can make a nice place for a picnic.)

To get there, take Kuamo'o Road (580) all the way until it becomes dirt. (A sign at the Keahua Arboretum says 4WD ONLY, but the road *may* not be bad. It depends on where they are in the maintenance cycle.) The pavement stops, but you won't. You'll cross over a bridge and *through* a stream and stay on the dirt road for over 2.5 miles. When you come to a Y, take the left fork and reset your odometer. Then at almost 1 mile is another Y, then a gate; take the left fork. (If the gate's locked, you have to walk an extra 0.3 miles.) At 1.3 miles is the second gate. The map on page 208 shows all of this. (This part of the road fluctuates between pretty good and utterly wretched.) If it's locked, park here and walk down the dirt road. The gate is on state land and was erected to prevent vehicles from going any farther, but it's perfectly legal to go through the gate and continue on foot. Near this gate is where they filmed the ENTRANCE GATE scenes in *Jurassic Park.* It probably won't stop a T-Rex, but it'll keep your car out. The views into Waiʻaleʻale Crater from this dirt road can be exceptional, especially in the morning.

After walking 10–15 minutes (0.5 miles) from the second gate, you'll come upon an ascent. There will be an old turnout on the left side. Listen for gurgling water here. The trail leading off to the left from this turnout immediately parallels for a short time a water ditch and passes through extremely lush territory. The ferns, birds and trees are abundant along this easy-to-follow but often slippery trail. A pleasant 10- to 20-minute trek up and over a 150-foot high ridge will bring you to a nice, freshwater pool, formed by the small dam. The area around the dam is covered with plant life and can be slippery. A wonderful, secluded spot to eat lunch.

If you don't want to walk *over* the hill to get to the falls, you can walk *through* it. Where the ditch becomes a tunnel (at a circular cement opening), you can access the tunnel that goes under the mountain. Most people will have to duck the entire 800-foot length and, of course, if the water flow rate should change while you're in there, you'd have a big problem to deal with. Hmm, maybe that over-the-hill trail isn't so bad after all. Anyway, it's an adventurous option that we've done (when the flow wasn't too high and we had a flashlight), and it's a hoot. Inner tubes and boogie boards are also fun in the tunnel.

The falls are actually formed by two streams. If you swim across the pool and climb the rocks, then take the right fork for only a few (slippery) minutes, you'll come to a small, hidden falls. At the base is something we call the **Jacuzzi**. During low to moderate stream flow the falling water creates bubbles and jets of air that feels remarkably similar to a spa (albeit a cold one). It's *wonderful* to soak in. Just stay out if the flow is too heavy, and read page 33 for precautions on swimming in streams. Use your own good judgment.

Hoʻopiʻi Falls Hike
(1 mile round trip)

Waterfalls have an amazing ability to bring peace of mind. Although Kauaʻi is studded with many waterfalls, most of them are inaccessible for one reason or

See map on page 61 to get here.

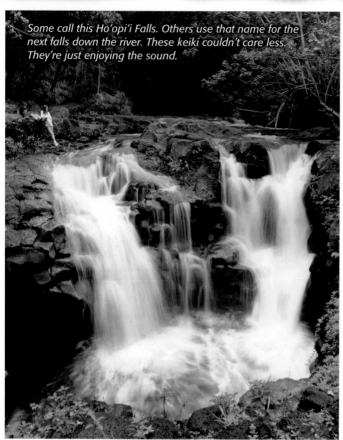

Some call this Ho'opi'i Falls. Others use that name for the next falls down the river. These keiki couldn't care less. They're just enjoying the sound.

another—but not this one. There are two falls on the Kapa'a Stream—and one of them is named Ho'opi'i. Some locals call the first one Ho'opi'i—government maps give that name to the second falls.

Look at the map on page 157. There are additional trails in this area, but the one shown is on state land. The top of the map on page 61 shows you where Kapahi Road is. An old *public* dirt road (now just a trail) is on your left as you come down Kapahi Road. Please be respectful of the neighborhood here. Residents don't want you driving faster than 15 MPH on Kapahi Road.

Walk down the trail, and when it comes to an intersection, go right. Head down-stream and eventually there's a side path leading down to the first falls. Wow, what a place! A flat lava bench offers a magnificent place to sit and breathe in the falls. The only way to get under those falls is either to go downstream and wade back upstream or jump into the pool as some of the daring locals do. (At your own risk; check out the water first to make sure there's nothing dangerous submerged.) This is a great spot to cool off on hot days.

The second falls downstream are no longer accessible due to the current leaser of the land closing the trails. Issues around illegal camping in the area had soured their mood, and now this area is off limits because of the actions of a few. This brings up a good example of why it is important for everyone—visitors and locals alike—to treat these places with respect. We hope that things will change in the near future with access to the the second falls, but in the meantime, it's off limits.

If you don't bring mosquito repellent, bring an extra pint of blood for the walk through the woods. Tennis shoes are OK. Bring water.

Hiking to the Top of Wai'ale'ale

A question we're often asked is *How can I hike to the summit of Wai'ale'ale?* Until fairly recently, you couldn't. In ancient times Hawaiians used to hike up a ridge on the northeast side of the crater (the ridge that's over the Tunnel Hike on page 208). Near the summit they had rope ladders for the final portion. A landslide and lack of use in the 1800s shut off that route. In the 1970s a person tried, with a helicopter overhead to give radio guidance, and he failed. In 2006 another person tried and had to be rescued by helicopter. But the construction of a pig fence across the Alaka'i Swamp has created an opportunity. It's a *beast,* however, and listed under Adventures.

SOUTH SHORE HIKES

Po'ipu Shoreline Sandstone Hikes
(4 miles round trip)

The lithified cliffs of **Makawehi** next to Shipwreck Beach, as well as the **Maha'ulepu** area, offer excellent shoreline hiking. The Makawehi cliffs are easily accessed by taking the trail from the parking lot between the Hyatt and the Po'ipu Bay Resort golf course (or simply walking to the east end of the beach). It's over half a mile long, formed from cemented sand dunes deposited here during the last ice age. The wind and salt have clawed and thrashed at these cliffs with impressive results. Part of the trail was destroyed by a landslide in 2006, so you'll get rerouted onto the golf course. Take your time, wander about and take a look at the remains of an old heiau. Look for (but don't remove) fossils in the sandstone, and enjoy the views.

Maha'ulepu is described in detail in Beaches on page 114. Another good hike is to start from the end of Gillin's Beach (see map on page 77). It's beyond the stream and past the last pocket of sand. It's wonderful to walk along here when the surf is raging. At one place there's a hole in the floor of the cliff, allowing you to see

the ocean exploding beneath your feet on the lithified bench below. This area looks like an alien landscape. Weekends bring fishermen who tend to leave reminders of their hobby here.

You could walk all the way to the Hyatt, if you wanted. The wind, pounding surf and beautiful cliffs create an amazingly relaxing walk, even if the ground is a bit lumpy. About two-thirds of the way to the Hyatt, the cliff gives way to a sandy pocket affording a luscious view of the cliffs.

HORSEBACK RIDING

If you want to let someone else do the walking while you tour the island, try horseback riding.

Silver Falls Ranch (828-6718) inland (mauka) of Kilauea is hands-down our favorite. Their 300-acre ranch looks more like a palm arboretum, and the guides seem thrilled to see you and show you around their little piece of paradise. The horses are well-groomed and the trails well-kept. This is how rides should be done if you're looking to be pampered in a stunning location (although it's nose-to-tail). $104 for the 1.5-hour ride. For $124 it includes another half-hour and a trip to their small waterfall and large pool. Swim and lunch there. The only downside is that their location is rainier than some of the others, so you take your chances with the weather. Their weight limit is fairly high at 300 pounds but also based on your height. The minimum age is 7, but special accommodations can be made for those as young as 5. The menagerie of animals at their barn is also a plus for the little ones and animal lovers. Experienced riders may be champing at the bit (wow, I finally got to use that horse phrase in the proper context!) for some more spark.

CJM Country Stables (742-6096) in Po'ipu has two rides available. The afternoon picnic ride is 2 hours of riding, 1 hour for lunch. The ride is mostly along or near the coast to a "secret" beach (it's Ha'ula). $150 per person. Then there's a 9:30 a.m. and 2 p.m. Scenic Beach & Valley Ride—2 hours of riding on mountains and along the coast. If you're thirsty on the trail, your only choice is passion/orange/guava juice. (If you want water, bring your own or buy it at the office.) $110 per person. 230-pound weight limit. Minimum age of 8 and no riding with adults. (You're on your own, kid.) The amount of narration depends on your guide, but the nose-to-tail orientation for up to 24 people (in four groups) means only those near the guide will hear it. The leader may spend the entire trip on his cell phone, which has happened to us *repeatedly*. (They wrote to us saying, "our guide was discussing safety"—yeah, whatever. They have no way of knowing when we *anonymously* review them.) The fact that they are the only outfit offering rides along a beautiful beach with fantastic scenery offsets most of the shortcomings the company may have. They take lots of riders and feel a bit like a rider processing machine, but the rigid structure might make beginners feel pretty comfortable.

At check-in you may get a lesson in… paniolo wisdom, which some may find endearing while others will be put off. One caveat: They say no experience is necessary, but we have been on tours with horses that aren't as docile as those used by other companies. We were glad to have enough experience on horseback to keep in line with the tour.

Esprit de Corps Riding Academy (822-4688) in Kapa'a is mostly for lessons, experienced riders and those wanting a private event. Call for prices and offerings.

Princeville Ranch Stables (826-7669) is a working cattle ranch without the nose-to-tail aspect. You're encouraged to spread out. The terrain is mostly flat, and there's no running. Though most companies have weight restrictions, they have a *height-to-weight ratio* restrictions, so go onto their website if you're in doubt. The three tours all offer something a little different with a minimum age of 8 (or 10 for a ride that includes a zip tour).

The Paniolo Ride is a 2-hour tour through the working ranch and its cattle herd for $119. The 3-hour Ride and Glide tour interrupts your horseback tour with a few zipline rides for $149. They also have a 3.5-hour ride to a "secret" waterfall. $149 per person; includes 1 hour for swimming and lunch. Bring your camera and something to swim in. Overall, nice scenery on this ranch. Past mile marker 27 on Hwy 56.

JET SKIING

Jet ski rentals are outlawed on Kaua'i. So if this is what you came here to do, you *sure* picked the wrong island.

A kayak can be a marvelous way to see Kaua'i. The quiet, peaceful nature of kayak travel appeals to many. There are four rivers on Kaua'i you can kayak and, of course, there is the open ocean.

River Kayak Trips

We've kayaked all the rivers in several kinds of craft. We prefer the rigid two-person, self-bailing kayaks for beginners, single person self-bailers for those who have kayaked before. Some use canoes, but we're not as fond of them since they can fill with water if tipped. (Inflatables are terrible since they are easily deflected by wind—called weathercocking, in case you're taking notes.)

Of the four rivers, the **Wailua** is by far the most popular. (See map on page 61.) It's very scenic, and there's a waterfall called **Secret Falls** on the north fork you can hike to if you like. (Some brochures call it the most spectacular waterfall on the island. That's bunk, but it's a nice one just the same.) There's a more dubious trail just before the falls that goes to the top and exposes you to the more beautiful upper falls, but the trail is pretty sketchy and not recommended. It's 5 miles round trip and takes most people about 3 hours to paddle plus stopping or hiking time. Since large boats take passengers to the Fern Grotto, kayakers should always stay on the north side of the river. If you want to visit the Fern Grotto, consider pulling ashore *after* the docks at the so-called kayak landing area. To be honest, the grotto is not the same

as it used to be and is barely worth the effort to get there. The best part about kayaking this river is the scenery and hiking to the waterfall. Just enjoy the Wailua for its lushness, and watch out for the large boat tours.

Past the Fern Grotto, is a cliff-jumping area at a well-known swimming hole. (The state had an ongoing war with pesky rope swing builders there. State workers, with marching orders from their lawyers, relentlessly cut 'em down almost as fast as people put up new ones. Finally the state simply cut down the trees.) People line up to jump off the cliff into the water there, despite a state sign warning them not to. If you do, too, make *sure* there's nothing under the water first. The African village scene from *Outbreak* was filmed on a secluded plain here on your right; look for it. The

When kayaking the Wailua River, the furthest reaches are the most serene.

wind will probably be in your face coming back, so hug the north bank tightly to minimize the wind. The earlier you leave, the less wind coming back, and you'll avoid crowds on the river and at the waterfall. (We start at 7 a.m. and strongly suggest you do, even if you gotta rent the kayak the afternoon before.) To kayak this river *on your own*, which we prefer, there are special logistical considerations—see RENTING A KAYAK FOR THE RIVER below. No kayak renting on Sundays except Kamokila Hawaiian Village, which makes for a super-short kayak trip.

The **Hanalei River** is the longest and goes mostly through plains. (Beautiful plains, but plains.) It takes about 3 hours (6.75 miles) round trip for most people to kayak this peaceful river. After a heavy rain, waterfalls etched in the distant valley walls can enhance the trip. The wind usually helps you a little coming back.

The **Huleʻia Stream** in Lihuʻe is 5 miles round trip (2 hours or more). It starts from Nawiliwili Harbor, and the water flow is not great, so expect ickier water here. There are majestic mountains on your left as you go out, and you will pass the easy-to-miss Menehune Fishpond and an area where they filmed the swing-on-a-vine-to-the-waiting-airplane scene from *Raiders of the Lost Ark*. (Keep an eye out for the opening to the fishpond.) Lots of jumping fish in the shallow parts of the pond. The last navigable part is our favorite part of this river. This river goes through a wildlife refuge, but you'll see and hear more birds on the Hanalei River. The wind will probably be in your face coming back. If you're doing this on your own, you'll run into large guided groups at times.

The **Kalihiwai** is short but *very* sweet. You can kayak it in an hour (taking your time) if you decide not to do the additional 10-minute hike (more like a grope up the river, then through the jungle on the right side) to Kalihiwai Falls. Put in at Kalihiwai Beach. You might not see the waterfall from where you stop kayaking. The scenery is the best of the four, and you might want to do it if you have any juice left after a Hanalei River trip. Expect to be hassled if you visit the beautifully manicured falls in any way that doesn't bring money to the horseback company that leases the land where the falls occupy.

Renting a Kayak for the River

You can rent a kayak and paddle any river you like, *except* the Wailua River. The state has rules making it harder to rent a kayak *on your own* to kayak the Wailua (which is the best one). They want you to go on a *guided* tour. (It's not a safety issue; it's a political one—long story.) So although we recommend doing river trips *on your own*, this may be harder to do on the Wailua. Companies that have permits can only rent six kayaks per day, and they might *pull* those from the rental pool if they can make more money putting a guided passenger in it. Of the companies mentioned below, **Kayak Kauaʻi**, **Wailua Kayak Adventures** and **Wailua Kayak & Canoe** have them for rent for the Wailua River. (The last one is the most expensive, but they're right on the river and open at 7 a.m.) Call a week in advance to maximize your chances of getting one. An alternative is **Kamokila Hawaiian Village** (823-0559), which rents kayaks for $35 from a location so far up the Wailua River, that your paddle to Secret Falls is probably less than 10 minutes. They also rent them on Sunday. (Nobody else is allowed.)

All the other rivers on the island you can kayak on your own without a guide.

Prices change a lot in this competitive business, and prices for rentals on the Wailua cost more. For single-person kayaks (which are getting harder to find) consider **Pedal 'n Paddle** in Hanalei or **Wailua Kayak Adventures**—rent for $20–$50 per day. Two-person kayaks are $40–$95 per day. Sometimes they are cheaper if you are willing to arm wrestle timeshare salesmen. Most cars will hold two or three kayaks on the roof, and staff will help you strap them on.

Guided River Trips

For guided tours of the Wailua River, see a list of companies below. Most companies charge around $85 *per double kayak.*

Although the Wailua is our favorite *unguided* kayak trip, the best *guided* river trips are up the Hule‘ia River in Lihu‘e. **Outfitters Kaua‘i** (742-9667) has a 7-hour Hule‘ia River kayak/hike/zip trip called the Kipu Zipline Safari. About 2 miles of kayaking, then a half mile of hiking to a small falls with a rope swing. Then you're on a tractor-pulled wagon to two ziplines (the second one is 0.25-miles long) and lunch. Finally, you finish it off at a place they call "blue pool," which has a water zipline. Then back to an outrigger canoe that brings you to your car. The hiking and paddling are not overly tough, though you'll get wet and muddy, and some of the trail involves boulder-hopping. The guides do a good job, they're great with kids (who *love* the part where they feed some pigs and peacocks), and they don't rush you during the trip. However, they may have some accuracy issues in their narrations, and you need to know about the water you're swimming in. See page 187 for more on that. It's not cheap at $189 per person ($149 for kids), 20 people max, and you'll be tired and happy at the end. The only downsides are mediocre food,

and the wait for the second zipline can be over half an hour. Bring shoes that can get wet.

If a kayak and zip combo aren't adventurous enough, how about a paddle followed *by a rappel* down a 30-foot waterfall? That's what **Island Adventures** (246-6333) does. This is one cool experience. The paddle is similar to Outfitters. Then you hike 10 minutes or so to a van, a short ride, followed by instructions on how to rappel. You don't have to have experience—they know what they're doing. And with their safety gear and a fireman's belay at the bottom, you don't have to worry about falling. The guides are great, and the opportunity to rappel a waterfall after a kayak trip (and visit and play around a 60-foot falls) makes this a pretty exotic experience. 5.5 hours, felt-bottomed shoes (so you don't slip) and lunch included for $180 total ($158 kids 6–11). Tours on Tuesdays and Fridays.

Kayak Hanalei (826-1881) offers guided trips that start in the Hanalei River and go out into Hanalei Bay, eventually landing on a beach for some snorkeling. The 4.5-hour tour starts at 8:30 a.m. is $109 for adults and $99 for kids (5–12). Deli lunch included.

Ocean Kayak Trips

Ocean kayaking can be an experience of a lifetime. The crown jewel is a summer Na Pali Coast trip. *National Geographic* named it the second best adventure in the United States. (Rafting the Colorado was number 1, and dog sledding in Alaska was number 3.) Na Pali can be an *incredible* trip for those who can do it, either guided or unguided. We try to do it every summer and camp along the way. Because paddling Na Pali is so involved, we have a complete description in Adventures on page 192.

In addition to Na Pali, **Outfitters Kaua'i** (742-9667) has a Kukui'ula Harbor to Port Allen trips in the winter for $159. There's usually a tailwind on this 8-mile, 4–5 hour paddle. Certainly not the most interesting shoreline on the island, but the Lawa'i Bay stop is nice. During peak whale season (late December–February) you stand a good chance of seeing humpbacks.

If you want to do this by yourself, you can stop at remote Palama Beach on the way down and, once at Port Allen, call a cab to take you back to your car at Kukui'ula.

What if I want to rent a kayak and paddle the ocean on my own? Well, unlike all the other Hawaiian islands, Kaua'i is a very difficult place to rent a kayak *for the ocean.* Whether it's because companies want to make more money guiding you or because Kaua'i's ocean waters are not as calm (probably a little of both), most will turn you down cold if you tell them you're taking a kayak into the ocean. Of course, if it's the sit-on-top variety (which most here are) as opposed to canoe-types, that's what we use on the river or ocean anyway. If you have some experience and good judgment, there's no one to stop you from taking it to the ocean.

Kayak Companies

The companies described below provide a variety of services.

Kayak Kaua'i (826-9844) in Wailua from April through September has one-day guided Na Pali tours for $216 per person. Lunch included at either Miloli'i or

On the Wailua River, first you kayak, then you hike...then you frolic!

Nuʻalolo Kai. For the Wailua River they have doubles to rent for $64. Guided Wailua trips with lunch for $95 *per person*. The more involved the trip, the better it is to call them in advance, *especially* for Na Pali.

Outfitters Kauaʻi (742-9667) in Poʻipu has summer Na Pali trips for $249. Guided Wailua River kayak tours with lunch are available for $109 *per person*, as well as the awesome trip described under GUIDED RIVER TRIPS. Outfitters is a big company with lots of offerings beyond kayaking. They do things well, for the most part. Our biggest complaint is that their guides seem pretty fast and loose with their "facts" lately, and narrations have lots of factual errors.

Kayak Hanalei (826-1881) rents kayaks right on the Hanalei River from their private dock. You don't need reservations, but they start renting them out at 8 a.m., so get there early. $35 per day for a single kayak, $60 for a double and $75 for a triple.

Pedal ʻn Paddle (826-9069) in Hanalei specializes in one-stop shopping. They rent kayaks for the Hanalei, camping supplies, beach cruiser bikes and snorkel gear.

Wailua Kayak & Canoe (821-1188) operates near the Wailua River, and you'll probably be able to walk your kayak down to the boat launch on a kayak dolly. Their gear (seats and such) are not as good as others, and customer service is scant. Doubles rent for a pricey $90 (it's $50 for a single), and you can only keep it 5 hours. Guided Wailua trip is $90 per person and includes deli-style lunch.

Wailua Kayak Adventures (822-5795) has river kayaks for rent—$35 for single kayaks, $70 for doubles. Guided Wailua trips are $60 per person, snacks only. (Ask if they'll offer cash discount.)

Kamokila Hawaiian Village (823-0559) is located far up the river, less than 10 minutes from the Fern Grotto and the trail to Secret Falls. Good for families with kids or anyone who wants a short paddle. They rent kayaks, canoes and stand up paddleboards for $35, which also includes admission to the village.

Kayak Wailua (822-3388) is a no-frills family operation. They don't offer you lunch (they suggest you eat before and after), and you'll pay an extra $5 for a seatback upgrade. Their price for guided trips, $60, includes tax and marina fee. That's still pretty cheap.

Aliʻi Kayaks (241-7700) is a local outfit that does tours of the Wailua for $55 per person. They meet at Wailua Visitor Center at Hwy 580 (Kuamoo Road) and Hwy 56.

In addition to standard bus tours, there are other land tours that may be worth considering.

Aloha Kauaʻi Tours (245-6400) provides tours of areas not easily accessed by most visitors. In their large, 4WD vans you'll explore either the Kilohana area (which is private and gated) or the mountains behind Wailua town (which are open to the public but require 4WD). Prices are $77. The Rain Forest Tour includes a 3-mile hike—weekdays only.

Roberts Hawaiʻi (245-9558) offers a **movie tour** in their smaller shuttles that will take you to several popular filming locations while showing you clips en route. Recommended for movie buffs but probably not a good choice for those with young children. Includes pickup, dropoff and lunch. Keep in mind that you won't be visiting any *exclusive* locations—you're only stopping at spots that anyone can get to, but you have a guide to give you the stories behind the movies that were filmed there. $122 for adults, $64 for kids age 4–11.

If you're interested in chocolate, there are two farms offering tours: **Lydgate Farms** (821-1857) and **Garden Island Chocolate** (634-6812). The tours are similar—each is 3-hours and includes extensive chocolate-tasting sessions. You'll also get to sample other fresh, tropical fruits found on the farms as well as learn about a football-shaped fruit pod becomes the magical delight we call chocolate. Lydgate Farms has tours daily, except weekends. Garden Island offer tours on Mondays, Wednesdays and Fridays. Lydgates's tour is $95 (kids 12 and under free), and Garden Island's is $75 ($29 for kids 4–12). Kids will enjoy the samples, but those younger than 7 may get antsy during the educational parts. Overall, we find Lydgate Farms the better of the two for their professional approach. (Garden Island Chocolate can get a little preachy.)

Lawa'i International Center (639-4300) is the site of 88 Buddhist shrines from the early 20th century. This site has been the home of a Hawaiian heiau, a Taoist temple, a Shinto shrine and a Shingon Buddhist temple. Free 2-hour tours on the second and last Sunday of every month at 10 a.m., noon and 2 p.m. (Though you can call to make separate arrangements.) The shrines are on the side of a hillside, and the winding path is easy. They have a new, hand-carved temple that they are very proud of, and overall, it's a relaxing way to spend a couple of hours. History and culture buffs will get the most out of this. Off Hwy 50 near Lawai Rd. on Wawae Rd.

Garden tours are numerous here on the Garden Island. You can either do them on your own (and set your own pace but

learn less) or have a guide, many of whom stretch things longer than necessary.

The big daddy is the **National Tropical Botanical Garden** (742-2623) in Lawa'i. Rich and lush with remarkably varied plants and abundant birds, tours here are guided and last about three hours. The fee for the tour is $30 per person (self-guided) for McBryde, $50 for the guided, more exotic and photogenic Allerton. We've seen some shaky facts from some of the guides, but most are good. Reservations are required. Kids 6–12 years old are $15 at McBryde and $25 at Allerton; 5 and under are free for both tours. They won't take you as far as the beach or the old Allerton home. For that you have to take the sunset tour, but that one is $95 and will cost you some of the time in the garden. Personally, we'd skip the sunset in favor of the regular tour. The self-guided McBryde garden is more of a park atmosphere, and you've got room to roam for around 1.5 hours. A pretty nice garden. Don't be late for your tour; they will *not* be accommodating.

In Ha'ena on the north shore, **Limahuli Garden** (826-1053) has good guides and is the most educational regarding native plant life, but those looking for a multitude of colorful tropical plants might be disappointed. $40 for the 2.5-hour (no bathroom break) guided tour, which is better than the $20 self-guided tour. Tuesdays through Saturdays only.

Na 'Aina Kai Botanical Gardens (828-0525) near Kilauea is described on page 50. The garden is beautiful and the setting dreamy. Guided tours only, and their pace is exceptionally slow. Lots of sculptures and very manicured. $35 for the formal garden walking tour. If you prefer riding, it's $50. (Don't do the walk/ride combo.) The family tour is the same price as the formal tour but is definitely recommended if you have little ones. You'll get to spend an hour at one of the best playgrounds in the state. Call for reservations.

Princeville Botanical Gardens (634-5505) near Princeville is small (8 acres) but packed with exotic tropical plants and fruits (which they are generous in letting you eat), including their own chocolate. They spend 3 hours covering the acreage (kids under 6 will probably stage a mutiny—not the best tour for them), and it's a bit overpriced at $69, but you can feel the family pride (and they have some of the best fruit we've ever tasted).

When Hollywood needs a beautiful, remote coastline studded with majestic cliffs and glorious valleys to film movies, they often choose Kaua'i's Na Pali Coast. *Pirates of the Caribbean 4, Six Days/Seven Nights, King Kong* and others have all used a Na Pali backdrop to convey an idyllic paradise. From the sea, this area of the island takes on a magical quality. Many people dream of seeing the Hawaiian Islands by sea. The Na Pali region is surely the most popular area to cruise, but there are others as well. This can be a fantasy trip. Rough seas are rarely part of the fantasy, but they can be part of reality, depending on conditions.

Seeing Na Pali by boat is an incredible thrill that we highly recommend. Soaking up this coastline and being on a boat are exquisitely relaxing. You can see it by leaving from the west side or the north shore. They are two very different experiences.

If you leave from the **west side**, you'll only see half of Na Pali (and not the best half), and three-quarters of the trip isn't even along Na Pali. The boats that leave from Port Allen travel 23 miles along the relatively uninteresting (by sea) Mana Plain, then head up the dry side of Na Pali before turning around at Kalalau. (Boats that leave from Kikiaola Harbor shave 9 miles off the duller part—see map on page 86.) If boats would cruise past Kalalau to Hanakapi'ai, we'd be much happier, because that short stretch has some beautiful sights. But most turn back at Kalalau. On the pro side, the seas tend to be calmer from the west side, especially on the return trip. Also, spinner dolphins are prevalent along the coast here—you're almost guaranteed to spot them.

A few companies, however, have permits to leave the **north shore**. Those boats that leave from Hanalei or 'Anini on the north shore have a *far* better and more exciting route, though the return trip is usually into head seas (meaning into the swells) and headwinds, so it can be bumpy.

Some west shore companies switch to south shore tours in October and return to Na Pali in April; others can do Na Pali year-round. Some combine it with a trip to Ni'ihau. If you do Na Pali in winter, expect bigger seas.

There are two main snorkeling spots: Nu'alolo (which is pretty good) and a spot near Polihale that the bigger boats often use called Makole (which is pretty bad). If you're at Makole, the best snorkeling is away from shore, not toward it. If you want to *land* at Nu'alolo and walk around and see some archeological remains, only **Captain Andy's**, **Kaua'i Sea Tours**, and **Na Pali Explorer** have the permits to come ashore.

Some of these boating companies give you discounts for booking online.

What & Who

We've spent a lot of time anonymously reviewing these boats, and here's the deal.

If it's May through September and you really want to see Na Pali, you want to do this from the north shore—*period*. That means you want **Na Pali Catamaran, Captain Sundown, Na Pali Coast Hanalei, HoloHolo** or **Na Pali Sea Breeze**, or if you want no frills, **North Shore Charters**. As mentioned before, *nothing* a west side company can do can compete with the route these guys take. They could probably *flog* you on this trip, and they'd still be better than any boat leaving from Port Allen. If you can't book these or it's not these summer months (April and October are borderline), we recommend **HoloHolo** and **Liko Kaua'i**.

North Shore

Our favorite is probably **Na Pali Catamaran** (826-6853). Their 35-foot power cat (no sailing) takes up to 18 people, has a slender enough profile to go into most of the sea caves, and plenty of shade. (That overhead protection comes in handy when the captain pilots the boat under a waterfall, but if you're feeling adventurous, they will let you sit on the bow.) $233 for a 4-hour tour, which includes snorkeling at Nu'alolo. The crew seems to genuinely care about making sure guests have a good time. They encourage passengers to get up and move around the boat to take pictures, and offer drinks (soda and juice) throughout the trip. If conditions are good, they often let you stay in the water for more than an hour, even though you are only guaranteed 45 minutes of snorkeling.

Another good north shore catamaran, **Captain Sundown** (826-5585),

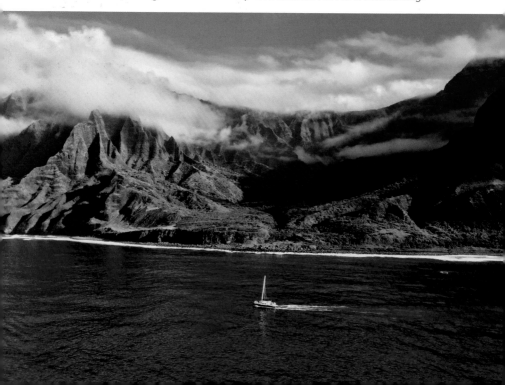

These passengers know what Hollywood knows... Na Pali is mesmerizing.

uses a 40-foot sailing catamaran. They'll usually sail part of the way down the coast far from shore, then motor back a bit closer. They tend to keep narration pretty light, and when they do talk, it's more personal stories than legends (some might seem like both). The boat feels roomy and comfortable even when they have the maximum of 17 passengers (they'll usually keep it to 15, which is even better). They feed you pretty well here, too—fruit at breakfast, deli sandwich at lunch, chips throughout for grazing. Consider riding the net (trampoline) on the way out. (The way back is much wetter and bumpier.) They like to troll for fish along the way (up to four lines) and will let you reel one in. Their tours are about an hour longer than others. The ding is that the 60-foot mast means they can't go into any of the caves, which is a highlight with the smaller boats. You're paying for the *sailing* experience, which most tour boats don't offer. Morning 5–6 hour trip is $205. No credit cards.

Na Pali Coast Hanalei (826-6114) also has a good product and a fun crew. Their 32-foot power cat (called UFO II) is small enough to poke into nearly all of the sea caves, and the crew does a good job. Morning tours are best with around 4 hours to sightsee, snorkel at Nu'alolo and eat a deli lunch for $239, while the 2-hour sunset tour does *not* include snorkeling and comes with snacks only for $189. Up to 18 passengers; minimal shade. Wear waterproof (or none at all) shoes to wade out to the boat at the Hanalei River. Grab a seat on the left (OK, OK, *port*) side going out for the best views. March–October is their season from the north shore. They also launch their older, slightly smaller boat from the west side (Kekaha) year round for a similar snorkel tour but for only $148.

All the above tour companies are good about letting you venture away from the boat a bit during your snorkel at Nu'alolo.

Next on our list would be **HoloHolo's** (335-0815) summertime (March–October) RIB boats, holding up to 25 passengers. Things start off rocky with their agonizingly long process of getting everybody from the Tahiti Nui Restaurant (meeting spot) to being under way. But the fast (though loud) boat gets closer to the shore than Captain Sundown, and they'll stop in a couple of caves on the way back. Deli lunch and cookies, with snorkeling at the less-preferred Makole for $199. Shade available to deploy upon request. Good crew.

North Shore Charters (828-1379) leaves out of 'Anini Beach *in the summer* with 14 passengers in their 27-foot boat. It has inflatable sides but with a hard hull—amazingly smooth and fast for a Zodiac. No frills, no shade, deli sandwiches, and you'll snorkel at Nu'alolo for $150. The best route of the RIBs.

Napali Sea Breeze (828-1285) uses a 34-foot power cat and gets *Flakiest of the North Shore Operators* award. (Multiple failed attempts to book were blamed on bad weather when other operators went out—we suspected that too few people were booked.) They carry 16 people at most (which can still feel crowded), and they snorkel at Nu'alolo. $195, which includes a deli lunch. Their narration is fairly spot on, but you need to be right next to the captain's tower to hear it. They depart from 'Anini (you'll have to wade to the boat), it takes 10 more minutes to get to Na Pali than the Hanalei guys, but you get to see some of the hidden beaches below Princeville. It would be easier to like them if the owner wasn't so tough on the employees in front of the guests.

West Shore

HoloHolo Charters (335-0815) has a large, 65-foot power catamaran. They can feel a bit like a processing machine, but do a pretty consistent job on all their tours. Their trips are distinguished in that they go to the "forbidden" island of Ni'ihau. For $215, the 7-hour trip leaves in the morning from Port Allen and makes a beeline to Kalalau Beach on Na Pali. In light seas they're close to shore; heavier swells call for greater distance. Then they tour part of Na Pali before heading to Ni'ihau where they snorkel. (Clean, clear water and lots of fish, but currents can sometimes make snorkeling there more work.) Continental breakfast and a good deli lunch included. After the snorkeling, the open bar serves beer and wine, but they refuse to serve cookies until they're 5 minutes from port. (Maybe they're afraid you'll toss them otherwise.)

There are two large trampolines at the bow for sunning, but they and the entire bow section are off limits most of the time while motoring. Easy steps into and out of the water from the boat. HoloHolo is a good outfit and is easy to recommend. The boat is good, pretty stable, there's plenty of shade available, and the crew is very professional. They have a freshwater shower hose and adequate snorkel gear but no wetsuits available. Our only complaint is that the boat design makes it feel crowded on nice days. Most of the seating is inside, but when it's reasonably calm and sunny, most people want to be outside, which is somewhat spartan and lacking in seating, so people tend to crowd around the railings.

Their sunset tour is $129 for appetizers, beer, wine, mai tais and champagne.

They also have a smaller cat called the Leila, but we don't recommend it as much.

Liko Kaua'i Cruises (338-0333) offers a relaxing 5-hour tour of Na Pali on a 49-foot power catamaran with 32 people. (By the way, a lot of companies claim to be the largest boat able to enter sea caves. Liko actually is, beating the competition by 1 foot in length.) You'll leave from Kikiaola Small Boat Harbor near Kekaha and cruise north up the coast, often going as far as Ke'e Beach if the weather's good. (That's farther than any other west shore power cat goes, which pleases us greatly.) On the way back you stop and snorkel at Nu'alolo Kai or sometimes lousy Makole. Liko, a native Hawaiian, narrates with legends and stories. $126 for adults, $86 for keiki (kids), it includes water, sodas and sandwiches. One of the better priced ocean tours if you have small children (3 and under are free). They do a great job of following the mood of their guests and seem to genuinely enjoy having kids aboard. Afternoon/sunset tours also available in the summer. Their sister company, **Makana Charters** (338-9980) uses a 32-foot power cat that holds 12 people. The cost is also $135, and the experience is just as relaxed and a little more personable—the Liko tours can lose some of their personal touch when their boat is packed.

Catamaran Kahanu (645-6176) is a small boat (18 max, which would be pretty tight) run by a gruff but likable Hawaiian captain. This is a small outfit, and what they lack in cushion (literally) is made up with their family feel. And just like family, the stories and anecdotes you'll be treated to are either endearing or patronizing, depending on your outlook. Overall, a pretty good trip, with a tasty lunch. Morning 5-hour trips from Port Allen are $149. They also do a 4-hour sunset dinner cruise along the Na Pali shore for the same price from April until the end of October, weather permitting, for the same price. -

Na Pali Experience (635-1131) is a small outfit that operates only during the summer months (May–September) and takes only six passengers on their 24-foot power cats. They venture almost all the way to Ke'e Beach unless the ocean is too rough. Then they turn around at Kalalau and snorkel at Nu'alolo (they keep good, updated snorkel gear). Being in a boat this small means you're able to get into all the sea caves (seas permitting), and it also means you'll get to know your captain fairly well. They keep things more lighthearted than other operators and do a pretty good job of reading their passengers' humor and tastes. Speaking of tastes, the only ding we feel is that the small size of the boat means less room for food. A 5-hour tour on the water with snorkeling works up an appetite—all they provide are snacks (like chips) and fruit. If you want something more substantial, you'll need to bring it and endure the resentment of your fellow passengers. Otherwise, it's a good product. We like the fact that they leave from Kikiaola—it's way better than Port Allen. They offer three tours throughout the day, $179 and each 5 hours.

Other Big Boats

Captain Andy's Sailing Adventures (335-6833) is the biggest operator on the island, leaving from Port Allen, and they tend to run pretty tight ships. They have three types of boats—their luxury catamaran (Southern Star), regular catamarans and their rigid hull rafts. The Southern Star is large (65 feet), plush and comfortable, and their 5.5-hour snorkel tour has a good BBQ lunch and free beer and wine for $179. If they take their full load of 49 people, it's *a bit* tight. But otherwise, it's an easy trip to recommend. Their 5.5-hour Na Pali trips in the smaller catamarans are $159. Snorkeling when conditions permit, but at lousy Makole. Deli lunch with free beer and wine. It would be a better product if they

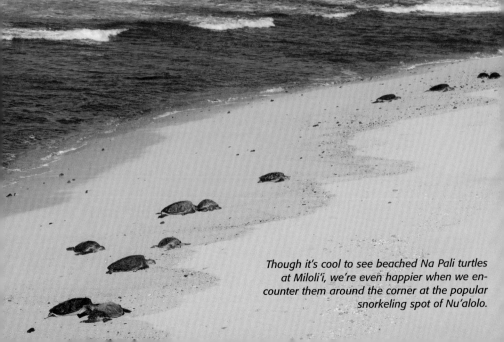

Though it's cool to see beached Na Pali turtles at Miloli'i, we're even happier when we encounter them around the corner at the popular snorkeling spot of Nu'alolo.

didn't pack up to *49* people on their nice 55-foot catamarans (and it *feels* crowded). You're best off if there's *more* than 49, because then they'll split the group onto two boats. These are sleek sailing cats, but they only sail a short time, and when they *do* raise the sail, it seems to activate the cookie-tossing instinct in some people, especially if they're using the indoor shade. (The crew is helpful and discreet with those who are nauseous.) But they are pretty capable sailboats, which will excite sailing enthusiasts. They also have a few Zodiac tours—including one that *lands* at Nu'alolo Kai for $205. Their excellent dinner cruise is described in ISLAND DINING on page 251. With so many boats, they have *way* too many options to describe here.

Kaua'i Sea Tours (335-5309) leaves from Port Allen for Na Pali trips for $165 (cheaper online). They have a 60-foot power/sailing cat called the Lucky Lady, which rides well. Think of this as a power cat, because at best they'll probably only raise the sails *while motoring* downwind. (The sails are more for decoration since this type of vessel sails like a pig.) They also have a water slide that keiki love—just watch out for back-flop entries. Continental breakfast plus a deli lunch. They also use a 24-foot rigid-hull inflatable (RIB) that lands at Nu'alolo (in the summer) for $165, but it's not in the same league as Na Pali Explorer's nicer inflatable. This 6-hour tour also includes a deli lunch. They have a dinner cruise described on page 251.

A sea cave—with a hole in the ceiling—and a waterfall. Even Hollywood couldn't make this stuff up.

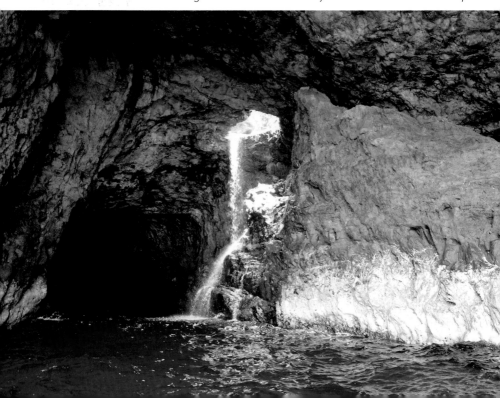

Blue Dolphin Charters (335-5553) has two catamarans called Blue Dolphin I and II, similar to the Lucky Lady above with similarly ineffective sailing prowess. Up to 49 people, continental breakfast (good cinnamon rolls) and deli lunch, good beer, wine and mai tais. They have a slide into the water to thrill the kids. $157 for Na Pali trips. You can SCUBA for an extra $39, which is quite reasonable. They also have intro to SCUBA where first timers can see what it's like under the sea for $75. We don't recommend going with Blue Dolphin if you've never dived before—stick with actual dive companies for that. The product feels tacked on rather than an emphasis on introduction. If you do dive, be sure to get a wetsuit—a warm, comfortable diver usually has more bottom time. Some days they also offer a Ni'ihau trip similar to HoloHolo's for $209. The crews are pretty good and their narrations fair. Plenty of shade, but avoid the inside seats at the front of the cabin. You never sail; at best they'll motor sail downwind. Po'ipu sunset tours (winter only) are $89.

Rigid-Hull Inflatables (RIBS)

Na Pali Explorer (338-9999) leaves from the west side and heads north in their 48-foot boat. There is some shade on board. $149 for the morning 4.5-hour Na Pali snorkel trip. They also have a less impressive 26-foot boat with no shade, but it is able to *land* at Nu'alolo Kai for $187. These trips include a light, deli-style lunch. You can get a decent discount if you pay with cash rather than credit.

Na Pali Riders (742-6331) has a 4-hour trip out of Kikiaola Harbor, but it's a decidedly mixed bag. They have less of the frills and more of the thrills. On the pro side, during the summer season they go all the way to Ke'e on the north shore, so

you'll see all of Na Pali. (Winter is whale watching heading south.) When they encounter dolphins, they get amazingly close. Also, inflatables can be fun on calm seas. But if seas aren't reasonably smooth, it's a rough ride because you'll feel every bump. On the con side there's no shade or restroom, if the boat is full it can feel crowded, and they only serve drinks and snacks. Price is $159—less if you pay with cash. We recommend the morning tour. An afternoon trip with snottier seas in a Zodiac ain't fun.

Boating Tips

Many companies offer morning and afternoon trips. Morning trips usually have snorkeling and better food on board. Morning is also when you're more likely to encounter smoother seas and better weather, so that's what we recommend.

Be wary of the information given during narrations. Many boat companies, like their helicopter brethren, are particularly prone to repeating inaccurate nonsense in their attempt to "educate" you, and we've seen some who literally made it up as they went along.

Seasickness can strike anyone. If you're concerned that it will be a problem, strongly consider taking Dramamine or Bonine at least an hour *before* you leave. (The night before and morning of are best. It's useless to take it once you're on the boat.) Also, avoid any alcohol the night before. (A *big* no-no.) No greasy foods before or during the trip. And some think that citrus juices are a cause of seasickness. Ginger is a very good preventative/ treatment. Below deck or in anything enclosed is a bad place to be if you're worried about getting seasick. Without a reference point, you're much more likely to let 'er rip. Scopolamine patches work but have side effects, including (occasionally) blurred vision that can last a week. (Been there, done that, on a 10-day boat trip.) If you're feeling sick, put something cold on the back of your neck. As far as the Ni'ihau trips are concerned, we've had people tell us they were prone to seasickness and ask where they should sit. The answer is...on land. The boats can be mighty rockin' in that channel between the islands, and if you have a history of easy-queasy, that trip might not be for you. Coming back from Ni'ihau is almost always rough.

From the west shore, the best views are off the right (starboard) side going out to Na Pali and off the left (port) side coming back. It's the opposite when you leave from the north shore. Also remember that most boats are a lot smoother in the back than the front, but you may inhale diesel fumes back there. Just slightly ahead of the back seats is our preferred position.

People come off these trips *toasted*, especially in the summer. Make sure you slather on the sunscreen early and often and consider having a wide-brimmed hat and light shirt to cover up with when not in the water, or you'll be sorry for the rest of your trip.

Since most trips involve driving early in the morning, consider doing the trip early in your vacation—when your body clock is still on mainland time, and it's easier to rise early.

Most companies make you remove your shoes. Also, agendas are not carved in stone. Weather, seas and opportunities along the way can alter the best laid plans. So be flexible.

There are a number of smaller boat companies with smaller boats that are crowded and have no shade, and we don't recommend them for these waters.

PARASAILING

Parasailing is outlawed on Kaua'i. Hey, *that* was easy.

River trips up and down the Wailua River take you to the Fern Grotto, a fern-lined amphitheater.

RIVER TRIPS

Kauaʻi is the only Hawaiian island to offer river trips, and there are two ways to do it. You can take a riverboat ride up the Wailua River (often referred to as the only navigable river in all Hawaiʻi, but this is a relative term) or paddle your own kayak. **Smith's Motorboat Service** (821-6892) goes 3 miles up the Wailua River and stops at the Fern Grotto, a large natural amphitheater with ferns all about. This is a popular place to get married. It's 30 minutes each way with entertainment and interesting information provided throughout. They spend 30–45 minutes at the site. $25 per person, and they leave many times each day in their 100-plus passenger boats. If you've heard of the Fern Grotto before and seen photos, be forewarned that those photos, even in current ads, might be *very* old. Hurricane ʻIwa in 1982 thinned out the ferns, and the closing of the nearby sugar company—and its leaky reservoir above the cave that accidentally created the grotto in the first place—has resulted in a greatly diminished attraction. They've tried to rejuvenate it somewhat, but it's still a bit of a letdown.

You can also rent a kayak at any of several places and paddle the Wailua, the Hanalei River, the Kalihiwai River or the Huleʻia Stream. The best thing about kayaking the Wailua River isn't the Fern Grotto. (In fact, they discourage landing kayaks there.) Instead, it's the overall scenery and a hike to a waterfall, if you like. See KAYAKING.

Kauaʻi is justly famous for many things: its incomparable lushness, gorgeous beaches and balmy nights. But Kauaʻi is not famous for its diving. This is a shame because Kauaʻi has some very good dive spots. Turtles are common, and many of them are downright gregarious. Lava tubes, ledges and walls are sprinkled around the island. Fish are abundant and varied. Coral growth is not as good as around the Big Island—at 22 degrees latitude, Kauaʻi is on the fringe of the coral belt. Kauaʻi's many rivers and streams cut visibility in some areas, but you can still see more than 100 feet on good days. The reefs on the north shore have been struck by a disease in recent years that is killing some of the coral, but the rest of the island hasn't suffered.

Granted, you might find better conditions on the Kona coast of the Big Island or around Lanaʻi. It is dryer there and the lava's porous, so the ocean receives virtually no runoff. But this should not dissuade you from enjoying the wondrous underwater sights the Garden Island has to offer.

Kauaʻi's ocean pattern is small summer surf on the north shore, larger summer surf on the south shore, and the opposite during winter months, so you should plan your diving activities accordingly. Summer is very popular, and the best companies book up early, so call them as soon as you know when you want to dive. The dive boat operators conduct their tours on the south shore year-round since the local government doesn't allow the boats to moor on the north shore. Some also have dives on the west side at Mana Crack and at Lehua Rock off the coast of Niʻihau. Those dives are generally considered advanced due to the depths and currents involved, and prices are higher than the spread we show in the table. The Niʻihau dive in particular involves at least 4 hours travel time (round trip), so those who get seasick (and those who aren't sure) should take Dramamine or Bonine *before* they depart.

Off Ni'ihau, however, you're treated to ridiculously clear water, lots of big life (sharks, rays, dolphins and your best chance at a Hawaiian monk seal) and a close view of the "Forbidden Island." (The Robinsons, who own Ni'ihau, *hate* it when you call it that.) See page 179 for more on this dive. Book in advance to ensure space.

So you'll know **our perspective** when we review companies, we should tell you what we do and don't like when we go on a dive. On a bad dive, the dive master takes the group on a non-stop excursion that keeps you kicking the whole time. No time to stop and explore the nooks and crannies. Good outfits will give you a briefing, tell you about some of the endemic species here, what to look for and will point out various things on the dives, keeping it moving but not too fast. Bad outfits kick a lot. Good outfits explain the unique qualities of Hawai'i's environment. Bad dive masters may tell you what *they* saw (but *you* missed). Good companies work around your needs, wishes and desires. Bad companies keep everyone on a short leash. Good dive masters know their stuff and share it with you. Bad dive masters don't know squat but imply they know it all in order to impress you. As divers, we tend to like companies that wander toward the boat for the latter part of the dive and allow you to go up when you are near the end of your tank, as opposed to everyone going up when the heaviest breather has burned up his/her bottle.

During times when we feel the diving conditions are bad (poor vis or big swells), we like to call around and ask about conditions. We appreciate the companies who admit it's bad, and we hold it against those who tell us how wonderful conditions are.

If You've Never Dived Before

If this is your first dive, the recommendation is a no-brainer. **Fathom Five** wins by default since other companies have poor systems. For instance, **Seasport**

Dive Operator	Services Available	Price of Dive	Rent Gear For Shore	Boat Size / Passengers	Dive Computer	Ni'ihau 3-Tank Dive	Dive Certification	Rx Masks
Bubbles Below 332-7333	Dive Shop & Boat Dives	$140–$180 (2 tank)	No	36' / 8 32' / 6	Extra	$350–$395	$520	No
Fathom Five Divers 742-6991	Dive Shop, Boat Dives & Shore Dives	$140–$180 (2 tank)	$67	25' / 6 35' / 6	Included	$355–$395	$495	Yes
Garden Isle Divers 631-7447	Boat Dives & Shore Dives	$170 (2 tank)	No	29' / 6	Included	None	$550	No
Kaua'i Down Under 742-7422	Boat Dives & Shore Dives	$189 (2 tank)	No	25' / 6	Included	None	$550	Yes
Seasport Divers 742-9303	Dive Shop, Boat Dives & Shore Dives	$143–$179 (2 tank)	$55	32' / 12 48' / 18	Included	$350	$525	Yes

Divers soaks up too much pre-dive time since they make you do a pre-dive class in Kukui'ula Harbor before taking you on a *boat* dive. If you don't do well in the harbor, they won't take you on the boat. We don't think that such measures are a good idea. Most first timers in Hawai'i do fine going straight to a protected part of the ocean, *if* the instructor does a good job, which, fortunately, **Fathom Five** does. They will take you directly out for an introductory *shore* dive for $115 (one-tank) or $155 (two-tank). Companies such as Seasport that do intros off their boat use a concept we disagree with, since shore dives make beginners *far* more comfortable than jumping from a boat into water over their heads with unfamiliar gear.

Kaua'i Down Under (which operates under multiple names) has a one-tank shore intro for $129 or $155 (two-tank) including all your gear—a pretty good deal.

Garden Isle Divers offers a two-tank shore intro for $190, but their relaxed attitude (which might be a bit charitable) might not keep first timers comfortable.

If you're interested in getting **certified** or did your book work on the mainland and want an open water referral, **Fathom Five** or **Bubbles Below** are your best bets. The open water referral method allows you to do your class work at home, saving your Kaua'i vacation for the *fun stuff*.

Recommended for Certified Divers

As anonymous certified divers (who sometimes pretend to be novices), we are able to experiment with different operators. The outfit we recommend are **Fathom Five** for boat and shore dives. They are well-qualified, professional and knowledgeable. We've been impressed at how they run their boat dives, and the personalized service really shows. They'll try to take you where *you* want

to go, not the other way around. They feed you better than anyone else, get you on the boat quicker and have a good ascent policy. They use a 25-foot and 35-foot six-pack, so they're able to keep the groups smaller and respond more to what individual divers want. They tend to use one for more experienced divers and the other for rustier divers, so they don't mix the two unless you want them to. (Certifieds will love that.) As for their shore dives, they aren't as organized as we would like, we still prefer their thoroughness and accuracy. In addition to standard two-tank dives, they have twilight dives, night dives, premium three-tank dives and Ni'ihau dives.

Bubbles Below has discovered many of the island's great dive spots, but they have recently been slipping in quality. (One of the biggest dings is the fact that instead of individual water bottles, you get reusable flasks to share—without cups. We ain't *that* comfortable with our fellow divers.) As far as the diving goes, they focus on the west side more than the others, including Mana Crack off Na Pali, and they offer a Nitrox intro for this dive to maximize bottom time. They're engaging with customers, but calling themselves naturalists is a bit generous. (Some of their information on sea life is questionable.) These guys are are more willing to do Ni'ihau in the winter, but that usually entails a harder channel crossing. They'll take a maximum of eight on their 36-foot Radon (which has a hot shower). They also have a 32-foot power catamaran that takes six people. Na Pali and North Shore dives are pricier.

Garden Isle Divers is a two-man team that more experienced divers who don't want any hand-holding might appreciate. They are very laid back and the opposite of a diver processing machine—you'll feel more like you're tagging along with a knowledgeable buddy than on a SCUBA tour. Their boat leaves from Port Allen and focuses on south and west shore dive sites. They seem particularly adept at finding rare critters like frogfish. A maximum of six on their 29-foot mosquito-hull boat.

Sometimes it's tempting to go with the cheapest dive operators. Remember that if you're herded in and out with a cheap company that doesn't know the underwater terrain, you may find that your "better deal" was no bargain at all. The spreads in our price table often reflect a short boat ride vs. a long trip to the north shore.

Dive Shops

There are a couple of dive *shops* (as opposed to dive operators) on the island. Although not the biggest, the best is **Fathom Five**. Their shop is on the small side, but they consistently update the gear. We also like how they'll rinse and store your personal gear, if you dive on multiple days. They're on Po'ipu Road in Koloa.

Seasport Divers in Po'ipu (with a smaller satellite office in Kapa'a) is the largest shop on the island with the best selection if you're looking to *buy* gear, but we don't recommend their boat dives as much, except perhaps their Ni'ihau trips in the summer.

Kaua'i Down Under's "shop" is really just a small outlet at the Sheraton Kaua'i in Po'ipu. Their boat dives are off a Zodiac, and they also offer scooter dives.

For **renting gear**, either of the two shops will do fine.

For the heavy breathers among you, **Bubbles Below, Fathom Five,** and **Seasport** have 100s available, so feel free to *suck 'em up.*

Dive computers are available for your own *independent* dives and can only be rented from **Fathom Five**. *Disposable*

underwater cameras in a watertight box for snorkeling are available at most grocery stores and sundry shops. If you have a GoPro, consider getting a red lens filter when shooting underwater—it will bring out the colors of fish and coral. **Fathom Five** rents better still cameras for SCUBA, and **Seasport** carries lots of underwater GoPro gear.

Some of the dive boats on Kaua'i feed you little or nothing between dives. I don't know about you, but I'm tempted to gnaw on the side of the boat after a dive. Bring a package of cookies with you. You'll probably be able to sell them to other hungry divers at prices confiscatory enough to pay for your dive. *I have a bid of $8 for a chocolate chip cookie... Do I hear $9?*

Shorties are usually sufficient for most people *in the summer only.* Surface water temperatures range from a low of 73.4 °F in February to a high of 80 °F in October. Any company that will *only* provide you with shorties doesn't seem to care much about your comfort. Or maybe we've just lived here too long and have gotten wussy about the cold.

Between morning and afternoon dives, morning is almost always best.

Nitrox (or enriched air) is available at **Fathom Five, Bubbles Below** and **Seasport Divers**.

Kaua'i has many boat dive spots. Since the more resourceful operators are always finding new spots, and since you basically go where the boat operators go, we'll forgo a detailed description of all boat dive destinations. Suffice it to say that Sheraton Caves, General Store, Brennecke's Ledge, Turtle Bluffs, Amber's Arches and Fishbowl are all popular. Some sites, such as Sheraton Caves, are nice but a bit over-dived.

Remember not to drive up to Waimea Canyon or the Kalalau Lookout after diving. As far as your nitrogen level is concerned, you're flying.

Below is a list of the best shore dives on the island:

- **Ke'e Beach, north shore**—If the seas are flat on a calm summer day, this area offers interesting shallow relief. The area near the reef drop-off is good, again on calm days.
- **Tunnels, north shore**—Easy access, lots of turtles, reef sharks, lava tubes, caves and nice underwater relief. Tunnels' allure is not its visibility, but the dramatic underwater topography. *If* you dive with someone who really knows the reef, this is unquestionably the best shore dive on the island and is often better than a boat dive. Low tide is best.
- **The Hole, north shore**—Located just off the St. Regis Resort. Like the name says, a hole in the reef. Acceptable underwater relief and easy access.
- **Kahala Point, east shore**—Entry and exit is a bugger on the lava rocks with crashing surf. Underwater relief is good, and there are lots of fish. Near Anahola Beach Park.
- **Koloa Landing, south shore**—Easy entry, usually calm conditions year-round and decent coral near the shore. After slightly murky water on entry, the sea is usually quite clear. High tide is best.

Ni'ihau Dives

For SCUBA divers looking for clean, clear, virgin waters, several dive operators offer three-tank dives near the privately owned island of Ni'ihau, mostly off Lehua Rock north of the island. (For more information on Ni'ihau, see INTRODUCTION chapter.) Since this island is in the rain shadow of Kaua'i, there are no permanent streams on the island (and conse-quently, no run-off). So visibility is often *well* over a hundred feet. This is some of the most exciting diving in the state.

The waters are rich in critters, arches, caves and pelagics. There's a good chance you will share the water with sharks, so be prepared. The dive requires a 70-mile round trip (if you leave from Port Allen) boat ride and involves drop-offs, currents and sometimes rough seas. This is not for the inexperienced diver. Dives are usually deeper here and often drift dives. Summer is best. Coming back into the wind is *always* a rough trip. We like **Fathom Five** (and are grateful for the shade and extra amenities) and **Bubbles Below** the best. It's a very good idea to book a month in advance to ensure space. **Seasport Divers** trolls for fish the whole time, which takes longer coming back, plus their boat is more crowded. **Garden Isle Divers** falls somewhere in the middle—not much shade but less crowded and they like to troll for fish.

Skydiving is available at Port Allen Airport on the west side.

We were not able—actually, more like *unwilling*—to re-review the company here, **Skydive Kaua'i** (335-5859), for this edition. We've reviewed them multiple times before and wrote that, "The plane didn't inspire confidence (their website referred to it as a 'state-of-the-art Cessna,' which was true—when *Lyndon Johnson* was president.)" We were also concerned with a general lack of instructions on what to do during a jump, and the fact that Port Allen is notorious for shifting winds. I know the wind conditions well there since it's where I first learned to fly. But the final straw was in 2016 when

Hawaiian Reefs—*Why is it that…?*

What is that crackling sound, like bacon frying, I always hear while snorkeling or diving? For years this baffled people. In the early days of submarines, the sound interfered with sonar operations. Finally we know the answer. It's hidden snapping shrimp defining their territory. One variety is even responsible for all the dark cracks and channels you see in smooth lobe coral. A pair creates the channels, then "farms" the algae inside.

Why are there so few shellfish in Hawai'i? It's too warm for some of the more familiar shellfish (which tend to be filter-feeders, and Hawaiian waters don't have as much stuff to filter). But Hawai'i has more shellfish than most people are aware of. They hide well under rocks and in sand. Also, people tend to collect shells (which is illegal), and that depletes the numbers.

Why do coral cuts take so long to heal? Coral contains a live animal. When you scrape coral, it leaves proteinaceous matter in your body, which takes much longer for your body to dispatch.

Why do some of the reefs appear dead? Much of the "coral" you see around Kaua'i isn't the kind of coral you're used to. It's called coralline algae, which secretes calcium carbonate. It's not dead; it's *supposed* to look like that. We do have a disease though, that is killing some of the coral on the north shore, which is being investigated.

What do turtles eat? Dolphins. (Just teasing.) They primarily eat plants growing on rocks, as well as jellyfish when they are lucky enough to encounter them. Unfortunately for turtles and lucky for us, jellyfish aren't numerous here.

Is it harmful when people play with an octopus? Yes, if the octopus gets harmed when someone tries to get it out of its hole. Best to leave them alone.

Why does the ocean rarely smell fishy here in Hawai'i? Two reasons. We have relatively small tide changes, so the ocean doesn't strand large amounts of smelly seaweed at low tide. Also, the water is fairly sterile compared to mainland water, which owes much of its smell to algae and seaweed that thrives in the bacteria-rich runoff from industrial sources.

Why is the water so clear here? Because relatively little junk is poured into our water compared to the mainland. Also, natural currents tend to flush the water with a continuous supply of fresh, clean ocean water.

Why do my ears hurt when I dive deep, and how are scuba divers able to get over it? Because the increasing weight of the ocean is pressing on your ears the farther down you go. Divers alleviate this by equalizing their ears. Sounds high tech, but that simply means holding your nose while trying to blow out of it. This forces air into the Eustachian tubes, creating equal pressures with the outside ocean. (It doesn't work if your sinuses are clogged.) Anything with air between it gets compressed. So if you know people who get headaches whenever they go under water…well, they must be airheads.

Getting up close and personal with our fishy friends.

they suffered a crash on takeoff that killed everyone aboard. Frankly, we're done reviewing them. We suggest Oʻahu if you want to skydive in Hawaiʻi. But if you still want to try, it'll run you $239 plus $2 for every pound you weigh over 215 pounds, up to 250 pounds.

If you have ever looked into a saltwater aquarium and marveled at the diversity of the fish life, snorkeling is an experience you might want to try. Anyone who has ever hovered over hundreds of colorful fish can attest to the thrill they felt being in their environment.

Where to snorkel depends on how good you are and what kind of experience you want. The best place for beginners is **Lydgate Beach Park** in Wailua. There you will find an area protected by a ring of boulders that shields you from the strong ocean. But visibility and fish

count have not been good for awhile. See page 112 for more. The intermediate snorkeler will find **Keʻe** or **Tunnels** on the north shore to be fabulous during the calm, warmer months. **Hideaways** is also great during calm seas. **Poʻipu Beach Park** on the south shore usually offers good snorkeling and calm seas in cooler months on either side of the tombolo. The BEACHES chapter has a description of all the beaches and the different characteristics they possess.

As far as gear goes, there are numerous places to rent gear on the island. We always snorkel wearing water shoes and divers' fins (which fit over water shoes). This way we can enter and exit the water without worrying about stepping on anything. Cheap water shoes can be found at many places, including Walmart. Bootie socks or women's thin, ankle-length socks will keep you from rubbing the top of your tootsies raw. Divers' fins can be rented at most dive shops. If enough people ask snorkel companies about them, they will start to carry them, too.

If you're looking to buy snorkel gear, you can pick it up pretty cheap at Walmart on the highway in Lihu'e.

Many people prefer to rent gear when they get here and leave it in the trunk, so they may snorkel when the opportunity arises. Your hotel or condo may have gear available. If they don't, try any of the following:

North Shore Rentals

Hanalei Surf Company (826-9000) has pretty good equipment for only $6 per day, $22 per week. *Rx* masks available for nothing extra.

Pedal 'n' Paddle (826-9069) in Hanalei will rent you gear for $5 per day, $20 per week.

East Shore Rentals

Boss Frog (822-4334) on the highway in Kapa'a has decent gear for $5–$10 per day, $10–$35 for the week. *Rx* masks available for more.

Seasport Divers (823-9222) on the highway in Kapa'a has similar rates, and

they also have divers' fins (the kind worn over water shoes) available.

Kapa'a Beach Shop (212-8615) next to Chicken in a Barrel in north Kapa'a has some great deals with full snorkel sets for $7 per day as well as wet suits for $7 per day. (Get either for $15 per week.)

Snorkel Bob's (823-9433 or 742-2206) has two locations: one on the highway in Kapa'a and the other located on Po'ipu Road past Koloa. You're likely to be drawn by the $2.50 per day gear, but be tempted by the $10 or even *$11* gear. Although the equipment is pretty good, it's not *that* good. $10 gear is your best bet. Weekly rental is $9–$68. *Rx* masks available for more. You can also rent on Kaua'i and return equipment at Snorkel Bob's on another island.

South Shore Rentals

Nukumoi Beach & Surf Shop (742-8019) rents beach equipment, including snorkel gear, boogie boards and the like. A good selection. Convenient, since they are right near Po'ipu Beach Park. $8 per day, $24 per week.

Stop bothering me! I'm trying to bond with the fish.

Fathom Five (742-6991) in Po'ipu has gear for $8 per day, $40 per week. Divers' fins available.

See also **Snorkel Bob's** listed above.

Snorkel Lessons

If you've never snorkeled before and desire lessons and assistance, **SeaFun Snorkel Adventures** (742-2734) offers guided snorkel tours for $85 per person (children 5–12 cost $68). They are great with kids, but it's really the adults who have never snorkeled who benefit from their guidance. We once tried to teach a friend to snorkel and were unsuccessful at even getting her to put her face in the water (she was terrified). We were very impressed that in only a few minutes they had her snorkeling like an expert. Even *non-swimmers* go out with them. For $5 extra, they'll pick you up at *some* south shore hotels and take you to a place like Lawa'i Beach and provide you with gear, wetsuit (which helps you float), drinks, snacks and assistance. Prescription masks are available.

Snorkel Tips

- Tropical gloves make snorkeling much more enjoyable. You can grab rocks to maneuver in shallow or surgy areas. (Please don't grab coral, however.)
- Use *Sea Drops* or another brand of anti-fog goop. Spread it *thinly* on the inside of a dry mask, then do a quick rinse. The old-fashioned method of spitting in the mask is not very effective. (It's particularly frightening to see tobacco chewers do this. Yuck!)
- Don't use your arms much, or you will spook the fish. Kick with gentle fin motion. Any rapid motion can cause the little critters to scatter.
- Fish are hungriest and most appreciative in the morning (before their coffee).

- If you have a mustache and have trouble with a leaking mask, try a little Vaseline. Don't get any on the glass—it can get *really* ugly.

If you've always wanted to see what it's like to SCUBA dive but are a bit worried or don't want to go through the hassle, try SNUBA. That's where you take an air tank and place it on a raft that floats above you. Anyone 8 or older can SNUBA. From the raft there's a 20-foot hose attached to a regulator. There you are, underwater up to 20 feet deep, no tank on your back, no hassle. You'll have some instruction before you (and up to seven other divers) go under, and the dive master stays with you the whole time. It can be an exciting way to see the underwater world for the first time. **SNUBA Tours of Kaua'i** (823-8912). They do their thing off Lawa'i Beach on the south shore. $75. Half hour underwater and an hour above for instruction. Video available.

If you're looking to be pampered, there are several spas on the island worth mentioning, and the range is huge. You can go from a spoiled, opulent setting to someone's house where clothing throughout your experience is optional. Please note that massages in Hawai'i are *much* more expensive than what you're used to.

The grandest tropical experience by far is **Anara Spa** (742-1234) at The Grand Hyatt in Po'ipu, and their fabulous 45,000-sq.-ft. full-service spa is guaranteed to turn you to jelly. It's pricey, but their attention to detail and overall surroundings make it worth the splurge. (You'll love their lava rock showers and optional thatched huts for outside treatments.) You also get full use of all spa facilities, including lap pool, steam and saunas, gym, etc.

The most opulent is **Halele'a Spa** (826-9644) at the St. Regis Princeville. Super rich decor (you won't want to leave the showers), and they really sweat the details. Though the surroundings are not particularly Hawaiian or tropical unless you're really paying attention, their services are top of the line. They have adequate gender-specific lounges, but the co-ed lounge is the one with all the trimmings. Also, if you get a massage, you're allowed to come back later in the day and continue to enjoy the spa's amenities.

Spa by the Sea (823-1488) at the Waipouli Beach Resort in central Kapa'a is your next best bet. The facilities are nice (though there are no day spa facilities), and with your ($100 or more) treatment, you and one other person can access their incredible meandering pool with its waterfalls. Good shower and locker room facilities and professional staff.

Spa at Koloa Landing (240-6622) in Po'ipu is relatively small but with large, nicely appointed rooms. If you have not had a Hawaiian lomi lomi massage—with long, gliding motions—they do it well here. Because they are small, if the gender of your practitioner matters to you, tell 'em on the phone or you might get a surprise. The two couples rooms have large Japanese soaking tubs. They have a cabana in front of the Sheridan that is oceanfront, but it's on

There's something undeniably cool about yelling the word, "Pull!"

the walking path and can be loud at times. Their pool is available before and after your treatment. A 20 percent tip is added to your bill.

(Aunty) Angeline's Lomi Kaua'i (822-3235) in Anahola is in a category all by itself. Forget the grand spa facilities of the resorts. This experience takes place in Angeline's home/farm, and the atmosphere is casual, open and co-ed. This is not for the bashful since nudity is common for your treatment, which includes the co-ed steam room. (They will work with the more modest as best they can.) Hawaiian chants start things off, and for $160 you get two hours of treatment, including a four-handed lomi lomi massage. Gruff on the phone but nice inside, family-run, and they've been around for decades. But don't be surprised to hear house noises throughout your treatment. BYOT.

Sport Shooting

If you came to Kaua'i for our big game hunting...well, then you were misinformed. We don't have any of that here. But what we *do* have is a pretty well-run sporting clay business called **Kaua'i Eco Sporting Clays** (651-6690). Whether you're into shooting or not, there's something oddly satisfying about saying *pull* and blasting a clay disk launched into the air by one of eight different traps. My problem was I didn't really know how to shoot. That's why I was so impressed with these guys, because you can tell they *really* want you to bag some targets, and they do a great job teaching you. It's $118 for the intro course, which lasts 60–90 minutes. You'll get 25 shells and have to pay another $10 to have the 20-gauge shotgun cleaned. (They have 12-gauge as well,

but it's really overkill.) When you're done, you'll have a smile on your face and never think of the phrase *cheek fat* the same way again. On Maalo Road heading toward Wailua Falls. Call in advance. This is a small outfit, and they sometimes don't run on time. But they're super friendly. Anyone 12 and up can participate.

Ho, braddah, da shreddin's da kine! (Just trying to get you in the mood.) Surfing is synonymous with Hawai'i. And why not? Hawaiians invented *da bugga*. Learning isn't as hard as you may think. Depending on conditions, they may put you on a large, soft board the size of a garage door (well...almost), so it's fairly easy to master, at least at this level.

Hanalei Bay is justly famous island-wide as one of the best and *most challenging* in Hawai'i. The chapter on BEACHES can assist you in picking beaches with surfing possibilities. **Cannons, Hanalei Bay, Kalihiwai, Kealia, Kalapaki, Infinities (Pakala Beach)**, are all well-known surf spots. If you want lessons, the best teacher we've seen is **Learn to Surf** (826-7612). For $55 they'll spend 90 minutes with you at whichever beach has the right conditions. Good attitude and good place to rent a board.

Most of the companies on the south side teach at Kiahuna Beach. They might seem distracted and disinterested, but that's only because they're distracted and disinterested. But you'll probably eventually ride a wave here. Companies there include **Hoku Water Sports** (639-9333) and **Kaua'i Surf School** (651-6032). **Titus Kinimaka Hawaiian School of Surfing** (652-1116) teaches out of Hanalei Bay, and you won't have the same

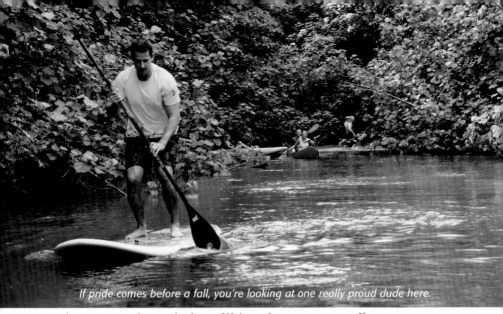

If pride comes before a fall, you're looking at one really proud dude here.

crowd issue as on the south shore. With the sandier bottom at Hanalei (the south shore is reefier), it might be worth the higher price ($65 for 90 minutes).

Hawaiian Surfing Adventures (482-0749) has 90-minute group lessons for $65, $150 for private. We found them patient and eager to get you riding your first wave. They mostly go out of the north shore, too.

If you just want to rent a board (about $20–$25 per day), contact your hotel activity desk or any of the following: **Po'ipu Surf** (742-8797) and **Nukumoi** (742-8019), both in Po'ipu, **Hanalei Surf Company** (826-9000) in Hanalei. **Kaua'i Surf Rentals** (651-0541) has a nice variety of boards and will deliver free to north and east shore as long as you spend $80 or more. Contrary to what you see in the movies, beginners should look for crumbling waves, not the picturesque, breaking waves that slap the water.

By the way, a collection of surfboards is known in surfing lingo here as a *quiver*. A little kid surfer who doesn't have a job or car yet is called a *grommet*. Double *overhead* is when the waves are really big, and if you get good enough, you might get a chance to visit the *green room*. If someone says your girlfriend is *filthy*, it's a compliment. And a *landshark* is someone who says he surfs...but doesn't.

Stand Up Paddling, or **SUP**, is the latest craze in the surfing world. The hardest part about learning to surf is standing up on the board while it's moving. This sport has made things easier by giving you a board big enough to dance on. SUP boards are wider, thicker and longer than the biggest longboards people commonly learn to surf on. SUP instruction focuses on keeping your balance while using a tall paddle to move you into the waves. (This provides an excellent central core workout, with your feet—of all things—hurting the most.) The sight of people standing and dipping long paddles in the water has earned SUP surfers the subversive title "janitors" or "moppers" from traditional surfers. The size of the board, as well as the fact that you are already standing up, gives you an advantage in catching waves early. You don't have to drop in exactly where the wave is breaking. Moppers can catch waves behind the lineup, but all surfing rules apply once you've caught the wave. Traditional surfers will be more inclined to drop in on your wave since they'll feel that you didn't work as hard to get it as they did.

Most of the surfing companies give lessons in SUP. Lessons start in the Hanalei River. If you're comfortable on the board, you'll want to ask for a Stand Up *Surfing* lesson. We've had good luck with **Hawaiian Surfing Adventures** (482-0749). Small groups up to four; $100 for a private 1-hour lesson, $75 for two or three people, $65 per person if there are four. **Titus Kinimaka** (652-1116) has 90-minute lessons for $65. **Hanalei Surf School** (826-9283) charges quite a bit more and has an elaborate pricing structure. You might consider their 15-minute land lesson for $50, then take the board for 2 hours.

An alternative is **Outfitters Kaua'i** (742-9667). They have a trip that paddleboards 2 miles up the Hule'ia River (usually downwind), then adds 1 mile of hiking in beautiful jungle and lunch at a waterfall with a deep pool to jump or zipline into. You motorboat back upwind. Only downfall is that your paddling instructions are practically nil. You won't learn much about the sport. Also their guides are friendly but are often factually challenged with their narrations. And though your group may repeatedly be told that the waterfall and "blue pool" (which is *not* blue) you're playing in is pure and clean, "straight from the top of Mt. Wai'ale'ale," analysis of topographic maps appear to us (we're not certified topographical surveyors) that the feeder stream water you're playing in comes from Haupu and through the Kipu cattle ranch. But it's a fun 5 hours for $129. Bring shoes that can get wet.

Tubing is where you sit in an inner tube and slowly drift along an old irrigation ditch. (We think their website makes

Local surfers combing the beach for the perfect morning wave.

things look *much* more exciting than the reality of the tour.) It's actually quite relaxing and calls for so little physical expenditure that you'll be tempted to look for your remote control and a can of beer while you're sitting there. Overall, however, we're kind of lukewarm on this. It's semi-lame, and there doesn't seem to be enough bang for your buck.

Kaua'i Backcountry Adventures (245-2506) does their tubing in an old sugar cane field between Lihu'e and Kapa'a. They'll pick you up in Hanama'ulu and drive you out to the area, narrating along the way. Then they'll put a helmet and gloves on you (wetsuits are extra), plunk you and 17 other people in inner tubes and off you go. This is *not* a whitewater adventure. Builders of these ditches didn't want to give up precious elevation quickly. So you'll putt-putt along at about 2 miles an hour. The best parts are the five tunnels, which represent about half your trip. They're dark, and the sounds of you and your fellow tubers bounce around in there.

Overall, the company does a pretty good job with what they have to work with, but they can be pretty disorganized at times. You won't see much in the way of views—the ditch banks block most of that. Deli lunch is included, but you'll be forgiven if you think the price—$110 per person—is pretty darned steep considering you're only in the water an hour. People with bad backs might not like the posture they're in for the ride. Note that there's a 300-pound weight limit. They also have kid-size tubes, but they'll ride at the adult-sized price. They must be at least 5 years old and 43 inches tall.

A kitesurfer soars overhead. Though Kaua'i waters are difficult for beginners, more advanced kiters can snag as much as 50 feet of air.

At **Kaua'i Waterski & Surf Co.** (822-3574), you can waterski the Wailua River. They rent a ski boat for $195 per hour, $100 for half hour. This includes the boat, driver, ski equipment and lessons, if you wish. Since you pay for the boat and not for skiing, non-skiers come along for free, up to five customers in the boat. If you've never skied before, it's *much* more tiring than it looks, but it's gobs of fun. By reservation only.

Although Maui sees more whales than Kaua'i, they are still very common here. Whales work in Alaska in the summer, building up fat, then vacation here from December or January to March or April, when the females give birth and the males sing the blues. Only the males sing, and they all sing the same song, usually with their heads pointed down. Humpbacks don't eat while they're here and may lose one-third of their body weight during their Hawaiian vacation. (I doubt that many *human* visitors can make that same claim.) These gentle giants are very social and have been known to come right up to boats to check out the sightseers. Regulations prohibit the boat companies from initiating this kind of intimacy, but they get close enough to enjoy the whales. If you want to go on a whale watching boat tour, see OCEAN TOURS for a description of the tour boat operators. Whale watching is mostly an opportunistic event here. Those boat companies that do a good job with their other tours (snorkeling, sunset cruises, etc.) are the ones that will give you similar treatment during whale season as well. If you hope to spot them from the land, elevation helps. Consider the Kilauea Lighthouse and the sandstone hikes along Po'ipu. Less wind on the water makes it easier to spot 'em.

WindSurfing

If you want to try windsurfing, you'll find that your options are limited on Kaua'i. Higher winds and more reefs mostly favor the experienced. A notable exception is 'Anini Beach. Celeste at **Windsurf Kaua'i** (828-6838) specializes in lessons for beginners on the north shore. Rates are $125 per person for 2 hours of lessons and practice. $35 for an hour for rental. Inquire about a rental if you already know what you are doing and want to skip the lesson. Take it to Maha'ulepu or Salt Pond on the south shore, if you like. The west side just south of the Pacific Missile Range Facility can also be very exciting for the experienced. There the winds that wrap around Na Pali can create ideal conditions.

Kiteboarding/Kitesurfing

We're hesitant to give this sport its own section because so many people still don't know what it is, and because it's an offshoot of windsurfing. It's all the rage here in Hawai'i and is called **kitesurfing** or **kiteboarding**. Imagine a modified surfboard, shorter and boxier than a normal board, with fins at both ends and straps for your feet. Then let a special, controllable, two-line kite drag you along. Like windsurfing, you don't have to go the direction the wind takes ya—you have control (though not as much as on a windsurf board). It's harder to learn than windsurfing, but *oh,* what fun it is! More fun than windsurfing, if you can get over the steeper learning curve.

The problem for Kaua'i visitors is that it takes a big investment of time and money to learn, and we haven't found a reliable source for lessons or equipment rental. Your best bet is **Aloha Surf School** (639-9283), which charges $275 for a 3-hour lesson in Hanalei Bay on the north shore. **Kiteboard Kaua'i** (951-415-0261) operates on the east side and prices vary based on skill level, but scheduling is difficult—the owner recommends booking one to two *months* in advance. If you have your heart set on kitesurfing, you're better off doing it on Maui where there is a larger learning infrastructure.

Ever seen movies where military commandos don a harness, hook a pulley onto a steel cable and zip down into the action? This is similar—without the hostile fire at the end.

There are lots of companies companies doing ziplines on Kaua'i. All have weight limits. Don't lie, or you might get turned away and still charged.

Probably our favorite is **Koloa Zipline** (742-2894). They may make a rotten first impression at the shop, but once on the course we've had good luck with the guides. The setting is around the Waita Reservoir, and the second half of the course has some knockout views. Three of the eight zips are over 1,000 feet with the final one—where I got up to 48 MPH—an impressive 2,150 feet long, not 2,500 feet as mentioned on their

website. (Most zipline companies seem to exaggerate their length of their cable—must be a guy thing.) They'll take up to 12 people, and they'll even let you hang upside-down if you're so inclined. There's about a mile of hiking during the tour, and you should bring water since they are kind of skimpy with it. $149, includes snacks. Minimum age is 7 and maximum weight is 280 pounds.

Outfitters Kaua'i (742-9667), our second favorite, has a nine-zip tour on Kipu Ranch near Lihu'e for $158, which includes lunch. The longest is 1,800 feet and has two lines so couples can race each other or snap each other's picture during the zip (to a degree, because the bigger they are, the faster they fall). The zips are varied and fun, and the company does a good job. One thing we didn't like is that some of the lines are pendulum style, meaning you come to an anticlimactic stop rather than a more dramatic landing. Afterward, they take you to a swimming hole and waterfall, but see our comments on page 187 before swimming there. 275-pound weight limit.

Princeville Ranch Adventures (826-7669) has nine lines. Most are under 500 feet, which is too short. The last three are the best. There's not much hiking except on both sides of the last and longest line, King Kong. At 1,200 feet long, I got up to 30 MPH—not bad. Their scenery isn't as nice as the others, but they have a decent swimming hole with small waterfall, and their lunch is probably the best of the bunch. (Swimming at a waterfall and lunch in addition to the zipping for $159. Zipping only is $139.) We've had issues with guides who were *too cool for school* previously, but they've gotten better lately. You'll need to weigh between 75 and 280 pounds.

Kaua'i Backcountry Adventures (245-2506) has seven lines, the longest of which is 950 feet. But they're all over the same valley, and they seem so preoccupied with "safety" that it takes some of the fun out of it. It's $125, which includes snacks and swimming in a stream. You'll need to weigh between 100 and 250 pounds. Tours are Monday through Friday only.

In the arms race to build faster, longer, and more thrilling ziplines, **Skyline Eco-Adventures** (518-2579) in Po'ipu lags behind the competition. The tour guides do their best to keep things fun on this eight-zip course with a distant ocean view, but you should hope that some of your group only paid for the five-zip option—fewer people means less waiting between rides. Speeds are tame, with most lines barely hitting 25 mph, if that. (We topped out at 30 mph on the seventh zip.) This is a no-frills experience; we were offered water from a jug at two drinking stations, and if you want to borrow a hip pack to store your stuff, you'll have to ask. Weight range is 80–260

pounds $140 for the eight-line zip course; $110 for the five line.

Just Live (482-1295). Let's start with the positive. They are friendly folks who started the company to bring team building and life skills to local youths, schools and community groups, only later expanding to the visitor market. Gotta admire their mission. But you're here to zipline, and compared to their competition, they come in last because of their location. In short, you spend almost all of your time in a few acres of Cook Island pine trees without many views. The average length is just 300 feet, and you go from tree to tree. If your group is full, it's pretty crowded up on their tree platforms. They are the cheapest at $79 for three zips and two bridges. No lunch and no swimming. For $149 you do three zips, two bridges, rock wall climbing, a little rappelling and get to go on their 60-foot swing, which is a scream (literally). In Puhi. You'll need to weigh between 70 and 250 pounds and have lived 9 years or more.

Ziplining can bring a new perspective on how you view the world.

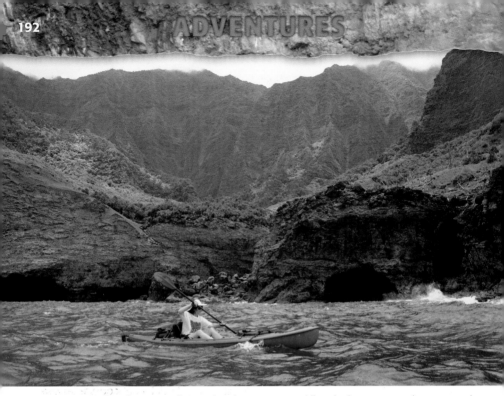

OK, so 16 miles along Na Pali Coast is a long way to paddle, whether over one day or several. But the wind, current and luscious scenery help propel you along.

The activities described below are for the serious adventurer. They can be experiences of a lifetime. We are assuming that if you consider any of them that you are a person of sound judgment, capable of assessing risks. All adventures carry risks of one kind or another. Our descriptions below do not attempt to convey all risks associated with an activity. These activities are not for everyone. Good preparation is essential. In the end, it comes down to your own good judgment.

NA PALI KAYAK TRIP

If you really want adventure, consider a kayak trip down the Na Pali Coast. June through August are normally the only months where ocean conditions permit kayak transit. Kayakers put in at Keʻe Beach on the north shore, exiting at Polihale Beach on the west shore, a total of 16 miles. Along the way you'll encounter incomparable beauty, innumerable waterfalls and sea caves, pristine aquamarine seas, turtles, flying fish and possibly dolphins.

If you're doing this as a maverick trip (below), at night you can camp on beautiful beaches, sleeping to the sound of the surf. The experience will stay with you for a lifetime.

There are two ways to do this trip—either on a guided tour or on your own. Guided tours do the entire trip in one day, offering a more structured—though less leisurely—way to see the coast. These trips, usually led by experienced guides, offer the *relative* safety of an expert. The drawbacks to this method are a lack of independent movement, a more brisk paddling pace (it can be *tough* to do in one day) and the lack of an opportunity to camp. Na Pali Kayak (826-6900), Kayak Kaua'i (826-9844) and Outfitters Kaua'i (742-9667). Of the three, we like Kayak Kaua'i for their deeper expertise. Expect to pay around $240. They bring the gear, food and know-how; you bring the muscles.

If you want twice as much cost and hassle but *ten times* the gratification, you can do a maverick trip. Na Pali Kayak and Kayak Kaua'i will give you a personal guide who will travel with you to Kalalau and then make a judgment call as to whether you're up to continuing on your own. You'll need a valid camping permit *with a kayak landing stamp* for Kalalau or Miloli'i before even applying for this service. See page 196 for info on permits, and expect to pay between $155 and $400.

Doing it on your own allows *you* to set the pace and the schedule. You go when you like, how you like, where you like and at the speed you like. You can rent a two-person kayak, if you desire. Consideration of this method necessitates a dispassionate evaluation of your skills, abilities, strengths and weaknesses. Although you don't need to be an expert kayaker, it doesn't hurt to have experience. Though we try to do this trip every year, when we *first* did it on our own, our only kayaking experience had been a 3-hour trip up the Wailua River. On that first trip we experienced ideal conditions, which don't always occur, even during the summer. Please bear in mind that this trip is not for everyone. The Na Pali Coast is wild and unpredictable, and you are exposing yourself to the ocean's caprice. The usually calm June through August seas can become difficult with surprising suddenness. Most of the Na Pali boat companies can tell you stories about kayakers who had to be rescued when they got in over their heads (so to speak).

Sunset from the caves of Kalalau is your rich reward for a morning's paddle.

If you decide to do it on your own, here are a few things to keep in mind:

- Learn as much as you can about kayaking. (*Paddling Hawai'i* by Audrey Sutherland was our main reference when we made the first trip.) Proper paddling and loading techniques are *vital*.

- In addition to other essentials, make sure you bring water-resistant sunscreen, a hat, sunglasses, Chapstick and possibly Dramamine.

- Apply for camping permits for Na Pali *well in advance* (as much as 6–12 months). Only permits valid from May through September include kayak landings.

- Think through your food requirements. (You *won't* be living off the land.)

- Any water source you utilize along the way will require water treatment pills to avoid possible contraction of leptospirosis. Water filters that don't use chemicals are not considered reliable due to the corkscrew shape of the leptospirosis bacterium. (We've used and trusted Sawyer filters and First Need XLE Elites, which purifies down to 0.1 micron, but you have to decide for yourself if it's good enough.) Fresh water is present at the following beaches along the route: Ke'e, Hanakapi'ai, Kalalau, Honopu, Miloli'i and Polihale, as well as some waterfalls that fall right into the ocean.

- Typical June through August conditions mean that the wind and currents are both pushing you in the direction you want to go, but *typical* doesn't mean *always*. Monitor ocean conditions by calling the National Weather Service (245-6001).

- Paddling in the early morning usually offers the calmest seas (sometimes like glass, if you're lucky) and easier launchings.

- Unless you spring for pick-up service, you'll have to rent an extra car for a couple days and leave one at Ke'e Beach and one at Polihale.

Here's some of what you can expect...

From Ke'e, Hanakapi'ai Beach is slightly over a mile. With campgrounds and a freshwater stream, Hanakapi'ai is a favorite place for hikers to camp, but it's too soon for kayakers. Past Hanakapi'ai, you will start to see caves and waterfalls straight out of your dreams. Some of the caves are horseshoe-shaped, with separate entrances and exits. Explore 'em all if conditions are safe.

Keep an eye out for dolphins and turtles, which become more plentiful as you get farther down the coast. At Kalalau, you have paddled 6 miles. If you're on your own, this is a good place to camp with half a mile of sand, fresh water and portable toilets. We like to pitch our tents in the caves (hoping rocks won't fall on us) at the far end of the beach, and walk a few minutes to a waterfall to shower. Kalalau is as far as hikers can go, so from here on you are in exclusive company.

Less than a mile past Kalalau is Honopu Beach. Landing crafts of all types, including *surfboards,* are prohibited. The only legal way to visit Honopu Beach is to swim there from Kalalau Beach (which can be hazardous if there's surf), or you can anchor your craft offshore and swim in (which can also be hazardous).

In all the Hawaiian Islands, and perhaps in all the world, you'll never find a more glorious, moving and mystical beach. Unspoiled Honopu is only accessible by sea. It is actually two beaches, separated by a gigantic arch carved into Na Pali by Mother Nature's furious waves. During the summertime when the pounding Na Pali surf weakens, Honopu is reclaimed from the sea. As you approach by kayak, you're left speechless by the sheer majesty of what unfolds before you. *Vertical* walls 1,200 feet high are the first characteristics you see from the sea. If you're lucky enough to visit here, the giant arch draws you toward it like a magnet. As you approach it, you can just make out the cascading waterfall around the bend. This is no mere trickle. This immense cataract can knock you down with its force. The stream continues through the arch and out to sea, providing a superb way to rinse off the saltwater. The southern beach of Honopu actually makes a better kayak landing than its northern counterpart, but the northern beach is the most dramatic, and its unfolding vista will surely stay with you forever.

Past Honopu, listen for goats. Although considered pests by island officials, it's charming to hear them from your position on the water. At 9 miles you come to a pair of reefs fringing a beach called Nu'alolo Kai. The waters inside the reef offer good snorkeling during calm seas (and you wouldn't be here if the seas weren't calm, right?). From your kayak, when the two signs onshore are aligned, you're heading toward the deeper channel and to shore.

In times past, the Hawaiians mostly lived in the hanging valley above the beach. Access required scaling the vertical wall (actually, it's worse than vertical; it leans outward!) up a ladder and along a "trail" in the cliff, which was often nothing more than cubbyholes for your feet. Worse yet was a large rock in the "trail" that was very difficult to get around. The Hawaiians even had a name for this dangerously placed, immovable rock. They called it "fat man's misery."

Next, Miloli'i is 11 miles into your journey. Camping and fresh water make Miloli'i an inviting respite. There is a reef all along the beach and the same system to mark the channel as at Nu'alolo. You need a permit to camp at Miloli'i.

After Miloli'i, you will see a radio transmitter on top of a mountain belonging to Pacific Missile Range Facility. From the radar transmitter (helicopter pilots avoid getting too close to it, claiming they can feel their *da kines* cook), it's only 3 miles to Polihale. After your surf landing there, you can look forward to dragging your kayak through 500 feet of sand in searing heat, a task that would make a Himalayan Sherpa weep. (Good thing you were smart enough to spring for pick-up service from your kayak company.)

Congratulations—you have now joined an elite club of adventurers who have braved the Na Pali coast. A not-so-quick shower at Polihale Beach, and you are ready to dance all night. Or maybe not.

An open-ceiling cave along Na Pali is one of the many places to poke your kayak into during your voyage.

THE KALALAU TRAIL

So you don't like paddling or the surf is raging. You can still see Na Pali. Because the ultimate hike is also the most famous hike in all Hawai'i—11 miles of switchbacks, hills and beautiful scenery. See map below. Much of the trail is narrow and not without hazards—hiking boots or at least closed-toe trail shoes are recommended. The trail calls for several stream crossings (some extra water shoes are handy for this). Don't cross if the water is too high. Don't go if overnight hikes are a problem. To get the proper permits, contact: Hawai'i DLNR, State Parks in Lihu'e at 274-3444. (Our website has a link to a page where permit applications can be filled out online.)

Our map is an accurate, computer-generated, shaded relief map drawn at a 45-degree angle to give you a perspective of when and how much climbing is involved—altogether about 5,000 feet round trip.

The first 2 miles of the trail leads to Hanakapi'ai Beach (sandy in the summer, bouldery in the winter). There are plenty of slippery and muddy sections, and the second mile is steep downhill (and tough coming back up). It's tricky in spots if you're a beginner hiker, but it's worth it. The views along the coast are exceptional. Hanakapi'ai is a beautiful but treacherous beach to swim, and it takes most people 1.5–2 hours to hike each way. From here, there is a fairly tough 1.8-mile side trail upstream to Hanakapi'ai Falls, one of the more spectacular falls and pools on the north shore. There are lots of false trails, and it's easy to miss some of the river crossings, but you're in a valley, so you shouldn't stray more than a couple hundred feet from the stream. Many people like to reward themselves by swimming in the pool under the falls. Watch out for falling rocks.

This is as far as you can go *without* a permit. The authorities assume anyone going past Hanakapi'ai will be camping. If this is your plan, and you have your state camping permit, keep going. Four miles ahead at Hanakoa, you have the choice of either camping, continuing to Kalalau or taking the half-mile side trip to Hanakoa Falls, which is even lovelier than Hanakapi'ai. You'll cross the Hanakoa Stream and take a left at the trail near a shelter. After 50 yards take

Indicates Foot Trails
3 Miles into Trail
⚑ Campsite

Kalalau Trail

Hanakapi'ai Falls

22°11.200
159°36.913
Hanakoa Falls

Half-mile side trip to Hanakoa Falls

Nearly 2-mile side trip to Hanakapi'ai Falls

Hanakapi'ai Valley

Limahuli Stream

22°13.224
159°34.984
End of the Road

Kalalau Trail

Ke'e Beach

Hanakapi'ai Beach

Ho'olulu Sea Cave

Waiahuakua Sea Cave

Kalalau Trail

© 2017 Wizard Publications, Inc.

So you'll know what's involved on this trail, the vantage point of this map is looking at the trail offshore from the air.

Wild, raw and unforgettable—the Kalalau Trail.

the left fork for 15 minutes. Watch for falling rocks at the falls. If you've come as far as Hanakoa, go see the falls. It's worth the walk.

Back on the trail, your toughest stretch is the last. From here to Kalalau Beach you'll find lots of switchbacks and a narrow trail at times. The stretch 7–8 miles into the trail has a couple of dicey spots,

but they're not as bad as they used to be. The views are stunning. Persevere and you will be richly rewarded. Wow! This is the glorious valley you see from the top of Waimea Canyon Drive at the Kalalau Lookout. The beach, the valley and the isolation all make Kalalau a magical place. There is a 2-mile trail inland, which takes you to "Big Pool," a large natural pool in the stream.

Have you ever read *Koʻolau the Leper* by Jack London? It's based on the true story of Koʻolau, who fled to Kalalau in the 1880s after authorities refused to let his wife accompany him to the Kalaupapa leper settlement on Molokaʻi. On July 2, 1893, a ship carrying 12 police, 14 soldiers, the sheriff, many rifles and a howitzer came ashore to capture Koolau and the other lepers who had joined him. After Koʻolau shot two of the soldiers dead and a third accidentally shot himself in the head (oops), the authorities decided to leave Koolau alone. He died in Kalalau in 1896 from his affliction.

As you stand on the beach at Kalalau, it's amazing to think that the entire valley

Kalalau Lookout

Kalalau Valley

550

Map continued on page 147

22°09.903
159°38.079
Big Pool

Honopu Valley

22°10.289
159°39.572
Falls

10

Kalalau Beach

Caves

Honopu Beach
& Honopu Arch

Open Ceiling Cave

E S
N W

was once populated. It was only in 1919 that this isolated valley was finally abandoned as people sought the life available to them in Lihu'e and other towns.

This is as far as you can go. A half mile farther down the coast is the most beautiful beach in all the islands, maybe in all the Pacific—Honopu Beach. There is none finer. Period. The only legal way to visit the beach is to swim there. If you do this, beware that the current is against you coming back. Only during calm seas, only with fins and only if you're a strong swimmer. In late summer Kalalau Beach snakes its way closer to Honopu, and people walk on the rocks and sand most of the way. Beware of unexpectedly large waves if you do this. For more information on Honopu, see NA PALI KAYAK TRIP above.

Kalalau has composting toilets. The waterfall provides fresh water, which should be treated before drinking as should your en route sources at Hanakapi'ai and Hanakoa streams. In fact, *all* fresh water in nature should be treated to avoid possible bacteriological contamination from animals or people polluting the stream.

AIRPLANE TRAIL

Physically, this is the least demanding of the Na Pali Coast ridge hikes. Running down the southwest rim of the Kalalau Valley, the trail is less than a mile (one-way) and only takes about 45 minutes to get to the end, where you'll get an awesome view of the beach and ocean 3,585 feet below. But don't let that fool you—we put it in the ADVENTURES chapter for a reason.

This unofficial trail is well-defined but not maintained. It's narrow, much of it runs along a cliff, and it's steep. (The Hawaiian name is Kalepa Ridge, but most people call it the Airplane Trail, presumably because one wrong step and you'll be flying.) On top of that, it's often wet thanks to frequent cloud cover rolling in and out of the valley. Steep and slippery are a bad combination when you are hiking close to the edge of a several-hundred-foot drop. But it's also magical when it is filled with clouds, then watching them fade away, revealing the splendor of Kalalau. And seeing the waterfalls across the valley, and knowing that there is no surface source to them—they are fed by a massive spring coming out of the mountain.

Before choosing to attempt this trail, take a realistic assessment of how experienced a hiker you are. Is there a mountain goat in your family lineage? Don't assume that just because this is an adventure that the view is better. Each of the ridge hikes are amazing and incredible in different ways. The view at Nu'alolo is the most expansive; you can see all the way up the Na Pali. Sharply-eroded Awa'awapuhi is the most dramatic. Honopu (all three on page 147), opposite a massive cliff face, is the most impressive. This one, Kalepa Ridge, with its birds-eye view of lush green Kalalau, is the most mystical. So no matter which you pick, you're not missing out.

The trail starts at the Kalalau Lookout near mile marker 18 of Waimea Canyon Road (Highway 550). There is a short fence with a gate to the left. The trail is unmarked, but it's fairly obvious once you walk over—just follow the fence and then head down toward the ocean. If it isn't dry, pick a different hike. The beginning stretch is the steepest—you'll lose 190 feet in the first tenth of a mile. (Total elevation loss is 660 feet.) The remainder of the trail is easier going.

At 0.9 miles, you'll come to a slight rise leading to a small flat patch of dirt that is perched above magnificent green spires. Stop here and think about the passengers in the tour helicopters flying *beneath* you—while they zoom past, you can take time to savor the view. Return the same way you came. (As if you had any choice.)

MAKALEHA HIKE

This hike is in the ADVENTURES chapter because it is only for the advanced hiker. The trail goes along a beautiful stream, through a bamboo grove and offers lush scenery. There are a number of places along the way to bathe in the stream, which can be deep in spots. Past the end of the trail are waterfalls just for you. The problem is that the trail is a trail-of-use and is not officially maintained. As a result, it is splendid in some parts, wretched in others. Some big steps up and down and mud spots keep it interesting. You will have to walk in the stream in some places, so we usually bring tabis (fuzzy mittens for your feet that work well on slippery rocks). Even without the waterfalls, you will get a real Indiana Jones feel for this part of God's country.

The trail starts at the end of Kahuna Road in northern Kapa'a. (See top of map on page 60 to get there.) From here, you park and walk past the water tank to the trail. At one point, the trail on the right (northern) bank veers away to a water tunnel. Don't go there, but instead cross the main stream at the remains of an old concrete dam. Follow the trail close to the stream as much as possible. From here, enter the bamboo grove. You'll see three large trees; behind the one on the far right is a trail that ascends into the bamboo, skirts the cliff edge and gives some opportunities (take the second one) to return to the river below. Remember that place for your return hike. From

Hike through bamboo, cross the stream several times, step in mud, walk on wet rocks. All this just to marvel at Makaleha. It works for our hiker friend pictured here.

here, it can be muddy if it's been raining (and it probably has been). This is the real Kaua'i—lush, wet and beautiful.

When the bamboo ends, you have a choice of walking on the trail (which will be muddy and thorny and fern-filled), or walk in the stream on the rocks. (Many will find rock-hopping in the stream *the whole way* their best solution.) At one point the trail dumps into the stream, and you'll have to cross it onto an island in the river. Walk the length of the island, cross the stream to the left, and pick up the trail again. Follow it until you come to some large boulders that form a wall. Go over the wall and cross the stream. The trail gets difficult from here. Look for machete marks in the annoying hau trees that cross the trail, sometimes forming a jungle gym of limbs. You should always be able to hear the stream, but if you get into trouble, there probably won't be

anyone coming along to help. Bring mosquito repellent or don't go. Footwear should include hiking sandals or boots and tabis (preferable) for stream walking. Bring water. You'll have to walk in the stream the last 50 yards before you come to a fork (where three streams converge at a stunning vista). A waterfall is up the left-most stream. *If you're feeling lucky,* a better waterfall is 20–30 minutes of rock-hopping to the right. It's an easier walk in a tall, narrow canyon, and the falls are two beautiful tiers with good swimming at the base. But that narrowness opens you up to the possibility of getting hammered by falling rocks, if one lets loose above you. Regardless, allow ample time to get back. In all, it's only 1.5 miles each way, but the going is pretty slow in many spots, and it *can* take much of the day.

HONOPU RIDGE TO A DROP-DEAD VIEW

Imagine a trail that cuts through forest, ventures down a ridge and culminates in one of the most inspirational views on the island. For two decades that's exactly what you had to do...*imagine* it. Back in 1982 one of Kaua'i's most delicious trails was damaged by a hurricane. State Parks folks, ever grumbling about budgets, decided not to put in the effort to reopen it. Over the course of more than two decades it became unrecognizable. But thanks to a few unsung volunteers, today Honopu Trail is available to ambitious hikers. Why ambitious? Because, although it's only just over 2 miles each way, much of the trail is still overgrown (largely due to disuse) making portions unpleasant, and there's opportunity to wander off the correct path if you're not careful. Most of the trail is obvious, but there are a few hunter trails (especially at the beginning) that might lead you astray. (See maps on pages 147 and 142.)

Makaleha Hike

Waterfall

Waterfall

22°06.430
159°23.925

Intermittent Stream

Trail indistinguishable from here—walk in the stream to waterfall.

Island
22°06.209
159°23.574

Makaleha Stream

One mile into hike

Water Tunnel

Bamboo Grove starts here

W N S E

Water Tank

End of Kahuna Rd

Map continued on page 60

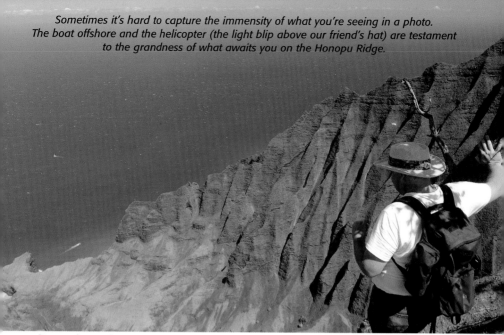

Located on the west side, you take Hwy 50 to Waimea Canyon Drive (550). At 0.4 miles past mile marker 17 (not far from the end of the road at Kalalau Valley) there's a turnout on the curve about 100 feet past a telephone pole. Park there, and the unmarked trail a short way up the hill heads left toward the coast. After just 120 yards you come to your first confusing intersection. The trail to the left is the correct path. (Don't go straight.) At 0.2 miles the trail comes to a T intersection at a tree whose branches all point to the right. Turn right. (The incorrect faint left leads down to a stream bed.) From here you'll *really* be grateful for long pants, because the native Pacific false staghorn ferns tend to claw at your legs. (Jeans can feel heavy—we've become fond of light pants with zip-off legs.)

It's mostly the first half mile that has the confusing intersections. Tips to staying on the correct trail include following the most beaten path, looking for logs or other barriers placed to block side trails and staying on the trail that has the most tags (ribbons) on trees. The easiest thing is to download our smartphone app and use the GPS map feature, rather than wasting time navigating a crisscrossing maze of trails.

Soon most of your 1,000 feet of elevation loss will occur. (You actually climbed a bit until now.) Always stay on the most worn path. About 1 mile into the trail (it will seem like more) you'll be on a wide ridge that will eventually get narrow enough to see Honopu on one side and Awa'awapuhi on the other. Eventually the trail comes to a glorious lookout on a dirt bluff. The vista into Honopu Valley is so magnificent that it defies description. The entire heavenly valley is before you. Honopu Beach and the Pacific are to your left 3,000 feet below. The scene is so intense that it literally looks unreal. If clouds are in the valley, wait a while. They tend to come and go. The trail continues another 15 minutes, terminating at a point where the ridge takes a drop down to a razorback spine (which you *don't* want to visit). From the end you're treated to a tasty view of Na Pali coast.

While on the trail, if you take a wrong turn, keep track of where you've been and backtrack. Nothing's worse than being lost in the forest. Our first time in (when the trail was more vague than it is now) we made two wrong turns, realized our mistakes, and returned to the intersection to find the right way. Also, make sure you're back at your car *at least* 1.5 hours before sunset. It will take most people 1.5–2.5 hours each way, and the trip back up is fairly strenuous. Bring gobs of water down, suck 'em up at the overlook, and bring only what you need back up. The trail has a few areas where there's opportunity to fall or twist an ankle. One short stretch is on the side of a dirt hill that may make some nervous. This hike is in the ADVENTURES chapter because of the poor trail conditions in a few scattered areas and because of the potential to get off the trail. Coming back, the quarter-mile closest to your car seems to present new opportunities to wander off the same trail you already took on the way down.

RAPPEL OFF A 60-FOOT WATERFALL

In Hawai'i, as elsewhere, ziplining has really taken off. But what if you want a *real* rush? That's where rappelling comes in. Da Life Outdoors (246-6333) has two waterfalls in Lihu'e that you'll get to rappel down. Think about it: You're at the top, you lean back and literally walk backwards down a waterfall. First a 30-footer. Then the big dog—a 60-foot falls that involves walking as well as sliding down. I know what you're thinking: *What if I fall?* They have all the safety gear as well as a fireman's belay at the bottom. That means they will give you the freedom to do it by yourself (rather than completely mothering you), but all it takes is a gentle tug on your rope from the other guy *at the bottom* to increase the friction and stop you from falling. Which gives you the best of both worlds. Book in advance.

They'll lend you felt-bottomed shoes (tabis) to keep from slipping, give you lots of training and practice on a wall before heading out to the wilderness. The guides are knowledgeable and genuine. The whole experience takes about 4 hours and involves a little hiking and swimming. Lunch is included. $179.

4WD MILOLI'I RIDGE ROAD

The southern, dryer part of Na Pali is defined by a series of ridges. The map on page 86 shows roads such as Ka-uhao and Ka'aweiki that wind their way along the ridges to the edge of Na Pali. Unfortunately, these are hunter roads, always closed during the week, and you're supposed to get a hunting permit to drive on them on weekends. But Miloli'i Ridge Road (see same map) is open all week long and, if you have a 4WD and it's not raining, you can probably drive to the end where you'll get a beautiful view of this part of Na Pali. Once at the road's end, look for a trail to the left that goes around and up a hill. Intrepid hikers might want to brave the ridge as far as their nerve takes them. (The ridge ends rather conclusively—right above Miloli'i Beach, a dramatic 1,400 feet below you.)

Here's the deal: The road is maintained by State Parks, which means it may be rutted, nasty, impassible or even closed if they feel like it. Or it might be fine. Either way, when you get to some picnic tables (shown on the map), you've come to the last part you should consider driving if it's *been* raining or you *think* it will. Because after that the road gets steeper, and you might have problems returning if it's too slippery. All told it's just over 5 miles of 4WD each way. You access Miloli'i Ridge Road 0.3 miles into the paved Makaha Ridge Road between mile markers 13 and 14 on Hwy 550 (Waimea Canyon Drive).

VISIT THE SUMMIT OF WAI'ALE'ALE

In every edition we've ever had of *Ultimate Kaua'i Guidebook*, we've always had to warn adventurous readers that it

He said, "Hey, babe. Take a walk on the wild side..."

wasn't possible to hike to the summit of the highest point on the island, one of the wettest spots on earth. All of that changed with the construction of a conservation fence. You see, until that fence was built, bagging the summit meant walking through miles of unnegotiable swamp in usually horrid conditions. Getting lost was almost assured, even with a GPS. But recent efforts to build a pig fence around the summit area also created an opportunity. Now, once you find the fence, getting lost is less of an option.

We need to stress, however, that this is still an *incredibly* taxing effort. We're talking a 20-mile round trip, nearly all of it above the 4,000-foot level, drilling your way into a wet, soggy, inhospitable world that will likely be ensconced in rain, wind and clouds. This could potentially take two days (though we know some über-hard

core elites who can do it in one day), and odds are the only photos you get will be from a rain-spotted lens of a mostly treeless landscape. Rescues would be very difficult because you'll probably be in the clouds, and helicopters can't land in a cloud. Most people should simply turn the page at this point. Hopeless idiots (of whom I include myself) should read on.

OK, we gotta start by saying you need to download our smartphone app. Not trying to pressure you into buying more Wizard products, but without the app, there's simply no easy way for us to describe where to find the arrow log. (More on that later.) And besides, you're gonna want to *know* if you're still on the trail to the fence, and the app is the only way.

You'll start by using your 4WD to get to the trailhead of the Mohihi-Waiʻalae Trail in Kokeʻe. (See page 148 for directions

From the summit of Waiʻaleʻale, the Wailua River is more than a half mile below your feet.

and info on that trail.) The Sugi Grove campground near the trailhead is a good option for starting this hike as early as you should (before sunrise).

The mile markers end before you are 4 miles into the trail, at which point the trail descends rapidly into a drainage. The footing getting down can be slippery if it's been raining (and it *has* been), and there are times you should face the mountain and actually climb down the trail. At the bottom you will find a river with a small waterfall and large boulders that make for a decent pit stop, especially before climbing back up on the way out. The trail is directly across on the east bank from where it ends on the west bank, and the boulders are aligned in such a way to make crossing easy.

Once on the other side of the stream, you head back uphill past a small cabin/shack used by hunters. It is from here that the trail gets harder to follow. The main trail *should be* flagged, and you should not go more than 5 minutes without seeing a flag marking the way. Again, we're assuming you have our smartphone app, because it's impossible to describe the entire trail, and parts are difficult and tricky.

At 5.5 miles, keep an eye out for an easy-to-miss arrow carved into a log on the ground, pointing the direction from which you came. That log will mark the spot where you will split from the main trail. Step over the log and slightly left. You'll see a faint trail and possibly some flagging tape. This is the trail you're looking for. It can be difficult to make out in places.

Once on the trail past the arrow log, you want to continue the same technique you have been perfecting over the last mile and half—look for the flagging tape, and always take the uphill path when applicable. Use the app to make sure you're on the trail. The terrain will be generally the same as what you have been seeing with some increased swampiness and the need to use whatever logs or roots you see to stay on solid ground.

About 0.75 miles along this path, trees begin to become more widely spaced, and you'll notice more shrub-like plants. You will suddenly burst out into open, Alakaʻi Swamp land with the hog-wire fence right in front of you. The change in scenery is very dramatic and exciting, giving the promise of the extreme landscape ahead. This is a good place to clean your shoes and clothing of any alien hitchhikers to avoid tracking them any farther.

When you approach the fence, turn right and follow it to its end. It is approximately 3 miles of a circuitous fence line over varied terrain until you reach your ultimate goal. You won't find anything more difficult than you have already encountered, but there will be some steep climbs to keep you on the ridge tops and heading toward the summit. There is always the fence itself to help keep your balance in some areas. You're probably cold. You're *certainly* wet. A great, potential spot to wait through the night *might* be found within a quarter mile of your encounter with the fence. It is the old staging area for construction of the fence, and it offers a flat area with minimally squishy ground. This area allows you to have a better idea of whether you will have a clear day at the summit when the morning comes. Early mornings are your best chance of seeing the summit cloudless.

The summit of Waiʻaleʻale is an otherworldly place. Other than a few clumps of sickly looking 6- to 10-foot trees, there is nothing over a foot tall for more than a mile in any direction. Not even the ubiquitous ferns are genetically programmed to deal with so much rain and cloud cover. So the dominant features carpeting the ground are moss, lichen and short grasses. The 3,000-foot cliffs plunging into the crater define the eastern portion, which is so shear, you can literally walk up to it and look nearly straight down to the crater over a half mile beneath your feet.

Walking around is a bit awkward. The sponge-like ground is constantly threatening to steal your shoes. It takes about 2 hours just to go from one end of the summit to the other. No mosquitoes live up here, but huge dragonflies are everywhere. Only a handful of birds can be heard, some of them endemic—found nowhere else in the world except on this watery mountaintop.

Please be mindful of the cultural sacredness of this spot, and make sure you bring everything out that you take in. Be careful not to disturb the remains of the heiau in any way.

Return the way you came. (Those five words…Easy to type, a buggah to do.)

SECRET TUNNEL TO THE NORTH SHORE

Imagine that you're in an east shore valley. You come upon a tunnel that's a *mile* long. From the moment you enter, you can see the light at the other end. When you emerge, you're in the virtually inaccessible back of the north shore's Hanalei Valley, surrounded by nearly vertical mountains, a perfect river and no people. Aside from a few hunters, almost no one on Kaua'i had even *heard* of this tunnel until we revealed it. Those who had heard of it considered it one of those urban legends, a myth. Well, it's no myth.

In the 1920s a sugar company was seriously coveting the abundant water flowing out the Hanalei River. They needed the water for their east shore sugar. So for $300,000 they cut this tunnel and diverted 28 million gallons of water a day under the mountain and into

a series of ditches to quench their thirsty crops. But times change. As sugar production dwindled on the east shore, they found that they no longer needed the north shore's water. So, years ago, they stopped diverting the water and abandoned the dam. The flume to divert the water is no longer there. They couldn't divert water into this tunnel even if they wanted to without doing major reconstruction on the dam. But the tunnel, blasted out of solid rock, remains.

Getting there will be a sloppy affair. It involves walking 2.5 miles along a trail through muddy conditions. (It rains about 160 inches annually here, spread fairly evenly throughout the year.) The footing, terrain, overgrowth, washed-out trail sections and ferns hiding pockets of nothingness make it one of the harder 2.5 mile stretches you'll find in Hawai'i. Bring a low-profile pack to reduce snagging vegetation during the many incidences of ducking under brush.

A Few Basics

Driving to the trailhead means taking a dirt road (see map). A regular car can go part of the way, but it's hard to say how far. There's an old truism—*What's the difference between a 2WD rental car and a 4WD SUV? A 2WD rental car can go anywhere!* Meaning, it depends on how much you're willing to punish it. This road is sporadically improved, and it depends on your timing. But for our purposes, 4WD is the way to go here. See directions to the Jungle Hike on page 156, and stop *just before* the first gate. Accept from the get-go that there's *no* way to keep your feet dry. Spiked tabis (described on page 139) work best, and you might find them at Discount Variety in Koloa or Walmart. The down side is that your feet will feel a bit tender when you're done. Long pants are also recommended. Ferns have a habit of sticking out in the trail, scratching at your legs. Jeans are OK, but they get heavy and stick to your legs, making it harder. Lighter pants are preferred. Look for delicious red thimbleberries along the way. (The redder, the better.) Bring a flashlight/headlamp (or two) for the tunnel. Also bring water and snacks.

The trail to the tunnel is a hunters' trail, and it's *always* muddy. The first 100 yards are very sloppy with a permanent puddle near the place where you park. Several short stretches are on uneven terrain, and caution needs to be taken. In the first 5 minutes you'll have to cross the Wailua River twice. *Usually* it's done by hopping across a couple of rocks. If it's too deep and you aren't comfortable, don't go. If it's been raining a lot, don't go. During very heavy rains you may find that the river isn't crossable coming back, presenting you with a dilemma. Just after the first crossing, go diagonally upstream about 150 feet and look for a trail in the bamboo thicket. (It's not the trail going straight *ahead* from the river). Bamboo is the best natural material there is for walking sticks, and it's a good idea to have one on this hike. (It makes a good spider stick in case there are webs across the trail.) Cut it so that a knuckle is near the bottom, acting as a natural stopper, preventing dirt or mud from filling the hollow tube. Shortly after the bamboo thicket the trail becomes more vague—keep an eye out for where it bears right.

The trail is intermittently "paved" with 'ohi'a tree logs looking like railroad ties from long ago. Avoid false trails. Remember, you'll never go more than 15 minutes without seeing the 'ohi'a logs. (Hunters— and their dogs—who use the trail mostly on weekends and Mondays often put their own tags on trees, and following them might help, or they might take you off the main trail.) You've gone almost a mile

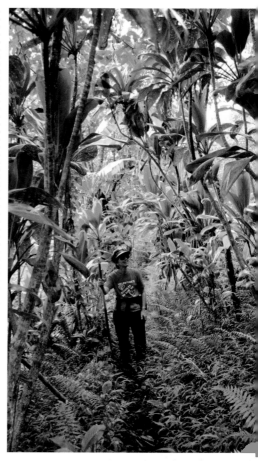

A hiker marvels at the richness of Kaua'i, which is ever-present on this trek.

when you see your first old, abandoned wooden power pole. Just after this you come to a flat muddy area and a trail to the left. We've walked through the flat part and sunk 3 feet into a bog. You'll cross a couple of smaller streams (a foot wide) and a slightly larger stream.

After 1.5 hours or so, when the trail encounters a large stream again, it seems to end. This is where people get lost. It actually veers slightly left, away from the stream and over some rocks. Pick your way over the boulders, staying on the left

Tunnel & Jungle Hikes

5243'
Waiʻaleʻale Rain Gauge, 4664'
World's Wettest Spot

Waiʻaleʻale Crater

Hanalei Valley

Tunnel Entrance
22°05.473
159°28.410

4300'

Tunnel Openings

Beautiful Waterfall

Blue Hole
22°03.977
159°28.971

1540'

Old Dam

Jungle Hike on page 156

Wailua River

Tunnel Entrance
22°04.850
159°27.688

1100'

1.8

Tunnel
Small Waterfall

2295'

Tunnel

1200'

1.3
Gates

830'

Trail to Tunnel
(2.5 miles) 1000'

1200'

Skinny plank bridge

.95

.75

0.15

Set odometer to zero here. It's 2.7 miles from the Arboretum.

0.0

Wailua River

Gate

Powerline Trail

Electrical Substation

Keahua Arboretum

600'

Kuilau Ridge Trail

Wailua Forestry Management Road is simply an extension of Kuamoʻo Road (580) in Wailua. To get here, turn onto Kuamoʻo from the highway in south Wailua (at Coco Palms) and continue for 7 miles to the Arboretum.

.... Tunnel
〰 Trail
〰 Dirt Road
1000' Elevation
0 ____ 1/2 MILE

Map is shown at an angle to give you a perspective of the mountains.

W
S · N
E

Map continued on page 60

© 2017 Wizard Publications, Inc.

side of the bank, and look for muddy stains on the rocks—they will lead you to the trail in the tall grass ahead. It crosses the stream where the stream makes a right turn. Once you cross, pick up the trail *directly* on the other side, and it's not far before you walk on a skinny plank bridge over a ditch. The trail goes to the left (and uphill) to the gauging station and tunnel. You'll notice a tunnel to the left and a little farther on, one to the right. You want the long one on the right (the left side is shorter and doesn't lead to anything). It takes us 2–3 hours *to* the first tunnel, and about 45 minutes *in* the tunnel. You'll gain about 600 feet with all the ups and downs.

Once in the tunnel, you'll notice that there's water standing in it. That's from the small amount of water that drips from the ceiling. It's just the right amount to keep about 4–8 inches of water fresh. The tunnel is about 6 feet wide and 7–10 feet high with an occasional need for a head duck on the straight portion. The bottom is flat and lined with small rocks, which makes for fairly straightforward walking. The tunnel reverberates with the ever-constant sound of the splashing of your feet in the ankle-high water. About 900 feet above you is the ridge that the ancient Hawaiians used to walk on to reach the summit of Waiʻaleʻale where the remains of their altar, at one of the wettest spots on Earth, may still be found. As you approach what appears to be the end, you see an odd sight: railroad tracks in the shallow water, probably used to haul the debris out of the tunnel during construction. At the light at the not-quite-end of the tunnel, you can step outside momentarily to visit a small waterfall waiting for you. Then it's back in the tunnel for the remaining 0.25 miles. That latter portion is partially lined with cement and shorings, requiring anyone 6 feet tall or more to duck for a bit. At the real end you need to follow the now-exposed ditch for a hundred yards or so, keeping an eye out for a faint trail on the right that goes over a ditch. It goes down for about a minute to the Hanalei River. During good weather the scenery is magnificent. The mountains tower all around you. Wai'ale'ale plateau is above and to your left, its side etched with waterfalls. The river, with some impossibly large boulders, makes a perfect place for lunch.

Most will be more than satisfied with this destination. But if you started early (hiking by 7 or 7:30 a.m.), there is one more challenge for the intrepid. You've been through a mile of tunnel already and are at the river. Directly across from the giant boulder and deep pool (you'll see it), there's a *very* faint trail on the other side of the river that leads 5–10 minutes upstream to *another* 0.7 mile-long tunnel. It's more dicey.

Follow the trail across from the boulder, past a bamboo grove where your route looks more like a game trail, until it meets an old diversion dam (that looks like a waterfall, which you'll hear). From the top of the dam look upstream, then turn to your right. You should see a vague trail going directly uphill. It will take you to a cement wall (part of the next ditch). The next tunnel entrance is over the wall to the right.

Once inside the tunnel (known to hunters as Ka'apoko Tunnel), there's lots of head ducking, and it has a more rickety feel. When the tunnel ends, there's an offshoot to the left. Not far from there, you come to a low-ceiling incline with water gurgling down. Scoot up and you'll emerge in a Shangri-la that will make you giddy with joy. A cathedral of 200-foot sheer walls is so steep they actually lean *inward*. Water drips from above, creat-

ing an exotic backdrop. To the left is a pounding waterfall. The setting is unbelievable and worth all the effort you went through to get here.

Besides enjoying the sheer beauty of the scene, look for a third tunnel across the river. There is a small stream trickling down from the entrance. The tunnel takes another 10 minutes and gives different perspective on the valley.

The trail conditions seem to get worse every year, and at the risk of sounding self-promoting, you'd do well to purchase our smartphone app to keep from veering off the trail. It's geo-aware, and we GPSed this trail (and all Kaua'i trails) ourselves to make sure the track is spot on.

Needless to say, you'll have the opportunity to get big-time muddy, slip on your 'okole, bump your head, twist your ankle, etc., on this adventure. Use your best judgment. This trail and tunnel are not maintained for this purpose, so please don't complain to *anybody* if you have any

Hikers entering the tunnel.

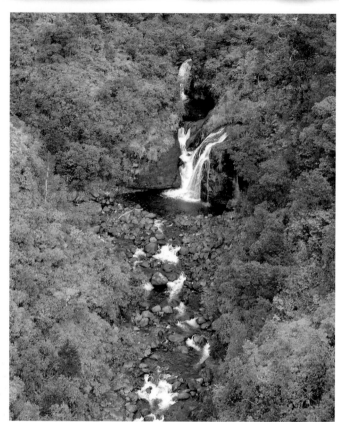

It takes time, a 4WD and wet feet to get to the so-called Blue Hole.

stead of looking for that trailhead, keep going on the road 0.4 miles until it ends at a concrete diversion dam. If the water is turbid and nasty, it's an indication that heavy rains have occurred, and this ain't the day for you. (Of course, *any* river can flash flood at *any* time.)

Walk across the dam and take the trail *up* the river. You're on the right side and the trail stays close enough to the river to hear it, so veer to your left at early intersections. You'll think at several points that the trail peters out. Keep looking, it goes on. At 0.4 miles you come to an island, where the river splits. You'll work your way up the island and when it ends, cross to the left side and pick up the trail. In 0.25 miles (it's impossible to describe the spot, but if you have our app, the geo-aware map shows where) you cross to the right side and will stay on it to the end. Mud (occasionally over a foot deep) is common, and fallen trees and branches make it more challenging at times, but it's better than boulder-hopping your way up in the water. You'll be gaining 440 feet of elevation. Tabis or shoes with aggressive tread are recommended.

It takes 3 hours round trip for *good* hikers, twice that long or more for sketchier trekkers, or if you can't find the adjoining trail segments.

At last you arrive at your goal. Three streams come together with two of them forming a glorious split waterfall. It's like

problems. This is a strenuous, exciting and memorable adventure with absolutely *no* guarantees. *That's* why it's an adventure.

HIKE TO THE BLUE HOLE

The term *Blue Hole* is widely used on Kaua'i yet is oddly ambiguous. Some use it to refer to Wai'ale'ale Crater. Some use it for the dam at the end of the dirt road that marks the trailhead. And others say Blue Hole is the pool at the end of an arduous hike. Let's go with the latter.

Getting to the trailhead can be difficult if you don't have 4WD. Read the directions to the Jungle Hike on page 156. In-a scene from heaven. You've been on the trail for less than 1.5 miles, but you'd *swear* it's more than that. (We're positive about that number, we promise.) Soak it all in (easy to do since you're already wet to the bone from your two stream crossings), and return the way you came.

For those who are tempted to continue into the crater, you should think *real* hard about that. If you've read our books to the islands, you know the tone of this warning is unusually strong for us. It's only 3 more miles (round trip) from the falls, but it is a *very* difficult and much less defined 3 miles that will exhaust even the toughest hiker. It has more potential for injury, more potential for bad weather (because it's much rainier in the crater) and more uncertainty of outcome. (All that in such a short distance? Yup.) It's muddy, undulating and filled with obstacles. Also, GPS signal degrades in parts of the crater due to the massive walls, so even our smartphone app might fail you. So if all this doesn't dissuade you, and because we *know* people will see this hike on the Internet and try anyway, the photo of the crater shows the route. Don't say we didn't warn you. Don't do this unless you start at sunrise. And don't forget that when you come to a 3,000-foot wall in front of you at the back of the crater, you still gotta come back. See page 10 for a photo of that wall.

Because of the length of the description to the Weeping Wall, we have it only in our app.

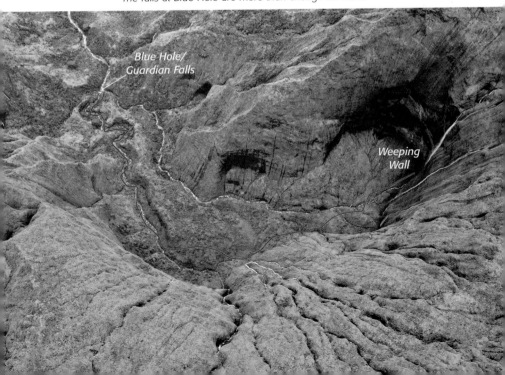

Looking down the 3,000-foot walls of Wai'ale'ale Crater, the line approximates the route to the back. It's difficult, and only for the hardiest of hikers who are on the trail at sunrise. The falls at Blue Hole are more than enough for most.

Blue Hole/
Guardian Falls

Weeping
Wall

First a day at the beach, then a romantic evening at the Sheraton Kaua'i.

By their very nature, restaurant reviews are the most subjective part of any guidebook. Nothing strains the credibility of a guidebook more. No matter what we say, if you eat at enough restaurants here, you will eventually have a dining experience directly in conflict with what this book leads you to believe. All it takes is one person to wreck what is usually a good meal. You've probably had an experience where a friend referred you to a restaurant using reverential terms, indicating that you were about to experience dining ecstasy. And, of course, when you go there, the food is awful and the waiter is a jerk. There are many variables involved in getting a good or bad meal. Is the chef new? Was the place sold last month? Was the waitress just released from prison for maul-

ing a customer? We truly hope that our reviews match your experience. If they don't (or even if they do), please drop us a line. Readers help us *tremendously* in keeping tabs on the restaurants, and we read and digest (so to speak) every e-mail.

We often leave out restaurant hours of operation because they change so frequently that the information would be immediately out of date. These decisions are usually made quite capriciously in Hawai'i. If you're going to drive a long way to eat at an establishment, it's best to call first. Restaurants that stand out from the others in some way are highlighted with this ONO symbol.

In some restaurants around the island you'll see guidebook recommendation plaques, guidebook door stickers and signed guidebooks, but you won't see ours. The reason? We *never* tell them when we're there. We review everything on the island *anonymously*. We're more interested in being treated like everyone else than in copping a free meal. How could you trust our opinion if the restaurant *knew* who we were?

By their reviews, many guidebooks lead you to believe that every meal you eat in Hawai'i will be a feast, the best food in the free world. Frankly, that's not our style. Kaua'i, like anywhere else, has ample opportunity to have lousy food served in a rotten ambiance by uncaring waiters. In the interest of space, we've left out some of the dives. We did, however, leave in some of the turkeys just to demonstrate that we live in the real world.

For each restaurant, we list the price *per person* you can expect to pay. It ranges from the least expensive entrées to the most expensive, plus a beverage and usually an appetizer. You can spend more if you try, but this is a good guideline. *The price excludes alcoholic beverages since this component of a meal can be so variable.* Obviously, everyone's ordering pattern is different, but we thought that it would be easier to compare restaurants using actual prices than if we used symbols like different numbers of dollar signs or drawings of forks or whatever to differentiate prices between restaurants.

When we give **directions** to a restaurant, *mauka side* of highway means "toward the mountain" (or away from the ocean). The shopping centers we mention are on the maps to that area.

Very few restaurants care how you dress. A few discourage tank tops and bathing suits. Some of the fancy resorts like the St. Regis Princeville, Sheraton or Grand Hyatt have dress codes. Their dress codes require **resort wear**, meaning covered shoes and collared shirts for men (nice shorts are *usually* OK), dressy sportswear or dresses for women.

It's legal to bring your own alcohol to restaurants in Hawai'i, and many restaurants, especially inexpensive ones, have no objections to letting you BYOB.

Local food can be difficult to classify. Basically, local food combines Hawaiian, American, Japanese, Chinese, Filipino and several other types and is (not surprisingly) eaten mainly by locals.

Pacific Rim is sort of a fusion of American and various countries around the Pacific, including Hawaiian and Asian. We used to categorize them separately, but it's a fine (and subjective) line between American and Pacific Rim, so we just lumped them in with American because even *we* were confused. We don't have a separate **Seafood** section because nearly every restaurant on Kaua'i serves some kind of fish.

Below are descriptions of various island foods. Not all are Hawaiian, but this might help if you encounter dishes unfamiliar to you.

ISLAND FISH & SEAFOOD

'Ahi–Tuna; raw in sashimi or poke, also seared, blackened, baked or grilled; good in fish sandwiches. Try painting 'ahi steaks with mayonnaise, which *completely* burns off when BBQ'd but seals in the moisture. You end up tasting only the moist ocean steak. Generally plentiful Apr.–Sept.

Lobster–Hawaiian spiny lobster is quite good; also called "bugs" by lobster hunters. Maine lobster kept alive on the Big Island are also available.

Mahimahi–Deep ocean fish also known as a dolphinfish; served at lu'au; very common in restaurants. Sometimes tastes fishy (especially if frozen), which can be offset in the preparation.

Marlin–Tasty when smoked; otherwise, can be tough; the Pacific Blue Marlin (kajiki) is available almost year round.

Monchong–Excellent tasting deepwater fish, available year-round. Usually served marinated and grilled.

Onaga–Also known as a ruby snapper; excellent eating in many preparations.

Ono–(Wahoo); *awesome* eating fish and can be prepared many ways; most plentiful May through October. Ono is also the Hawaiian word for delicious.

Opah–(Moonfish); excellent eating in many different preparations; generally available April through August.

'Opakapaka–(Crimson snapper); great tasting fish cooked several ways. Common October through February.

'Opihi–Using a specialized knife, these must be pried off rocks at the shoreline, which can be hazardous. Best eaten raw mixed with salt.

Poke–Fresh raw fish or octopus (tako) mixed with seaweed (limu), sesame seed and other seasonings and oil.

Shutome–Swordfish; dense meat that can be cooked several ways. Most plentiful March through July. The word comes from Japan and literally translates to *mother-in-law*.

Walu–Also goes by other names such as butterfish and escolar. Be careful not to eat more than 6 ounces. The Hawaiian nickname for this oily fish is maku'u, which means—*ahem*, this is awkward—"uncontrollable bowel discharge." Eat too much, and you may pay more dearly than you intend.

Hanalei Dolphin (826-6113) buys from the fishing boats and has a market that sells fresh, locally-caught fish. Other places include **Foodland** (822-7271) and **Safeway** (822-2464) in Kapa'a, **Fish Express** (across from Walmart) in Lihu'e, **Konohiki Seafoods** in Hanama'ulu and the **Koloa Fish Market** in Koloa.

LU'AU FOODS

Chicken lu'au–Chicken cooked in coconut milk and taro leaves.

Haupia–Coconut milk custard. Tasty, but too much will give you the… *ahem*.

Hawaiian sweet potatoes–Purple inside; not as sweet as mainland sweet potatoes but very flavorful.

Kalua pig–Pig cooked in an underground oven called an imu, shredded and mixed with Hawaiian sea salt (outstanding!).

Lomi salmon–Chilled salad consisting of raw, salted salmon, tomatoes and two kinds of onions.

Pipi kaula–Hawaiian-style beef jerky.

Poi–Steamed taro root pounded into a paste. It's a starch that will take on the taste of other foods mixed with it. Consider dipping your pipi kaula in it. (Now *that* sounds bad if you don't read it right.) Visitors are encouraged to try it at least once so they can bad-mouth it with authority.

OTHER ISLAND FOODS

Apple bananas–A smaller, denser, smoother texture than regular (Cavendish) bananas and a bit tangy.

Barbecue sticks–Teriyaki-marinated pork, chicken or beef pieces barbecued and served on bamboo sticks.

Bento–Japanese box lunch.

Breadfruit–Melon-sized starchy fruit; served baked, deep fried, steamed or boiled. Definitely an *acquired* taste.

Crackseed–Chinese-style spicy preserved fruits and seeds.

Guava–About the size of an apricot or plum. The inside is full of seeds and tart, so it is rarely eaten raw. Used primarily for juice, jelly or jam.

Hawaiian supersweet corn–The finest corn you ever had, even raw. We'll lie, cheat, steal or maim to get it fresh.

Huli huli chicken–Hawaiian BBQ style.

Ka'u oranges–Big Island oranges. Usually, the uglier the orange, the better it tastes.

Kim chee–A Korean relish consisting of pickled cabbage, onions, radishes, garlic and chilies.

Kona coffee–Grown on the Kona coast of the Big Island. Smooth, mild flavor. Better than Kaua'i coffee.

Kulolo–Steamed taro pudding. (Tasty.)

Laulau–Pork, beef or fish wrapped in taro and ti leaves, then steamed. (You don't eat the ti leaf wrapping.)

Liliko'i–Passionfruit.

Loco moco–Rice, meat patty, egg and gravy. A hit with cholesterol lovers.

Lychee–A reddish, woody peel that is discarded for the sweet, white fruit inside. Be careful of the pit. Good, small seed (or chicken-tongue) lychees are so delicious, they should be illegal.

Macadamia nut–A large, round nut.

Malasada–Portuguese donut dipped in sugar. Best when served hot.

Manapua–Steamed or baked bun filled with meat.

Mango–Bright orange fruit with yellow pink skin. Distinct, tasty flavor.

Manju–Cookie filled with a sweet center.

Methley plums–A wild fruit harvested with a permit at Koke'e State Park during the summer months.

Musubi–Cold steamed rice, often with sliced Spam rolled in black seaweed.

Papaya–Melon-like, pear-shaped fruit with yellow skin; best eaten chilled. Good at breakfast. Kaua'i has varieties called sunrise and strawberry papaya.

Plate lunch–An island favorite as an inexpensive, filling lunch. Consists of "two-scoop rice," a scoop of macaroni salad and some type of meat, either beef, chicken or fish. Sometimes called a box lunch. Great for picnics.

Portuguese sausage–Pork sausage, highly seasoned with red pepper. Tastes weird to some people.

Pupu–Appetizer, finger foods or snacks.

Saimin–Noodles cooked in either chicken, pork or fish broth. Word is peculiar to Hawai'i. Local Japanese say the dish comes from China. Local Chinese say it comes from Japan.

Sea salt–Excellent (and strong) salt distilled from seawater. Much of our sea salt comes from Salt Pond Beach Park.

Shave ice–A block of ice is "shaved" (*never* crushed) into a ball with flavored syrup poured over the top. Best served with ice cream on the bottom. Very delicious.

Smoothie–Usually papaya, mango, frozen passion fruit and frozen banana, but almost any fruit can be used to make this milkshake-like drink. Add milk for creaminess.

Taro–Found in everything from enchiladas to breads and rolls to taro chips and fritters. Tends to color foods purple. Has lots of fluoride for your teeth.

NORTH SHORE AMERICAN

Bar Acuda
5-5161 Kuhio Hwy • 826-7081
(ONO) Hanalei—A pretty unusual concept, it's called tapas food. (Yeah, we didn't know what that meant, either. It's Spanish food served in small, communally shared portions.) In this case, you order lots of small entrées and share them. The menu changes weekly and seasonally, so you'll have to

explore it on your own. Expect to see items *such as* (but they may not have) smoked trout, braised short ribs, mesclun salad, garlic green beans or chorizo sausage with chickpea stew *(particularly good)*. The food is pricey (and the drinks seriously overpriced), but the flavors are unusual and very effective, and you'll sample a number of them. The molten chocolate cake, when they have it, is incredibly earthy and wonderful—tiny but ONO. And the atmosphere, sort of a contemporary jazzy feel, works for us. **$25–$50** for dinner. In Hanalei Center. Reservations strongly recommended.

Bistro Kilauea
2484 Keneke St. • 828-0480

ONO Kilauea—A small, open air restaurant in Kilauea's Kong Lung Center that is a favorite among our readers. This is a great place to escape the midday heat thanks to the trade winds blowing through the restaurant. The lunch menu features a handful of pupus (consider the fish rockets), good salads, burgers and some seafood. Dinner expands things a bit with more seafood options and steaks. Service is normally quick, and the atmosphere is very comfortable. Happy hour tends to kick the activity up a notch inside. The desserts are tasty but on the pricey side. Overall, an easy recommendation. **$10–$20** for lunch, **$15–$40** for dinner. Live music Thursday and Saturday evenings.

Chicken in a Barrel Hanalei
5-5190 Kuhio Hwy • 826-1999

ONO Hanalei—The name refers to their method of smoking beef, pork, ribs and chicken in a barrel. As you might guess, chicken is your best bet here—it's *super* moist and flavorful. The only thing we wouldn't recommend

here is the shredded pork, which tends to be mushy. Otherwise, the ribs, brisket, local beef burgers and chili all make for excellent choices. You can get a lot of food for a reasonable price (the sampler easily feeds two, if not more), and it is stuff that even the pickiest of eaters (like kids) will enjoy. **$9–$20** for lunch and dinner. Near the entrance to Ching Young Village in Hanalei. There is also a location in Kapa'a (see East Shore Dining).

Duane's Ono-Char Burger
4-4350 Kuhio Hwy • 822-9181

Anahola—Duane's Ono-Char Burger is an institution on Kaua'i. After being mediocre for a few years, quality is back up, but you'll still have to endure *achingly* slow service. Think of it as burgers served on Hawaiian time. We still like the specialties, such as the teriyaki burger and the mushroom burger. Their milkshakes (especially the marionberry shake) are tasty. Most customers opt to eat at the cement outdoor tables, which are a bit stark. Marauding wild chickens and cats usually compete for your jettisoned French fries. Or consider taking your food down Anahola Road (south of Duane's) to Anahola Beach Park, where picnic tables at the beach make for a pleasant atmosphere. (Weekends at that beach, however, are a bit crowded.) Service can be gruff. **$8–$14** for lunch till 6 p.m. On the highway in Anahola; can't miss it. You may want to call in your order because you'll *never* wait less than 20 minutes, often *way* longer, if you order at the counter. Cash only.

Hanalei Dolphin Restaurant
5-5016 Kuhio Hwy • 826-6113
2829 Ala Kalanikaumaka, Po'ipu
742-1414

ONO Hanalei—This is a north shore tradition that has

much more consistent these days than what we've seen in the past. They have some outdoor tables on a lawn next to the Hanalei River—very nice at lunch or while waiting for your indoor table at dinner. They are often busy and don't take reservations—so if waiting bothers you, arrive early or you're out of luck. Their seafood selection is excellent. Pick a fish and a side item. The teriyaki 'ahi is awesome and best ordered med-rare, even if you're a medium kind of diner. *Love* it with the asparagus wraps. They have a seafood market, a good place to pick up fish for cooking back at the condo. And the western-style sushi is high quality. Bartending skills tend to be lacking—avoid the Blue Dolphin. This place (also called Dolphin Hanalei) pleases most of the time. But, perhaps because of the price, when they tank, they *really* tank. **$15–$20** for lunch, **$30–$60** for dinner. On the highway in Hanalei; can't miss it. Their other location at The Shops at Kukui'ula is called **Dolphin Po'ipu**. Same menu, smaller space and no view.

Hanalei Gourmet
5-5161 Kuhio Hwy • 826-2524
Hanalei—Quality comes and goes with this place. Currently, they're in the zone most days. Good fish tacos (available some nights), good fish and chips. Burgers, sandwiches and salads for lunch; steak, seafood, pastas and burgers for dinner. Promise us you'll avoid the nachos. "Gourmet" seems a bit generous, and much of the atmosphere gravitates toward the bar. **$13–$17** for lunch, **$20–$36** for dinner (less if you want a burger). In the Old Hanalei School across from Ching Young Village. Live music some nights.

Harvest Market Café
5-5161 Kuhio Hwy • 826-0089
Hanalei—In the back of Harvest Market

natural grocery store, Harvest Marthey have a soup and salad bar as well as hot plates, all sold by weight and made fresh daily. The items are fresh, healthy and surprisingly affordable (at least compared to the groceries in the store). The smoothies and juices are good options, but the baked goods are best when fresh in the morning. **$5–$12**. The café closes by 5 p.m. most days. The last building in Hanalei Center; can't miss it.

Kalypso Island Bar & Grill
5-5156 Kuhio Hwy • 826-9700
Hanalei—Items are hit or miss but rarely rise above acceptable. A lot of readers have told us how much they love the drinks and the food, and we can't help but wonder if the former influenced their opinion of the latter. (I've done more than my fair share of restaurant reviews where the food was *great*… after a couple of potent drinks, but less stellar with a clearer head.) The menu runs the gamut from American to Mexican to Italian to Pacific Rim. Burgers and the steak sandwich are your best bets, though they come with no sides. Breakfast is the one area where they bring their batting average up— good Eggs Benedict choices and French toast (very rich tasting). **$10–$25** for breakfast (weekends only) and lunch, **$18–$35** for dinner. On the Hwy; can't miss it.

Kaua'i Grill
5520 Ka Haku Rd. • 826-2250
Princeville—So there you are, at a restaurant with a great view overlooking Hanalei Bay, good food and pretty good service. Why no ONO from us? Because your net worth is now noticeably less, and you didn't walk away feeling pampered enough. Forget the $16 drinks and $25 appetizers. This is the place to get your tasty $60

lamb chops or a whole Kona lobster for $78. And the only thing you get with that steak is...a fork. All sides are extra. And if you order it medium and it comes out less than rare? And if the waitress takes so long to come over that you're halfway finished, you'll get an "I'm so sorry" and maybe even, "The chef is sorry, too." But no offer for a free dessert or a discount. We relay this story to illustrate that you can take great ingredients such as the location and food and still leave the customers wanting. Is it good? Yes. Is it *that* good? Not really. If money's no object, *you'd* give it an ONO. But for the rest of us mere mortals, it's short of the mark. **$45–$100** or more for dinner. In the St. Regis, Princeville. Their sister restaurant, **Makana Terrace**, has somewhat inferior food, an even better view and, sorry—no ONO there either. Closed Sunday and Monday.-

North Shore General Store
5-4280 Kuhio Hwy • 826-1122
Princeville—It's pretty rare that we'd be reasonably happy with food at a *gas* station. (Especially one with *their* prices.) Using quality lean Princeville Ranch beef, (which you can also purchase for grilling), these guys make one of the better burgers around. If you're into BBQ sauce, onion rings and bacon, try the Braddah's BBQ burger. Burgers range from $6–$8, a pretty reasonable price *in these here parts*. They also have fish and chips as well as pizza, which *tastes* like gas station pizza and is ridiculously priced at $6.50–$7.50 per slice. Hot dogs come split and on a hamburger bun. Their breakfast sandwiches are tasty at $6. Add a hash brown patty, which works best when you put it *in* the sandwich. A few tables outside or to take it to go. Service can be *slooooow*. In the 76 gas station at the Princeville Center. Breakfast is **$7–$10**, lunch and dinner are **$8–$15**.

Postcards
5-5075 Kuhio Hwy • 826-1191
Hanalei—A vegetarian restaurant that also serves fish. The food is distinctive and can be fairly well prepared. They use organic ingredients and have creative selections. Taro fritters make a good pupu, and the fresh fish is recommended. Ambiance is homey. The two areas that need work are the service (often slow), and the wine list is poorly chosen. **$20–$40** for dinner. On mauka side of the highway. Reservations required for parties of six or more. Closed Sunday and Monday.

Tahiti Nui
5-5134 Kuhio Hwy • 826-6277
ONO Hanalei—Tahiti Nui is a longtime Hanalei institution that has seen great highs and huge lows. Currently they have an energy that was missing for a decade. Food is pretty good (try the fish burger), their mai tai is one of the best on the island, and they have live music some nights. Behind the small dining room is their pizza joint, **Tiki Man Pizza**, and next door, the **Iti Wine Bar** is a tiny (iti) but atmosphere-rich cubbyhole that might serve Tahiti Nui food, or maybe tapas, or maybe something else. Hard to say here. Iti is so small that *you* may well define the atmosphere. Tahiti Nui is like a living entity, and it's hard to say what you'll find. That's part of the joy. It might be the place with great food and colorful characters, or over-the-top characters bordering on seedy. Either way, this is the center of north shore nightlife, both for visitors and locals. It's because of this we give them an ONO. If you're more of a high-end resort kind of traveler, this may not be your place. Dinner stresses seafood and only a few pupus, and at **$25–$35** is overpriced. Lunch is burgers and sandwiches for **$13–$22**. They

also have a lu'au on Wednesday nights that is different from any other found on Kaua'i (in a good way). On the ocean side of the highway.

NORTH SHORE ITALIAN

Kilauea Bakery & Pau Hana Pizza
2484 Keneke St. • 828-2020

ONO Kilauea—Delicious baked goods and breads. (Try the macaroons or macadamia shortbread cookies.) The pizza is pricey, but the unusual fresh ingredients and the flavor combinations of the whole pizza specials work well. An example: Their island-stylin' pizza is ham, pineapple, roasted garlic and chipotle peppers—much more interesting than traditional Hawaiian-style. More typical pizzas by the slice, which are too pricey given the less-glamorous toppings and tendency to get soggy later in the day. (At least the crust is very good.) And the Big Kilauea Salad is particularly good. Service can be friendly, but more often you'll be put off by their attitude—they sometimes seem to pride themselves on their surliness. We nearly pulled the ONO for this reason, but then had an eclair that soothed our grumpiness. They have a dozen tables split indoors and out. **$12–$22** for meals. Bakery is reasonably priced. In Kong Lung Center off Kilauea Road. Open 6:30ish a.m. to 9 p.m. Closed Tuesdays.

Tiki Man Pizza
5-5134 Kuhio Hwy • 826-6277

Hanalei—The pizza arm of the Tahiti Nui restaurant. It's not bad, but it won't leave you wanting more. **$17–$30** with most specialty pizzas on the high side of that range. (It's $22 for a 15-inch single topping.) By the slice (when they feel like it) for **$3**. On the ocean side of the Hwy

in Hanalei. Pick up or delivery for lunch and dinner, or you can dine on the Tahiti Nui lanai.

NORTH SHORE JAPANESE

NorthSide Grill & Sushi
5-5190 Kuhio Hwy • 826-9701

Hanalei—The entrées can be good here and they seem to be improving since our last edition. The sushi in particular has improved though we recommend sitting at the sushi bar—the chef tends to give the extra effort to those that sit and engage rather than order from afar. Service is good, though we've noticed their timing can be off with larger groups. The second-story, open-air setting overlooking the town and towering mountains makes window seats a treat. You'll find numerous fish dishes (which they do well) as well as burgers, chicken, ribs and some pasta. Consider the ono wrap with mango. Readers love their mai tais—they do pack a punch. **$10–$25** for lunch, add a few more bucks for dinner. Not quite an ONO but a decent place to grab a bite. In the Ching Young Village.

NORTH SHORE LOCAL

Hanalei Wake-up Café
5-5144 Kuhio Hwy • 826-5551

Hanalei—Restaurants around here tend to open late for breakfast, if they open at all. This place opens at 7 a.m. Very small menu and less-than-pristine surroundings—think *greasy spoon*. They're usually packed. Service is fast, but the food is hastily assembled, and they *hate* substitutions. Omelettes are avoidable and you'll probably find the coffee weak, but other items will fill the need. Decor is an homage to all things surfing. **$10–$20** for breakfast. On ocean side of the road.

Can't miss it. A little pricey for a place that's cash only.

Kilauea Fish Market
4270 Kilauea Rd. • 828-6244
440 Aleka Pl., Kapa'a • 822-3474
Kilauea—Besides the usual fresh seafood, they carry some pricey free-range beef. If you don't want to cook at home, we suggest their Andy Irons burrito or the fish tacos. They also have salads, plate lunches and unique specials. The outdoor seating is covered, so if you want some sun, take it to the beach. It's pricier because you're in Kilauea. Behind the Kilauea Plantation Center, kitty-corner from the Kong Lung Center. **$12–$19** for lunch and dinner. Closed Sunday. Their second location in Kapa'a is called **Sleeping Giant Grill**.

Village Snack & Bakery Shop
5-5190 Kuhio Hwy • 826-6841
(ono) Hanalei—Their baked goods are *excellent* and very reasonably priced. Ambiance is...well, they don't *have* any. But if you want a restaurant that has looked the same since the island rose from the sea, this is the place for you. Hearty, cheap food. Try the apple crisp—*very* ono and only $3. Or consider the chili pepper chicken or a tuna sandwich. **$6–$11** for breakfast and lunch. Not bad food for the price. Simple, homey and cluttered. In Ching Young Village. Open at 7 a.m.

NORTH SHORE MEXICAN

Federico's Fresh Mex Cuisine
5-4280 Kuhio Hwy • 826-7177
Princeville—We used to get positive feedback from readers about this place, but lately it's been the same mediocre to poor experiences we've had. They feature your usual suspects at Mexican restaurants, such as burritos, tacos and quesadillas as well as salads, tostadas and tortas. The tacos and burritos come in various styles with beef, chicken, pork or seafood options. The prices are good for Princeville, but note that you only get one taco per order, so be sure to get two if you're expecting a full meal. Service can be hit or miss, running from very friendly to downright hostile. No seating inside—you either get the food to go, or they bring it out to you in the shared food court. It's around **$10** for breakfast, **$6–$16** for lunch and dinner. Closed Sunday.

Tropical Taco
5-5088 Kuhio Hwy • 827-8226
Hanalei—If you're wondering why there's a likeness of a green truck inside this location, it's because the owner operated Tropical Taco out of one for over 20 years. Sadly, the food isn't up to par these days. (It's too expensive, the portions could be bigger, and they tend to overuse refried beans as filler.) You're better off hitting up one of the food trucks next door. Lunch and dinner are **$13–$15**. Closes at 4 p.m. on weekends. Located in the green Halele'a building on the ocean side of the highway in Hanalei.

NORTH SHORE THAI

Lotus Garden
5-4280 Kuhio Hwy • 826-9999
Princeville—This small Chinese/Thai restaurant in the Princeville Shopping Center shares the same outdoor space as Lei Petite. You'll find Thai and Chinese items as well as some fusions. No obviously fresh ingredients here—most of it apparently comes from Costco, including their only fish, sea bass. Nearly all meals are reasonably priced around $11. Noodle dishes, stir fry, soups and some Thai specialty dishes make up the menu. Hard to get excited. **$11–$15**.

NORTH SHORE TREATS

Kalalea Juice Hale
4390 Puu Hale • 346-0074

ONO Anahola—The orange colored shack across the road from Duane's Ono Char Burgers has some tasty treats. This family-run operation has local, organic juices, smoothies, açaí bowls and shave ice. In case you didn't get the health food memo, an açaí bowl is like a big fruit parfait with more fruit and a base of the superfood açaí berry. The attitude is right and the flavors are fresh—we haven't had a bad experience here though the smoothies are only as good as the combo you choose. Try the fresh-pressed sugar cane juice. It has a sweet yet earthy taste that tickles the taste buds. **$6–$15**. Closed Mondays.

Shave Ice Paradise
5-5183 Kuhio Hwy • 212-1653

Hanalei—Good shave ice—they keep the blade sharp enough for a nice ice consistency—but they are inconsistent on the syrup. Sometimes too much, sometimes too little. On the expensive side. **$5–$10**. Cash only. Across from Ching Young Village. Try Wishing Well Shave Ice instead.

Wishing Well Shave Ice
5-5080 Kuhio Hwy • 639-7828

ONO Hanalei—A long-time north shore landmark that shows how an ownership changes can breathe new life into a business. While the traditional flavors are still available, their local, organic syrups (which are chilled) have brought the experience to a new level. Definitely get ice cream in the bottom, or consider a snow cap (sweetened-condensed milk) and a fresh fruit topping. You'll have a treat that is so picturesque and delicious that it may break your social media page posting a photo of it. The traditional flavored shave ice starts at **$5**, while the organic starts at a pricey **$8**. The price is worth it, though. Organic flavors rotate depending on what's in season. We've even been impressed with their non-sweet flavors like coffee and earl grey tea. Find them in a truck on the ocean side of the highway in Hanalei.

EAST SHORE AMERICAN

Bubba's Burgers
4-1421 Kuhio Hwy • 823-0069
2829 Ala Kalanikaumaka, Po'ipu
742-6900

ONO Kapa'a—Funky place to get decent, but *small* burgers (might want to opt for a double), chili rice, etc., with a limited choice of burger toppings. Love the chocolate banana shake. If it wasn't for their sassy attitude, we probably *wouldn't* give them an ONO. Their motto is, "We cheat tourists, drunks and attorneys." So if you are a drunk attorney visiting the island, you're on your own, counselor. **$5–$10**. On highway in north Kapa'a; can't miss 'em. Also in Po'ipu's The Shops at Kukui'ula near the roundabout. Nothing stands out individually, but overall the place works fairly well at the Kapa'a location. The Po'ipu location is not as good. We should point out that our reader e-mail seems to be pretty split for Bubba's (some love it and some don't), so maybe we're being too generous with the ONO, even for the Kapa'a location.

Bull Shed
4-796 Kuhio Hwy • 822-3791

Kapa'a—A consistently solid place for fairly good grub and nice ocean views. Dinner only, quite popular with both locals and tourists, known for hearty beef and seafood and moderate portions. They do meat well here (the bone-in prime rib looks like something out of the Flintstones), but they lag on the sides. The window seats are particularly close to the water (we've been there when the waves actually splashed against the glass), but arrive 10–15 minutes before they open (they start serving dinner at 5 p.m.) to get one. All entrées come with a choice of salad or…salad. Sorry, no soup. (And slim pickings at the salad bar.) And if I may rant, you only get rice with entrées. If you pay extra and get a baked potato, they'll try to take the rice away. Hey, I'm *paying* for it. Leave it alone! (Whew, I feel better already.) **$15–$40**. Limited desserts such as coconut cream pie and a pretty good and reasonably priced wine list (which they pair well) along with a broad martini selection. On the ocean side of highway across from Kaua'i Village. Reservations only for six or more.

Chicken in a Barrel
4-1586 Kuhio Hwy • 823-0780

Kapa'a—The original, roadside stand in north Kapa'a and the only location where you can easily see the barrels used for smoking the chicken. And the smoked chicken is *delicious*. They also have beef and pork but don't seem to do them as well here as at their Hanalei location (see North Shore Dining). The menu is slightly smaller at this location with no fries or onion rings available. They are friendly here, and if you stick to the chicken, you won't be disappointed. For a better overall meal go to the north shore location. **$15–$20** for lunch and dinner. Across from the Kaua'i Products Fair on the ocean side of the highway.

Daylight Donuts
4100 Rice St. • 245-7414

Lihu'e—Small donut shop in strip mall behind Ace Hardware on Rice Street.

Horrid coffee and dull, overly processed donuts are something you can find in a gas station back home. Even though the prices are reasonable (get a dozen for $11), you'd do better to get the day old, discounted baked goods from the grocery store. Definite pass. Closed Sundays.

Deli & Bread Connection
3-2600 Kaumualii Hwy • 245-7115

ONO Lihu'e—An absolutely dandy place to get sandwiches (although you'll often have to wait a while at lunch time). Large selection of traditional meats and veggies, plus some extras. Try the TOPSS sandwich. **$7–$12**. In Kukui Grove next to Macy's. Some effective baked goods (though sometimes stale). But overall, a very steady place.

Duke's Kaua'i
3610 Rice St. • 246-9599

ONO Lihu'e—So before we talk about the food, we should mention that this is one of the better places on the island to have a tropical cocktail, downstairs outdoors on the **Barefoot Bar** overlooking Kalapaki Bay. We also like the indoor table by the small indoor waterfall. The menu downstairs includes flatbread pizzas, burgers, seafood and other items that are not as overpriced as most resort foods. Service there is only fair, and prices are **$12–$20**. Now as for the restaurant *upstairs*, the beef and seafood are very good. Consider the fresh catch prepared Duke-style. If the special is the fish sautéed in a miso bur blanc with mac nut and crab encrusted—*jump* on that. The prime rib is huge and delicious, and their salad bar is probably the best on the island. (Add it on for only $4.) The only ding on Duke's is that portions seem to get smaller every year. Lanai tables at the railing are best, offering a nice view of the bay. **$23–$35** (more if you spring for lobster), which ain't bad for the quality of the surroundings. Located at the Marriott. (You can park in their lot or next to Anchor Cove at the beach parking lot.) They also have free valet parking from the road next to Anchor Cove Shopping Center, but it often fills up. Reservations recommended.

Gaylord's Restaurant at Kilohana
3-2087 Kaumualii Hwy • 245-9593

(ONO) Lihu'e—This place has a lot of ambiance and history. Located in the courtyard of a former sugar baron's 1930s home, the old world feel and cozy outdoor setting really work. We've seen them go up and down over the years, and our ONO has come and gone. This time around they *barely* eked out an ONO despite spotty service. The menu brings a bit of fresh fish, cioppino, hoisin-glazed spare ribs and a good filet. Only dings are that sounds from the nearby lu'au sometimes intrude, and their bartending skills change with every visit. They make up for it with an extensive (and expensive) wine list and *sometimes* a good mai tai. Live music some nights, but the quality is hit or miss. **$14–$20** for lunch, dinner is **$25–$40**. Mauka side between mile markers 1 and 2 on Hwy 50 between Lihu'e and Puhi in Kilohana.

Greenery Café
3146 Akahi St. • 246-4567

(ONO) Lihu'e—Unique, easy to love and hard to find—just how we like it. Greenery Café serves soul food with an island twist. Ingredients are mostly local and organic. The blending of flavors works very well, and you can get a plate with cornmeal-crusted 'ahi, collard greens, black-eyed peas and kim chee—how's that for multi-ethnic cuisine? Their signature meat is the rosemary chicken (seasoned with rosemary from their herb garden), which is very good and downright addicting as rosemary chicken salad. Wraps, sandwiches, salads and plate lunches make up the usual menu, but be sure to check the specials. Good vegan options, too. **$6–$15** for lunch. Open some Saturdays, closed Sundays. Across the street from the Tip Top Café between Hardy and Ahukini Rd.

Ha Coffee Bar
4180 Rice St. • 631-9241

Lihu'e—Ha is the Hawaiian word for breath. (No they don't mean *coffee breath*; it's deeper than that.) The setting is comfortable, spacious and conducive to both relaxing and working. The coffee is pretty good, and the limited baked goods, though not made on site, are tasty when fresh. The staff is friendly and attentive. WiFi is free but only good for 30 minutes (hopefully, it was just a few emails you need to send). Perhaps our favorite things are the topographic map collections they have hanging up—we're map geeks. Not an ONO and not exactly on the way to many things, but we wouldn't steer you away. **$3–$6**. Closed Sundays.

Hukilau Lanai
520 Aleka Loop • 822-0600

(ONO) Kapa'a—Fish is their specialty, and they do it very well, though their non-fish items also hold up. The complex flavor combinations here are skillfully conceived. The sweet potato ravioli or the lobster and goat cheese wontons make killer appetizers. And don't overlook their bartending skills, which are unusually well crafted. The Hukilau Mixed Grill is a tasty selection of seafood items. And their meatloaf is deadly. The atmosphere and views of the courtyard are peaceful and romantic, and if you have kids, you could turn 'em loose on the large lawn adjacent to the dining room. Easy to recommend and always booked; get reservations well in advance. At Kaua'i Coast Resort, next to Coconut Marketplace. **$20–$35** for dinner. Closed Monday.

Java Kai
4-1384 Kuhio Hwy • 823-6887

(ONO) Kapa'a—A small coffee place loved by residents and visitors alike. They roast their coffee in-house daily and offer a good selection of Hawaiian coffees not seen in many other places (such as Moloka'i espresso), all of which can be purchased by the pound. If you're a true caffeine fiend, consider a Chemex Pour Over—it takes a while to make, but you'll be vibrating by the time you finish it. Smoothies, juices and granola bowls are also popular if you're more health conscious. Baked goods and breakfast bagels are pretty tasty, too. Lunch items include sandwiches and wraps. Indoor and outdoor seating is available, but the small space gets crowded quickly (which also slows the service down). If you're in a rush, take advantage of their to-go counter in the back, **Kai Bar Roasters**. **$8–$16** for breakfast, **$11–$20** for lunch. On highway in north Kapa'a. Open at 6 a.m.

JJ's Broiler
3416 Rice St. • 246-4422

Lihu'e—A longtime steak and seafood landmark. With their good location adjacent to Kalapaki Beach, they should be able to eke out an ONO from us, but don't seem to put in the effort. Perhaps being in the area where cruise ships dock creates complacency. Even readers who have gone against our warnings have written in to relate horror stories. They have a varied menu at dinner of steak, seafood, pasta, and carryovers from lunch with burgers, sandwiches and salads ($16

and up), which creates lots of choices. But prices are high, and extras such as appetizers and beverages (it's hard to get a glass of wine for under $10, and they don't even give refills on *soda*) are pretty overpriced. The atmosphere inside is more sports bar, with the outdoor tables overlooking Kalapaki Bay. (You won't hear the surf, only the sports announcers.) Their signature dish—Slavonic steak—seems to be an attempt to bury poor cuts of steak with sauces. **$15–$30** for lunch, **$15–$50** for dinner. In Anchor Cove Shopping Center.

Jo2
4-971 Kuhio Hwy • 212-1627

Kapa'a—They call themselves *natural cuisine*, but we don't know what that means. This is the most recent dining expression of a well-known Kaua'i chef with a long-time knowledge of local flavors augmented by high-end chef skills. That's a fancy way of saying the menu is impossible to define. Seafood plus some "from the land" options. Their hamachi sashimi is an amazing appetizer (even if you don't like raw fish, you might like this), and both the lamb and walu are good choices. Top it off with the warm apple pineapple cobbler—so much better than what you've had. So why no ONO? Great presentation, good, sometimes epic food, sometimes not and a surprisingly bad bar are what you should expect. When you pay this kind of money, you need consistency. We haven't observed that here. The variability is possibly related to the times the boss is in. **$35–$55** for dinner. Reservations are recommended. In Waipouli Conplex. Closed Sundays.

Kalapaki Beach Hut
3474 Rice St. • 246-6330

Lihu'e—A small shack that specializes in burgers made from Kaua'i beef (which they often undercook). They also have a couple of grilled sandwiches and fish and chips. Their taro fries are unusual but no more flavorful than any other taro preparation. They often have lines, and seating is at a long counter with a couple tables and a counter with an ocean view upstairs. Service can be slow and snotty—this ain't fast food. They also serve mediocre shave ice—how do you mess that up? Breakfast is **$8–$12** with a scant selection (good breakfast sandwich). **$9–$13** for lunch and dinner. Next to Anchor Cove Shopping Center. Open at 7 a.m.

Kaua'i Beer Company
4265 Rice St. • 245-2337

ONO Lihu'e—Kaua'i is certainly not known as a haven for craft brew beer. These guys might change that. Not only do they make the best beer on Kaua'i, but also some of the best in the state. They have six regularly available libations plus a rotating nitro tap (brewery regulars know what this is—try it if you don't), but the Bavarian-style Shwarzbier Black Limousine is a real crowd pleaser. The food's good, too. Most items are made in house with locally sourced produce, and the quality is top notch. Salads, sandwiches (such as Parmesan Chicken with Ulu Pesto Sandwich or a Cuban with a Pacific Rim twist) and other interesting entrées. If you have kids or a DD, they make home brewed root beer. Thursday nights feature a rotating roster of food trucks that come at dinner to serve you in the restaurant—super popular with residents. **$6–$20** for lunch and dinner. On Rice Street between Kress and Hardy. Closed Sunday and Monday.

Kountry Kitchen
4-1485 Kuhio Hwy • 822-3511

Kapa'a—A reliable breakfast standby (served till 1:30 p.m.) with a huge menu that includes lots of ways to deliver eggs, and the ambiance matches the name. Lunch also available but their DNA is breakfast-based. Omelettes here are hit or miss—consider the lu'au omelette. The pancakes, however, are very fluffy. Though the price ain't cheap, you're paying for a great selection and mostly good results (with exceptions, such as the tasteless cornbread or the biscuits and gravy). They have a separate section that is just coffee and Belgian waffles along with a big community table. *Almost* gave 'em an ONO. **$10–$18** for breakfast and lunch. On the mauka side of the highway in northern Kapa'a.

Lava Lava Beach Club
420 Papaloa Rd. • 241-5282

Kapa'a—This should be a no-brainer for an ONO since it's pretty much the only place on island you can actually eat *on the beach* without booking a private dinner. They accomplished this by bringing sand onto their property adjacent to the beach. (Being on the east shore also means that wind and rain can send people to the inside tables.) Good menu, but they rely too much on location. Food and service are adequate and not commensurate with the price. Their selection is mostly American fare with a definite Pacific-Rim bent. Breakfast is probably their strongest showing with options like benedicts and omelettes plus good breakfast cocktails. Lunch brings fish and chips, ribs, burgers, sandwiches and flatbread pizzas. Dinner expands the meat and seafood offerings. **$12–$20** for breakfast, **$15–$30** for lunch and **$19–$40** for dinner. (Don't forget your credit card in the Spam can.) Pick it up a bit, Lava Lava, and we will gleefully give you an ONO. And *please* put something on the bottom of the chairs so they don't sink so far into the sand. After it works its way down, I feel like a kid at the grown-up table for the first time. Behind the Coconut Marketplace at the Kaua'i Shores Hotel.

Mermaids Café
4-1384 Kuhio Hwy • 821-2026

Kapa'a—A brightly painted hole in the wall that serves healthy wraps, 'ahi tacos, a noodle plate or two and bountiful salads from their tiny menu. Portions are ample and flavors can be great if they don't overdo it on sauces. (Ask them to go light on any fish.) Really like the tropical fish tacos and the 'ahi cilantro wrap. Seating is cramped and limited. Bountiful salads. They have a number of tasty and unusual drinks, such as hibiscus lemonade. On Kuhio Hwy near 581. **$10–$16** for lunch and dinner.

9th Island Sports Bar & Grill
4-831 Kuhio Hwy • 822-7773

Kapa'a—They call themselves a Las Vegas-style pub, and items are named after Vegas stars and gangsters. (Vegas is sometimes called Hawai'i's *9th island* due to its popularity as a vacation destination for residents.) It's more of a small sports bar atmosphere. Half-pound burgers and sandwiches dominate the menu. The Butterfinger (teriyaki) burger is tasty as is the jalapeno burger. Patties are hand-formed with bread crumbs inside. In all, a slightly above average eatery. Biggest complaint is they can be slow. **$13–$18** for lunch and dinner. In the Kauai Village Shopping Center.

Oasis on the Beach
4-820 Kuhio Hwy • 822-9332

Kapa'a—They have an awesome, breezy location next to the beach in front of the Waipouli Beach Resort with a thatched, woody atmosphere. Small but well-chosen menus using fresh local ingredients with clever preparations. Breakfast has lots of recognizable favorites with a local twist (love the Oasis Hash made with short ribs). Lunch has good tempura fish and chips, local beef burgers, fish tacos and a few other items. Their drink called okolehao is tasty and potent, and we like their beer selection. Prices ain't cheap, but most of the entrées can come as a half portion for less money, and the results work for us. Dinner brings a small menu of steak and seafood plus many pupus. Service is usually (but not always) good. They have a pretty cool catamaran bar in back. You'll have to park on either side of the resort and stroll along a beachside path to the restaurant. **$11–$18** for breakfast, add a few bucks for lunch, and **$16–$35** for dinner. Live music every Wednesday.

Olympic Café
4-1354 Kuhio Hwy • 822-5825
2360 Kiahuna Plantation, Po'ipu
742-8717

Kapa'a—A funky, local standby that has stayed consistent through the years. The menu here is vast, and most portions are bulky. Breakfast scrambles are tasty, and the burritos and burgers work well at lunch. Dinner adds some more expensive items like steak, pasta and fajitas. For dessert, the tasty Kaua'i Pie has nearly a half-gallon of ice cream and can easily satisfy a table of four. Fridays they have a free taco bar during happy hour (3–7 p.m.), which can get really busy. It's a weird night, and you should stay away from the fish. Drinks, while not stellar, tend to be fairly well-crafted. If you order waffle fries, it's a buck if you want something to dip them into. **$8–$18** for breakfast, **$11–$20** for lunch, **$16–$30** for dinner. Service can be spotty.

Window seats overlook the highway. Across from ABC Store in downtown Kapa'a. The ONO doesn't apply to the Po'ipu Shopping Village location. It has the same menu but doesn't seem as well-executed.

Ono Family Restaurant
4-1292 Kuhio Hwy • 822-1710
Kapa'a—This is a long-time Kapa'a institution. Between this and Kountry Kitchen, Ono Family wins for most "homey" and slightly better food. (They tie for the weakest coffee, though.) Huge breakfast menu of various combos of eggs, meats and starches, many with local twists—the Local Girl omelette has fried rice and kim chee. The sweeter offerings of pancakes and French toast feature some tasty, fresh fruit combos. Fish such as ono and mahimahi can be added to most dishes. Lunch isn't as compelling, with average burgers, sandwiches and Mexican-style items such as burritos. Service has gotten friendlier but not faster. **$8–$20** for breakfast and lunch. On ocean side of Hwy just south of 581. Outside is **Ono Ono Shave Ice**, which is pretty good. They have a limited number of natural syrups made in house that often sell out.

Papaya's Natural Foods & Café
4-901 Kuhio Hwy • 823-0190
Kapa'a—A good health food store that also serves mostly veggie items, such as veggie lasagna, tofu, falafel and perhaps some sandwiches. Basically you pay $8 a pound for hot food and salad, and results are mixed. We've had some good meals here…and we've walked away with our inedible plates still full. Hard to say what you'll get. Good smoothies and fish tacos, though. **$8–$18** all day. Very limited seating out front, making it best to grab and go to a nearby beach park. Located in Waipouli Plaza. Parking is tight and full most of the time but there is more parking around back.

Sam's Ocean View
4-1546 Kuhio Hwy • 822-7887
ONO Kapa'a—Just a disclaimer. Your humble author happens to own the building, not the restaurant. He has *no* stake in the business, but he has had others review this place to keep it simple. One of the better views in Kapa'a that also captures the evening breezes, making for a cool and relaxed atmosphere. The food is pretty good, too. Like many restaurants around the island, Sam's has embraced local ingredients and serves them well. They feature steak, seafood and some pasta dishes plus more appetizers (such as boards of cheeses to be shared among a group and the crispy cauliflower—excellent when they use small pieces). The chocolate mousse cake truffle is deadly. Their bartending skills are high, and we recommend both their mai tai and the painkiller. It's a bit pricey, but you're paying for the killer view. (And I guess the landlord's rent…) **$16–$35** for dinner. Across the street from Hanai and Tamba Surf in north Kapa'a. Closed Tuesdays.

Small Town Coffee
4-1543 Kuhio Hwy
ONO Kapa'a—An artsy, hodge-podge red bus with personality. Their coffee is consistently good and organically grown. Powerful espressos, homemade hot chocolates and lattes. Some tasty baked goods and vegan items. Diehard regulars usually occupy the tables where they solve the world's problems among themselves. Open 6 a.m. (food starts at 7 a.m.). **$8–$12**. On mauka side of Hwy 56 in north Kapa'a in the parking lot across from the Kaua'i Beach Hostel.

Street Burger
4-369 Kuhio Hwy • 212-1555

Wailua—We like this place, but if you're expecting grass skirts and coconuts, then you'll want to head somewhere else. The stark industrial design is more befitting the downtown of a major urban area on the mainland than it is Hawai'i. (The change of pace is probably why those of us who live here enjoy it.) The gourmet burgers are good, but we've noticed the quality has been slipping since they first opened. And they won't let you upgrade to specialty fries, meaning if you want to try one of their more interesting flavor combinations, you have to get a separate side order that can run as much as $10 extra. The bar is well-stocked, and they stay open later than most other places here. **$10–$23** for lunch and dinner, open Tue.–Sat. 11 a.m. to 10 p.m. On the highway near Haleilio, just north of the river.

EAST SHORE CHINESE

Garden Island Barbecue
4252 Rice St. • 245-8868

Lihu'e—Despite the name, it's a Chinese restaurant with a local twist, *not* a BBQ. The selection is dizzying—over 150 items! (And no, we haven't tried every one.) Portions are good, and the price is reasonable. There will almost certainly be something that interests you. Service is lightning fast. Although the food's not the greatest, you ain't paying for the greatest. You're paying for a large selection, large portions, and you want to get in and out fast. So you're getting what you pay for. **$10–$14** for lunch and dinner, plus a cheaper special. At Rice and Hardy.

Ho's Chinese Kitchen
3-2600 Kaumualii Hwy • 245-5255

Lihu'e—We don't want to sound mean, but since our very first edition this has

been the most consistently hideous food on the island. Plus, the service is only slightly better than the food. We've taken "friends" here just to punish them. But Ho's is still here, so they must be doing something right. We just don't know what it is. **$10–$12**. In Kukui Grove Center.

Super No. 1 BBQ & Chinese
4-361 Kuhio Hwy • 823-1268

Wailua—Because we have a responsibility when giving a review of a company, we make *multiple* visits before giving a review as strong as this one. (It ain't all fun and games and mai tais, folks.) They would seem to bring the use of MSG to new heights (or lows, depending on your perspective). Anything that we didn't immediately spit out, should have been—it sits like a rock in your stomach. Their name is *No. 1*, but after eating here and sampling their flavors, what comes to mind is more like *No. 2*... **$5–$12**. Next to Brick Oven Pizza in Wailua.

EAST SHORE INDIAN

Shivalik Indian Cuisine
4-771 Kuhio Hwy • 821-2333

ONO Kapa'a—Good food that has stayed consistent over the past couple of editions. (Bear in mind that this is the only Indian restaurant on the island, so we can't be too picky.) Lunch consists of *thali* plate lunches served on metal trays. Choose either vegetarian or non-vegetarian dish. Both come with basmati rice, yellow dal, vegetable curry, small salad and naan. Lunch runs from **$10–$13**, drinks are extra. The flavors are good, the ingredients usually taste fresh, and you get to choose your "heat" level. Dinner is off the menu (except Wed. and Fri. night buffets). We love the lamb vindaloo and sabzi jalfrezi with large chunks of fresh veggies. Dinner buffets ($18) are their weak point—they tend to lose some flavors trying to please everyone's palate. In Waipouli Town Center near Foodland. $18–$30 for dinner. Closed Tuesdays.

EAST SHORE ITALIAN

Café Portofino
3481 Hoolaulea Way • 245-2121
Lihu'e—Their view alone creates a very tasty atmosphere for those fortunate enough to get a railing table. Kalapaki Bay waves create a background hum that can enhance any food. The owner is Italian, and some of the flavors smack of the real Italy, for good and bad. (After spending a month in Italy, we came to expect good wine and bad bread—just like this restaurant.) The quality has been improving since last edition. They're not quite back to the ONO status, but we won't steer you away either At the Kaua'i Marriott. $25–$50 for dinner.

Kaua'i Pasta
4-939B Kuhio Hwy • 822-7447
3-3142 Kuhio Hwy, Lihu'e • 245-2227
ONO Kapa'a—A pretty easy place to like for the most part. Expect a few pastas and four sauces, plus panini and Parmesan for lunch, add pizzettas and some specials at dinner. Seafood options are almost nonexistent here, so look elsewhere if you're in a fishy mood. The quality is good for the price and portions ample, except for the tasty bread that they are so stingy with. Their lunch salads are very large, so consider ordering only one per couple. Entrées have a $3 split charge. You can add chicken breast or meatballs to any pasta for $6 or shrimp for $9. Well-chosen wine and beer list, while their cocktails are simple but well conceived. (The Smoking Italian goes well with pasta dishes.) Lunch is $15–$21, dinner is $15–$30. On Kuhio Hwy behind Taco Bell. If you walk

through the restaurant, they have another dining room and nice lounge in the back. The atmosphere seems to be most casual in the front. They also have a location in Lihu'e on the highway that goes by the name of **KP Lihue Italian Grill & Bar** and serves equally good food, with some variations on the above menu in a trendy urban-style atmosphere.

Pietro's Pizza
3501 Rice St. • 245-2266
ONO Lihu'e—This is like two restaurants rolled into one. By day, it's a New York-style pizza joint where you order from a window. By night, an Italian-style, wood-fired oven, Neapolitan pizza restaurant. The daytime pizza is passable—it's better taken to go and reheated, for some reason—but the nighttime digs are where the ONO comes in. Nice ambiance, good drinks, cool sit down bar with USB ports so you can linger with pizza and beer, and simple yet flavorful food. Nearly all the ingredients are Italian in origin (the cured meats in particular) while tomatoes are an Italian variety. Consider the Mario Bomba appetizer. The pizzas are baked in their homemade oven with kiawe (mesquite) and cedar woods. They aren't huge (you get six slices), and there are several types with bases of either red or white sauce—all of which we've liked. We really enjoy the extra mile they go with Italian beverages, be it sodas, beers or liquor. (Try some Grapa or Limon-cello). Easy to recommend for dinner, not so much for lunch. $15–$20 for lunch and dinner. In the Harbor Mall in Lihu'e. Closed on Sundays.

Scorpaciatta
4-1306 Kuhio Hwy • 634-3061
ONO Kapa'a—A food truck serving Neapolitan-style, wood-fired pizza. It's served very quickly, and the ingredients are locally sourced. What's not to like? One pizza is enough to share with

two if not three people, making it one of the better deals on the island. Classic flavors like pepperoni and margarita, but consider the fig and pig—kalua pork with fig jam. (Crazy, but it works.) **$10–$15** per pizza. Next to Wailua Shave Ice in downtown Kapa'a.

EAST SHORE JAPANESE

Kikuchi's
3501 Rice St. • 855-5789

ONO Lihu'e—This is one of the better food trucks on the island. It features a fusion of cuisine that ranges from Japanese to Pacific Rim to American, and it all works well. The biggest hits are their steam bun sandwiches and sushi sandwiches (really more of a giant sushi roll) as well as some tasty salads. The ingredients are always fresh and local when possible. The ginger fried chicken steam bun sandwich is a definite crowd pleaser, but the 'ahi sushi wrap makes us want to stop every time we go by—the fresh sprouts inside give it a nice crunch, and we could almost drink the wasabi soy sauce dressing. It's Hawaiian time for lunch, meaning they don't always follow their posted hours. **$10–$15** for lunch. On the mauka side of the road, across from Anchor Cove Shopping Center.

Kintaro Restaurant
4-370 Kuhio Hwy • 822-3341

ONO Wailua—This has been a reliable place for many years, but they have been slipping, and the ONO is marginal. They have a sushi bar (try the Hanalei rolls), a large teppan-yaki section (that's where the food is prepared in front of you by a talented, knife-wielding chef), full bar and a pleasant atmosphere. Filet mignon for those who don't want Japanese food. In fact, they have the best steak and lobster on the island. It's cubed

and cooked in front of you, and it melts in your mouth. A bit pricier than others, but worth it. (Occasionally they get overenthusiastic with the salt.) The sushi is super popular with locals—love the *rock 'n' roll*. But they have been shaky lately with the teppan-yaki chefs. Just north of Kinipopo Shopping Center not too far from the Wailua River on Hwy 56. Dinner only, **$20–$50**. If you want reservations for teppan-yaki you must call during business hours at least a day (two or three is better) in advance. Closed Sunday.

EAST SHORE KOREAN

Korean BBQ
4-356 Kuhio Hwy • 823-6744

ONO Wailua—A good place to try some Korean food plus a lot of local items. The combo plates are the best deal. One or more meats—Korean-style BBQ beef, kalbi (short ribs), etc.—plus plenty of side dishes—rice, mac salad, kimchee, etc. The Korean seaweed soup is excellent but it tastes terrible if you eat it with the meats. Overall, consistently good, except for the disappointing chicken katsu. **$10–$20** for lunch and dinner, except for a couple of much pricier items. In the Kinipopo Shopping Village in the south part of Wailua on Hwy 56. Closed Monday and Tuesday.

EAST SHORE LOCAL

Fish Express
3-3343 Kuhio Hwy • 245-9918

ONO Lihu'e—A long-time local favorite, this is the place to get your seafood fix to go. Along with lu'au foods and salads (both very good), they make some wicked fish specials. Seven different preparations are paired with a fresh fish that changes daily. You can't go wrong with macadamia nut-crusted fish with liliko'i, or have it sautéed with garlic and herbs. Get brave and try some of the unusual but tasty seafood creations at the deli counter. The 'ahi poke is a good place to start. One of the best deals on the island is their fried chicken and shrimp plate, which is enough food for two to share and only costs around $7. **$9–$12**. Across from Walmart on Hwy 56. Open 10 a.m. to 5 p.m. (Grill closes at 3 p.m.) Closed Sundays, and sometimes no grilled items on Saturdays.

Hamura Saimin Stand
2956 Kress St. • 245-3271

(ONO) Lihu'e—Universally loved by locals and forewarned visitors alike, they've been here since 1950 and have some of the *best* saimin on Kaua'i. (See page 216 for definition of saimin.) It is wildly popular, and people come from other parts of the island to eat here. Their selection is scant, but the food is good and cheap. Consider the "special" saimin, which has more ingredients and is tastier. Their only dessert—liliko'i pie—is light and fairly good but sells out early. Food is served lunch-counter style—so seat yourself and smile at your neighbor on the bench. Though dumpy, it'll be here forever unless the sodium police raid the place. Makes for good takeout, but it's so hot that transporting it almost necessitates a hazardous materials permit. (Spill any on you, and you may burst into flames.) **$7–$11** for lunch and dinner. Kress is off Rice Street. See map on page 67. Cash only.

Kalena Fish Market
2985 Kalena St. • 246-6629

Lihu'e—Sort of out of the way and hard to find, which in this case is OK. 'Cause the food is not worth searching for. Plate lunches, chicken katsu and some Korean BBQ items served with avoidable results. Oh, and by the way, despite the name, it's not a fish market. **$8–$13**. On Kalena (south of Kress St.) near Rice Street. Cash only. Closed Sunday.

Kaua'i Family Café
4-361 Kuhio Hwy • 822-3288

(ONO) Wailua—An excellent and affordable Filipino restaurant that also serves local and American food. If you're unfamiliar with Filipino food, they are more than happy to explain what things are. The pork and peas is particularly good as is the pancit noodles. You can also find loco mocos and decently priced hamburgers, too. Breakfast brings more familiar American dishes, but consider the tortang talong—a tasty eggplant omelet. Be sure to try their house-made, chili garlic sauce. Top it all off with the Filipino version of shave ice, halo halo. **$8–$15** for breakfast, **$10–$17** for lunch and dinner. In the strip mall next to Brick Oven Pizza in Wailua. Closed Sunday.

Mark's Place
1610 Haleukana St. • 245-2722

(ONO) Puhi—One of those places that you'd never know was here if someone didn't tell you about it. They often serve the best local food on the island, but they've been a bit variable lately and we're keeping an eye on them to make sure they still rate an ONO. The prices are reasonable and the portions ample. Consider the mixed plate with chicken katsu, teriyaki beef and beef stew for around $12. The loco moco is really good as is their burger. Be sure to check their daily specials, which often feature fresh fish. They now carry the locally made Ono Pops as well, which are a real treat with unusual flavors. This is local-style food, so don't expect low calorie or low cholesterol. And don't expect to eat in; everything's to go. But if you want to eat what many locals eat and don't want to spend much, this is the place for you. **$5–$12** for lunch. From Hwy 50, take Puhi Road, right on Hanalima. Closed weekends.

Pono Market
4-1300 Kuhio Hwy • 822-4581

Kapa'a—One of our readers' favorites, the friendly folks here serve a great plate lunch with lots of aloha. If you don't know what an item is, they take the time to explain. It's the perfect place to try some local dishes like lau lau or kalua pork. Their 'ahi poke is arguably the best on island. It can get busy around lunch, but they run the place like a well-oiled machine. **$7–$15** with some cheaper sandwiches. They also have a small coffee bar on the side with espressos and so-so ice cream. On the ocean side of Hwy 56 in downtown Kapa'a. Closed Sunday.

R & J Bakery
4303 Rice St. • 245-7520

Lihu'e—This small Filipino bakery and lunch counter is one of those places that's easy to overlook. It really feels like stepping into a small lunch shop in a foreign country. The family that owns and operates the restaurant has a great passion for their food and are helpful in explaining dishes and giving recommendations. They specialize in Filipino comfort food, and everything we tried, we liked. Plates are priced by size with the smallest only $4 and the largest $7. The baked goods selection is mostly sweets, such as danishes, muffins and mochi. Good, cheap, local grub. **$5–$10** for breakfast and lunch. In the Rice Shopping Center.

Tip Top Café
3173 Akahi St. • 245-2333

Lihu'e—Eating here is something of a cul-tural experience. It is recognized by locals as an outstanding bargain for breakfast and lunch. The menu includes some non-traditional breakfast items, such as beef stew and oxtail soup served first thing in the morning. Try the pineapple pancakes—very tasty. Diner-style weak coffee. Great cream puffs and pastries in the morning (pass on the cookies, though.) Eggs are their weak spot, and the hash browns are hard and greasy—stick with pancakes. Clean, unpretentious heartiness, less-than-bubbly service. Readers are split—some *love* the place, others (including us) are less happy. Let us know if you think we were wrong. **$8–$17** for breakfast, **$9–$17** for lunch. Closed Mondays.

EAST SHORE MEXICAN

Happy Taco
4-1395 Kuhio Hwy • 631-9810

Kapa'a—This food truck next to Mariachi's at the north end of town has all the right parts—homemade tortillas, fresh ingredients and good prices. Unfortunately, the food isn't much better than their poorly conceived, brick-and-mortar neighbor. They serve the usual lineup of Mexican food, but you really need to use their homemade hot sauce to bring out the dull flavors in any of the dishes. They have a few tables, umbrellas and potted plants to up the ambiance, though it's still the side of the road. They're friendly folks here, and we wanted to like 'em, but the food doesn't rate. **$7–$15** for lunch and dinner.

Mariachi's
3501 Rice St. • 246-1570
4-1387 Kuhio Hwy, Kapa'a • 822-1612

Lihu'e—The menu here is a broad selection of standard Mexican items plus some Mexican seafood dishes. Quality is slightly below average, and prices are too high for what you get. The portions are disappointing on some items. Service isn't as quick as you'd expect with Mexican cuisine, but they've put a disclaimer on the menu stating that it takes time, so we can't rightly scold them for it. The combination plates are a good deal if you get them "as is." Otherwise, they'll nickel and dime you with extras. For dessert, try their home-made sopaipillas. **$12–$14** for breakfast, **$14–$24** for lunch and dinner. Upstairs in the Harbor Mall. Also in Kapa'a on Kuhio Hwy just north of Hwy 581.

Paco's Tacos
4-1415 Kuhio Hwy • 822-9944
4460 Hookui Rd., Kilauea • 828-2999
854 Puu Rd., Kalaheo • 332-5792
Kapa'a—Paco's has a hard location and several trucks that float around, including the one in Kilauea. Traditional Mexican fare such as tacos, burritos and quesadillas. They use fresh fish, and the authenticity is there. The burritos are dense and tasty. Avoid the enchilada unless it comes with their mole sauce. There might be a language barrier, so speak clearly when you order your food. The restaurant location stays surprisingly cool inside. **$10–$15** for a meal and a drink. In North Kapa'a between the Bank of Hawai'i and Déjà Vu. Also at Kukuiolono Golf Course in Kalaheo.

Tiki Tacos
4-971 Kuhio Hwy • 823-8226
ONO Kapa'a—"No rice, no beans, no chips and salsa." Just an appetizing selection of tacos and quesadillas at the small shop in Waipoili Complex. Lots of different innards from spicy steak to fish and shrimp to pork to lamb, all on hand-made tortillas. Tacos are stuffed and tasty. (Make *sure* you make use of their sauces.) Snag one of the few indoor or outdoor tables, or take it to go. **$7–$13** for lunch and dinner.

Verdé
4-1101 Kuhio Hwy • 821-1400
ONO Kapa'a—A small Mexican joint that features less typical items. They call it New Mexican, and the results are probably the best Mexican food on the island. Familiar Mexican flavors with refreshing ways to deliver them. Love the stuffed sopaipillas, and the stacked enchiladas *really* work, especially with chunks of pork. Flavors are bold, and they're proud of their chilies. Add fish burritos and tacos and limited bar items (a half dozen tequilas, beer and a variety of margaritas), and you have the kind of place that is easy to return to. To go items don't travel well, however. **$10–$20** for lunch and dinner (which can get slammed and you may have to take it to go). In Kapa'a Shopping Center on mauka side of highway.

EAST SHORE THAI

Lemongrass Grill
4-871 Kuhio Hwy • 821-2888
Kapa'a—Despite being right next to the road, ambiance here is really nice—something of a throwback to Hawaiian Tiki bars. The eclectic menu is a bit hard to classify, but we stuck them in Thai. (Think of it as Pacific Rim with Thai tendencies.) Lots of fresh seafood dishes, curries and prime rib that all hit their marks pretty well. (Even their duck dish is well executed.) Cocktails are strong but tasty—consider the mango mai tai, which uses real fruit pureé. Live music most nights adds to the atmosphere and almost keeps the road noise from being

noticeable. Biggest dings are that service can be slow, and the portions are a bit small for the prices. **$20–$30** for dinner. On the mauka side of the highway, just north of Kaua'i Village Shopping Center and the whale mural.

EAST SHORE TREATS

Hee Fat General Store
4-1354 Kuhio Hwy • 823-6169
ONO Kapa'a—This is currently one of our favorite shave ices on the island. They carry a limited number of natural syrups these days, and they hit those flavors out of the park—guava is particularly good. Their lava flow is an interesting combination with a snow cap of melted vanilla ice cream on top. Only wish they'd chill the syrups because their ultra-fluffy ice melts fast. We admire that they sweat the ice before shaving. While we highly recommend the shave ice, everything else in the store is *waaay* over priced. **$3–$7**. North Kapa'a on Hwy across from the ABC Store.

Kaua'i Fruit & Flower
3-4684 Kuhio Hwy • 245-1814
Lihu'e—On Hwy 56 near the airport. *$12 for a pineapple!* Minimum purchase is two. Closed Sundays. Need we say any more?

Shave Ice Tege Tege
4-1620 Kuhio Hwy
ONO Kapa'a—Tege Tege means "just right" in Japanese, and this hand-made organic shave ice is just that. It's a tiny operation. They use a hand crank ice machine called the Hatsuyuki from Japan to create the closest thing to snow we have ever seen on Kaua'i. This is *not* your ordinary shave ice, and there are no artificial colors or flavors. We like the mango honey—real honey, handmade

mango syrup and real organic mango cut up and piled on top. Be sure to get there early, because once they make 100, they're pau for the day. **$7–$9**. Open *most* every day from 11:30 a.m. until whenever. If there are more than three people ahead of you, expect a *loooong* wait. Ocean side of the Hwy on the north (toward Anahola) side of town. They often close for the winter months.

Skinny Mike's Hawaiian Ice Cream
3501 Rice St. • 245-9386
Lihu'e—There really is a skinny Mike, and we don't know how he stays that way operating this place. Ice cream (made in Hawai'i, but not on Kaua'i), sorbet, vegan-style ice cream, smoothies, shave ice and coffee drinks round out the offerings here. The ice cream is mediocre, though they fill a good niche if you've been down at Kalapaki Beach. They bill themselves as an internet café with free WiFi, but not much of the space is set up for really taking advantage of this. It works if you're just using it on your phone while waiting for ice cream, but don't expect to write your vacation blog from one of their limited seats. **$4–$10**. On the ground floor of the Harbor Mall.

Tropical Dreams
4-831 Kuhio Hwy • 822-1010
ONO Kapa'a—This is simply the best ice cream we know of, and we're thrilled to get it on Kaua'i. Made on the Big Island, flavors and texture are superb. It ain't cheap, but if you're really looking to indulge yourself, you won't find a better place. In the Kaua'i Village Shopping Center. **$5–$8**.

Wailua Shave Ice
4-1306 Kuhio Hwy • 634-7183
ONO Kapa'a—A shave ice joint with a great creative bent.

They don't offer things a traditional shave ice shop does—ice cream for the bottom being the most glaring difference. They make up for this omission with fresh, local flavors and unique toppings. We've liked everything we've tried, especially the coconut x coconut x coconut which features coconut milk, haupia foam and roasted coconut flakes—subdued flavors that work. **$6–$8**. On the ocean side of the highway in Kapa'a near mile marker 0, sandwiched between buildings in the red food truck.

EAST SHORE VIETNAMESE

Pho Kapa'a
4-831 Kuhio Hwy • 823-6868

Kapa'a—Good, authentic Vietnamese food that is priced right. The folks here are friendly, attentive and especially helpful in showing you how to get the most out of your meal with all those mysterious sauces on the table. Their namesake pho soup is very good as are the vermicelli noodle dishes such as lemongrass beef. However, it is their $7 bahn mi sandwich that keeps us coming back. **$6–$12** for lunch and dinner. In the Kaua'i Village Shopping Center. Closed Mondays.

SOUTH SHORE AMERICAN

Beach House Restaurant
5022 Lawai Rd. • 742-1424

Po'ipu—A longtime south shore landmark, they have the best oceanfront location on the island—and they *know* it. Consequently we've seen them rest on their laurels and charge high prices for mediocre food and so-so service. An ownership change with a proven restaurateur has brought in the potential to return to their glory years. We are withholding the ONO, until we see a pattern of consistency

in line with the prices. Nice sunsets from here. Tables are reasonably spaced. Vast wine list. Steak and seafood dinner will run you **$30–$45**. Lunch is more reasonable at **$13–$23**. On Lawai Road in Po'ipu on way to Spouting Horn. Reservations *strongly* recommended days in advance.

Brennecke's Beach Broiler
2100 Hoone Rd. • 742-7588

Po'ipu—Their motto says, "right on the beach" (actually they're across the street from Po'ipu Beach Park). Brennecke's is one of those places that has made a great living off their view. Opened in 1983 after Hurricane Iwa opened their view of the ocean across the street, they sailed along and continued to have a great vista after Hurricane 'Iniki pruned the trees across the street in 1992. But it's been a long time since the gardener visited, and the park vegetation has seriously encroached on their view of the ocean. Still good, but pretty limited. As for the food (mostly seafood with steak and a cheaper pasta), many flavors are muted and not worth the high prices. At least they tend to cook fish well, and their guava plum BBQ sauce makes any of the pork dishes worth a try. Their mai tai is good but has a funny aftertaste. The large selection of nonalcoholic drinks makes it a pretty good choice if you've got kids. **$15–$25** for lunch, **$15–$35** at dinner. Brennecke's is not a *bad* choice, but it *is* an overpriced one.

Downstairs and next door, **Brennecke's Deli** has breakfast items before 10:30 a.m., sandwiches, hot dogs and bad shave ice. Though the food's certainly not gourmet, it's amazing how much better it'll taste if you take it across the street to one of the beach park tables and gaze at the delicious scenery. **$6–$11**.

Dolphin Po'ipu
2829 Ala Kalanikaumaka • 742-1414
Po'ipu—See Hanalei Dolphin review on page 217.

Eating House 1849
2829 Ala Kalanikaumaka • 742-5000

(ONO) Po'ipu—A rustic chic atmosphere that is open and loud with good food and mostly good service. First of all, the tables near the bar must be for decoration only, because the servers and bartenders will almost certainly ignore you. And once you're inside, the service is good but often forgetful. But the food makes up for it. Menu is seafood and steak with some Asian. In fact, the kamameshi (hot pot rice bowl) with butterfish is incredible, and the crispy cauliflower and brussel sprouts—which I dreaded as a kid—are awesome. Flavors are bold. Ask your server about more popular dishes, which taps you into what nearby local residents find most pleasing. Nice selection of wines (including 50 under $50), good signature cocktail (love the Hawaiian martini, which is better with Hangar One than Skye) and beer choices. Consider the warm apple volcano dessert. We have had disappointments here, but overall great food, mostly good service and an interesting environment with distant ocean views makes it ONO worthy. **$25–$60** for dinner. At the Shops at Kukui'ula. Reservations recommended.

Garden Island Grille
5404 Koloa Rd. • 639-8444

(ONO) Koloa—A good stop for food and drinks if you're exploring Old Koloa Town. Casual, open atmosphere with a familiar menu of sandwiches, burgers, salads, tacos, seafood and pricey appetizers. The food is good (they cook fish nicely), but it's their cocktails that really shine. Try their mar-

garitas made with local, fresh squeezed juices (such as tangerine or grapefruit). The owners will probably come by and check on you while you're dining, and many people staying on the south shore make repeat visits for the service. Their kids' menu is simple but good quality for the price. Live music nightly from 6 to 8 p.m. **$10–$22** for lunch and dinner. Almost directly ahead as you enter Koloa from the north.

Gourmet Pizza & Burgers by Merriman's
2829 Ala Kalanikaumaka • 742-2856

(ONO) Po'ipu—A nice, casual atmosphere with good, but pricey, food. They follow the farm-to-table trend and feature high-quality ingredients seen in most Merriman's locations. Besides the namesake items, you find salads, tacos and a few desserts. The pizzas are good, about 8 to 10 inches and enough for two to share, especially with an appetizer. (Consider the roasted Hamakua mushroom.) Burgers are big but don't come with with any sides. (The truffle fries are worth the upgrade.) If you are *fearless* in the face of cholesterol, consider the BKE burger—beef, kalua pork and a fried egg plus a kim chee and pickled fern topping. (Ask for the sriracha aioli to dip it in.) They make a strong, flavorful mai tai that'll leave its mark. **$10–$25** for lunch and dinner with burgers alone at $14–$18. In the Shops at Kukui'ula.

Ilima Terrace
1571 Poipu Rd. • 742-1234
Po'ipu—All right, enough is enough. We love this location at the Grand Hyatt but had to pull the ONO. They offer good food in a beautiful, open-air setting near a resort waterfall. But the breakfast is crazy overpriced. How else can you describe

$11 for *half a papaya* or $21 pancakes? And at lunch you have grilled chicken BLTs for $23 or pricier dinner-style entrées for more. Their once-mighty breakfast buffet has basically been cut in half for selection but not price—**$39**. Admittedly, the setting is fantastic but not enough to justify the price. If you're doing the buffet, watch for thieving birds attacking your unattended plate. **$21–$32** for lunch. Reservations recommended.

Kalaheo Café & Coffee Co.
2-2560 Kaumualii Hwy • 332-5858

ONO Kalaheo—Comfortable coffee house ambiance with lots of room, quality breakfast choices and a large list of coffee drinks make this a good spot to stop on your way to a boat tour on the west side. (One of the best Bloody Marys on the island, too.) Order at the counter and grab a seat. Great omelettes. We like the bonzo burrito and the bagel benny. Their cinnamon knuckles are deadly and best eaten hot. Sandwiches and salads at lunch. Dinner offers an eclectic menu from Thai veggie curry to fresh fish tacos to turkey meat loaf. The coconut shrimp appetizer will keep us coming back. **$8–$16** for breakfast and lunch, **$18–$33** for dinner (Tues.–Sat.). Open at 6:30 a.m. On highway in Kalaheo. Across from Brick Oven Pizza.

Kalaheo Steak & Ribs
4444 Papalina Rd. • 332-4444

ONO Kalaheo—A woody, western/paniolo atmosphere that sets a beefy tone. They have a typical steakhouse menu with a token fish. Their namesake ribs are meaty, and the house BBQ sauce is pretty good. They do steaks fairly well, though they *start* at $28. The French onion soup is sweet but tasty. If you're there during happy hour, they include their tasty Moloka'i sweetbread

pudding dessert. Avoid the poorly executed garlic mashed potatoes. Super friendly service. **$16–$40** for dinner. On the biggest cross street in town. Can't miss it. Closed on Monday.

Kalapaki Joe's
1941 Poipu Rd. • 742-6366
3-2600 Kaumualii Hwy, Lihu'e • 245-6366

Po'ipu—A local watering hole with a sports bar atmosphere. Huge selection of burgers, sandwiches, tacos, gobs of salads, hearty dishes and seafood. Results are mixed, especially with appetizers, as some ingredients taste cheap. Burgers tend to be your best bet, and the variety of toppings keeps things interesting. Breakfast has plenty of eggs and meats with local twists, but it's pricey for what you get. Service manages to be friendly yet uncaring at the same time. They seem perpetually understaffed. Good beer selection, though. In all, not quite an ONO, but it's above average bar food for a decent lunch and dinner price. We won't steer you away. **$11–$18** for breakfast, **$12–$24** for lunch and dinner. Nowhere near Kalapaki Bay (but it *used* to be). On Poipu Road between Hoowili and the Koloa–Po'ipu Bypass. The Kuku'i Grove Mall location is very popular during football (or any sports) season.

Keoki's Paradise
2360 Kiahuna Plantation • 742-7534

ONO Po'ipu—This is a special sort of place that people either love or hate (we love it). The ambiance is the story here with plants everywhere, a large fish lagoon, waterfalls and thatched roof booths (try to say *that* three times fast). It's the South Pacific that never really existed except in movies. The exotic bar area serves burgers, sandwiches, ribs and *very* cold beer at lunch and dinner for **$12–$17**. The tables in the main area are arranged on several levels. Purists will sniff that the ambiance is not real—so what?! It's still exotic inside. If you are in the right mood, this is the sort of place you will remember for a long time. As for the food, it's a steak and seafood restaurant with above average food and (usually) good service. Many styles of fish and steak plus their signature prime rib (including a 32-ouncer for those who swam here from O'ahu). The hula pie is equally large. The place can get pretty busy. This can have an effect on the service, which can be their weak point. Reservations recommended. **$28–$42** (more for steak and lobster) for dinner. They haven't changed over the years, but if it ain't broke, don't fix it. In the Po'ipu Shopping Village.

Koloa Deli
5476 Koloa Rd. • 742-9998

Koloa—A good place to grab a meal on your way to the beach. They use Boar's Head meats to fill their huge sandwiches, but most everything else they offer is made in-house. From the fresh baked bread and pastries to the desserts and the homemade salads, you will get quality food from these guys that will have other beachgoers envious of your lunch. You can build your own sandwich or choose one of their specialty sandwiches (the Godfather is our favorite). They always have seasonal baked goods ready to go, and be sure to check their daily plate lunch-style specials. Good coffee, too. Friendly service and reasonable prices, and you have a place that works. **$8–$12.** Closed on Sunday.

Living Foods Gourmet Market & Café
2829 Ala Kalanikaumaka • 742-2323

Po'ipu—The deli within the organic grocery store in The Shops at Kukui'ula is a bit pricey but worth a stop. Besides the high-end market items, they feature a number of freshly made breakfast and lunch/dinner dishes. From brioche egg sandwiches and pancakes to pastrami sandwiches and small pizzas, they cover the bases of café fare. You can take it to go, or eat at one of the small tables outside. If they're busy, expect to wait a long time for food. **$7–$18** for breakfast, lunch and dinner.

Merriman's Fish House
2829 Ala Kalanikaumaka • 742-8385

Po'ipu—A gourmet fish house that has picked it up in recent years. Only a few lanai tables (requestable) have views of the distant ocean. Crazy good chocolate purse dessert goes well with their entrées, most of which are very good, but some are underwhelming. (Stick with the fish—hence the ONO.) Awesome mojitos. Service has historically been snotty but has improved of late. **$30–$53** for dinner. In The Shops at Kukui'ula.

Plantation Gardens
2253 Poipu Rd. • 742-2121

Po'ipu—A very relaxing tropical orchid, cactus and bromeliad garden setting with mostly outdoor tables (which are preferred). The menu is a small but carefully selected array of fresh fish and a few red meat entrées with a bent toward local preparations. Prices are pretty reasonable given the setting, good service and beautiful presentation. The food *sounds* and *looks* fantastic, but too often we find ourselves describing the entrées as, "just OK." However, where they fumble with flavors in dining, they pick up the slack with their cocktails, which are well conceived. We *want* to love the place for the ambiance alone, but can't quite rate it as ONO. **$17–$35** for dinner. At the Kiahuna Plantation resort.

Puka Dog
2360 Kiahuna Plantation • 742-6044

Po'ipu—Hard to believe we'd give an ONO for a $8.49 hot dog. Granted, it's overpriced. But these are very good hot dogs served in an unusual way. The dogs are roasted (giving them the slightly crunchy skin), then embedded in a wraparound bun served with a choice of sauces inside, from mild to habañero. Get the fresh fruit relish—more like chutney—to smear on the tip each time you bite. (Love the mango.) Only two dogs—a Polish sausage and a veggie dog. But with their sauces and fixin's you'll be pleased. For a beverage get their lemonade...or bring your own drink. In the Po'ipu Shopping Village. It's about **$13** for a dog and lemonade.

Red Salt
2251 Poipu Rd. • 828-8888

Po'ipu—The name derives from the strong red Hawaiian sea salt that accompanies most items (and the bread with the unsalted butter). Ambiance is modern with splashes of Asian and tropical. Breakfast is a more traditional menu with items like eggs and pancakes, all with top-quality ingredients. Try the mac nut Belgian waffles. Dinner is very good and very expensive. Entrées range from red salt-spiced seared 'ahi, wagyu New York steak and lamb to their Big Island vanilla bean mahimahi. They lean toward seared, so if you want it cooked through, let 'em know. Most nights they also offer excellent sushi. They have uncommonly good mixed drinks. Our biggest ding is that their ads show a cleverly photographed oceanfront location, when, in fact, ocean views are poor and fairly distant. **$30–$55** for

dinner, more for the wagyu steak options. In the Ko'a Kea Hotel. Reservations recommended.

RumFire
2440 Hoonani Rd. • 742-4786

Po'ipu—What a difference a couple of years makes. When we reviewed RumFire last edition they were firing on all cylinders. Since that time we have received complaint after complaint from disappointed readers, and we have to say—we agree. They serve an American/Pacific Rim fusion that has become hit or miss. The food preparation has lost that loving feeling with the high price being more memorable than the flavors. We still recommend the Maui onion soup, and they at least still do a decent job with fish—the crab-crusted catch of the day hits the mark. Ambiance is modern, and the layout of the restaurant is spacious but doesn't embrace the island's surroundings—some may find it cold rather than modern and hip. We're pulling the ONO and hoping they can get things back to where they were. **$22–$45** for dinner. In the Sheraton Kaua'i Resort.

Savage Shrimp
2829 Ala Kalanikaumaka • 742-9611

Po'ipu—This one-time food truck grew up to be a brick and mortar restaurant. The name is in reference to the locally sourced shrimp, while the savage part...just get one of the spicy items and you'll find out. Ordering is pretty straightforward. You either get a plate of 10 shrimp (which includes rice and coleslaw) or shrimp tacos (baja style with five shrimp in each taco). If you get a plate, then you choose the sauce, and the shrimp are cooked in it. They have eight different styles that run the gamut of garlic scampi to tangy, Thai-like sauces (we like the Aloha and Savage styles best). They also have a few fried versions such as coconut shrimp and some fish and chips. Not as pricey as most of the other eateries in the Shops at Kukui'ula. **$11–$17** for lunch and dinner.

Tidepools
1571 Poipu Rd. • 742-1234

ONO Po'ipu—Located at the Grand Hyatt Po'ipu, their best feature is a very romantic atmosphere. A thatched roof, a stocked freshwater lagoon next to your table and flickering tiki torches outside provide a calm, quiet dinner environment. The limited menu concentrates on fresh fish (their specialty), with some beef and at least one vegetarian item. (Very good crab cakes.) **$33–$55**. Service can be on the slow side. Reservations recommended. Dinner only.

SOUTH SHORE ITALIAN

Brick Oven Pizza
2-2555 Kaumualii Hwy • 332-8561
4-361 Kuhio Hwy, Wailua • 823-8561

ONO Kalaheo—We have a lot of affection for this place and we eat here often, but we have to admit that it's overpriced. Though not baked in a real brick oven, they pride themselves on making their own sauce, sausage and other ingredients. The crust is thin with scalloped edges and brushed with garlic butter with tasty results. You can get gluten-free crust only on small pizzas. The sauce is simply perfect. Simple Italian atmosphere, attentive, friendly service and excellent pizza. But the prices—it's just shy of *$40* for a large four-topping pizza. It's still a great place for pizza and sandwiches, but the only reason we keep the ONO is because the pizza can't be beat. Prices are **$10–$35**. No reservations. Kids are given a wad of pizza dough to play with—nice touch. (And fitting, since

adults will *spend* a wad of dough.) Located on mauka side of highway as you enter Kalaheo or the mauka side as you enter Wailua from Lihu'e. Buffets some nights for $19. Note that the ONO does *not* apply to the Wailua location. It's poorly run, and the recurring incompetence can kill the experience. Closed Tuesdays.

Dondero's
1571 Poipu Rd. • 742-1234

ONO Po'ipu—Regional Italian food. Entrées change too often to recommend a specific one here. Pastas, veal, fresh fish and lamb, usually expertly prepared. Outstanding wine list. Elegant dining; their dress code requires resort wear, meaning covered shoes, collared shirts for men, etc. Dondero's never seems to disappoint, but you *pay* for that consistency. Dinner is **$30–$50**. In the Grand Hyatt. Reservations recommended. Closed Sunday and Monday.

La Spezia
5492 Koloa Rd. • 742-8824

Koloa—A hip, contemporary Italian wine bar atmosphere, the two-person tables are pretty small. This somehow creates the weird condition that when they are *slow and empty*, it feels claustrophobic. But as they get busier, it's less so. (I know that sounds odd, but trust me on this.) Appetizers are pretty good. The chicken with 40 cloves somehow makes the chicken light and fluffy. And the flatbread pizza appetizer is tasty if a bit filling. Dinner has offerings, such as winter squash risotto, pork tenderloin over capellini and a slightly disappointing lasagna. Spaghetti with arancini (crispy mozzarella risotto balls) zucchini noodles is bold and unusual like other dishes, has flavors that be described as divisive—you 'em or hate 'em. What t rethink is their service. Friendly, but the tiny kitchen creates such terrible bottle-necks that we've waited as much as an hour and a half for entrées, even when we were early-comers. **$17–$30** for dinner. Across from the Post Office in Old Koloa Town.

Pizzetta
5408 Koloa Rd. • 742-8881
 Koloa—Although the name stresses pizza, their broad menu includes lots of pastas, parmigianas, ribs, some fish and other items. Prices for non-pizza items are pretty high; the pizzas are more fairly priced except the $9 by-the-slice (which includes a side salad). The lasagna is thin but tasty and generous. Overall, entrées are pretty dependable, and the variety ensures that one person can get the BBQ chicken pizza, the other the seafood fettuccine, and both will be happy. Good Tuscan chop salad. The mozzarella sticks in focaccia bread are kind of cool, but avoid the watery spinach and artichoke dip. They also make a pretty decent mai tai (but pass on the lame mojito). It can get pretty hot inside unless you get one of the few lanai tables. **$15–$25** for lunch and dinner (lunch items can bring it down to $11). On the main road in Koloa Town.

SOUTH SHORE JAPANESE

Makai Sushi
2827 Poipu Rd. • 639-7219
—A small counter simple menu of fresh usually either 'ahi or erything is made to ed out surprisingly re good and come orilla. 'Ahi is your gorilla style is a akame (seaweed)

salad, spicy sauce, green onion, fish roe and toasted sesame seeds layered and beautifully presented. Easy to recommend. No place to sit; take it to go. **$12–$18** for lunch. In the Kukui'ula Store next to Seasport Divers in Po'ipu.

SOUTH SHORE LOCAL

Koloa Fish Market
5482 Koloa Rd. • 742-6199
Koloa—Ordering can be intimidating. You're standing at the counter with locals who *know* what they want. You, however, are trying to figure out what the items are. They serve plate lunches like laulau, kalua pig, etc. (Take a look at island foods on page 215 for help.) Small selection but decent quality. **$10–$14**. In Koloa. Closed Sunday. Cash only.

SOUTH SHORE MEXICAN

Chalupas
3477 Weliweli Rd. • 634-4016
Koloa—These guys are an example of how a captive audience can ruin good food. This is a taco truck next to Koloa Zipline, which is where a lot their customers come from. What was once one of the best tacos in town has become inferior with joyless service. Some items still hold their flavor, like the carnitas, but the fish tacos are disappointingly bland. **$8–$15** for lunch. A few covered tables here, but watch out for the aggressive chickens looking for a handout.

Da Crack
2827 Poipu Rd. • 742-9505
Po'ipu—Great *crack in da wall* for Mexican grinds, brah. Order your food through their small take-out window next to Outfitters Kaua'i. They offer massive burritos, tacos, nachos and quesadillas, big enough to feed two.

(Consider the keiki menu if you want a single portion.) The burritos are stuffed with your choice of beef, chicken, pork or local vegetables, and they proudly claim that they use no MSG, hydrogenated oils or lard. Best Mexican food for the money on the south shore. Grab it to go. **$8–$15.**

Tortilla Republic
2829 Ala Kalanikaumaka • 742-8884

(ONO) Po'ipu—It's like two separate restaurants here. Downstairs serves as the margarita bar and features a pupu-driven menu as well as tacos, burritos and salads. Upstairs is the slightly more formal, sit-down grill with a full dinner menu featuring Mexican dishes prepared in distinct regional styles. Both have a hip, contemporary cantina feel. The margarita bar has lots of small tables both inside and out as well as a long bar inside where you can order their various margaritas and other creative cocktails (such as the horchata colada). The upstairs bar, made of white onyx with deep, dark wood trim and floors, is worth a gander The portions are good, and the food is more hit than miss. They pride themselves on their enchiladas and do a pretty good job with them (the mole poblano enchilada is very good). Their tableside guacamole is excellent and prepared right in front of you. They also serve a pretty good brunch on weekends (love the carnitas hash). Overall, we like this place but always privately whine about the prices, which are a bit too high. (They have some decent deals during happy hour and Taco Tuesdays.) **$15–$25** for lunch, **$25–$40** for dinner, **$10–$18** for brunch. In The Shops at Kukui'ula.

SOUTH SHORE THAI

Bangkok Happy Bowl
2360 Kiahuna Plantation • 742-9888

Po'ipu—Good idea, badly executed. A Thai restaurant that also has a sushi bar. First time we've seen that done. But we have yet to try an item that tasted good. Which is a shame, because we really wanted to like the place. Instead of exciting food, it is fairly tame—Americanized in its flavor and presentation. (They don't crank up the spice no matter how much you assure them you want it to set off fire alarms.) Avoid any of the fried appetizers as they are way too greasy. Portions are small for the price. **$14–$20** for lunch, up to **$30** for dinner. In the Po'ipu Shopping Village.

SOUTH SHORE TREATS

Fresh Shave
3540 Koloa Rd. • 631-2222

(ONO) Lawai—Enjoying shave ice has never looked so hip. Served from a vintage trailer, this operation uses fresh juices, purées and toppings not usually seen. All the flavors are named after different mustache styles. (Fresh shave, get it?) Flavors such as Fu Man Chu, which is strawberry purée and diced apple bananas, is a crowd pleaser, but we like the Dirt Squirrel—it has cold brew coffee from Ha Coffee Bar. **$6** for any flavor. Monday through Saturday at Warehouse 3540 near the Hawaiian Trading Post in Lawai.

Koloa Mill Ice Cream & Coffee
5424 Koloa Rd. • 742-6544

Koloa—Rather ordinary ice cream, but they make a mean blueberry cheesepie (like a cheesecake) as well as some other baked goods. Smoothies aren't bad. In Koloa Town. **$4–$7.** Be warned that none of the neighboring shops want you to bring ice cream in with you.

Koloa Shave Ice...& More
3450 Poipu Rd. • 742-5200

Koloa—This small shave ice stand also

serves smoothies and a limited variety of coffee drinks. That's about all we can say that's positive. They open late for a coffee shop (9 a.m.) and, despite having fresh fruit toppings, all their syrups are artificial (behind the curve as far as Kaua'i shave ice goes). The ice cream they use isn't very flavorful, they're stingy on napkins, and (if I may rant) the spoon they give you is smaller than the ones you get at Costco for free samples. It's pricey for what you get, service is indifferent, and to top it off, they don't even have a garbage can to throw away the massive cup they serve the shave ice in—you have to walk next door to the Chevron to find one. They're very visible if you're heading south on Po'ipu Road, but do yourself a favor—keep driving and find a treat elsewhere. $4–$10, cash only. Next to Fathom Five in the Old Koloa Town.

Lappert's Ice Cream
2829 Ala Kalanikaumaka • 742-1272
ONO Po'ipu—A beautiful ice cream shop in The Shops at Kukui'ula. Lappert's went from great locally made ice cream to mediocre to good quality again. Compelling flavors and some stupid-rich gelatos, including a nearly radioactive chocolate. (Better than their chocolate *ice cream*.) $4–$8.

Papalani Gelato
2360 Kiahuna Plantation • 742-2663
ONO Po'ipu—Outrageous gelato made on the premises as well as dairy- and sugar-free frozen concoctions. It ain't cheap, but it's utterly delicious. $4–$9. Next to Bangkok Happy Bowl in Po'ipu Shopping Village as well as various restaurants all around the island, but it doesn't seem *quite* as good as getting it from the source. (We can only attribute to perhaps the way it's stored.)

The Right Slice
2-2459 Kaumualii Hwy • 212-5798
3501 Rice St., Lihu'e
ONO Kalaheo—Think pie. Did you visualize sweet, like apple or pumpkin? Or savory like chicken pot pies? They have both here, and they do 'em right. They have over 50 flavors of sweet pies (plus gluten free), many of which are made with fresh, local ingredients (love the mango liliko'i). Only a handful of flavors are available fresh at any given time, but call ahead and your options increase. Buy them whole, by the slice or as one of their smaller variations. We think their savory pies are the real treat, though. For around $10 you can take one home and bake, or call an hour ahead and get one baked to go. (They also have family-sized pies that serve six to eight but require 24-hour notice.) They always have chicken pot pie and shepherd's pie available as well as specials for that week. Their value packs are a good way to get a picnic lunch to go and require calling ahead as well. $5–$15 for most single items, up to $55 for family-sized. In Kalaheo on the mauka side of the road just before the streetlight or in the back corner of the Harbor Mall in Lihu'e. Closed Sunday and Monday.

Uncle's Shave Ice
2829 Ala Kalanikaumaka • 742-2364
4454 Nuhou St., Lihu'e • 246-4454
Po'ipu—So here's the deal. Their signature shave ice is their poorest offering. They're not keeping the blades sharp enough, and we keep getting ice that's too coarse. But the real reason to come here is the shave *snow*. They mix the water with dairy and syrup, then freeze it. Must not be as hard as pure ice because the result is ultra light and fluffy with a nice consistency, especially if you have 'em put a cap on top. $4–$8. In The Shops at

Kukui'ula. Also in Hokulei Village Shopping Center, Lihu'e.

WEST SHORE AMERICAN

Da Booze Shop
9883 Waimea Rd. • 338-9953
ⓄⓃⓄ Waimea—If you're looking for tasty booze preparations made with skill and care...well, you came to the *wrong* place. They don't have any. Instead, they have a sign saying, *We serve God Instead of Alcohol.* So let's move onto the food. It's a local joint that serves burgers, salads, lunch plates with BBQ ribs and/or chicken plus some surprisingly good wraps. This is local comfort food that's popular with hunters, those who have just hiked around Waimea Canyon and anyone else looking for good food with large portions at reasonable prices. Our only complaint is that the inside is a bit cramped and can get pretty stuffy midday. Best to take your food across the street to Cook Park and enjoy some shade. Look for their Underground menu for specials and out-of-the-ordinary offerings. Lunch and dinner are **$6–$15**. In the middle of town next to Big Save. The ONO is for the value. Closed Sunday.

Island Taco
9643 Kaumualii Hwy • 338-9895
2360 Kiahuna Plantation, Po'ipu
742-7045
Waimea—A cursory glance might leave the impression of a hole-in-the-wall gem— and it *can* be. But they've been dropping the ball lately, and we've had to pull their ONO. They still make tasty, homemade tortillas, but the filling is hit or miss (the mahimahi is consistently overcooked and bland). Taco plates are a bit pricey. Choose from options such as the Cajun or seared wasabi 'ahi (say *that* one out loud) in your tacos or burritos. We recommend

getting your burrito wet for the extra dollar. The atmosphere is bare bones (indoor counter and outdoor tables). The staff can be hot or cold toward their customers. On the mauka side of the highway toward the west end of town. (They close at 5 p.m., so keep that in mind if you're hiking). **$11–$25** for lunch. The Po'ipu Shopping Village location closes at 9 p.m.

Kaua'i Island Brewery & Grill
4350 Waialo Rd. • 335-0006
Hanapepe—A brewpub with a large vaulted ceiling, warehouse-style dining room that is nicely done in soft wood. There is upstairs table seating or on the rail if you want a great vantage point for people watching. The main dining room is alive with hustle and bustle with hit-or-miss service. As for the beer offerings, the "hoppiest" of their brews were fairly homogenized with one being mostly indistinguishable from the next. However, their Paniolo Brown and especially their Cane Fire Red are both standouts. All the brewing is done on site, and you can glimpse some of the process through the viewing window to the production floor. Salads, soups, wraps, sandwiches, burgers and entrées of fish, ribs and steaks. The food's not stellar (with appetizers being the weakest attempt), but it's not bad, and you came for the brew and atmosphere, especially after a long day on a snorkel boat tour. **$13–$25** for lunch and dinner. On your left before the Port Allen Harbor.

Koke'e Lodge
3600 Kokee Rd. • 335-6061
ⓄⓃⓄ Koke'e—The best (and only) place to grab a bite to eat around Waimea Canyon. Though you might not expect a park concessionaire to shine, the food's actually pretty good. If the cool weather is getting to you (well, cool to us wimpy Hawai'i residents), con-

sider the cornbread and chili or the Portuguese bean soup. They also serve breakfast all day, plus burgers, sandwiches and a couple of salads. Their coconut pie is excellent. Don't expect to be treated like old friends, 'cause you ain't one. **$7–$12**. Located *waaaay* up the road in Koke'e on Waimea Canyon Road past mile marker 15. They have a cool-looking bar and fireplace adjacent to the dining room, and they make a good Bloody Mary. That may be most folks' drink of choice since they're only open 9 a.m. to 4 p.m. (Get there by 3:30 p.m.)

Shrimp Station
9652 Kaumualii Hwy • 338-1242
4-985 Kuhio Hwy, Kapa'a • 821-0192

ONO Waimea—A good place for a plate of shrimp with rice or fries. Some items, like the sweet chili garlic shrimp (very tasty), you'll have to peel. Others, like the coconut shrimp, come peeled. Most items are **$13**, though some are less. On the ocean side of Hwy 50 in Waimea just before Waimea Canyon Road. Just some outdoor picnic tables (flies can be a problem). We're a bit less happy with their Kapa'a location on Kuhio Hwy. The ONO applies only to Waimea.

Wrangler's Steakhouse
9852 Kaumualii Hwy • 338-1218
Waimea—Well, with a name like Wrangler's, you ain't a'lookin' for no Mongolian food, and you ain't a'gonna find it here. (Cowboy twangs are hard to do in print.) The dinner menu is steak, which they do reasonably well (the pulehu steak is our favorite, but sauté anything in butter and garlic, and you'll make us happy) and seafood. All entrées come with soup and a trip to the tiny salad bar, which features some unfamiliar items, such as pickled daikon radish and boiled peanuts.

Lunch is burgers (which is the only beef from local ranches), steak and some specials. Some outdoor tables in sunny Waimea can make for a pleasant meal. Their biggest issue is service—you have a better chance of signaling a passing helicopter than your server. **$11–$17** for lunch, **$20–$40** for dinner. On the ocean side of the highway in Waimea. Saturday is dinner only, closed Sunday. The adjoining bar, **The Saddle Room**, is open only Thurs.–Sun. and is consistently better than the steakhouse in terms of food, service and overall experience. Overall, not quite an ONO, but we won't turn you away either.

WEST SHORE LOCAL

MCS Grill
1-3529 Kaumualii Hwy • 431-4645
Hanapepe—A popular spot with locals that has decent food for a reasonable price. Even when food isn't stellar, they really shine when it comes to seasoning. Steak, chicken, some fish, burgers, fries, even the mac salad is tastier thanks to their salt and pepper mastery. The onion strings appetizer is pretty good and is more than two people can comfortably eat. Dinner brings a few pasta dishes, but it's steak they do the best. It looks like a warehouse from the outside (because it's part of one), but the interior has diner written all over it. **$10–$18** for lunch, couple more bucks for dinner. On the main highway in Hanapepe next to Kaua'i Kookie. Closed Sundays.

WEST SHORE TREATS

G's Juicebar
9681 Kaumualii Hwy • 639-8785
ONO Waimea—After trying one the fresh juices here and noticing all the other patrons enjoying the acai bowls, we tried them. Gotta say, they

are really good and give you a surprising amount of energy. We've tried acai bowls at numerous places but have yet to find one as good as G's. Give the Gandhi a try to see if you feel the same way. **$6–$8.** This small, cosmically themed juice bar is across from the West Inn in Waimea.

JoJo's Shave Ice
9734 Kaumualii Hwy • 378-4712
5-5190 Kuhio Hwy, Hanalei • 378-4612
Waimea—The most prominent shave ice shop in Waimea. Long time visitors will remember the cramped, almost dingy conditions of the building that still managed to almost always have a line out the door. A change of ownership brought a new look and crazy high prices. Other shave ice companies get away with high prices by offering organic syrups, often made by hand. Not here—they have over 60, good, old-fashioned artificial colors and flavors. The closest to natural flavors they have is coffee (which JoJo's does better than other companies—it's not too sweet). **$8–$12.** On the main highway in Waimea almost across from mile marker 0. There is outdoor seating under a shade cloth (much appreciated in the blazing Waimea heat). They have a second location in Hanalei at Ching Young Village that has fewer flavors.

Kaua'i Chocolate Company
4341 Waialo Rd. • 335-0448
'Ele'ele—Homemade chocolates, fudge and ice cream. None are great; none are bad. It's solidly mid-level quality. In the Port Allen Marina Center. **$3–$6.**

ISLAND NIGHTLIFE

I know what you're thinking. "Gee, this section sure is small." True. Let's face it— Kaua'i won't be confused with Las Vegas when it comes to nightlife. That's part of our charm. But hey, it's not like we spend *all* of our nights rearranging our sock drawers. (Usually just Fridays, and *oh, what a crazy time that* is!) Besides, if you did most of the things in the previous two sections, you're too pooped to party.

That said, there is probably enough nightlife on Kaua'i to satisfy *most* people's needs. Many of the restaurants feature entertainment at night, but the schedules are always changing. You can select a restaurant from the listings above and inquire about their entertainment.

People have different desires when it comes to nightlife. Here we simply try to describe what's available and let you pick what you want.

Po'ipu
On the south shore, nightlife is mostly a resort affair. (So to speak.) **Stevenson's Library** at the Grand Hyatt is designed to appeal to anyone who ever wanted to visit the private library of one of the Rockefellers. Richly decorated, bookcases filled with the classics, pool tables (not billiards), large aquarium, chess tables and a terrace with great ocean views. The bar is the center attraction and is beautifully crafted out of strips of koa and monkeypod. Pupus are available, as is sushi some nights. Good but pricey cocktails. The Grand Hyatt's **Seaview Terrace** commands a fabulous view of the resort and can be a relaxing place to have a drink after a long day. Early music nightly.

Outside the resort, your best bet is **Keoki's Paradise** at 742-7534 in the Po'ipu Shopping Village. They have Hawaiian entertainment in their nice-looking lounge most nights. Hula demonstrations in the shopping center's courtyard some nights. Also consider ambling through **The Shops at Kukui'ula** to see what's happening.

In Koloa, **Garden Island Grille** has live music by local artists nightly from 6–8 p.m.

Lihu'e

Duke's Barefoot Bar at the Marriott is a great place for a drink; sporadic music offered. **Rob's Good Times Grill** (246-0311) on Rice Street offers entertainment every night. Mostly a local spot; sometimes a bit rough. **Kaua'i Beer Company** (245-2337) is especially lively on Thursdays when food trucks take over the dining experience.

Kalapaki Joe's (245-6366) often has lots of sports on TV.

Moviegoers can call the **Kukui Grove Cinema** at 245-5055 for a listing of their features.

Kapa'a

Trees Lounge (823-0600) behind Coconut Marketplace in Kapa'a is currently *the* place to go on the east shore for live music, pupus and cocktails. Most of the local musicians featured are pretty good, and the food is better than you'd expect at a lounge. When Trees closes, some of the crowd goes to **Big Wave Dave's** (822-3362), is a sports bar on the Hwy north of the ABC Store where the atmosphere can be younger and more local. **Oasis on the Beach** at the Waipouli Beach Resort across from Safeway in Kapa'a has a good *near*-beach bar and a good selection of rums. (Try the Ron Zacapa on ice when they have it. If you mix it with Coke, we don't want to know about it.) **Makai Lounge** at the Courtyard Kaua'i at Coconut Beach (320-3655) is a decent place for a beverage near the pool. Some like to grab a drink here and stroll along the beach. We also like to grab a drink at the Sand Bar poolside at **Islander on the Beach** and sip it on the beach, watching the waves.

North Shore

Hanalei Gourmet (826-2524) across from Ching Young Village sometimes has live music but is only recommended for those on the prowl. **Tahiti Nui** (826-6277) in Hanalei is the center of north shore nightlife. You never know what you're gonna get there, but some of the live music is pretty good. **Happy Talk Lounge** (431-4084) in Princeville has a good variety of live music nightly, offers beautiful views of Hanalei Bay plus tasty (but pricey) pupus and drinks.

West Shore

In Hanapepe, every Friday night is **Art Night**, where you can walk the streets, find good food, listen to live music and peruse the galleries. One of the best, regularly occurring events on the island.

In Waimea, find a bright light bulb and watch the geckos eat the mosquitoes—you crazy party animal, you.

LU'AU & DINNER SHOWS

If you've ever seen a movie that takes place in Hawai'i, odds are there was a lu'au scene. This is where everyone stands around with a mai tai in one hand and a plate of kalua pig in the other. There's always a show where someone is twirling a torch lit at both ends, and, of course, the obligatory hula dancers. And the truth is that's not far from reality. The pig is baked in the ground (called an imu) all day and is absolutely delicious. Shows are usually exciting and fast moving. Although lu'au on O'ahu can make you feel like cattle being led to slaughter, Kaua'i's lu'au are somewhat smaller and more pleasant.

All in all, a lu'au can be a real blast. If your time allows for one, it is highly recommended. On Kaua'i, the lu'au are all different, so your choice might be easier than on the other islands. Kilohana is high-production, story-line oriented; Grand Hyatt is more traditional; St. Regis is super pricey with great views and food but a lousy show, and Smith's is a blend of the three.

Lu'au Kalamaku at Kilohana (245-5247) is one of the largest lu'au in the state. Their 20,000-square-foot pavilion can hold nearly 1,000 people. You may not see it at maximum capacity, as some nights are cruise ship-only performances. Instead of waiting in line at the entrance, you're encouraged to roam their manicured grounds, visit the vendor booths, and grab a drink while the line diminishes. They also offer a 30-minute train ride for $20 (leaves the station at 5:30 p.m.). This as well as a number of hands-on cultural activities (such as Hawaiian stone bowling) makes Kalamaku the best choice for those with small children.

Seating is assigned, and there's hardly a bad table in the house. Considering the cost of this lu'au, we expected the food to be better. The main dishes are simple, and there's little variety in the side items. Dessert is very weak, and waiting in line for 20 minutes to get it (which has happened to us) makes it worse. At least the bar is accommodating, but it closes at 7:30 p.m., just as the show begins. There are only eight women's restroom stalls, meaning on a full night it comes to 62.5 women per stall. So get it done quickly, gals. Someone is waiting and giving you stink eye.

The show is energetic, captivating and highly entertaining. Instead of the traditional Polynesian revue, they offer a theatrical production of the Polynesian migration to Hawai'i. There is a plot to the show, and each element is presented with quality sound, inventive lighting and a level of intensity that remains constant throughout the show (also good for keeping the attention of keiki). The fire knife dance is especially exciting but is marred somewhat

by a protective net. Shows are Tues. and Fri. (Tuesday is less crowded). **$108** for adults, $72 for teens, $42 for kids 3–12. The show only, no food, is $54.

We also like **Smith's Tropical Paradise** (821-6895). Lu'au are Mon., Wed., and Fri. plus other days during parts of the year. The food is not the star; it's the marvelous setting. (And they need more desserts.) Smith's is surrounded by a huge garden area. Though the garden could use a little polishing, the site works perfectly for a lu'au. After dinner, you move to a separate show area where a small pond separates the audience from the stage. While not authentic by any means, it's dazzling, well-choreographed and quite entertaining, complete with an erupting volcano. **$98**. Free open bar, but it closes at 7:30. Allow 30 minutes for a garden tour before the imu ceremony. You can also attend the show alone, without the food, for $15. The only ding is the lack of enthusiasm by a lot of the staff. The host, at least, is more enthusiastic.

If you'd rather have a more intimate experience, **Tahiti Nui Lu'au** (482-4829) gives you the feeling of being invited into a (very talented) family's home. Instead of an audience of several hundred people, you're in a dining hall next door to the Tahiti Nui bar with 60 (usually fewer). The seating is shared, the entertainment is decidedly low-tech, and the food selection only takes up two tables. The food isn't as varied as others but seems higher quality (even the poi tastes better here), and the pig they pull out of the imu is always what you'll be fed. Having the restaurant's well-conceived mai tai rather than the watered-down alternative found at most lu'au might affect our judgment, but we still appreciate their different approach. The show only has four dancers, and they

Most kid-friendly

cover traditional hula all the way through Samoan fire dance. The only ding is that they start charging for drinks at 6 p.m., so suck 'em up early. All in all, one of the better and more affordable lu'au on Kaua'i. Wednesday nights in Hanalei for **$80**.

Next on our list is the **Grand Hyatt Kaua'i Lu'au** (240-6456). The line to get in can be long, and they serve only fruit punch until you're inside. The food is well-prepared. When they have the lu'au in their Ilima Garden, it's a nice setting. But when it's in the courtyard or ballroom, it suffers. And there's no way to know which one they'll use in advance, so it's lu'au roulette. It has a more comfortable dining experience than Smith's and a more traditional MC-dominated show. The performances aren't as polished as other lu'au, but everyone seems to actually *enjoy* being there. Seating can be confusing; grab a table in the front center. Free, open bar all night, plus table service for drinks. They do a good job with desserts here—try the guava mousse cake. Wednesdays and Sundays for **$108**.

'Auli'i Lu'au (634-1499) at the Sheraton in Po'ipu sits solidly in the mid-range of Kaua'i's lu'au. The food selection is wide and of pretty good quality. We like that they have appetizers out before the full buffet (no imu ceremony, though). The show is the more traditional, MC-driven type. What really shines here is the setting—this is the only lu'au that is next to the ocean. This makes for some beautiful ambiance, especially as the sun sets. They start feeding you mai tais while you're in line, which are free through the show. There are a few craft vendors around but not much in the way of cultural demonstrations—mostly they encourage you to get comfortable and talk with your neighbors. Mondays and Thursdays plus Saturdays during summer and winter holi-

days. **$109** for adults, $74 for teens, $52 for kids 3–12.

Lu'au Maka'iwa (800-763-0120) is held under big tents next to the Courtyard Kaua'i at Coconut Beach in Kapa'a. They say it's oceanfront, but you won't be able to see the ocean from where you sit. The seating is open unless you sprung for VIP, which is not worth it here because everyone has a good view of the stage. Things feel a bit disorganized before the food is served. There are some craft vendors and even quasi-cultural demonstrations that seem more like the dancers getting warmed up rather than an interactive experience for guests. The food is good (though no imu ceremony here), but be sure to get it while it's out—they start clearing it away by 7:30, and if you're one of the last tables to eat, you won't be able to get seconds. Also, make sure you load up your drinks as the bar closes at 8 p.m. The show itself is heartfelt, featuring several generations of practitioners representing Tahiti and Hawai'i. The MC-driven show feels a bit stiffer than most. Overall, adequate. Thursdays and Sundays. **$99** for adults, $65 for kids 4–12 (VIP is $129 and $79).

Mailani Dinner Show (826-2746) at the St. Regis Princeville is a wallet-choking **$159** for tables on the outdoor terrace and much inferior indoor seating. The positive traits are the great food with killer desserts and stellar views from the outdoor tables. On the negative side the show is pretty bad and takes place on a microscopic stage. And it's the only lu'au where you pay *at the end*, with a clear expectation of a tip, adding salt to the wallet wound. Offered seasonally. Call if you have your heart set on it.

DINNER CRUISES

Maui and O'ahu have multiple choices when it comes to dinner cruises. On

Kaua'i the pickin's are more slim. Fortunately, there's a winner here. One of **Captain Andy's** boats is a beautiful 65-foot catamaran called **Southern Star** (335-6833) adorned with nice touches such as wooden decking and lots of high-end furnishings. Food is excellent (though you should eat that steak fast because the breeze will chill it). Open bar. Though the boat cuts through the water well, this is still Kaua'i, so some will get seasick. You'll probably power upwind toward Po'ipu then sail downwind, but they *may* go up to Na Pali. Don't get too comfortable in the back; suck up some of the breezes on the bow. Some of the narration is classic Captain Andy bad, but the staff is warm and helpful, and the experience easy to recommend. $159 for 4 hours. They also have a 4-hour tour with a buffet on a smaller boat that goes to Na Pali (though most of the trip is along the bland Mana Plain). Better scenery on *part* of this one, but poorer boat and food for $129.

Kaua'i Sea Tours (826-7254) has a 4-hour trip with more modest food and beverages for $130. The boat's not as cushy, and the bar serves only beer, wine and mai tais, but it's all included. **Blue Dolphin** (335-5553) has a very similar product and boat for $130 as well as one that includes snorkeling or scuba for $157 (Only from June through September).

DINNER ON A BEACH

The **Grand Hyatt Kaua'i Resort** (742-1234) features the *Share the Stars with Someone You Love* dinner for $675 per couple (though not *technically* on the beach). It's in a gazebo overlooking their pool. What a perfect way to make up for forgetting your anniversary.

The **Kaua'i Marriott Resort & Beach Club** (245-5050) will serve you near their beach fire pit for $700 and up per couple plus all kinds of heavy surcharges. **St. Regis Princeville** at 826-9644 (being the St. Regis) will do it for you for a *mere* $1,900. When you add *mandatory* gratuity and tax, it's gonna be around $2,400 for two people. If you're good with that, please contact our corporate office because, boy, do we have an investment opportunity for you.

Sheraton Kaua'i (742-1661) offers a more affordable option. Their Halelani Romantic Dinner is $355 per couple for a three-course meal or $430 for the four-course. You are closer to the beach than at the Hyatt, but the table doesn't feel quite as private. Not available on Sundays or Mondays.

ISLAND DINING BEST BETS

Best Local Food—Pono Market
Best View—Beach House Restaurant
Best Phony but Exotic Ambiance—
    Keoki's Paradise
Best Shave Ice—Hee Fat General Store
    or Tege Tege.
Best Saimin—Hamura Saimin
Best Lu'au—Smith's Tropical Paradise
Best Steak and Lobster—Teppan-yaki
    Tables at Kintaro
Best Inexpensive Baked Goods—Village
    Snack & Bakery Shop
Best Place to Lower Your Net Worth—
    Kaua'i Grill
Best Place for a Romantic Dinner—
    Tidepools or Dinner on a Beach
Best Gelato—The insanely good
    chocolate at Lappert's
Best Fish on the Go—Fish Express
Best Vietnamese Food—Pho Kapa'a
Best Tapas—Bar Acuda
Best Name for a Place that Does NOT
    Serve Alcohol—Da Booze Shop

Hotels shown in this color. Condominiums shown in this color.

Rental Agents⚓

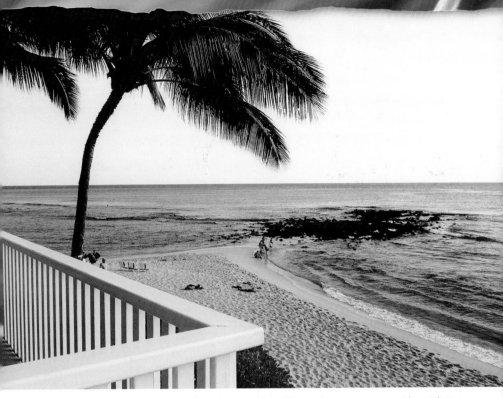

Wanted: Visitor seeking room with a view. Must be willing to burn your return airline ticket.

Your selection of where to stay is one of the more important decisions you'll make in planning your Kaua'i vacation. To some, it's just a place to sleep and rather meaningless. To others, it's the difference between a good vacation and a bad one.

There are four main types of lodging on the island: hotels, condominiums, bed and breakfasts, and single family homes. The vast majority will stay in one of the first two types. But B&Bs and single family homes are often overlooked and can be very good values. If your group or family is large, you should strongly consider renting a house for privacy, roominess and plain ol' value. There is a list of rental agents in the WHERE TO STAY INDEX, each

willing and happy to send you a list of homes they represent. We also have a B&B referral service listed there.

We have *brilliantly* labeled the four main sections of Kaua'i as North Shore, South Shore, East Shore and West Shore and listed the resorts geographically within in each section. **Hotels are in green** and **condominiums are in blue**. Hotels usually offer more services but smaller spaces with no kitchens. Condos usually have full kitchens, but you won't get the kind of attention you would from a hotel, including daily housekeeping. There are exceptions, of course, and we will point them out when they come up. You can find their locations on the various maps.

See all Web reviews at: www.hawaiirevealed.com

All prices given are RACK rates, meaning *without any discounts*. Tour packages and direct internet booking will often bring better rates. Most resorts offer discounts for stays of a week or more, and some will negotiate price with you. Some won't budge at all, while others told us *no one* pays RACK rates. These prices are subject to taxes of around 13.5 percent.

The gold bar indicates that the property is exceptionally well priced for what you get.

SOLID GOLD VALUE

A REAL GEM

The gem means that this hotel or condominium offers something *particularly* special, not *necessarily* related to the price.

These are subjective reviews. If we say that rooms are small, we mean that we've been in them, and they feel small or cramped to us. If we say that maintenance is poor, we mean that the paint might be peeling, or the carpets are dingy, or it otherwise felt worn to us.

HOTELS

All hotel rooms described **(shown in this color)** have air conditioning, an activity or travel desk, telephones, small refrigerators, lanai (verandas), cable TV and have cribs available upon request. None has room service unless otherwise noted. If you are a smoker, call about smoking policies because most hotels in Hawai'i are designated non-smoking.

CONDOS

One of the confusing aspects about renting a condo **(shown in this color)**, cottage or house on Kaua'i is the fact that there's no central rental source for many individual properties. Most condo complexes, whether large or small, consist of individually owned condominiums. Individual owners have the prerogative of renting their units through any rental agent they choose. Consequently, a 50-unit condo resort might be represented by many rental agents. Usually (but not always), prices for comparable units within a given resort are equivalent through different agents. When we describe a particular resort, we will often give the names or phone numbers of one or two companies that dominate the rental pool. But realize that this does not always do justice to the *entire* property. When we describe rates, it is for the larger rental agents. Different agents have different policies for the same complex.

Once you have decided where you want to stay, you can contact the resort. You may also want to contact some of the rental agents on page 252 to determine if they represent any units from the property you have chosen.

Also realize that condominium owners usually have complete autonomy in how they furnish their individual units. Consequently, a resort that we describe as a good deal might have individual units that are not as hot. (Notice how we neatly cover our 'okoles, so that if you get a less-than-charming condo in a resort we recommend, we can always say you got one of the few duds there.)

Many condos have minimum stays—usually three nights. We don't always list this because it changes with different rental companies. More and more rental agents also require you to pay *all* of your condo rental costs and cleaning fees before you arrive. It may make you nervous, but you might not have a choice if you're intent on staying at a particular place.

Three bedroom/two bath units are described as 3/2, two bedroom/one bath

Some resorts may be booked at: www.hawaiirevealed.com

units are described as 2/1, etc. Differentiation between half baths and full baths is not made. The price spread for rooms of a given size is due to different views, different locations within the resort and seasonal fluctuations. So when you see that a 2/2 unit rents for $140–$180, you should figure that $180 units have a better view or are closer to the water. The terms Oceanfront, Ocean View and Garden View are used rather capriciously in Hawai'i, so you should be skeptical of them.

Unless otherwise noted, all rooms come with telephones, complete kitchens, washer/dryers in unit, coffee makers, lanais (verandas), cable TV, ceiling fans and have cribs available upon request. Housekeeping is usually not available, and none has air conditioning unless otherwise noted. (On Kaua'i, trade winds often make a/c unnecessary, and few opt for it.) Most condos also have an additional cleaning fee and charge more at Christmas. If you are a smoker, you will want to check policies before you book. Most condos don't allow smoking in the units, and some even restrict you from smoking on the lanai and property grounds, too.

BED & BREAKFASTS

Rather than describe the countless B&Bs scattered about the island, you're better off calling **Hawai'i's Best Bed & Breakfast** (808) 885-4550. We have lots of links to B&Bs on our website, but it's not practical to personally review them the way we do other accommodations.

RENTAL AGENTS

Nearly all the rental agents on the list on page 252 also represent private home vacation rentals, as well as condominiums in various resorts. Contact them in advance to obtain lists of rentals available or hit their websites. (We have links to all of them from our site.) Many great bargains can be found this way.

WHERE SHOULD I STAY?

What part of the island you want to stay on will dictate, to a degree, what kind of vacation you have. Although Kaua'i is small enough to do a driving tour in one day, where you stay will dominate certain activities.

The **north shore** is probably the prettiest part of the island and is dominated by one large hotel and lots of condos and vacation rentals. The weather is usually great in the summer and can be quite a bit wetter in the winter. Though the scenery is incomparable, the down side is the remoteness you'll feel when you want to venture to other parts of the island.

The **east shore** is the most geographically convenient. Trips to the north or south shore don't feel as daunting. There are plenty of hotels and condos and the most dining and shopping options. The down side is traffic in Kapa'a (especially heading south on Hwy 56), and the scenery and beaches aren't as good as the north shore.

The **south shore** has better weather year round and some great beaches. Several big hotels and lots of condos dominate. But the backdrop isn't as nice as the north or even east shores, and there aren't as many dining or shopping choices as the east shore. Also, construction of new condos will be ever-present.

Finally there's the **west shore**. It's nearly always sunny, it's the hottest and driest part of the island and has only one resort plus a few vacation rentals to choose from. If you plan to spend all your time hiking in Koke'e and Waimea Canyon, it's convenient. Otherwise, it's isolated and remote.

See all Web reviews at: www.hawaiirevealed.com

WHERE ARE THE REST?

You'll notice that some of the resorts listed here don't have full reviews. When we review a place to stay, we don't just want to list bare bones information on them. After all, you can get that kind of info on the internet. We wanted to tell you what we really *think* about a place, and that takes space. Also, we wanted to include aerial photos of the resorts. After all, a picture speaks a thousand words (and a thousand words takes too long to read, anyway). But in the end we only have so much space we can devote to accommodations.

We had a choice—give you *less* info on *all* of them or do *detailed* reviews on only a *portion* of them. Neither choice seemed palatable.

So we came up with a *third* way: List minimal info on all (including if they are GEMS or SOLID GOLD VALUES), print detailed reviews on *most,* and post full reviews of all on our website, **www.hawaiirevealed.com**. After all, most people use this section before they come to the islands. And with the internet (which has infinite space), we can do more, like post larger aerial photos of the resorts with specific buildings labeled when appropriate, provide constant updates when necessary, and put links to book hotels right on the website. You should remember, however, that resorts post photos to lure you in, and some aren't above posting modified or overly flattering shots when they were new and sparkling. Our aerials don't lie and are designed to give you a feel for their ocean proximity (does oceanfront *really* mean oceanfront?), so you'll know what kind of view to expect from a given location within the resort. Resorts whose full reviews are posted *only* on our website are identified with

Please remember that all these reviews are *relative to each other*. This is important. Even staying at a dump right on the ocean is still a *golly gee!* experience. In other words, *Hey, you're on the ocean on Kaua'i!* So if we sound whiny or picky when critiquing a resort, it's only because their next door neighbor might be such a better experience. It doesn't mean you'll be miserable, it just means that *compared to another resort*, you can do better.

NORTH SHORE

Hanalei Colony Resort
(800) 628-3004 or (808) 826-6235
5-7130 Kuhio Hwy

52 units, pool and spa, BBQs, coin-op laundry room, small day spa, art gallery, restaurant (lunch and dinner), free Wi-Fi resort-wide (and at restaurant with computers available), housekeeping every third day, wedding coordinator. No telephones, no TVs in rooms, free area shuttle to beaches, shopping and dining. This is the only beachfront resort on the north shore. Some of their units are as close to the water as you will get on Kaua'i *(25 feet).* We especially like units in A, F, G, I and the front J units. The resort is secluded and somewhat isolated, near the end of the road on the north shore. All units are two-bedroom (although the bed-

A REAL GEM

Some resorts may be booked at: www.hawaiirevealed.com

rooms aren't completely walled off, and second rooms have a single twin bed). This allows for only three people per room. Extra persons over 3 years old will add $50 per day to the room charge (maximum four people total). Room updates in 2015 included new furniture for all units and kitchen updates in premium units. Their location on Kepuhi Beach is outstanding, and the attention to detail is admirable, but you may find some rust on metal items in units. (Being this close to the ocean, it's *unavoidable*.) While the lack of room telephones might make arranging your day slightly awkward, others will welcome it. Cell phone coverage may be spotty, depending on your carrier. (You can use the phones by the small pool, which is also where the laundry facilities are, so you won't be bored between loads.) 2/2 units (850 sq. ft.) are $287–$586. Garden views are also quite nice. 2-night minimum.

Hanalei Inn
(877) 769-5484 or (808) 826-9333
5-5468 Kuhio Hwy
WEB REVIEW

St. Regis Princeville
(866) 716-8140 or (808) 826-9644
5520 Ka Haku Rd.
WEB REVIEW ♦

Hanalei Bay Resort & Suites
(877) 344-0688 or (808) 826-6522
(800) 826-7782 or (808) 822-4444
5380 Honoiki Rd.
WEB REVIEW

Pu'u Poa
(800) 222-5541 or (808) 826-6585
(866) 922-5642
5454 Ka Haku Rd.
56 rooms, tennis court, pool, free Wi-Fi, BBQ area, washer/dryer in unit. Units are

large (1,352–2,079 sq. ft.) and comfortable. Most units (especially higher floors) have commanding ocean views. Units vary depending on the care of the particular owner, but most we saw were nice. The great ocean bluff causes lots of seaspray-induced maintenance headaches. Many bathrooms have deep, round Japanese-style tubs or Jacuzzis next to the shower. Note that some of the unit owners have converted their lanai into a separate room (which they call an atrium). It's nice, but your upstairs neighbors will be able to see you through the glass...so behave yourself. 2/2 units from the first phone number are $325–$445. 3- or 7-night minimum. The second set of numbers has units mostly of similar quality and price. Kaua'i Pacific Real Estate also has units here.

Hanalei Bay Villas
(800) 367-5025 or (808) 245-8841
(800) 222-5541 or (808) 826-6585
5451 Ka Haku Rd.
WEB REVIEW

Pali Ke Kua
(800) 222-5541 or (808) 826-6585
(800) 367-5025 or (808) 245-8841
5300 Ka Haku Rd.
98 units, pool, spa, BBQ area, free Wi-Fi in most, washer/dryer in unit, restaurant. Some nicely furnished units, but they vary

See all Web reviews at: www.hawaiirevealed.com

Alii Kai I
(866) 922-5642
(800) 222-5541 or (808) 826-6585
3780 Edward Rd.

a lot. Nicely tucked away, offering privacy, but thin walls can make your visit less quiet if you have a noisy neighbor. Many units have very fine ocean bluff views, but it's a bit pricey at rates listed below. Some of the layouts are a bit strange, and the bedrooms feel small to us. Second bedrooms on upper floor units are lofts. Some are enclosed and others are open offering less privacy. There is a private path to the eastern part of Hideaways Beach below the cliffs, which is where the BBQ area is located. It can be awkward carrying food down there. (This beach is otherwise only reachable by swimming from the western part of the beach). Units 3–16 have mountain views. 1/1 units (683 sq. ft.) are $195–$225, 2/2 units (1,067 sq. ft.) are $200–$325. 3- or 7-night minimum. Kauai Pacific Real Estate also has units at this property.

Emmalani Court
(800) 325-5701 or (808) 742-2000
(866) 922-5642
5200 Ka Haku Rd.
WEB REVIEW

Villas of Kamali'i
(800) 367-5025 or (808) 245-8841
(800) 325-5701 or (808) 742-2000
4141 Lei O Papa Rd.
WEB REVIEW

63 units, BBQ area, pool, free Wi-Fi in most, washer/dryer in unit. Most of the **SOLID GOLD VALUE** buildings are perched on the sea cliffs (except numbers 1 and 2). Bldgs. 3, 4 and 5 have the best views and can be quite dreamy, though the mountain views from 1 and 2 are really pleasing. Layouts of these 2/2 units are good with even the second bedrooms often having ocean views. Sounds do carry in these buildings. Decor varies *a lot* here from unit to unit—some feeling more dated than others. It's worth it to splurge for the ocean view here. Don't confuse this resort with Alii Kai II next door. Units (886–1,086 sq. ft.) are $119–$215. 3-night minimum.

The Cliffs
(800) 367-8024 or (808) 826-6219
(800) 222-5541 or (808) 826-6585
3811 Edward Rd.
WEB REVIEW

Nihilani at Princeville Resort
(800) 325-5701 or (808) 742-2000
(800) 367-5025 or (808) 245-8841
4919 Pepelani Loop

102 units, pool, spa, a/c, BBQ area, free Wi-Fi, washer/dryer in unit, garages (some not available to renters). These 34 triplex buildings were completed in 2008. The close proximity of the buildings, lack of any decent views

Some resorts may be booked at: www.hawaiirevealed.com

and roads (with noise) on three sides of the grounds give the property a claustrophobic feel. If you can get past all that, the interiors are pretty nice. Big bathtubs and separate showers in many of the bathrooms. Very pleasing layouts in the single-story 2/3 units, which at 1,567 sq. ft., make them very livable. We like the large dens and separate living rooms. The two-story 2/2 (1,406 sq. ft.) units are our least favorite layout here. They show Bali Hai views on their property map, but the views of it are not great, and only a few units can see Bali Hai, mostly buildings 16–19. (Even in some of those we had to walk out onto the second floor lanai to see it.) 2/2s or 2/3s (1,406–1,567 sq. ft.) are $175–$200, 3/3s or 3/4s (1,874–1,972 sq. ft.) are $175–$300. 3-night minimum.

Plantation at Princeville
(800) 222-5541 or (808) 826-6585
(800) 325-5701 or (808) 742-2000
4771 Pepelani Loop
WEB REVIEW

SeaLodge
(866) 922-5642
(800) 585-6101
3700 Kamehameha Rd.
86 units, pool, BBQ, free Wi-Fi in most, coin-op laundry, most units have washer/dryers. Most units have incredible ocean bluff views at *extremely* reasonable

prices. You'll never get tired of gazing at the extensive offshore reef. Building A will require the most walking to your car. Bldgs. B

SOLID GOLD VALUE and F have the poorest views but also the cheapest rates on the property. Units vary *considerably* in terms of quality from both agents listed. The "BBQ area" leaves a lot to be desired and requires a short but steep walk and your own charcoal. At these prices it's an easy place to like due to the location. 1/1 units are 567 sq. ft. and are a good deal at $119–$185, 2/2 units (second bedroom is a loft, making it 754 sq. ft.) are $110–$175. 3-night minimum from first phone number. Also note that both of these rental agents are based on the mainland, not Kaua'i.

Kamahana
(800) 222-5541 or (808) 826-6585
(866) 922-5642
3800 Kamehameha Rd.
WEB REVIEW

The Westin Princeville Ocean Resort Villas
(866) 837-4254 or (808) 827-8700
3838 Wyllie Rd.
WEB REVIEW

Puamana
(800) 222-5541 or (808) 826-6585
3880 Wyllie Rd.
WEB REVIEW

See all Web reviews at: www.hawaiirevealed.com

Mauna Kai
(800) 222-5541 or (808) 826-6585
(800) 826-7782 or (808) 822-4444
3920 Wyllie Rd.

WEB REVIEW

EAST SHORE

**Hotel Coral Reef Resort
on the Beach**
(800) 843-4659 or (808) 822-4481
4-1516 Kuhio Hwy

21 rooms (6 more planned), pool, juice/ sandwich bar, free Wi-Fi in rooms and lobby, free room safes, BBQ area, a/c, refrigerators, **SOLID GOLD VALUE** coin-op laundry, lanai on all (but some suites), coffee makers with free coffee daily. The rooms have a fresh, tropical feel. The oceanfront unit's bathrooms have deep Jacuzzi tubs. Good oceanfront location, and the grounds were looking great on our recent visit. Free coffee, fruit and pastries in the lobby in the mornings where you can "talk story" with other guests and staff. Free bikes, beach gear, coolers and DVDs available on site. A third story was planned at press time on the oceanfront building with an elevator, along with room updates. Overall, a friendly place to stay. Rooms and suites (approx. 200–600 sq. ft.) are $125–$245. Discounts available if you call direct at certain times of the year (or during construction) make this a SOLID GOLD VALUE.

Honu'ea International Hostel Kaua'i
(808) 823-6142
4534 Lehua St.

WEB REVIEW

Kaua'i Kailani
(800) 367-5004 or (808) 822-3391
4-856 Kuhio Hwy

WEB REVIEW

Waipouli Beach Resort & Spa
(800) 688-7444 or (808) 823-1401
(877) 465-2824 or (808) 651-0040
4-820 Kuhio Hwy

196 units, pool with keiki pool, 3 spas, fitness room, restaurant, business center, a/c, day spa, free laptop-sized room safes (from first agent), Wi-Fi resort-wide, washer/dryers in all but studios, BBQ area. **A REAL GEM** Finished in 2006, this resort has the most upscale condos on the east shore. The area is very congested, and traffic into and out of the property may be an issue at times. Once you are within the grounds, you won't notice that much, as most of the resort is oriented toward the pool and beach. The rooms are richly appointed and furnished. They include dark, imported hardwood trim, granite counters, oversized Wolf ovens, etc. On the plus side, the bedrooms and baths are large. The baths have deep tubs and separate showers. On the negative side, the living area is relatively small. They didn't

Some resorts may be booked at: www.hawaiirevealed.com

plan for a dining area, which is usually just a small table often shoved against a wall (an issue if you have more than four people staying in a room). We were told that the developers planned to have all the dining on the lanai, but with possible passing showers that is not always practical. The oceanfront units have the best layouts with roomy lanai and dreamy views. Second story and above are better, because first story oceanfront units have plantings in front of them that may block some of your view of the beach. The hotel-type rooms have a coffee maker, fridge, microwave and are closest to the road. The bathrooms in those units have showers only—no tubs, and no coin-op laundry available on property, but they will change your towels.

The pool is the star here. It is a saline, two-acre, river-like pool that meanders through the entire courtyard of the property. One end is sand-lined for the kids (since the beach is not very swimmable), and it has two waterslides. There are three spas, each with a sandy bottom, and one is suitable for kids. The day spa, which is pleasant for a resort of this size, also rents beach gear and bikes.

There is a *mandatory* resort fee of $25 per day for parking, internet and use of fitness room regardless of the booking agent. Hotel-type rooms (395 sq. ft.) are $165–$239, 1/2s (898 sq. ft.) are $205–$419. 2/3s (1,279–1,853 sq. ft.) are $245–$480. 2-night minimum. The second set of phone numbers has one- and two-bedroom units for about the same price and a 3-night minimum.

Courtyard Kaua'i Resort at Coconut Beach
(800) 321-2211 or (808) 822-3455
650 Aleka Loop
WEB REVIEW

Plantation Hale Suites
(800) 775-4253 or (808) 822-4941
525 Aleka Loop
WEB REVIEW

Islander on the Beach
(877) 997-6667 or (808) 822-7417
440 Aleka Place

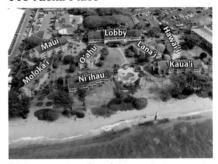

200 rooms, pool and spa, BBQ area, coin-op laundry, poolside bar, empty refrigerator, microwave, coffee maker, Wi-Fi in rooms, lobby and by the pool, coin-op laundry. Wonderful open, plantation-style setting adjacent to Wailua Beach with very relaxing grounds. The Kaua'i and Ni'ihau buildings are fairly close to the ocean, allowing you to fall asleep to the sound of the surf. Grab a beverage from the poolside bar (2–9 p.m.) and sip it at the beach, or enjoy live music some nights. Relaxing thatch-covered daybeds by the pool are free. The resort was converted to a condotel (meaning the rooms are all individually owned), but decor is consistent, pleasing and well-maintained. They charge a *mandatory* $20 per day "amenity" fee, which covers daily coffee, room safe, local and toll-free calls, DVD and PS3 rentals, internet, daily coffee and a few other items. Rooms are smallish at 311 sq. ft. and go for $319–$379. 1/1 Suites at 622 sq. ft. (with full kitchen) are $469. They have lots of specials, and few ever pay the price we listed (and we're assuming you won't either).

See all Web reviews at: www.hawaiirevealed.com

Kaua'i Shores
(800) 222-5642 or (808) 822-4951
420 Papaloa Rd.

WEB REVIEW

Lae Nani
(800) 688-7444 or (808) 823-1401
(800) 367-5025 or (808) 245-8841
410 Papaloa Rd.

84 units, lighted tennis court, pool, coin-op laundry, free room safe (from first agent listed), washer/dryer in unit, BBQ area, Wi-Fi in some. Though this gated resort is still a gem, it's a bit overpriced (from first agent listed), so we're hoping that you're getting a discount off these RACK rates. Pleasant grounds and a very nice oceanfront location. They have a Hawaiian heiau on the premises, as well as a wonderful boulder-enclosed ocean pond for the keiki (kids). Building 5 has oceanfront units. 1/2 units (808 sq. ft.) are $319–$379, 2/2 units (1,072–1,368 sq. ft.) are $409–$439. The second agent listed has much cheaper prices.

A REAL GEM

Lanikai
(808) 821-9555
(800) 367-5025 or (808) 245-8841
390 Papaloa Rd.

WEB REVIEW

Kapa'a Sands Resort
(800) 222-4901 or (808) 822-4901
380 Papaloa Rd.
24 units, pool, BBQ area, guest laundry for

a fee, free room safes, free Wi-Fi in units. This is a good bargain. They have ocean-front studios (some have a pull down Murphy bed— these are recommended for more living space). Small, but they make good use of the space. You are as close as 30 feet from the water on a small beach (down some steps) in the oceanfront units. The beach may have large driftwood on it. Resident offshore turtles will keep you entertained at dusk. The property feels very intimate and tropical. Some of the oceanfront units (numbers 1–2) are partially blocked by trees. Some units could use updating. Studios (approx. 380 sq. ft.) are $135–$177 (definitely spring for the ocean-front), 2/2 units have a two-story layout (728 sq. ft.) and are $175–$235. 3- or 7-night minimum. Discounts on 14 nights or longer stays.

SOLID GOLD VALUE

Wailua Bayview
(800) 882-9007
(800) 367-5025 or (808) 245-8841
320 Papaloa Rd.

WEB REVIEW

Hilton Garden Inn Kaua'i
(844) 672-2149 or (808) 823-6000
3-5920 Kuhio Hwy

WEB REVIEW

Some resorts may be booked at: www.hawaiirevealed.com

Kaha Lani
(800) 367-5004 or (808) 822-9331
(800) 367-5025 or (808) 245-8841
4460 Nehe Rd.

74 units, lighted tennis court, BBQ area, pool, computer in office, free Wi-Fi, coin-op laundry, room safe in some, housekeeping every fourth day. The grounds are well-tended, and the area is less built up than some places on the east shore. The buildings themselves feel cheaply built (and sound carries pretty efficiently), but they are well-maintained. Most of the units are reasonably decorated, though you still have lots of variation in terms of updating. However, all the units are very clean. We prefer units on higher floors for a better ocean view, though views still feel a bit distant. Adjacent to Lydgate State Park and the beach path. RACK rates have a large spread, so we hope you got a good deal. The staff is helpful here. 1/1 units (739 sq. ft.) are $168–$289, 2/2 units (996 sq. ft.) are $214–$369, 3/2 units (1,183 sq. ft.) are $311–$479.

Kaua'i Beach Villas
(800) 367-5025 or (808) 245-8841
4330 Kauai Beach Dr.
WEB REVIEW

Kaua'i Beach Resort
(866) 940-2782 or (808) 245-1955
4331 Kauai Beach Dr.
350 rooms, 4 pools, 2 spas, 7 conference rooms, valet parking, room service, day spa and beauty salon, 24-hour fitness room, a couple of shops, Wi-Fi throughout, 3 restaurants, lounge with outdoor firepit, coin-op laundry, empty refrigerator, coffee maker with free coffee daily, laptop-sized room safe, 24-hour business center, free airport shuttle.

A REAL GEM

We just like the feel of this place on every visit. It's relaxing, laid back and not too big. This resort has been through many management changes, but its latest is one of the better ones. The resort has renovated most of the rooms, lobby and common areas. The new room decor (now called "Deluxe") is modern and makes the space feel much larger than its 320 sq. ft. They have left some rooms unrenovated, but those are still very well-maintained and can be had for a better rate. The lanai are small here, just barely room for chairs. If you opt for ocean view, ask for one of the ocean-facing end units in Bldg. 4. Otherwise, spring for a pool view, most of which can catch a view of the ocean. Adjoining rooms available.

This resort, located between Lihu'e and Wailua, is near a pretty but relatively unswimmable beach. (A short walk farther north leads to better parts of Nukoli'i Beach.) The saline pools are the star

See all Web reviews at: www.hawaiirevealed.com

here. They've augmented their other 3 pools with a wonderful half-sand-lined pool and a water slide complete with man-made waterfalls. They have added more umbrellas around the pool for extra shade. (If it gets too hot, head over to their shave ice/ice cream stand—a sweet touch! Stick with the keiki size.) Service has improved markedly, to the point that it competes with higher-end resorts (but you may need to head over to the pool bar for a drink since there's no poolside service), and they keep things *very* clean. The staff is *very* warm here. They charge a *mandatory* $25 per day "amenity" fee, which includes internet, valet or self-parking, local calls, room safe, fitness room, weekly manager's cocktail party and some other items. Lots of daily activities here.

RACK Rates are high at $338–$498, but few pay them. Suites (655–1,253 sq. ft.) are $600–$1,300. Many good discounts and packages are available.

Tip Top Motel
(808) 245-2333
3173 Akahi St.
WEB REVIEW

Motel Lani
(808) 245-2965
4240 Rice St.

Motel Lani

8 rooms, a/c, BBQ area, no laundry on site. They claim this "was probably the first hotel on the island." It's pretty disheveled with old furnishings, and it's on

SOLID GOLD VALUE

a busy intersection. They were painting rooms on our recent visit. Rooms are small (most under 200 sq. ft.), have bathrooms and fridges but no phones or TVs. $55–$70. Cash only in advance. If you stay more than two nights, the rates drop, but you pay in full *in advance*. They have an old piano in the lobby, but we doubt you'll find Billy Joel playing here. The reason for the SOLID GOLD VALUE is there are not many places with a private room, a/c, and bath for this kind of money on the island, but don't expect much more than that.

Kaua'i Palms Hotel
(808) 246-0908
2931 Kalena St.

28 rooms, coin-op laundry, free Wi-Fi throughout. No phones, no lanais. This is probably your best bet in Lihu'e (but it is a bit pricier). It has small, clean rooms and few amenities, but the present owner has made an effort with the decor and property. They provide free coffee and tea in the mornings. Rooms (108–250 sq. ft.) are $85–$95, kitchenettes (250 sq. ft.) are $105. Larger rooms (275 sq. ft.) with full kitchens are $110. The $85 rooms do not have a/c and are on the second floor, but they do have ceiling fans. In summer you will probably want to spring for a/c to sleep comfortably.

Marriott's Kaua'i Lagoons Kalanipu'u
(800) 845-5279 or (808) 632-8202
3325 Holokawelu Way
78 units, pool, spa, BBQ area, firepits, a/c,

Some resorts may be booked at: www.hawaiirevealed.com

Kaua'i Marriott Resort & Beach Club
(800) 220-2925 or (808) 245-5050
3610 Rice St.

WEB REVIEW 💎

Garden Island Inn
(800) 648-0154 or (808) 245-7227
3445 Wilcox Rd.

WEB REVIEW ▬

Banyan Harbor
(800) 422-6926 or (808) 245-7333
(800) 767-4707 or (808) 245-4711
3411 Wilcox Rd.

WEB REVIEW

Kaua'i Inn
(800) 808-2330 or (808) 245-9000
2430 Hulemalu Rd.

WEB REVIEW

SOUTH SHORE

Grand Hyatt Kaua'i Resort & Spa
(888) 591-1234 or (808) 742-1234
1571 Poipu Rd.

free Wi-Fi in the rooms (if you book direct), 42-inch TVs, daily housekeeping, full-size washer/dryer in unit, free room safe, business center, elevators, free 24-hour fitness center, small convenience market. **A REAL GEM** Though opened as timeshares in 2010, they often have vacation rentals available. These buildings sit overlooking very pretty mountains, golf course and more distant ocean views (along with some ongoing construction of another property in the distance). Overall, the views are best from higher floors. The units are modern and spacious with high-end appliances, granite counters and large lanai. The two- or three-bedroom units (all have king beds) can accommodate two or three couples nicely as each room also has a TV, and the kids can use the pull-out sofa in the living room. Bathrooms have large showers and separate tubs. The two-level pool by building C has a nice layout, but may become crowded when all the units are booked. There is a free shuttle to run you back and forth to the Kaua'i Marriott Resort to enjoy the beach (not the pool or lounge chairs), but you do have signing privileges at their restaurant by the pool. There is a 10 a.m. checkout, but they will store your luggage, and you may use the pool and showers before your flight. Parking is $15 per day if you are not in a timeshare. 2/2 units (1,300 sq. ft.) are $569–$619. 3/3 units (1,600 sq. ft.) are $799. Discounts available.

602 rooms, multiple pools and spas, 2 tennis courts with pro shop, golf course, 24-hour room service, 6 restaurants, 55-inch TVs, free Wi-Fi throughout and high-speed in rooms, 4 cocktail lounges, 9 shops, Camp Hyatt **A REAL GEM** children's program, 23 conference rooms, valet parking, 24-hour fitness center, empty refrigerator, coffee makers with free coffee daily, coin-op and valet laundry, lu'au, complete business services and a 45,000-sq.-ft. day spa with beauty

See all Web reviews at: www.hawaiirevealed.com

salon and lap pool. It's hard for us to review this resort without sounding like drooling sycophants. But the reality of the Hyatt is that they did almost everything right. Put simply, it's our favorite big resort on the island.

As you walk into the lobby and see the ocean framed by the entrance, you realize that here they really sweated the details. The grounds are as exotic as any you will find in all the islands, complete with parrots and other birds. Their pools are incredible. Gallon for gallon, they're more fun than any we've seen on the island. The upper swimming pool seems to meander forever. It even has a slight current and hides such goodies as caves tucked behind small waterfalls (they're easy to miss). Take your time exploring as it winds through lush vegetation. At the end of the upper pool, you can take the "elevator" (a free and respectably fast waterslide) to the bottom. There you will find what they call the action pool, complete with a volleyball net, waterfalls, spas and an area for children. An island there hides a hot tub. Above is the adult pool. Across from the lower pool are several *acres* of saltwater lagoon. If you want saltwater without the waves, here it is. The "sand" is actually more like gravel and is imported. (It's hard on tender tootsies but makes a good loofah.) Inside the lagoon are several landscaped islands.

The grounds are lush, very well maintained and feature a smashing waterfall below the Seaview Terrace Lounge. The resort is located on a so-so beach called Shipwreck Beach. They have covered casabella chairs (two chairs with retractable cover) on the beach for $165. They're coveted, and the Hyatt could use more. If you're lucky enough to be under one in the evening during a passing shower, it's something you will long remember. Cabanas by the beach are $275 and include water and some amenities like cookies or fruit. Casabella chairs are $140 around the lagoon. Large hammocks and loveseat swings are scattered throughout the grounds. Their shops run the gamut from fine art to housewares. They have wedding coordinators on site, and guest services are good.

The Hyatt's an easy GEM, and their awesome grounds put them in a class by themselves. Rooms are pleasant and modern. Rooms with a king bed have a walk-in shower with a hand-held showerhead and bench. Rooms with two queen beds have a tub/shower combination.

They have a *mandatory* $35 per day resort fee covering local calls, self-parking, fitness center, laptop-sized room safe, unlimited fitness classes at Anara Spa, tons of daily activities from Otterpop eating contests to 'ukulele lessons and some other things. Valet parking is $30.

If your intention is to come to Kaua'i and never leave the resort (which we hope you *won't* do), the Hyatt is the place to come. You'll never get bored here. This is a *great* place to bring the kids, but adults will enjoy it, too. Camp Hyatt provides an extensive children's program for kids age 3 (if potty-trained) to 12 for $125 per day. Anara Spa is massive and complete with couples' "treatment hales," lava rock showers, steam rooms and baths. So what's the catch? Well, amenities like this don't come cheap. Rooms (500 sq. ft.) are $480–$1,030. Suites (1,055–2,463 sq. ft.) are $1,100–$5,200. Be aware they have an early departure fee if you opt to trim some days off your stay.

Makahuena

(800) 367-5004 or (808) 742-7700
(800) 325-5701 or (808) 742-2000
1661 Pe'e Rd.
78 units, small pool, spa, BBQ area, free

Some resorts may be booked at: www.hawaiirevealed.com

Wi-Fi, free room safes (from first agent listed), washer/dryer in unit, lighted tennis court. The developer seems to have spared... well, lots of expenses, actually. Like the endless concrete stairs at every turn, cheap-looking fixtures, etc. Some of the units are fairly nice inside, some are not. We've never felt very warm toward Makahuena. The location out on the point will expose you to *lots* of sea spray-laden wind, so don't expect the windows to stay clean. Those winds, however, tend to keep the units cool. There are eight different floor plans, so it's hard to say if you'll get a good one. Second floor units are better for views, whereas many first-floor units are partly below ground. 2/2 units (1,157–1,217 sq. ft.) are $233–$509, 3/3 units (1,380 sq. ft.) are $341–$569. The second agent listed has some units with better prices.

Po'ipu Makai
(800) 325-5701 or (808) 742-2000
(800) 367-5025 or (808) 245-8841
1677 Pe'e Rd.
WEB REVIEW

Po'ipu Crater Resort
(800) 367-8020 or (808) 742-7400
(800) 325-5701 or (808) 742-2000
2330 Hoohu Rd.
30 units, pool, sauna, BBQ area, tennis court, free Wi-Fi in units and by the pool, washer/dryer in unit. Located in the bottom of a small crater, the grounds are

pleasant and well maintained, but there is no view. (Technically speaking, you're in a hole.) When the trade winds aren't blowing, it can get pretty hot in there, and sounds bounce around in an odd way. Lots of rental agents have units here, not just the numbers listed. (The first agent charges for local calls.) 2/2 townhouse units (1,240 sq. ft.) are a pretty good deal at $116–$212. 4-night minimum. Prices decrease if you stay longer than 7 nights.

SOLID GOLD VALUE

Po'ipu Palms
(800) 325-5701 or (808) 742-2000
(800) 742-2260 or (808) 742-2233
1697 Pe'e Rd.
WEB REVIEW

Sunset Kahili
(800) 367-8022 or (808) 742-7434
(800) 367-5025 or (808) 245-8841
1763 Pe'e Rd.

35 units, pool, free Wi-Fi in a few and in rec room, BBQ area, elevator, washer/

See all Web reviews at: www.hawaiirevealed.com

dryer in unit. Built in 1968 (you'd swear it was the '50s), it's old but fairly well-kept in the common areas. The units all vary, but mostly they are in need of updating. They all have nice ocean views, with the third floor and above being particularly good. Units ending in 01 and 08 are 2 bedrooms. Master bedrooms are only shut off by shoji doors, which creates less privacy. It's very popular with seniors and long-time repeat guests. An average value. 1/1 units (766 sq. ft.) are $125–$175, 2/2 (1,028 sq. ft.) units only available from second agent listed are $170–$255. 4-night minimum and 3.5 percent for credit card payments from first agent listed.

Po'ipu Shores
(800) 367-5004 or (808) 742-7700
1775 Pe'e Rd.

39 units, pool, BBQ area, free Wi-Fi in rooms and on most of the property, free room safes, washer/dryer in unit, elevator in Building A, limited housekeeping every three days. Most (not all) units have been nicely updated here. The grounds aren't much, but the property is well-maintained. However, expect sea spray on your windows, even though they clean them daily. That's what you're paying for—the extraordinary proximity to, and sound of, the ocean—not the size of the rooms. (Some people actually *complain* that the ocean is "too loud.") The townhouse units in building C are the quietest. The one-bedroom condos are the only units without

A REAL GEM

the master bedroom on the ocean side, but all units have great ocean views. Very nice staff here. 1/1 units (698 sq. ft.) are $317–$529, 2/2 units (912–1,036 sq. ft.) are $359–$649, 3/2s (1,041 sq. ft.) are $419–$699. They often discount. The 1,955-sq.-ft. penthouse is $479–$799. It was originally built for the developer, is glass-walled and has one of the grandest views on the south shore.

Po'ipu Plantation
(800) 634-0263 or (808) 742-6757
1792 Pe'e Rd.
WEB REVIEW

Nihi Kai Villas
(800) 325-5701 or (808) 742-1412
1870 Hoone Rd.

70 units, pool, keiki pool, free Wi-Fi, free room safe in some, 2 tennis courts and a paddle ball court (sort of mini tennis), BBQ area, washer/dryer in unit. Well-maintained grounds. The rooms seem to vary *a lot*. The two-story townhouse units have an annoying layout, but single-level 2/2 units are an acceptable value. Many of the units have been remodeled; others need updating. Buildings 1, 2, 4 and some units in 5 and 8 are your best bet for a glimpse of the ocean. The rest are strictly garden views. The agent above rates their units into premier plus, premier, deluxe and island casual. We didn't find much differ-

Some resorts may be booked at: www.hawaiirevealed.com

ence between premier and deluxe. Island casual units have not been updated but are still clean. 1/2 units (792 sq. ft.) are $175–$250, 2/2 units (1,221–1,531 sq. ft.) are $150–$425, 3/2 or 3/3 units (1,808–1,821 sq. ft.) are $315–$550. 3-night minimum.

Hideaway Cove Villas
(866) 849-2426 or (808) 635-8785
2307 Nalu Rd.

Regency II
(800) 325-5701 or (808) 742-2000
(800) 367-8020 or (808) 742-7400
1831 Poipu Rd.

Po'ipu Kai Resort
(800) 367-8020 or (808) 742-7400
(877) 997-6667 or (808) 742-7424
1775 Poipu Rd.

The Villas at Po'ipu Kai & Regency Villas
(866) 407-0249 or (808) 742-8410
2373 Hoohu Rd. & 2387 Hoohu Rd.

Marriott's Waiohai Beach Club
(800) 845-5279 or (808) 742-4400
2249 Poipu Rd.

Ko'a Kea Hotel & Resort
(888) 898-8958 or (808) 828-8888
2251 Poipu Rd.
121 rooms, saline pool, spa, 24-hour fitness room, a small shop, restaurant, lounge, poolside snack bar, empty refrigerator, *Nespresso* makers, resort-wide Wi-Fi, laptop-sized room safes, valet-only parking, small day spa,

A REAL GEM

24-hour room service, 42-inch TVs, hospitality room, coin-op and valet laundry. This was originally the Po'ipu Beach Hotel built in the 1960s and whacked by hurricane 'Iniki in 1992. It was left abandoned until the current owners rebuilt this upscale boutique-type hotel on the original footprint of the old buildings in 2009. The resort is airy and modern with themes of ocean life in bright colors scattered about. Most rooms are dark chocolate and white with a splash of hot pink, orange or teal and feel larger than their listed size. They've thought of many nice touches you don't often find at hotels of this size, such as *Nespresso* machines (unlimited pods supplied), ceiling fans in every room so you can leave the doors open and enjoy the ocean sounds, reading lights, Egyptian cotton sheets, down feather beds and pillows (which they can remove if you don't like them), keyboard height pull-out desks on wheels, and showers with rain shower heads mounted in the ceiling and wide benches to sit on. The oceanfront deluxe rooms and suites, which are larger, have separate deep soaking tubs and even HDTVs. The oceanfront views are excellent and very close to the water. Their beach is small and varies in width, so you won't have many people parked in front of your room. Since they are on a fairly protected cove, the snorkeling can make up for the minimal sand. Their small day spa offers many treatments for individuals or couples. If you stay here, opting for an oceanfront or a courtyard view is worth the

See all Web reviews at: www.hawaiirevealed.com

money (if you can swing it). The garden views tend to be quieter, but on the side facing the Marriott's Waiohai, they are less private. They have a *mandatory* $37 per day resort fee, which covers valet parking, local calls, fitness room, internet and a few other items. Overall, we found it relaxing, peaceful and appreciated the intimacy with the ocean. Rooms (335–445 sq. ft.) are $500–$900. Suites (585–680 sq. ft.) are $1,625–$2,575. Few pay these RACK rates.

Kiahuna Plantation Resort
(800) 367-5004 or (808) 742-2200
(800) 688-7444 or (808) 742-6411
2253 Poipu Rd.
WEB REVIEW

Sheraton Kaua'i Resort
(866) 716-8109 or (808) 742-1661
2440 Hoonani Rd.
WEB REVIEW ◆

Po'ipu Kapili
(800) 443-7714 or (808) 742-6449
2221 Kapili Rd.

60 units, pool, 2 lighted tennis courts, elevators, free Wi-Fi in rooms, coin-op laundry (washer/dryers in all two-bedroom units and some 1/1s), BBQ area, some units have a/c in bedrooms, linen service for seven or more nights. Well-maintained and sculptured grounds, very spacious rooms for the money, and a second-home atmosphere

A REAL GEM

make this an easy recommendation. Buildings 1, 2, 6 and 7 (all 2/3s) have very nice ocean views and are two-story townhouses. You can pick herbs from their garden if you choose to cook. Linen service for 7 or more nights. The staff is top-notch here. 1/2 units (1,120–1,250 sq. ft.) are $250–$425, 2/2 or 2/3 units (1,400–1,820 sq. ft.) are $325–$600. They also have elegant 1,800-sq.-ft. penthouses for $425–$575 with large lanais. 3-night minimum. Special discounts available throughout the year.

Alihi Lani
(800) 742-2260 or (808) 742-2233
2564 Hoonani Rd.
WEB REVIEW

Koloa Landing Resort at Po'ipu
(844) 556-7226 or (808) 240-6600
2641 Poipu Rd.
WEB REVIEW ◆

Waikomo Stream Villas
(800) 325-5701 or (808) 742-7220
2721 Poipu Rd.

60 units, pool, keiki pool, free Wi-Fi in units, nice BBQ area, washer/dryer in units. Pretty, well-kept grounds and large

Some resorts may be booked at: www.hawaiirevealed.com

rooms (all garden views). Some of the garden views are quite lovely with small streams. Lots of privacy. The rooms are rated by the **SOLID GOLD VALUE** above agent as premier plus, premier, deluxe and island casual. We felt the premier or deluxe units were really not that different—both were very nice. Opt for island casual if you want clean but not updated. 1/1 units (1,050 sq. ft.) are $150–$300, the 1,500-sq.-ft. 2/2 units (second bedrooms are a loft with limited privacy and units are on third floor) are $200–$375. Very nice staff here. 3-night minimum.

Whalers Cove
(800) 225-2683 or (808) 742-7571
(800) 325-5701 or (808) 742-2000
2640 Puuholo Rd.

39 units, pool, spa, daily housekeeping, elevator, BBQ area, free daily coffee, free room safe, free Wi-Fi in rooms and lobby, washer/dryer in unit. This is a lovely property **A REAL GEM** and very serene. The grounds are well-manicured, and the setting for the pool is outstanding. Though individually owned and decorated, units are well-furnished with koa wood doors and even koa floor trim in the closets. Back in the day, the units were some of the most expensively furnished in the area, and even today most have been updated and still compete. The resort is very quiet, and they provide more personalized service than you will find elsewhere.

(They will even do your grocery shopping before you arrive and stock your refrigerator.) Some units have Jacuzzi bathtubs, many overlooking the ocean. They are not on a beach, but there is a snorkeling cove nearby. Units from first agent listed have a *mandatory* $15 per day resort fee, but they don't charge a cleaning fee, so things may even out. You'll have optional access to the Poipu Beach Athletic Club (and even a shuttle back and forth), including fitness center, pool with keiki pool and restaurant for $100 per unit per week. In all, it's expensive but worth the money if you get a deal. 1/2 units (995 sq. ft.) are $366–$850. (These actually have 2 bedrooms, but you are limited to 2 people and charged as if it were 1/2.) 2/2 units (1,390–2,060 sq. ft.) are $375–$744. 3/3 units with all bedrooms facing the ocean (2,090 sq. ft.) are $750–$975. 2- to 7-night minimum.

Kuhio Shores
(800) 543-9180 or (206) 938-5802
(800) 367-8022 or (808) 742-7555
5050 Lawai Rd.

Prince Kuhio
(888) 747-2988
(800) 742-2260 or (808) 742-2233
5061 Lawai Rd.
72 units, pool, coin-op laundry (washer/dryers in *some* units), free Wi-Fi in units, BBQ, a/c in studios facing pool. Grounds are very **SOLID GOLD VALUE** well-tended, and the pool and BBQ area are very pretty. Built in 1962, the resort's clean for its age, but in some places its age does show in things like rusty gutters. Some units are more updated than others, and they vary *a lot*. Located across the road from the ocean, this used to be a hotel but was converted to condos, so expect some bizarre room

See all Web reviews at: www.hawaiirevealed.com

layouts and bathrooms with showers only—some big, some *tiny*. The ocean views here are not that great, but if you want a glimpse, get a unit above the first floor and closer to the road. Larger one-bedroom units are in the middle section of the building ($10–$20 more than the ones at the front of the building), while studios are in back. If you are looking at studios with numbers ending in 30–37, then you may want to opt for a park-facing, odd-numbered unit for a more pleasant view than the interior courtyard, but you won't have a/c in those. Some long-term rentals here. Studios (338–450 sq. ft.) are $70–$120, 1/1 units (600–720 sq. ft.) are $105–$155. There is also a 2/1 penthouse (875 sq. ft.) with a large roof deck for $200–$275. 3-night minimum from first phone number, which is for a large group of owners. Prices decrease for longer stays, and because you are dealing directly with the owners, they may be more flexible with the price. The second set of numbers has similar rates. Other agents also have a few units here.

Kalaheo Inn
(888) 332-6023 or (808) 332-6023
4444 Papalina Rd.
WEB REVIEW

WEST SHORE

Inn Waimea
(808) 652-6852
4469 Halepule Rd.
WEB REVIEW

The West Inn
(808) 338-1107
9690 Kaumualii Hwy
WEB REVIEW

Waimea Plantation Cottages
(800) 716-6199 or (808) 338-1625
9400 Kaumualii Hwy

59 units, pool and keiki pool, restaurant, Wi-Fi throughout with a computer in lobby for guest use, a/c in most bedrooms, DVD rentals, **SOLID GOLD VALUE** room safe, laundry facility, a conference room, a small shop, BBQ areas and also charcoal grill upon request, volleyball, and housekeeping every three days. At this 27-acre former plantation, peace and privacy are yours—the trade-off is relative isolation given the location on the extreme west side. There is much feeling of 'ohana (family) here, and you will definitely experience the aloha spirit. With their location so close to the mouth of the very reddish Waimea River, swimming in the murky ocean water is pretty poor at this marginal beach. The coconut grove, banyan trees and hammocks scattered about add to the quiet charm of this property, and this is a good place to

Some resorts may be booked at: www.hawaiirevealed.com

watch the sunset over the private island of Ni'ihau.

Many of these cottages were once plantation workers' homes, and each is as different as their former owner's tastes. We had a hard time coming up with adjectives to describe the rooms. They have old-style floors and furniture, just like from the plantation days. Units vary tremendously in decor, price and proximity to the ocean. Rooms have been refurbished with modern amenities, but they retain the old-style feel inside, without feeling *too* old and worn. They are very clean. Most bathrooms have showers only, so if you need a tub, request one when booking. All rooms have a full kitchen.

There's a *mandatory* $25 per day resort fee, which covers local and long distance calls, internet, room safes, daily coffee and DVD rentals and many other items you may have thought were included anyway. Prices have come down with the new management making this an easy SOLID GOLD VALUE. Studios (300 sq. ft.) are $139–$199, 1/1s (approx. 594 sq. ft.) are $195–$429, 2/1s (approx. 726 sq. ft.) are $239–$465, 3/2s (approx. 1,088 sq. ft.) are $279–$499, 4/3s (approx. 1,250 sq. ft.) are $399–$599, 5/4s (4,020–4,240 sq. ft.) are $659–$839. Discounts available.

The Cabins at Koke'e Park
(808) 652-6852
Koke'e State Park
WEB REVIEW

YWCA Camp Sloggett
(808) 245-5959
Koke'e State Park
30 beds in the bunkhouse, cottage and lodge, huge firepit (bring your own wood), BBQ area, pay phone (bring change

because your cell phone probably won't work), covered lanai with Ping-Pong table, volleyball and other games. This property was built in 1925, this is a clean, no-nonsense camp with a no-nonsense attitude: "Leave it as you found it." The grounds are isolated, but the scenery is quite beautiful with a small stream. It's $20 per tent for camping with access to toilets and hot showers. The Bunkhouse can be rented in two halves, each half sleeping up to 15 people (bring your own bedding and towels), and there is a kitchenette available. There is no laundry on site. Community restrooms and showers for campers and bunkhouse. The Bunkhouse rents for $180 for each half. They have a cottage available for $150 for up to four people. The lodge has a commercial kitchen and bath and can sleep up to 15 people for $250. Or you can rent the entire facility for $900. They closed in 2015 for a deep cleaning and painting of the facilities. They often rent to large groups, so be sure and call two weeks or more in advance for availability. The cabin and lodge often are reserved up to a year or more in advance with summer being the busiest season. 2-night minimum for all but tent camping. They charge a cleaning fee of between $100–$500 for the facilities, but if you leave it clean, it should be returned to you.

SOLID GOLD VALUE

INDEX

Island Dining Index on page 212, Where to Stay Index on page 252.

INDEX

275

Island Dining Index on page 212, Where to Stay Index on page 252.

INDEX

Island Dining Index on page 212, Where to Stay Index on page 252.

INDEX

Island Dining Index on page 212, Where to Stay Index on page 252.

INDEX

Island Dining Index on page 212, Where to Stay Index on page 252.

INDEX

Island Dining Index on page 212, Where to Stay Index on page 252.